"Neiman's book offers engaging and illuminating insights into both the causes of persistent inequality and productive steps for change. What makes this book especially compelling is its insistence that understanding unequal economic, racial, and gender structures in contemporary America holds promise of more opportunities, freedom, meaning, and healing for every individual. *Rich White Men* can help everyone think anew about luck, hard work, leadership, opportunity, and repair."

—Martha Minow, Harvard Law School
professor and dean 2009–2017

"In this well-researched and moving narrative, Neiman centers his critique on the 'compounding unearned advantages' possessed by rich white men like himself, which cause dismaying societal inequity, lack of opportunity for other individuals, and a psychological pain in those who realize that the luxuries they enjoy are often acquired at the expense of others. *Rich White Men* makes plain a number of truths that you simply cannot unsee. It also proposes revisions to the rules of the game, making this book an essential read for any capitalist who would dare."

—Julie Lythcott-Haims, councilmember for the City of Palo Alto and *New York Times* bestselling author of *Your Turn*

"Blending scholarship and moral urgency, *Rich White Men* cries out for Americans with the deepest pockets to dig into their pants to build a better world. One only can hope they will heed to call."

—William Darity Jr., professor of public policy, African and African American studies, and economics at Duke University and author of *From Here to Equality: Reparations for Black Americans in the Twenty-First Century*

"*Rich White Men* is an exposé and hopeful polemic. It takes the reader on a journey and shines a light on the biases of the philanthropic elite. An insider, Neiman shares fascinating reflections and raises sharp questions about the nature of race and democracy. The book powerfully weaves together personal narrative and offers the privileged a path for how they can transform themselves from being part of the problem to being part of the solution."

—Megan Ming Francis, associate professor of political science at the University of Washington and author of *Civil Rights and the Making of the Modern American State*

"Neiman's book disrupts the narratives of mediocrity and deservedness that are deployed to justify extreme inequity and white dominance. A great read, chock-full of insights, *Rich White Men* urges the privileged ultrawealthy to humbly walk away from unearned advantage and come home to authentic community and reciprocity."

—Chuck Collins, Institute of Policy Studies, author of *Born on Third Base* and *Altar to an Erupting Sun*

"With *Rich White Men*, Neiman has challenged me—and inevitably many others—to think harder about what it takes to build an America with far less identity-based adversity—and what that would unlock for all of us."

—Dr. Laura Huang, Harvard Business School professor and author of *Edge*

"*Rich White Men* is more than a book. It's a blueprint for revolution in a focused little package."

—Melody Talcott, member of the International Repatriation Coalition

RICH WHITE MEN

What It Takes to Uproot the Old Boys' Club and Transform America

GARRETT NEIMAN

LEGACY
LIT

NEW YORK BOSTON

Legacy Lit
Hachette Book Group
1290 Avenue of the Americas
New York, NY 10104
LegacyLitBooks.com
Twitter.com/LegacyLitBooks
Instagram.com/LegacyLitBooks

First edition: June 2023

Legacy Lit is an imprint of Grand Central Publishing. The Legacy Lit name and logo are trademarks of Hachette Book Group, Inc.

The publisher is not responsible for websites (or their content) that are not owned by the publisher.

The Hachette Speakers Bureau provides a wide range of authors for speaking events. To find out more, go to hachettespeakersbureau.com or email HachetteSpeakers@hbgusa.com.

Legacy Lit books may be purchased in bulk for business, educational, or promotional use. For information, please contact your local bookseller or the Hachette Book Group Special Markets Department at special.markets@hbgusa.com.

Library of Congress Cataloging-in-Publication Data

Names: Neiman, Garrett, author.
Title: Rich white men : what it takes to uproot the old boys' club and transform America / Garrett Neiman.
Description: First edition. | New York, NY : Legacy Lit, an imprint of Hachette Books, [2023]
Identifiers: LCCN 2022057863 | ISBN 9780306925566 (hardcover) | ISBN 9780306925573 (ebook)
Subjects: LCSH: Wealth—United States. | Men, White—United States—Economic conditions. | Rich people—United States. | Equality—United States.
Classification: LCC HC79.W4 N45 2023 | DDC 305.5/23408909073—dc23/eng/20230324
LC record available at https://lccn.loc.gov/2022057863

ISBNs: 9780306925566 (hardcover), 9780306925573 (ebook)

Printed in the United States of America

LSC-C

Printing 1, 2023

For Ayan, and the next seven generations

The Seventh Generation Principle is based on an ancient Haudeno-saunee philosophy that the decisions made today ought to result in a sustainable world, for people and planet, seven generations into the future.

The mine owners do not find the gold, they do not mine the gold, they do not mill the gold, but by some weird alchemy all the gold belongs to them.

—BILL HAYWOOD, GOLD MINER AND UNION LEADER

The world has enough for everyone's needs, but not everyone's greed.

—MAHATMA GANDHI, INDIAN LAWYER AND
NONVIOLENT REVOLUTIONARY

CONTENTS

FOREWORD   XI

MY CLASSIST, RACIST, AND SEXIST PREFACE   XV

INTRODUCTION   XXV

PART I
HOW THE OLD BOYS' CLUB REPRODUCES ITSELF

CHAPTER 1:   Compounding Unearned Advantage   3

CHAPTER 2:   Wealth and Opportunity   15

CHAPTER 3:   White Advantage   29

CHAPTER 4:   Male Advantage   45

CHAPTER 5:   Intersectional Advantage   61

CHAPTER 6:   The Exception Factory   73

CHAPTER 7:   The People of Color Ranking System   83

CHAPTER 8:   Blaming the Victim   97

CHAPTER 9:   The Luck Defense   115

PART II
BECOMING EQUITABLE

CHAPTER 10: Intersectional Equity   133

CHAPTER 11: Antimonopoly   151

CHAPTER 12: Abolishing Poverty   167

CHAPTER 13: A Culture of Repair   183

CHAPTER 14: A Healing Society   201

CHAPTER 15: Embracing Feminine Leadership   221

CHAPTER 16: Restoring Connection   235

CHAPTER 17: Transforming the Power Structure   255

CONCLUSION   279

About This Book's Relationship with Wealth and Power   289

Ten Actions the Advantaged Can Take to Help Construct
     an Equitable America   293

Acknowledgments   297

Resource List   301

Endnotes   305

Index   345

FOREWORD

Dr. Robin DiAngelo

When I first introduced the term *white fragility* in an article by the same name in 2011, I had no idea the extent to which it would speak to people across a range of racial identities. When I turned that article into a more accessible book, countless newly awakened white people—moved by the racial uprising during the Summer of 2020—found it an invaluable guide to understanding our socialization into and collusion with systemic racism.

In the few years that have passed since that book was released, I have been heartened by the increased commitment of many white people to racial justice and their turning toward Black, Indigenous, and other peoples of color for leadership and guidance. But sadly, I have not been surprised by how fleeting that commitment so often is—and the racial arrogance and lack of humility so many "aware" white people default to, confident that our work is over and that we already know all we need to know. The ideology of individualism allows us to exempt ourselves, seeing racism as residing in the white person next to us, but rarely ever in ourselves.

As someone who has been engaged in antiracist work for several decades, I am clear that antiracism is a lifelong journey, a destination at which we will never fully arrive. For every inch we gain in challenging our conditioning into this system, the system is pushing right back. The comfort and advantage that systemic racism offers to those of us who are white are seductive. We must be relentless and vigilant and proceed with humility.

One of the great challenges to resisting the seductive forces of racism is how they interact with other systems of oppression that are also forceful and unyielding. Kimberlé Crenshaw, bell hooks, and Audre Lorde, among many other women of color, have written deeply and insightfully about the dynamics of intersectionality. Also enlightening are the contributions of those who have studied white masculinity specifically, including Tim Wise (*Speaking Treason Fluently*, 2008), Michael Kimmel (*Angry White Men*, 2013), and Ijeoma Oluo (*Mediocre*, 2020).

As a white cis woman who grew up in poverty and was the first in my family to go to college, I have also felt firsthand the oppressive power wielded by wealthy white men, a subset of Americans who author Garrett Neiman describes in this book. I have witnessed countless interactions through which rich white men abuse their societal power to avoid accountability for harm they cause. I outline these deflections in *White Fragility*, including: social taboos against talking openly about race; the "good/bad binary" that tells us that only some people are racist, and those people are bad; the idea that white men are objective and worked hard for everything they have; and a deeply internalized sense of superiority.

While rich white men don't typically manifest their white fragility through literal tears as many white women do, they still do so, albeit in more aggressive ways. Their fragility most commonly shows up as varying forms of dominance and intimidation, including:

- Control of the conversation by speaking first, last, and most often
- Arrogant and disingenuous invalidation of racial inequality via "just playing the devil's advocate"
- Simplistic and presumptuous proclamations of "the answer" to racism ("People just need to ...")
- Playing the outraged victim of "reverse racism"
- Accusations that the legendary "race card" is being played
- Silence and withdrawal
- Hostile body language
- Channel switching ("The true oppression is class!")
- Intellectualizing and distancing ("I recommend this book ...")
- "Correcting" the racial analysis of people of color and white women
- Pompously explaining away racism and the experiences of people of color

All these moves push race off the table, help white men regain control of the discussion, end the challenge to their positions, and reassert their dominance.

I am clear that white women have not consistently shown up for racial justice. But I am also clear that when white people do show up, it is overwhelmingly white women. Sexism makes it easy to express contempt for and critique of white women—one example in the present moment being the countless "Karen" memes—but this allows, yet again, for rich white men to skate under the radar and distract us from who truly controls the halls of power.

Rich white men need to be educated and challenged on their complicity in a system that grossly and obliquely overadvantages them at the expense of others. And *Rich White Men* does just that. Garrett Neiman provides reflections and a model for personal transformation that other wealthy white men—as well as other white people—can learn from. *Rich White Men* is a powerful exposé from within the belly of the beast, a location he uniquely has access to. The book makes a major analytical contribution to the racial and social justice movement by exposing that belly, yet it is also a very personal journey that embeds a commitment to reckoning and accountability that is informed by Neiman's conviction that an equitable America is in everyone's self-interest, including this nation's morally, relationally, and spiritually impoverished rich white men.

What most distinguishes Garrett's voice is not solely his insightful analysis—though he has much to offer on that front—but rather his humility and vulnerability. Garrett courageously and generously shares his collusions and mistakes, those uncomfortable moments that shined a light on his ignorance and or arrogance, and the lessons learned. He speaks from his own lived experience and describes himself as someone who is part of the system, not outside it. Garrett is crystal clear that he hasn't "arrived" in his consciousness or practice because this is a lifelong process. In so modeling, he provides a framework for how rich white men might begin to engage.

Rich White Men is among those rare books that makes the case for an equitable and just America while offering hard-earned insider insights that inform how our movement can win. I am especially excited that he takes on the intersections of class and gender and speaks back to the common claim that the equitable distribution of wealth will simultaneously end racism and all other forms of oppression. May it get into the hands of those who need it most.

—Dr. Robin DiAngelo, author of the
New York Times best seller *White Fragility*

MY CLASSIST, RACIST, AND SEXIST PREFACE

You get to a certain age and you realize that somehow the world's problems are yours to solve and if not us—who, if not now—when?

—JIM COULTER, AMERICAN BILLIONAIRE AND
COFOUNDER OF TPG CAPITAL

MYTH:

Rich white men approach the issue of inequality objectively and benevolently.

The master's tools will never dismantle the master's house.

—AUDRE LORDE, AMERICAN WRITER,
FEMINIST, AND CIVIL RIGHTS ACTIVIST

REALITY:

Rich white men often prioritize solutions that protect our wealth and power.

When I arrived at Edward's corner office—I'll call him Edward, because he buys and sells companies like Richard Gere's character in the 1990 movie *Pretty Woman*—I was awestruck. As a nonprofit CEO, I'd seen many fancy offices while fundraising. Still, Edward's setup was unique. Millions of dollars in abstract art lined the walls. And outside the panoramic, floor-to-ceiling windows, New York's Central Park was visible in all its splendor.

I suppose I ought not have been surprised. Because of his entrepreneurial success, Edward had secured a slot on the Forbes 400, the list of America's richest people. His high profile meant that his investment decisions could make or break billion-dollar companies. The success of the nonprofit I was leading—and the futures of the additional students we'd be able to serve if he made a large donation—was resting at that moment largely on his whim.

The first half hour of the meeting was smooth sailing. I told Edward about CollegeSpring, the national nonprofit I'd cofounded with my Stanford classmate Jessica Perez in 2008. I shared how we'd grown from a volunteer-run effort to a three-office staff of twenty-five, and how our programs were empowering thousands of students of color from high-poverty communities. Program participants improved their SAT scores from, on average, the twentieth to the fortieth percentile, and those higher test scores enabled many of them to become the first in their families to go to college. I emphasized that the Obama administration had invited us to the White House and heralded CollegeSpring as a promising model for supporting academic achievement in communities of color; we'd also receive praise from national media and then Facebook COO Sheryl Sandberg, who had written about us in her number one bestseller *Lean In*.

Edward seemed impressed. *We're going to get this donation*, I remember thinking.

Then, seemingly out of the blue, he asked a question about the students we served. "So, this program of yours," he began. "When you go into the schools, you offer the program to all of the students at the school?"

Many people I'd met appreciated the fact that our program did indeed serve all students, so I was surprised by his negative tone, which suggested it might be a leading question.

When I confirmed that his understanding was correct, Edward groaned. "Well, my problem is, most of the kids in *those* schools are lazy," he said. "I only support high achievers. That's why I fund scholarships at my alma mater," he explained. "I don't want my money going down the drain on the lazy kids."

He wasn't specific about what he meant by "those" schools, but he didn't have to be. It was obvious he was talking about Black and brown kids who went to school in high-poverty neighborhoods.

My mouth fell open. By that point, I had gone to thousands of fundraising meetings with hundreds of wealthy people, mostly rich white men. It certainly wasn't the first time a prospective donor had said something ignorant. Nor was it the first time I'd needed to transform a bizarre comment into a fundraising opportunity.

In that moment, though, I was stunned—and tongue-tied. I couldn't decide whether to challenge his ignorance or try to spin his belief about the inferiority of our students into a reason why he ought to make a charitable donation. I was too surprised to be articulate, so I fumbled through a tortured response.

Within minutes, the train to the million-dollar donation that had been steaming ahead sputtered and ground to a halt. The initial positive energy and the rapport we'd developed over years seemed to leave the room all at once. The momentum was gone, never to be recovered.

The fundraising opportunity was lost. That door had closed.

At first, I blamed myself. After all, it was my job to successfully advocate for our program no matter what obstacles came my way. I had let our organization—and our students—down.

But then, I became angry. Here was a rich white man who might have never even visited the communities we were discussing, and somehow, he was dictating who deserved a better life. He could have helped, and instead he chose to stereotype our students. He felt it was only worth finding the exceptions that reinforced his biased view that most students of color are lazy. He believed that donations to support entire underserved communities were a waste.

It is tempting to dismiss Edward as an outlier or a "bad apple." In fact, when I've told this story in the past, people often assume he is a right-wing extremist. The truth, though, is that Edward *is* a "good" billionaire. He backs Democrats and many cultural, educational, and environmental causes. If he hadn't been among the "good" billionaires—a philanthropist committed to fighting poverty, which many wealthy people aren't—I doubt he'd ever have agreed to meet with me.

While Edward was ignorant about what life is like in high-poverty communities of color and may be embarrassed by my sharing this story, I don't intend to shame him here. After all, Edward's ignorance is by design. Today, the United States is as racially segregated as it was in 1970 and more socioeconomically segregated than at any point in its history.[1] And like most Americans, Edward was socialized in an educational system that whitewashes history and suggests that those who fail to secure the American dream are irresponsible.

I've spent the past fifteen years as a nonprofit leader and fundraiser, first as the CEO of CollegeSpring and more recently as a cocreator of Liberation Ventures, a Black-led philanthropic fund that is building grassroots power to accelerate momentum toward federal reparations in the United States. Through my roles, I've met dozens of white men who are at least as rich as Edward. I've also met hundreds more white men who are nearly as wealthy or otherwise wield significant power as elected officials, political appointees, university presidents, foundation leaders, or heads of other influential institutions.

Many rich white men have views similar to Edward's. Most aren't as explicit as Edward was in our exchange, but the perspective is common, maybe even typical. There are exceptions, but not many. Most nonprofit leaders don't share these kinds of stories because it would damage our credibility with donors, but behind the scenes and off the record, "philanthropist bias" is a common watercooler topic. "You think that's bad?"

one of America's most famous Black nonprofit leaders once asked me, after I recalled this story to him. "That's *nothing* compared to what I've heard come out of the mouths of donors over the years."

In a way, Edward's unusually explicit example of bias gave me an incredible gift, because it shook me out of my day-to-day. Looking back on it, that was the moment when it sank in for me that extreme ignorance dominates the viewpoints within America's political and economic elite. And it instilled in me a lifelong commitment to uprooting inequitable power dynamics.

After that interaction, I became increasingly critical of billionaire-led social change. But, I admit, it's easier to lay blame at someone else's feet than to look in the mirror. Perhaps what's most painful for me, looking back on that experience, is that Edward and I have much more in common than I could have admitted at the time.

The moment that started to become clear to me was at CollegeSpring's all-staff retreat in summer 2016 when—not long after my meeting with Edward—outside consultants facilitated a five-hour workshop with our entire team on diversity, equity, and inclusion.

If I were producing my own revisionist history, I'd say I championed the idea. But the truth is that the session only ended up on our agenda because our executive team and director of talent planned this intervention while I was away on my honeymoon. When I got back, I questioned whether five hours was necessary when we had so many other issues to discuss. I only relented because our senior team was strongly united.

When our staff of twenty-five gathered, I presumed the meeting would go well. After all, we were creating opportunities for Black and brown youth to go to college and improve their lives. We were on the right side of history. *I* was on the right side of history.

But once everyone felt free to talk, all kinds of problems came to the surface. Staff members were angry that I had not spread authority evenly across the organization and that people of color often left before they rose in our hierarchy. They were frustrated that our board and executive team were almost exclusively white. While we had some diversity further down in our ranks, at the top, our leaders were as homogenous as those in Edward's investment firm.

Even in our well-intentioned group, rich white men had a near monopoly on *power*. Most of our board members were wealthy white men, and theirs were the main voices heard at board meetings. If I couldn't even nurture a level playing field within our organization, how could I possibly expect to level it through our work?

The experience hit me hard. As CollegeSpring's founding CEO, I had the final say on key decisions and policies. My decisions had elevated some voices above others, and my unconscious bias had made it easier for wealthy white men like myself to thrive and advance. I didn't have the words for it at the time—nor would I have had the courage to admit it—but looking at the staff hierarchy, it was clear that I had built an institutionally classist, racist, and sexist organization. The realization made me sick to my stomach. Maybe I wasn't one of the good ones after all.

Through the eyes of the working-class women of color who worked for CollegeSpring, I started to see that I, like Edward, had the power to decide who deserved a better life and who was worthy of advancing. While I would have acknowledged even then that I benefited from many advantages—including my gender, race, and economic background—I had struggled to see how my location as a wealthy white man had shaped the ways I'd wielded power as CollegeSpring's young leader. Remembering how angry I was about Edward's power and how difficult it had been to challenge him in that moment helped me see the full impact of the power I was myself exercising. Some of the impact I'd had was positive, but I'd caused harm, too. The fact that I needed to tangle with a billionaire to gain that insight is itself telling.

When I came to see that CollegeSpring was structurally inequitable, I took some early steps such as supporting the creation of a staff diversity, equity, and inclusion committee and recruiting more board members of color. But deep down, I knew that I was fumbling over my good intentions, and didn't yet have the capabilities to lead the organization's transformation toward equity. That is a large part of why I decided to step down from my role in 2017, which created space for me to pass the baton to Dr. Yoon Choi, a seasoned executive who has enhanced College-Spring's effectiveness, financial stability, and equity practice ever since.

Looking back on it, it felt as if I had been handed the keys to a Lamborghini on my sixteenth birthday. The powerful engine helped me go fast, and it was an exhilarating ride, but on the dark and windy road of trying to build a more just world, people were bound to get hurt.

The rich white men who handed me those keys didn't tell me it was classism, patriarchy, white supremacy, and other systems of oppression that drove that powerful engine. I was given power that enabled me to skip classes in college and earn mediocre grades without anyone questioning my intelligence or work ethic. Power that enabled me to raise $15 million from almost exclusively white donors. Power that ensured that when I applied to Harvard's master in public policy / master in business administration joint-degree program, influential white alumni and faculty put in a good word. Power that insulated me from failure in ways that can't be fully measured because they are so deeply baked into this country's social and economic systems. Power that has enabled me to talk in recent years about big ideas, like providing a guaranteed livable income and reparations, without being suspected of looking for a handout. And, yes, power that is largely contingent on my prioritizing a path that does not threaten other rich white men's wealth or power.

It is true that I have always worked hard. But at every critical moment, the unearned advantages I have had as a white man raised in a wealthy family have given me a crucial edge.

When I arrived at Stanford in 2006, I was invited to, as Apple cofounder Steve Jobs once said, "put a dent in the universe." As a bright-eyed teenager, I didn't have the perspective to see that what was pitched to me as "thinking big" was actually "thinking small." Policy change and social movements, I was told, were the old way of doing things; Silicon Valley and social entrepreneurship was the *future*. Somehow I never questioned why, in an environment ostensibly obsessed with scale, the greatest scale solutions had been wiped from the board.

Over my years leading nonprofits, I started to see how I was—at least in some ways—a pawn in a larger game. I was, as Anand Giridharadas describes in his 2018 book *Winners Take All*, a sidekick to the plutocracy. In college, I was awestruck by the opportunities that Stanford offered, which led me to become eager to join "the elite." After I became a social entrepreneur, the guys in that club sometimes made jabs about how non-profits like mine didn't run as well as their esteemed private companies, but most of the time, I was treated with respect and welcomed. I relished the influence they had shared with me, which I'd imagined were enough to level the playing field.

Since I started exploring the possibility of writing this book in 2016, a lot has happened. Yet plutocratic power still won't yield. "Twenty million Americans lost their jobs in the pandemic," President Joe Biden remarked in a 2021 address to Congress. "At the same time, roughly 650 billionaires in America saw their net worth increase by more than $1 trillion."[2] Nearly all of these billionaires are white men. The recent widening of these chasms reflects the continuation of a long-term trend: since 1980, America's wealthiest 1 percent has become $28 trillion richer, while the bottom half hasn't gotten any wealthier.[3]

And unless things change significantly—and quickly—American inequality will get much worse. In a country that claims to value equal opportunity, baby boomers are inking wills that will pass on $36 trillion to their heirs over the next few decades.[4] White inheritors are poised to receive nearly all of that wealth, with white male heirs specifically controlling most of those assets.[5] How much of that $36 trillion will be used to further gut democracy, snuff out social mobility, and reproduce inequality? And how much of it will be deployed to transform the systems that currently protect rich white men's monopoly on wealth and power?

In the corner offices of billionaires and executives at Goldman Sachs, McKinsey, Stanford, Harvard, and other enclaves of mostly silver-spooned white men, I've seen wealthy white guys like me bring biased answers to these questions when we feel secure enough to express unguarded views. As a result, among the many things I've learned from my experiences is that a central barrier blocking America from becoming an equitable nation is a collection of myths that justify inequality, which many rich white men believe in and market to the public as conventional wisdom. These myths prey on the darker sides of human nature and are often subtle enough to sneak past those of us who benefit from them. Part of why I feel a responsibility to name and challenge these myths is that, earlier in my life, I used to believe every one of them.

As the flawed assumptions behind these myths have become visible to me, I have nurtured an alternative belief that my safety and well-being—as well as our collective safety and well-being—is best protected by an equitable America. I don't want to live in a nation where there is extreme inequality, even if I benefit from that inequality materially. Instead, I want to recover what living in such an unequal country has cost me, including meaningful relationships, my mental and physical health, a connection with my ancestral and cultural roots beyond whiteness, access to my true self, and the belonging I seek.

As civil rights activist Fannie Lou Hamer put it far better than I ever could, "nobody's free until everybody's free." The pages ahead reflect a culmination of what I've learned to date about how the system reproduces inequality, and what it takes to transform America into a nation that empowers every one of us to become free.

INTRODUCTION

The United States has always struggled to be egalitarian while resisting to uproot its elitist colonial underpinnings and rationalizations that were developed to justify building an empire on the lands of Indigenous Peoples and the backs of Black people's labor.

In 2023, this nation is at an inflection point. Disparities in wealth and power have become so extreme that marginalized groups are creating alternative pathways to restore their self-determination with growing intensity. And, due to the burgeoning visibility of social-justice movements, developing consciousness that politics as usual is ill equipped to address white supremacy and the crises that continue to impact all of us, such as the COVID-19 pandemic, and an intellectual renaissance in the field of liberatory scholarship, elites who are becoming aware of these disparities are confronting the suffering of the oppressed—and how that suffering is an existential threat to their own well-being and this nation's vitality.

As a cultural strategist, resource mobilizer, and cooperative entrepreneur, I've spent the past fifteen plus years at the nexus of transformative movements and privileged people who are trying to show up better in service of our collective liberation. As a former member of the Malcolm X Grassroots Movement, I organized locally in my birthplace of Newark, New Jersey, to deal with racial disparities in public health, safety, housing, and homelessness. I mobilized resources for the Freedom Ride to Ferguson, which catalyzed the global movement for Black lives. I also supported the mitigation of racialized violence inflicted by white nationalists in Charlottesville, through Within our Lifetime, a racial-justice and healing network. And I've indulged my entrepreneurial spirit as a cocreator of AdAstra Collective, a worker-owned movement consultancy; ZEAL, a social-impact studio and agency for Black creatives; and Liberation Ventures, a philanthropic fund and field-building effort—which I started with Aria Florant and Garrett Neiman—that is building power toward reparations for Black Americans.

Through these various efforts, I have interacted with hundreds of people in positions of privilege who are striving to work in solidarity with marginalized communities. I've also been part of many collaborations where privileged people have caused significant harm, many collaborations where privileged people have done real good, and many collaborations where they've done both. Along the way, I've helped shape and support progressive philanthropic institutions like the Solidaire Network and RESIST; I've also collaborated with wealthy white people like Garrett Neiman, who are dedicating their lives and resources in various ways to advance the liberation of our humanity. These relationships give me faith that it is possible for elites to transform their relationship with capitalism and contribute toward the building of an America that gets to go through a just transition in its culture, politics, and economy. However, since deep commitments from privileged people continue to be rare, I also know that such a future is not inevitable and requires further organizing and creative approaches to call people into what it means to practice being in solidarity and equitable with one another.

What is important to know about *Rich White Men* is that it illuminates pathways for the privileged to live and engage differently so that they can do more good and less harm. This book wrestles with important, complex questions that many other books about inequality have left on the sidelines in their attempts to address the root causes of issues, such as: Why are white high school dropouts wealthier than Black college graduates? What does it take to get white men in poverty on board with gender and racial justice? Why do many white women subscribe to patriarchy and capitalism playing against their own best interests and well-being? What does rich white men going to therapy have to do with advancing social justice? What can activists like Stanley Levison—a rich white man and Dr. Martin Luther King Jr.'s closest white adviser and friend—teach us about how the advantaged can live lives committed to equity? And what does it look like to build a society where rich white men are no longer on top yet are better off than they are today?

Rich White Men shines a light on the ideologies and behaviors of those who stand most forcefully in the way of this nation's healing and makes a convincing case for why elites also deserve liberation from racialized capitalism. Throughout this book, Garrett offers crucial insights from within the halls of power, articulates his ongoing personal transformation in illuminating ways, and provides a clarion call to transform America's culture and systems in ways that not only enable but sustain equity. I believe everyone can glean something valuable from the discourse this book will generate. I have deep gratitude for having had the opportunity to contribute this introduction, and hope that this project can support the restoration of our humanity—and guide our thriving beyond history's suggestions and consequences about who rich white men are destined to be.

—a. k. frimpong

PART I

HOW THE OLD BOYS' CLUB REPRODUCES ITSELF

CHAPTER 1

COMPOUNDING UNEARNED ADVANTAGE

People have got to know whether or not their president is a crook. Well, I'm not a crook. I earned everything I've got.

—RICHARD NIXON, THIRTY-SEVENTH PRESIDENT OF THE UNITED
STATES, DURING THE HEIGHT OF THE WATERGATE SCANDAL

MYTH:

Rich white men earned everything we have.

It is difficult to get a man to understand something, when his salary depends upon his not understanding it.

—UPTON SINCLAIR, AMERICAN POLITICAL ACTIVIST,
AND AUTHOR OF *THE JUNGLE*

REALITY:

Rich white men benefit from compounding unearned advantages.

The wealthy philanthropist I interviewed in 2019 is an incredible American success story.

I'll call him Mark, after Mark Zuckerberg, because he, too, is a tech titan. The odds were against this Mark becoming a CEO of one of America's most powerful companies. Mark describes his upbringing in a mostly white suburb in Colorado as "solid middle class, lower middle class," but after he sold his pioneering company for $3 billion, he now lives among the ultrarich in a $20 million mansion in Atherton, California, the moneyed suburb that houses much of the Silicon Valley elite.

Mark's family didn't have the resources to pay for college, but after he aced a scholarship exam, he was guaranteed a full ride to a number of universities. When he flew to New York City for college, his trip to campus marked the first time he flew in an airplane. A few years later, his sterling academic record and work experience as an intelligence officer in the U.S. Army helped him secure admission to one of the nation's top business schools. That put him on the fast track to join the American elite. Mark's next stop was IBM, a prestigious technology company that gave him the network, skills, and credibility to build his own company. Later in life, he started sharing his wealth through philanthropy. He has served on his alma mater's board of trustees and supports an array of good causes.

During our conversation, we discussed the notion, which has emerged in some circles, that philanthropy is undemocratic and unaccountable. Hearing that perspective angered him. "We give money away not for the tax benefit but to help," Mark emphasized. "For people to do anything other than say thank you when I write a sixty million dollar check is absurd."

Like many philanthropists, this man believes that society will be better off if his surplus resources are in his control rather than with the government. "I would pay higher taxes gladly," Mark told me, "if I had a high degree of confidence that the government would spend it well. I don't have that confidence.... Government is not something to be trusted."

Later in our conversation, it emerged that at least part of what was animating him was his belief that he deserved his wealth and power, that he earned every penny he gives away. "I earned everything I have today," he told me. "I worked hard and was appropriately rewarded."

Mark doesn't buy the idea that the system is "rigged" in ways that benefit people like him. "That's unadulterated horseshit," he said gruffly.

Ultimately, this rich white man seems to feel that drawing too much attention to the advantages some people have is unhelpful, even counterproductive. "'Rigged' means the wealthy cheated the system. That's not the reality," he told me.

On one hand, I understand where Mark is coming from. He came from relatively humble beginnings, worked hard, and secured a different trajectory than his friends back home. If the system were truly rigged, how could he have achieved so much more than his friends and neighbors? And how could he have become more successful than most of his university classmates, even though most of them grew up with many more advantages than he had?

But on the other hand, his belief that his success relies on his hard work alone seems to require some willful ignorance. If the system is truly fair, why are there such persistent and dramatic disparities in wealth among different groups in this country? In America, after taking into account the relative size of the populations, white men are 125 times as likely as Black women to become billionaires. And the only reason the disparity can even be calculated is because Oprah Winfrey—America's only Black female billionaire—found a way to become an icon.

How could Mark have earned everything he has today when countless other people worked just as hard but never had access to the basic supports he had, such as good schools, safe streets, a college degree, and job opportunities? Would acknowledging these advantages dim his own shining star? Would it hurt his self-image to admit that the playing field isn't level and that he benefited from that inequality?

Mark is among the many rich white men I've met who get uncomfortable when it is suggested that they benefit from *privilege*, a concept that scholar Peggy McIntosh popularized in a 1989 essay that refers to social advantages, benefits, prestige, and respect that an individual receives because they belong to an identity group. Those advantages are rooted in historical context, in which rich, straight, white, able-bodied, Christian men in the United States and other Western societies used their identities to justify their domination over other groups.[1]

Many of the rich white men I've met bristle at the idea that they are "privileged" because the term doesn't feel fully accurate to them. When many people hear the word, they seem to imagine aristocrats living in palaces in Old Europe; people who exude snooty affluence, flaunt gaudy jewelry, and have servants at their beck and call. That didn't square with Mark's experience: he didn't grow up living like a prince, and he had to work a lot harder than a nobleman to achieve his wealth and status.

Another reason for hesitation is the sense that many of the things that are described as privileges are things that everyone ought to have. In the current context of American inequality, having a roof over one's head, enough to eat, or access to a safe neighborhood might be a privilege, but many people believe—rightfully, in my view—that those things ought to be human rights, not privileges. Part of the defensiveness about privilege seems to be an interpretation that those labeled as privileged ought to have such basic rights taken away from them. If I put myself in the shoes of someone who brings that interpretation, I can see how the term could feel scary and threatening. That seems to be especially true for white people in poverty who are struggling to meet even their most basic needs, and certainly don't want their lives to get harder.

A different rich white man told me that he would like to replace the word "privilege" with "advantage." "It is absolutely true that it is an advantage to be born white," he told me. "But it is also an advantage to be born the son or daughter of a wealthy Black family."

In his view, a privilege is static, but a disadvantage can be overcome by education and hard work. "A privilege is something else again, like the caste system in India or the class system that used to dominate England," he emphasized. "We don't live in that kind of system, and it is a disservice to our young people to tell them that we do."

The Racial Equity Institute (REI)—an antiracism training and consulting organization founded in 2007 that works with organizations and communities to help them understand how systemic racism works—has grappled with all this complexity. In its trainings, REI emphasizes that while white Americans are less likely to be in poverty than people of color, it is still the case that—because of America's demographic makeup and poverty trends—two-thirds of Americans living in poverty are white.[2] So REI is sensitive to the fact that low-wealth white people have often struggled to see their lives represented in discussions about socioeconomics and race. Since privilege is most often associated with material wealth and resources, financially struggling white people naturally push back on the term and are often deeply insulted by it.

Both to reflect the reality of white poverty and to engage low-wealth white people in understanding how racism impacts their lives, REI introduced the concept of "white advantage," which speaks to the benefits that even low-wealth white people experience across various measures of well-being. By focusing on unearned advantage—advantages people receive because they possess certain identity characteristics—REI and other organizations have brought many more people to the table. The term "unearned advantage" has a no-fault appeal; to some, it carries less baggage and feels less loaded than "privilege." The goal here, as I understand it, is not to make those who benefit from unearned advantages comfortable but to find a starting point for a constructive conversation in which everyone feels invested in addressing inequality.

Research in recent decades has confirmed what marginalized people have always known, that identity-based unearned advantages exist. In their 2013 book *Blindspot*, psychologists Mahzarin Banaji and Anthony Greenwald popularized the idea of unconscious bias, which refers to how our likes and dislikes and our judgments about someone's character, abilities, and potential are shaped at the subconscious level. Unearned advantage is also detected in *audit studies*, an approach used in economics, sociology, political science, and psychology in which just one identity characteristic is altered in a pair of otherwise identical people. For example, two résumés might be identical except that one has a male-sounding name while the other has a female-sounding name. By examining whether the altered characteristic results in differential treatment, audit studies test for discrimination.

Through these studies, we have learned that white men with a criminal record are more likely to be offered a job interview than Black men without a criminal record; that men are seen as more likable and a better fit for leadership positions than women; and that job applicants whose résumés include upper-class interests like sailing and polo are more likely to be offered interviews than those who list working-class interests like pickup soccer and country music.[3]

A growing number of people are becoming familiar with this research. However, in the elite spaces I have inhabited the past fifteen years, there remains a disconnect. Over and over, wealthy white men have broached the issue with questions like this: *Sure, bigotry and unconscious bias are problematic, but there aren't that many bigots, and these unconscious biases are so subtle we aren't even conscious of them. So how can unearned advantage explain the massive disparities we have in American society? Maybe unearned advantage matters to an extent, but don't hard work, talent, and luck matter more?*

Earlier in my life, I would have agreed with them. But eventually I came to see something that marginalized people have tried to help wealthy white men like me understand for centuries: even seemingly small sources of unearned advantage powerfully shape our lives and bend the arc of the universe toward injustice.

I've come to think of the life-changing impact that occurs when unearned advantages intervene at key moments in our lives as "compounding unearned advantage." Similar to compound interest, unearned advantages people inherit gild their own paths and limit the opportunities of everyone else. When those with advantaged identity markers receive better treatment from teachers, police officers, doctors, professors, hiring managers, bosses, sponsors, politicians, and others who have power to bend trajectories, even seemingly small unearned advantages can swell into great advantages.

Compounding unearned advantage says nothing about how hard any individual works or the quality of their choices. Rather, it simply acknowledges that those who benefit from unearned advantages receive a premium on their positive efforts and a discount on their missteps.

And the basics of compound interest dictate that even a slightly higher return compounds into great advantages over time. The compounding nature of unearned advantage is the reason even the most subtle negative stereotypes and unconscious biases have massive pernicious effects.

If there's one thing that rich white men know like the back of their hand, it's compound interest. When I was a kid, my dad taught me the rule of seventy-two, which is a way to estimate the number of years it takes for an investment to double in value. The way the rule of seventy-two works is that you divide seventy-two by the rate of return you're getting on your investment. For example, an investment with a 5 percent annual return will double every fourteen years (seventy-two divided by five is about fourteen). By contrast, an investment with a 10 percent annual return will double twice as fast—every seven years. Over time, the differences compound. For example, a $10,000 investment with a 5 percent rate of return will be worth about $100,000 in fifty years. How much would that same investment be worth with a 10 percent rate of return? $1.2 *million*. Each incremental increase in annual return fuels an exponentially different outcome.

Unearned advantages have compound effects, too. When someone benefits from ongoing unearned advantage—because of their gender, race, socioeconomic status, or other identity characteristic—the unearned advantages compound and cause trajectories to diverge.

One of the ways that compounding unearned advantage manifests is that it impacts career trajectories within institutions. In most companies and organizations, those who have advantaged identity markers are promoted at higher rates.[4] When the "promotion game" is repeated sequentially, those who have advantaged identity markers increasingly benefit from compound effects. Say, for example, that the odds of a white man being promoted in a company at each level are one in two and that the odds of a Black woman being promoted in a company are one in three (many companies aren't so equitable). When these different rates compound, the person benefiting from unearned advantage becomes more and more likely to climb the ladder. If the "promotion game" is played ten times over a career, the white man *is fifty-seven times* more likely to reach the top post than the Black woman. That result reflects the present reality: just forty-four Fortune 500 CEOs are women, and just three are Black.[5]

I wasn't always aware of the ways unearned advantages have helped me get ahead. Initially, they felt invisible to me. But over time, I've listened to enough stories from people whose lived experience is different from my own to see how compounding unearned advantages have shaped my trajectory as a wealthy white man.

I was struck one day when Julie Lythcott-Haims, an American educator and author, described to me her experience with her elementary school's gifted and talented program.

Julie is a Black woman from a mixed-race family. When Julie asked to be tested for the gifted program, her school refused. Julie's continued persistence only led her white teacher to dig her heels in further. Only when Julie's enraged *white* mother came to the school to talk to the principal did the school finally acquiesce. When Julie finally was tested for the program, she scored in the ninety-ninth percentile. Students had already been slotted into classes by the time Julie received her results, so Julie joined late. On her first day in the gifted program, Julie's teacher introduced Julie to her classmates in a way she will never forget: "Looks like anyone can be in 'gifted' if you have a parent who complains," she told the class.

My experience with my school's gifted program was entirely different—but it, too, is seared into my memory. To be sorted as gifted and make it into the Gifted and Talented Education (GATE) track, I needed to surpass the ninetieth percentile on the second-grade gifted exam. GATE students received extra attention from the best teachers, and that advantage compounds. GATE was the gateway to a top university—and a better life.

The test's math and reading questions came easily to me, but I felt lost during the spatial portion. A few weeks later, my mom and I opened the results. I scored in the eighty-seventh percentile. It was close, but I didn't make the cut. I was devastated.

I was just starting to process the experience when I learned that my teacher had approached my mom with a proposition. There was a possible workaround: according to school district policy, teachers can submit a portfolio to the district on behalf of a student and request that student to be admitted into the gifted program. Even though I hadn't passed the exam, she felt I was a high-potential student who deserved to be in the gifted program, so she told my mom that she wanted to recommend me via the alternative process. It required significant time and paperwork, but ultimately, I was labeled "gifted." And I've been on the "gifted" track ever since.

That credential put me on the accelerated track and then the Advanced Placement (AP) track, prerequisites for my admission to Stanford. Stanford provided the credentials and network that got me to Harvard for two graduate degrees and empowered me to start four nonprofits.

At the time, I felt my teacher's advocacy had righted a wrong. I felt I *was* gifted—my test scores just didn't reflect my potential (heard that one before?). Today, I acknowledge that it's more complex than that. How was I different from an equally intelligent student in a high-poverty neighborhood whose teachers may have been too overwhelmed to offer such advocacy? How could I account for the fact that—as Johns Hopkins researchers found—white teachers like mine believe white students have more potential?[6] Or the analysis of former Google data scientist Seth Stephens-Davidowitz, who found that in their Google searches parents are two and a half times more likely to ask "Is my son gifted?" than "Is my daughter gifted?" which suggests that many parents see their sons as more intelligent or—at the very least—are more invested in their sons' being intelligent because intelligence typically offers more status and financial rewards for men than it does for women.[7]

It is true that if the GATE test had included just the math and verbal sections—without the spatial component—I would have passed with flying colors. So the issue is not necessarily whether I had gifts—I believe *every* child has gifts—but rather that an assessment was made to label me "gifted" even though I didn't meet the criteria that other children were asked to meet.

Since the advantaged can sometimes game the system, gifted programs have reproduced America's legacy of separate and unequal schooling.

Similar to how white flight in the 1960s whitened suburban schools and effectively reinstituted segregation,[8] gifted programs whitened classrooms *within* schools. And as elite university admissions have become more competitive, many wealthy parents now spend thousands of dollars not only to help their teenagers succeed on the SATs but to ensure their elementary school–age children meet eligibility requirements for gifted programs.

Unequal access to gifted and talented programs is among the many ways that the playing field favors rich white men. Any of the unearned advantages that worked in my favor—growing up in a wealthy community with well-resourced public schools, having white teachers who believed in my potential, having a gender many parents associate with intelligence—could have been enough to shift my trajectory. But with all three in play, that outcome was exponentially more likely.

Compounding unearned advantage is about more than opportunity; it's about surviving an America that prioritizes individual indulgence over collective well-being. I suspect that's why many of those who lack a single advantaged identity marker—such as wealthy white women, wealthy Black men, and low-wealth white men—have told me that they feel oppressed. Little protects wealthy white women from sexual assault in a society that allows rape kits to collect dust and leaves rapists unaccountable. Little protects wealthy Black men from police officers and rogue vigilantes who can murder without consequence. And little protects low-wealth white men from the violence of poverty, which kills 874,000 Americans annually, more than cancer.[9]

Yet still, unearned advantage can be a shield in a violent world. It's not easy being a wealthy white woman in a male-dominated society, but the compounding unearned advantages of race and class offer some protection. It's not easy being a wealthy Black man in a white-dominated society, but the compounding unearned advantages of gender and class offer some protection. It's not easy being a low-wealth white man in a wealthy-dominated society, but the compounding unearned advantages of gender and race offer some protection.

When I heard about the white woman who threatened to send police after a Black bird-watcher in Central Park in 2020,[10] I was angry. And I was angry at the white male Lyft driver I met in Cincinnati who spent the entire drive spewing racist and xenophobic views about people of color in his community. But I also wondered: If I were underneath the weight of patriarchy or poverty—or both—would I try to hang on to my unearned advantages for dear life, too?

And if I'm honest, there are still instances when I leverage my unearned advantages to make my life easier or advance my own agenda—like when I asked a wealthy white couple if I could borrow their lake house for a month rent free so I could write under ideal conditions.

I imagine that people from marginalized backgrounds are sick and tired of rich white men claiming that we've earned everything we have when it is far more complicated than that. In those moments when we succeed, we can feel proud to have risen above the crowd. But we can still acknowledge the inconvenient truth that most people have been shut out of the game we've been playing.

We don't need to feel guilty or fragile about that. I can feel secure about who I am as a person and my contributions without feeling like I fully earned every accolade and success.

"Not everything that is faced can be changed," writer and activist James Baldwin once said. "But nothing can be changed until it is faced."

Acknowledging the truth about compounding unearned advantages will do more to set us free than any lie we tell ourselves ever could.

CHAPTER 2

WEALTH AND OPPORTUNITY

To turn $100 into $110 is work. To turn $100 million into $110 million is inevitable.

— EDGAR BRONFMAN SR., BILLIONAIRE PHILANTHROPIST AND
HEIR TO THE SEAGRAM FORTUNE

MYTH:

America is a meritocracy that offers equal opportunity.

Anyone who has ever struggled with poverty knows how extremely expensive it is to be poor.

— JAMES BALDWIN, AMERICAN WRITER AND ACTIVIST

REALITY:

American capitalism favors those who have access to capital. And in America, access to capital is highly unequal.

M inh Pham is an aspiring financier. We became friends at a conference for college students who were interested in entrepreneurship.

Minh is a first-generation Vietnamese American. His dad grew up in Hanoi, Vietnam's capital, where his family owned several high-end restaurants; he immigrated to the United States for his M.B.A. and spent his career in sales at a large biotechnology company. Minh's mom came to the States from Ho Chi Minh City, Vietnam's largest city, where her family of twelve had shared a two-bedroom, one-bath apartment. She got a job in IT and later met and married Minh's father. They settled in a Michigan suburb and set about pursuing the American dream.

Their son attended the local public schools, which were excellent. His classmates were mostly upper middle class and white, though many of his fellow AP students were Asian American. Minh graduated in the top 1 percent of his class. His parents earned too much to qualify for the financial aid his family would have needed to send him to a private university, so they were thrilled when his high marks landed him a merit-based scholarship to the University of Michigan.

Minh maintained a 4.0 GPA in one of the university's toughest majors. Then, two years in, he switched his career path from engineering to business. He set his sights on securing a summer internship with one of the Big Four accounting firms.

"I felt totally out of my depth," Minh told me. "I remember going to an accounting jobs Q and A session at Michigan. The panel was literally eight white dudes who were all six feet tall. I remember thinking, *There's no way I am going to get a job at a top-tier accounting firm.*"

Even the company's informal coffee chats were intimidating to him. "The first thing anyone asks you about is sports," he said. "My parents don't know anything about football or basketball. I had to memorize all these facts about Michigan football. It was crazy."

But his efforts to assimilate paid off. He landed an internship at PricewaterhouseCoopers, one of the most prestigious accounting firms. Overall, he had a positive experience there. He got the job done, and built strong relationships with leaders in his office, though he did have to turn down golf outings because he didn't know how to play. And he ended up prioritizing projects led by white women, whom he found "easier to connect with as a minority than the white dudes."

After his summer at PwC, Minh decided he wanted to take a crack at investing, which he thought might be more interesting—and lucrative. After college, he secured an Analyst position at a highly regarded boutique investment firm in Chicago.

At his new company, Minh encountered an environment dripping with unearned advantage unlike anything he'd seen at PwC. Nearly everyone who worked there was a rich white man. For the most part, his colleagues' fathers were titans of industry—partners and founders of investment firms and executives and CEOs of major corporations. "It is an intimidating work environment," Minh told me. "The founder has an anger problem. I still remember—during my first month, after a deal I was working on fell through, he punched a wall and broke two bones in his hand."

Minh wanted to understand the hiring process, so he signed up to support recruiting—and learned how the world of finance really works. His company partnered with headhunting agencies to generate recruiting prospects. At every agency, the entire recruiting team was composed of blonde white women who had played a varsity sport at an Ivy League school, Minh told me. "Even the gatekeepers come from that background." And applicants were as likely to be sorted by wealth and family ties as they were by work experience or academic success.

Minh was one of six associates hired in his class. Like many professional service firms, the company had an up-or-out approach: during orientation, the firm's leaders made clear that only one analyst was likely to end up on the partner track; the rest would need to find a new place to work. If Minh worked hard for the next eighteen months, he was told, the promotion could be his.

Minh sensed that status and connections that he didn't currently have might be important for securing the promotion, but he tried to not let that deter him. He had played the game in high school, in college, and at

PwC. And every time, he had won. Climbing the ladder in investing was just the next puzzle to be worked out.

But then, a few months later, Minh learned that his friend Adam—one of his white male colleagues—had already been promised the promotion.

Minh's mouth fell open. "How could that be?" he remembers asking Adam directly. "I thought those decisions were going to be made much later?"

With a sheepish look on his face, Adam told Minh that the investment firm's founder was considering buying Adam's father's company—and that the founder and his father had discussed over dinner that Adam was being groomed for the promotion.

Minh still remembers the anger he felt when he first heard that. "I'm pretty sure no one ever took my dad out to a Michelin Star restaurant and discussed over Foie gras whether I ought to be promoted," he said wryly, trying not to let the unfairness bother him.

Like Minh, I have also noticed that the closer I've gotten to the heart of American power, the more such backroom deals seem to reign. However, I haven't heard many of the rich white men I know acknowledge how they've leveraged such practices to secure opportunities, or to build and protect their fortunes.

Instead, many of the rich white men I've met have suggested that America's economic and political system offers *equal opportunity*, with chances for advancement open to everyone and with every person getting an equal chance to compete. "You can never have equal outcomes," JP Morgan CEO and white male billionaire Jamie Dimon said in 2020, "but you can have equal opportunity."[1]

Billionaire financier George Kaiser took Dimon's claim a step further. "America's social contract," Kaiser wrote in a public letter announcing he would give away the majority of his fortune, "is equal opportunity. It is the most fundamental principle in our founding documents and it is what originally distinguished us from the old Europe."[2]

Equal opportunity is a sister concept to *meritocracy*, a system that offers power and resources on the basis of talent, effort, and achievement rather than social class. Part of the reason rich white men are so committed to the idea, it seems to me, is that the legitimacy of our power relies on the public's belief that America functions as a meritocracy.

Equal opportunity and meritocracy are alluring, aspirational ideas. It's convenient to believe we have nearly realized such a system. Most of the rich white men I have talked to say that, while there is still work to do to achieve these ideals, America is on the right path and will arrive soon. That implies that equality is inevitable, but history suggests otherwise. Historically, most rich white men have resisted true equality, whether the issue at hand was slavery, women's suffrage, child labor laws, or civil rights.

It's not just that inequality isn't getting better; it's getting *worse*. Today, the richest 0.1 percent take home 196 times more in income than the bottom 90 percent.[3] In recent decades, the top 1 percent doubled its share of income while American poverty rates held steady.[4] CEOs have especially benefited from these trends: while the typical worker's compensation grew 14 percent in real dollars from 1978 to 2019, CEO pay increased by 1,000 percent.[5]

The rise in income inequality has also corresponded to less *social mobility*, a term that refers to how fluid a person's class status is in a society. While most baby boomers—born 1946 to 1964—grew up to achieve higher living standards than their parents, future generations haven't been so fortunate. Recent trends show that two-thirds of families in poverty remain in poverty a decade later, while most high-income families stay in the top strata.[6]

It's not just that the ceiling is rising. The floor is also falling out from under the working class. More than 140 million Americans—nearly half of the population—live below the official poverty line or are living paycheck to paycheck.[7] Adjusted for inflation, the 2020 federal minimum wage is a third lower than it was in 1970.[8] That loss—worth $3.42 per hour in today's dollars—is among the reasons why America's working class has become the working poor. "If you want the American dream today," Ford Foundation president Darren Walker told CNBC in 2019, "you ought to move to Canada."[9]

Some economists and politicians say that the American dream is fading because the economy isn't growing as quickly as it once was.[10] That's a partial truth: GDP did grow more quickly in the 1950s and 1960s, when the American middle class blossomed.[11] However, faster growth wouldn't be enough to reverse social mobility trends. When David Grusky, who runs Stanford's Center on Poverty and Inequality, conducted simulations to predict what American inequality would look like now if today's GDP growth rates matched the growth rates that baby boomers experienced, he found that an uptick in GDP growth would make up for just one-third of the decline in social mobility.[12] What accounts for the rest? The widening distribution of incomes, which has become a gaping chasm over the past few decades.

But a focus on income inequality largely misses the point. *Wealth, not income, seems to be a much better predictor of life chances and mobility.* While few studies to date have explored the relative impact of income and wealth on long-term life outcomes, the Institute for Fiscal Studies has found that children born into wealthy families are six times as likely to be wealthy as adults, a disparity that is far greater than the impact of the income divide.[13]

In America, wealth inequality is more extreme than income inequality. While America's top 1 percent capture 19 percent of income, they hold 32 percent of the wealth—about $40 trillion.[14] When the World Economic Forum surveyed 103 countries in 2018, it found that the United States had the sixth-highest wealth inequality.[15] That level of inequality is on par with Russia—infamous for its oligarchs—and South Africa, which has struggled to dismantle its apartheid legacy.[16] Among "developed" countries, American wealth inequality is unique.

Wealth is the financial backbone of unearned advantage. While hard work is pitched as the key to financial success, the top 1 percent of American wealth holders—each worth $10 million or more—typically collect $500,000 or more from annual investment returns alone.[17] Because of lenient tax policies that allow most inherited wealth to be passed down, work is optional for wealthy Americans. That's a literal reinvention of aristocracy.

A significant portion of American wealth is unearned. Economists estimate that a third of American wealth—about $30 trillion—is inherited.[18] Of those born into the top 1 percent, 41 percent inherit an average of $4.8 million.[19] In fact, 21 percent of the Forbes 400 were "born on home plate," inheriting enough money to snag a spot on the list without any earnings of their own.[20]

Yet many beneficiaries of inherited wealth are reluctant to acknowledge how unearned wealth has shaped their lives and opportunities. For example, in a public letter that outlined his motivations for participating in philanthropy, Richard Edwin Marriott—heir to the Marriott fortune—said he and his wife Nancy decided to give back when they realized "how blessed we have been to be born and raised in this great country with the freedom to choose our paths in life and receive an appropriate reward for our efforts and ideas."[21] Is inheriting a multibillion-dollar fortune an *appropriate* reward for inheritors like the Marriotts?

Marriott

Even lesser fortunes confer meaningful advantage. As Warren Buffett's mentor Benjamin Graham has observed, the first $100,000 in wealth is the most difficult to secure.[22] So those who inherit even a relatively small sum still have a big leg up.

I am a beneficiary of inheritance. When my grandmother passed away, her will granted me $50,000, which I used to pay off my undergraduate student loans and put money down on a condo. Eliminating my student loans lifted a major psychological burden, which gave me more confidence that I could safely pursue an entrepreneurial career. While college graduates from low-wealth families spend their first decade—if they are lucky—getting their net worth out of the red, those who have access to intergenerational wealth, like me, are all but guaranteed the American dream from birth.

I also benefited from less-formal wealth transfers. Before my grandmother passed away, she paid for one-sixth of my Stanford tuition, worth about $30,000 at the time. These transfers enabled my parents to preserve wealth they have since invested and ultimately enabled me to graduate debt-free. Throughout college, my parents gave me a credit card attached to their bank account so I could live more luxuriously than the typical college student. I returned that credit card after college, but they continued to provide gifts at critical points—including helping my wife and me furnish our first home. Perhaps most importantly, I know I'd have my parents' financial support if I encountered a true emergency.

Some of my particularly wealthy Stanford classmates had even more generous arrangements. After college, I was surprised at how often friends told me that their parents paid their rent. Shortly after I graduated from college, a newly minted Goldman Sachs banker told me his parents paid his rent because "$100,000 is not enough to live on in New York City." One wealthy couple I know, whose son works at a New York hedge fund, gave their son $250,000 for the down payment on his condominium. That kind of assistance plays a critical role in wealth inequality because home equity is the primary source of wealth for the middle class.[23] *Circle of wealth*

And the benefits accrue all along the road to millionaire status, because buying a home in an affluent area is the surest path to the American dream. Wealthy communities generate more property tax revenue, which they reinvest into higher-quality public services.[24] American public schools are typically funded by local property taxes, so wealthy communities have resource-rich public schools. Many wealthy communities also supplement public dollars by establishing local education foundations. For example, Silicon Valley's Woodside School District has a private foundation that augments public spending with an extra $5,400 annually for each student.[25]

Wealthy families make extraordinary investments outside of school, too. According to a 2017 article in *Town & Country* magazine, affluent families spend an average of $1.4 million on each of their children before they leave for college.[26] That includes major investments in private school education and enrichment opportunities like music and art lessons, foreign-language tutors, travel sports leagues, SAT preparation, college counseling, cultural immersion programs, and service abroad programs. These eye-popping investments are a central reason why at five of the eight Ivy League colleges—Dartmouth, Princeton, Yale, Brown, and Penn—more students come from the top 1 percent than the bottom 60 percent.[27]

Some experts propose that low-wealth people ought to move to high-opportunity neighborhoods. There is some wisdom behind this approach: those who live in such neighborhoods get better outcomes, regardless of their individual wealth. For example, even after controlling for factors like socioeconomic status and race, children who grow up in DuPage County, a wealthy Chicago suburb, earn dramatically more than the national average.[28] However, most people can't afford to live in places like DuPage, which is Illinois's most expensive locale.[29] Nationally, homes near high-performing elementary schools are 140 percent more expensive than those near low-performing schools.[30]

And many affluent communities work hard to remain exclusive. A common practice is exclusionary zoning, like policies that permit only single-family homes—not apartment buildings, which are accessible to a more socioeconomically diverse population—in neighborhoods that have high-performing schools.[31] These dynamics perpetuate a cycle of compounding unearned advantage: affluent families move in, schools and services improve, property values increase, property taxes increase, schools and services improve even more, and even wealthier people move in. While wealthy parents are getting richer and their children are getting better schooling, low-wealth families are increasingly shut out.

The neighborhood I grew up in followed this pattern. When my parents moved to a Southern California suburb in the early 2000's, single-family homes cost about $500,000. Two decades later, those same homes have tripled in value. As housing has become more expensive, the community's public services have improved. That's led to a tangible shift in opportunity. For example, the first few years that my high school was open, Stanford accepted about one student from the school each year. Today, several get in. America has more than ten times as many high schools as Stanford has slots,[32] so my high school is increasingly getting more than its share. That's because students and the school have more resources, not because its students have more merit.

For millions of American families, unearned advantage buys access to these exclusive neighborhoods. Nearly half of homeowners in affluent counties receive financial help from family or friends to purchase their homes.[33] Many parents cosign on their children's mortgages, enabling them to secure lower interest rates and monthly premiums.[34] As a result, they pay off mortgages more quickly and have more money to invest elsewhere, which compounds.

If these unearned advantages weren't enough, federal policy further enriches the wealthy. For example, in recent years, the federal government doled out $200 billion annually in tax refunds to homeowners via the mortgage interest deduction.[35] This benefit is only available to those who itemize their taxes—typically middle-class and wealthy people—so most of the checks benefit the already-wealthy: 70 percent went to families who make $200,000 or more.[36]

The mortgage tax deduction is one of many "upside-down" tax policies that primarily benefit the wealthy. Each year, the United States issues $1.2 trillion in tax refunds via its tax expenditures program.[37] That's nearly double the government's military budget, which sustains eight hundred bases in seventy countries. While a few programs, such as the earned income tax credit, offer relief to low-wealth families, much of the $1.2 trillion subsidizes wealthy families. From mortgage and retirement subsidies alone, the typical member of the 1 percent receives over $18,000 annually, whereas middle-class people receive about $500.[38] Yes, the wealthy are more subsidized by the American government than the poor.

And the ultrawealthy benefit from unearned advantages that even everyday millionaires do not. Capital gains are taxed at half the top income bracket rate, which nets often already-rich people $130 billion annually.[39] Intergenerational wealth transfers also benefit from protections: $13,000 in annual gifts are tax-free, the first $10.9 million is exempt from inheritance tax, and capital gains are exempted when investments are passed directly onto heirs.[40] After they exploit every possible deduction and loophole, those in the top 0.001 percent—whose adjusted gross incomes exceed $62 million—pay a lower percentage of their income in taxes than secretaries, firefighters, and nurses.

For the ultrawealthy, even being a philanthropist can be profitable. There is, of course, the charitable tax deduction, which nets a cohort of mostly wealthy people some $50 billion a year, all of which can be reinvested. But there are also more opaque, ancillary benefits, like the fact that philanthropic circles offer access to proprietary information and social capital that yield financial benefits. "I am quite sure that I have earned financial returns from giving money away," hedge fund billionaire Bill Ackman declared in a public letter about his commitment to philanthropy. "Not directly by any means, but rather as a result of the people I have met, the ideas I have been exposed to, and the experiences I have had as a result of giving money away. A number of my closest friends, partners, and advisers I met through charitable giving. Their advice, judgment, and partnership have been invaluable in my business and in my life."[41]

The rich pay lower taxes in large part because most wealthy people prefer those policies. In a 2013 study, Princeton political scientists found that wealthy people are much more fiscally conservative.[42] While fifty-two percent of Americans think the government should redistribute wealth via heavy taxes on the rich, just 17 percent of wealthy Americans do. And while 78 percent of Americans think the federal government should make sure everyone who wants to go to college can, just 28 percent of wealthy Americans do. In the same study, researchers found that the policy preferences of wealthy Americans are highly correlated with the policies that are signed into law. Meanwhile, the policy preferences of the typical American do not have a statistically significant link to real-life public policy.

Given this disheartening finding, elites ought not to be surprised that many Americans are pessimistic about the ability of government to improve their lives and that resentment is building among low-wealth Americans of all racial backgrounds.[43] Politicians are literally ignoring everyday people's political preferences in order to secure donations they need from the wealthy to win elections. That's what happens in a plutocracy, not a democracy.

It also ought not to be surprising that in a capitalist system, beginning life with more capital is an advantage and a source of power. In such a system, those who start with more capital benefit from unearned advantage that they can convert into exponentially greater unearned advantage over time. *Compound interest*

Compound interest—which Albert Einstein described as "the eighth wonder of the world"[44]—is capitalism's greatest strength. It enables some people who start life without wealth to transform relatively modest savings into a sizable nest egg. And occasionally, it enables a small number of people—usually white men—to become the rags-to-riches stories that America loves to celebrate.

However, with respect to democracy and social mobility, compound interest is capitalism's Achilles' heel. It's tough to climb in capitalism without capital, and as wealth becomes increasingly concentrated, it becomes easier for incumbent wealth holders to hoard it. As a result, the descendants of wealthy people typically stay wealthy, whether or not we work hard—or, in many cases, at all.

After the civil rights movement secured legal rights for African Americans, that foundation could have enabled America to begin moving toward becoming an equitable society. Instead, America doubled down on wealth inequality, during both Republican and Democratic administrations. That approach has angered people who feel shut out of the American dream. For Black people, it has always been clear that the playing field is not level.[45] Now low-wealth white people are feeling resentful, too, tantalized by riches they feel entitled to but somehow still find are outside their grasp. The rich white movers and shakers want low-wealth people to think equality is just around the corner, but we keep moving the goalposts so that the more things change, the more they stay the same. If it all sounds pretty dire, that's because it is.

However, a growing number of Americans are fighting back. The Poor People's Campaign—a national social movement led by Rev. William Barber and Rev. Liz Theoharis—is calling for economic justice in America. Patriotic Millionaires is a group of high-net-worth individuals with annual incomes above $1 million and/or assets above $5 million who are committed to raising the minimum wage, combating the influence of big money in politics, and advancing a progressive tax structure.[46] One for Democracy is a collaboration of philanthropists, business leaders, and donor advisers committed to donating 1 percent of their wealth to supporting community organizers and protecting our democracy.[47] Over one hundred millionaires and billionaires from nine countries have signed an open letter calling for permanent taxes on the wealthy in order to reduce extreme inequality and raise additional recurring revenue for public services.[48]

My generation—the millennials—and subsequent generations are especially fed up with extreme wealth inequality. One organization that has tapped into that youthful energy is Resource Generation, a community founded in 1998 that now includes 1,200 members—all young adults under the age of thirty-five who are among the richest 10 percent of Americans *and* are committed to the equitable distribution of wealth, land, and power.[49]

Through my nonprofit work, I came to realize that I was indeed a "limousine liberal," a pejorative that refers to wealthy liberals who claim to advocate for everyday Americans yet live lavish lives. After I began to understand the costs of wealth inequality, any personal desire I had to join the rich white guys' club dissipated. I joined Resource Generation and other, similar circles, which helped me see how other wealthy people were organizing their families and networks to redistribute wealth in ways that reduce systemic inequality. That journey has led me to meet some inspiring people—like Chuck Collins, who gave away the money he inherited as a descendant of the Oscar Mayer fortune and now fights inequality full-time as the director of programs on inequality and the common good at the Institute for Policy Studies.[50]

For wealthy Americans, taking on wealth inequality requires facing the ways that our advantages were inherited, not earned—and the fact that those inheritances have historically been used to lock working-class people out of social mobility. But any material difficulties that wealthy Americans might encounter on the path to reducing wealth inequality are trivial compared to the hardships that Americans in poverty wrestle with each and every day.

CHAPTER 3

WHITE ADVANTAGE

Poor kids are just as bright and just as talented as white kids.

—JOE BIDEN, FORTY-SIXTH PRESIDENT OF THE UNITED STATES

MYTH:

If America addresses economic injustice, racial injustice will also be solved.

Color-blind racism is the new racial music most people dance to. The "new racism" is subtle, institutionalized, and seemingly nonracial.

—EDUARDO BONILLA-SILVA, AUTHOR AND SOCIOLOGY PROFESSOR AT DUKE UNIVERSITY

REALITY:

Among those with equivalent levels of wealth, whiteness still offers compounding unearned advantages.

In fall 2019, just before midnight, I flipped open my Apple laptop and opened my Gmail account. There I found an email from Connor, someone I had never met.

"You are the problem," the subject line read.

I was already on edge because of an op-ed I'd written about white privilege, which had run in the *Boston Globe* that day.[1] Most of the hundred-plus comments posted online were negative, including two dozen the *Globe* blocked because they included racial slurs or other profanities. There was doxing, too, like the comment that mentioned my wife and where she worked.

Apprehensively, I hovered my mouse over the email and clicked.

"Keep trying to stir that shit pot there pal! White privilege is bullshit!" the email began.

"Go fuck yourself," Connor wrote in closing. "You are a race baiter and only creating more hate, dividing us more."

In his message, Connor described his ancestry, lived experience, and perspective:

I am white 30 years old and come from a very low-income family of Irish Americans, my great grandfather was brought here to work on a power grid when he was 16 yrs old. He was far underpaid and discriminated against for lack of education, for being poor, and for his nationality. He worked hard his whole life and still struggled, where was the white privilege? Four generations of hard working, good men who all raised their children in poverty but taught them it is never right to judge anyone based on color, race, money or anything other than character and virtue.... [When I lived] in Hawaii I had to be very humble and give respect even when treated poorly, walking on eggshells is an understatement. Never once did your horse shit "white privilege" come through to bail me out or save me. Now if you want to talk about WEALTH PRIVILEGE then I agree, for that is what lies at the root of our problems. I have always been poor just as my great grandfather was, and have always worked hard but never been able to rise out of poverty. It's because I'm not wealthy, and do not have white privilege.

It was a difficult message to read. I felt attacked, and it troubled me that Connor so strongly denied white advantage. However, I also felt compassion for him. Clearly my article had struck a raw nerve. I am someone who has benefited from wealth advantages that Connor's family lacked. From Connor's perspective, I presume, I was yet another wealthy elite talking about how white people had too much, when he and his white family had very little at all. Why couldn't I see his pain? Why didn't I care that his family had struggled for generations? How could I say the deck was stacked in his favor when he could barely put food on the table?

For a couple of days, I weighed whether to reply to Connor's message. Other people who have written about controversial issues had advised me not to "feed the trolls." And Connor *had* cursed me out. Yet he didn't seem like a troll. Over time, I have learned that underneath anger, there is usually pain. I thought that it couldn't hurt to see if there might somehow be a way to bridge the differences in our perspectives. So I decided to reply.

When I responded to Connor, I thanked him for taking the time to write to me and sharing his family history. Then I validated his feelings and lived experience. I acknowledged that he seemed like a good person who cared about his family, and I told him I had compassion for his family's experience with intergenerational poverty. I shared that I agreed with him that wealth inequality is a central issue in American society, and I talked about how unearned wealth compounds and why I see that as unjust.

Then I challenged him. I told him that, while white advantage doesn't guarantee that a person will become rich, historical discrimination—like slavery and Jim Crow segregation—made it more likely that white people would become rich and then pass on those advantages to their children.[2] I also mentioned that even if white advantage doesn't enable a family to become wealthy, it is helpful in other ways; for example, low-wealth white people typically have more contacts who can offer help in a financial emergency and also receive better treatment from the various actors in the criminal justice system, including police officers, judges, and juries.[3]

I closed by affirming him again. Even though it is statistically true that white people are more likely to escape poverty than Black and Indigenous Peoples, I emphasized that it is difficult to break free of poverty, regardless of one's race. I also emphasized that it doesn't need to be this way; that policy ideas have been proposed that would help end poverty. The example I gave is "baby bonds," a policy idea championed by United States senator Cory Booker that would open a savings account with $1,000 in it for every baby born into a low-wealth family and add more money every year depending on household income.[4] When those children reach age eighteen, they can access that money for opportunities that support wealth building, like purchasing a home or enrolling in college. "I am looking forward to your thoughts," I wrote in closing. "I truly believe that no one should live in poverty, and I would like to partner with you to build a better and more just America."

Twelve hours later, Connor wrote me back:

> Wow. Sorry for attacking you like that, and thank you for enlightening me. I see that we actually agree where problem lies. The white privilege is more of a biproduct of wealth privilege as well as stain left behind after we washed the dirty history of slavery and real racism. I think it just bothers me on a personal level because most people use the term wrong and only in negative ways trying to make others feel certain ways. It is very broad term since there are many white skinned races. Anyways I truly appreciate your reply. Wish I could have gone to college so I could be more informed and also able to make a change.

I learned a lot from that interaction. Because of the bubbles I've lived in, I have few relationships with people who have a background like Connor's. And as I've often done when I lacked relationships with those whose lives are different, I initially judged him unfairly. Connor, his family, and other people in similar situations deserve better from rich white men like me.

I don't mean to suggest that anyone in Connor's situation would have reacted similarly to my response. America is a complex country. No cure-all can singularly mend this nation's vast divides. Still, paths forward are starting to emerge. When I read the 2010 book *Difficult Conversations* by Douglas Stone, Bruce Patton, and Sheila Heen, which came out of the Harvard Negotiation Project, I learned that it is often difficult for people to listen unless they feel heard. I've also found that when I validate people's emotions and lived experience—with the intention to understand and empathize, not to manipulate—I've built stronger relationships, which can spark productive collaborations. I've come to understand that it is exhausting for marginalized people to validate other people's pain when so often they don't get that validation in return. That's why I believe that the most advantaged are uniquely responsible for validating other people's pain.

For all the assumptions that I've heard rich white men make about working-class white people, a growing body of evidence that suggests that low-wealth white people can be recruited into the progressive coalition. In a 2021 experimental study, *Jacobin* magazine, YouGov, and the Center for Working-Class Politics found that populist, class-based progressive campaign messaging that names elites as a major cause of America's problems, invokes anger at the status quo, and celebrates the working class resonate with working-class voters.[5] Perhaps because of a perceived need to cater to wealthy donors, Hillary Clinton, Joe Biden, and other leaders in the Democratic Party establishment have largely steered clear of these framings.

I've also learned that white people in poverty have reason to be concerned when elites call for racial justice without mentioning economic justice. In a 2019 study, psychologists found that after liberal Americans contemplate white advantage, they are less sympathetic to white people in poverty, whom they perceive as failing to leverage white advantage.[6] When wealthy white men talk about a single oppressive system—even with the best of intentions—it can feel as if we are erasing America's many other oppressive systems that impact people's lives. That is dangerous because it can reinforce bigoted ideas about those who experience oppression we aren't naming.

Economic and racial justice doesn't need to be an either-or proposition, but from the very beginning, rich white men have driven a wedge between white and Black Americans in poverty. Growing up, the impression I'd gotten is that low-wealth white people and Black people never got along. So I was surprised to learn that, early on, before "white" was a term that defined social class in the United States, poor white and Black people developed close friendships on rich white men's plantations.[7] It took popularizing "whiteness" and explicitly racist policies to tear these friendships apart. In 1705, rich white men gave their white indentured servants a racial bribe: ten bushels of corn, thirty shillings, fifty acres of land, and a gun.[8] In exchange, these indentured servants were convinced to abandon their multiracial rebellions. Plantation owners also punished white servants if they allowed enslaved Black people to escape plantations, and offered rewards when they tracked down Black runaways and brought them back.[9] Over time, the bonds between low-wealth white and Black people withered. Similar to how the British Empire used divide and rule to control its colonies, rich white American men used the racial bribe to create the false impression that working-class white people had more in common with wealthy white planters than they did with their Black neighbors. That legacy has never been overthrown, so it persists into the present. The current system still treats low-wealth white people poorly—so poorly that many continue to cling desperately to their race-based advantages—while treating low-wealth Black people even worse.

We've already discussed how inheriting capital can, to say the least, come in handy while trying to succeed in America's capitalist system. What we haven't discussed is how access to capital varies greatly by race: while 10 percent of white families have no wealth, about 30 percent of Black and Indigenous families are in that situation.[10] The median white family is ten times wealthier than the typical Black or Indigenous family, and the average white family is seven times wealthier.[11] Both figures matter: the median is a proxy for the typical experience within a racial group, and the average is a proxy for that racial group's relative power.

That distribution of wealth is not a coincidence. During settler colonialism, rich white men stole 3.8 million square miles of land from Indigenous Peoples,[12] which is now occupied by real estate built that is valued at $70 trillion.[13] During slavery, white Americans extracted 410 billion hours of unpaid labor from enslaved Black people;[14] many Indigenous Americans were enslaved, too, a practice that continued decades after the Emancipation Proclamation under the guise of "civilizing the savages." No matter what hourly figure is used to quantify the value of that labor—which doesn't even account for damages that ought to be paid for assault, rape, and murder—the inevitable result is a figure in the trillions of dollars.

I grew up thinking that my own advantages were generated independently from America's racist systems. My socioeconomic advantages came primarily from my dad's side of the family, which had come to America from Hungary and Ukraine in the early 1900s, a half century after slavery. They settled in California, thousands of miles from the Jim Crow South. And, they were Ashkenazi Jews, who had immigrated to the United States to avoid persecution themselves.

On top of it all, the socioeconomic advantages I inherited were hard won by my ancestors. When he was in eighth grade, my great-grandfather Dave left school to take a job in Ohio's steel mills. Eventually, his family relocated to California, which required great resourcefulness on their part: to finance the move, Dave's parents started up small grocery markets in multiple towns along the way. They reached California when Dave was sixteen, which is where—a few years later—he met my great-grandmother Anne, whom he'd gotten to know while they were both working at Dave's family's bakery. After high school, Dave attended night school to get an accounting degree. Eventually, he learned to make pickles, and applied his business acumen by renting a storefront from his brother Jack to sell them.

After his brother Jack raised his rent, Dave decided he eventually wanted to go out on his own. He and Anne pinched pennies throughout the Great Depression, and by the mid-1930s, they'd saved enough to secure a business loan, which enabled Dave to buy an industrial building in Boyle Heights in East Los Angeles. The pickle factory he created there became a successful family business. That success generated some family wealth, which enabled Anne to purchase a six-unit apartment building, not far from downtown. Two decades later, Dave and Anne had saved up enough to move to Beverlywood, a more affluent neighborhood. Dave and Anne also acquired a love for investing, and—when they had money to spare—purchased some stocks that skyrocketed during the time they held them, including Edison, GE, and Philip Morris.

Dave's son Moe—my dad's father—married my grandmother Ann at eighteen. After he and Ann discovered that they were pregnant with my dad, Moe quit college and went to work for his father Dave in the pickle factory. Income from that job enabled them to purchase two homes consecutively, but they later downsized to an apartment in order to free up cash to buy a twelve-unit apartment building in Los Feliz, a neighborhood just east of Hollywood that—at the time—was in a redlined area that included racial restrictive covenants that prevented Black buyers.

When my dad was a sophomore in high school, his family moved out of the apartment and bought a home in Cheviot Hills (like Los Feliz, Cheviot Hills also had racially restrictive covenants to ensure that all buyers were white). My dad credits the efforts of his ancestors—including positive family values like diligence, financial responsibility, and an emphasis on education—as empowering him to become the first in our family to earn a graduate degree. And that advanced education unlocked more opportunities, including equipping him with the credentials, job experience, confidence, and skills to purchase and develop his own private day care and elementary school. For the first six months, he opened and closed the center himself: he'd arrive by 6 a.m., drive over to his day job as a school psychologist a couple hours later, and came back to the school until 6 p.m. That persistence enabled the center to become a thriving business that sustained our family for four decades, while also contributing to the growth and development of 4,000 children from a variety of backgrounds.

Ultimately, everything in that sequence enabled me to be raised in an economically secure family in a safe and well-resourced neighborhood that had high-performing public schools. It also enabled significant gifts from my grandmother, which enabled me to graduate from college debt-free and helped my wife and me buy a condominium in my twenties. I am incredibly grateful for the hard work and example set by my ancestors, who overcame significant adversities so that I could experience life with fewer stressors and more opportunities.

Eventually, though, I've come to see how for many Americans, hard work and persistence aren't enough. The person who most helped me grasp that reality is Josephine Bolling McCall, an elderly Black woman I met in 2018 who was born and raised in Lowndes County, Alabama, in the heart of the Jim Crow South. When I met Josephine as part of a Harvard Kennedy School study trip, I caught a glimpse of what our family story might have looked like if we hadn't been racialized as white.

When I met Josephine, she told us about her father, Elmore, who rose from poverty to build a trucking and farming business that employed many people and sustained his family. Elmore's business offered well-paying jobs for Black people, services valued and used by white business owners, charity for churches and individuals, and security for his own family.

It immediately struck me that my great-grandfather Dave and Elmore had a lot in common. The two men were born just a few years apart, Dave in 1905 and Elmore in 1908. Both started with just a few dollars to their names and became pioneering entrepreneurs.

Yet while my family acquired the American dream, Josephine's family endured what Malcolm X has described as the American nightmare. In 1947, angry white people, resentful that Elmore was winning business contracts they thought should have been theirs, shot Elmore dead. His life was cut short at thirty-nine. As Josephine documents in her book *The Penalty for Success*, Elmore's death unraveled his survivors in ways that have persisted for generations. Without a male breadwinner in a viciously racist and sexist era, the Bollings quickly depleted their wealth. They've been trying to claw their way back into the middle class ever since.[15]

Elmore was one of four thousand Black people lynched in the century after the Civil War and among the countless Black people targeted specifically for their success. Some Black people, like Elmore, were pursued individually, while others were attacked collectively through large-scale attacks like the 1921 Tulsa Race Massacre, during which white mobs destroyed Black Wall Street, murdered hundreds of residents, and burned a thousand homes to the ground.[16] The only terrorism on US soil more deadly and economically damaging were the 9/11 attacks. While many families like mine were building intergenerational wealth, many Black families' nest eggs were going down in flames.

Such extreme state-sanctioned white terrorism drove millions of Black people north, where they became forced migrants yet again. White people sought safety in the suburbs, but Black refugees were stranded in deteriorating urban centers. Instead of investing in these communities, authorities hired more police, built more prisons, and launched a war on Black people that politicians disguised as the war on drugs.[17]

When I've discussed with relatives our family's connection to white advantage, they acknowledge that Black people had it tougher at the time. But acknowledging white advantage feels more difficult, since they also feel—rightly—that they and their ancestors overcame hardships so their descendants could have a better life.

Like many white people in poverty today, my Jewish ancestors were trapped in the middle of a knotty American hierarchy: they were at the whim of oppressive rich white men like Andrew Carnegie, who ordered his steel mills to exploit countless children from families like mine. *And* my ancestors transcended poverty with wind at their backs from whiteness. "Yes, they had it easier," one family member eventually conceded to me, "but their lives were not easy."

Over time, I've come to accept both truths—that the exceptional unearned advantages I benefit from today are the result of my ancestors' hard work *and* a system that only enables certain Americans to convert hard work into intergenerational wealth and power. What I eventually concluded is that the system doesn't need to operate this way: my ancestors wouldn't have needed to overcome so much adversity had Gilded

Age robber barons not leveraged their power to crush equitable policy proposals such as higher minimum wages and child labor bans. It angers me that—a century later—millions of American families are still being put through a similarly barbaric trial by fire, perhaps in exchange for even fewer potential rewards.

When I've heard Americans suggest that this nation offers equal opportunity, I've found that it's usually other white people who are making that claim. Yet such a perspective leaves out that, due in large part to historic discrimination, 90 percent of inherited wealth in America flows to white people. Disparities in inherited wealth are among the central reasons why 95 percent of American millionaires and 98 percent of American billionaires are white.[18] It also helps to explain why, on average, white high school dropouts are wealthier than Black college graduates.[19]

Learning more about racial wealth disparities put my family's financial status in a new light. Since I grew up in a well-to-do white suburb and attended Stanford—which had many students from even wealthier families—I used to describe my class background as upper middle class. But after I learned that most Black, Indigenous, and Latinx families have hardly any wealth at all, I started to see that from the vantage point of most people of color, white families that own property in affluent white suburbs and have access to intergenerational wealth are *rich*.

When Harvard Business School classmates and I visited one of South Africa's richest people in Cape Town as part of a study trip, I also started to see how the compounding unearned advantages of whiteness also accrue to those of European descent in other nations.

Known for its natural beauty, Cape Town boasts some of the world's finest scenery, restaurants, and wineries. It is the largest city in a country that toppled apartheid in 1994 and elected Nelson Mandela as its first Black president of a new multiethnic government. Yet despite its progress, South Africa remains among the world's most unequal countries. Millionaires and billionaires live on large estates while a quarter of the population lives on less than $3.20 a day.[20] Almost all the millionaires are white, and almost everyone in poverty is Black.

From our hotel downtown, we drove up a winding road into the hills and stopped in front of a mansion, which is where I met the family's patriarch. I'll call him Cecil, after Cecil Rhodes, the British imperialist who was the benefactor behind the Rhodes Scholarship, which has held cachet ever since it helped launch Bill Clinton's political career. Buoyed by inherited wealth and two Ivy League degrees, this Cecil became CEO of one of South Africa's largest companies.

We came inside into a large sitting area. Fancy tapestries lined the walls. Black servants brought us a dizzying array of courses. Cecil asked what had brought each of us to Cape Town. I said I wanted to experience the country's natural beauty and inequality firsthand.

Inequality. The word itself was a trigger for our host. His defense of South Africa's racial hierarchy would dominate the rest of our group's evening.

Because the best defense is a good offense, he started by going after the United States. "Mexican immigrants aren't doing too great in your country," Cecil noted.

His point was that inequality was rife in the United States, too. I think he expected me to get defensive, but when I acknowledged their disadvantage, admitting that Mexican Americans faced significant discrimination and America needed to do better, he seemed flabbergasted.

"The Black South Africans do not work because they receive government grants," Cecil countered. His bravado had returned. His voice started booming, and he cited the *Daily Show* host in his defense. "If Trevor Noah were so oppressed, how did he become so literate?"

His wife was embarrassed, and she unsuccessfully tried to change the subject. Eventually she guided us to a different, less formal room, seemingly hoping that a change of scenery would shift the discussion. After we'd relocated, Cecil pulled me aside. "Come outside with me. I want to show you something," he said.

Cecil pointed to the neatly manicured grass in his backyard, which stretched into the distance. "Our gardener is from Malawi," he proclaimed proudly. "The Malawians are *very* hardworking. They aren't like Black South Africans," he said confidently.

I was disturbed. His comment reminded me of how many white

Americans I have met who believe it possible to distinguish between "good" immigrants and other people of color.

As he finished his comment, one of his servants walked by—a light-skinned Black man who would have been designated "coloured" by the apartheid regime, which insisted that he be treated worse than white people but better than other Black South Africans.[21] It was a classic implementation of divide and rule, elevating a portion of an oppressed population to get the working classes to fight amongst themselves instead of directing their anger at their oppressors.

"Tell this young man about the Black South Africans," Cecil directed his servant.

"Oh, yes, they are lazy. *Super* lazy," he told me. "I mean—most of them have water and electricity now, and they're *still* complaining."

It was a somber moment. Here was a white man and light-skinned Black man colluding together in a Cape Town mansion to perpetuate anti-Blackness. Perhaps the interaction was shaped by power dynamics—after all, the rich white man paid his servant's salary—but it felt as if they were aligned, rallied behind a shared political orientation. The narratives they deployed were nearly identical to how white American bigots describe Black Americans. If it sounds like they were working from the same playbook, it's because they were. As Trevor Noah himself notes in his 2016 book *Born a Crime*, South Africa's apartheid regime sought inspiration by studying Jim Crow.[22]

Due in large part to such internationally synchronized bigotry, North Americans and Europeans hold 57 percent of the world's wealth—over $200 trillion—while representing just 17 percent of the global population.[23] Meanwhile, Africans—who represent a similar percentage of the global population—hold just 1 percent of the world's wealth. Latin Americans hold 2 percent.[24] These global realities mirror the domestic racial wealth gaps between white, Black, Indigenous, and Latinx populations in the United States. Centuries of colonialism and white supremacy—in the United States and elsewhere—have reproduced white advantage *everywhere*.

In America and around the world, I've observed a tendency to paint

Connor/Cecil perspecties

all white men with the same brush. Some aspects of the white male experience are shared regardless of socioeconomic status, but there are also important differences between perspectives like Connor's and perspectives like Cecil's. Connor is seeking relief from financial distress and desperately wants his pain to be acknowledged and addressed. He is eager to see wealth redistributed so that he and his family have a shot at the American dream. Cecil, on the other hand, isn't interested in those kinds of policies. He thinks the system is fair, so he doesn't grasp why policies might need to change. Unlike Cecil, Connor was willing to acknowledge white advantage as soon as he knew I was sympathetic to the challenges he faced in a society overrun by wealth inequality.

In America, there is a hunger to sort out whether race or class is the principal cause of inequality. What some experts have helped me understand is that race *was* class until the Civil Rights Act of 1964. And because nearly all the wealth inherited before 1964 flowed to white people, the compounding unearned advantages of wealth are almost always attached to the compounding unearned advantages of whiteness. Therefore, wealth advantage is perhaps better understood as a *feature* of white advantage—available to a subset of white Americans—than as a distinct set of advantages. As a result, race and class continue to be deeply intertwined.

Many Americans believe that hard work and perseverance can lift anybody over economic barriers. My immigrant ancestors' rise seems to testify to that. Still, being white crucially shaped their experiences. I've met many rich white men who proudly claim that their ancestors came to America with nothing, but the truth is, we came with white advantage that offered exclusive access to opportunity in the greatest wealth-building era in the history of the world. And white men have used that advantage to subjugate people of color for centuries—commandeering land, exploiting unpaid labor, and decimating families and cultural bonds—in service of building a social hierarchy that persists into the present.

CHAPTER 4

MALE ADVANTAGE

If women wanted to be appreciated for their brains, they'd go to the library instead of to Bloomingdale's.

— MICHAEL BLOOMBERG, BILLIONAIRE PHILANTHROPIST AND PRESIDENTIAL CANDIDATE FOR THE DEMOCRATIC PARTY

MYTH:

Gender equality in America is just around the corner.

Women are graduating from film schools, law schools, and medical schools in equal numbers as men, but they are shut out when they get to the leadership positions. We have to think about why this is.

— MERYL STREEP, AMERICAN ACTRESS AND ACADEMY AWARD WINNER

REALITY:

Men benefit from highly durable compounding unearned advantages.

Pat Patriarchy

The founder of the leading hedge fund I was interviewing is known for his clarity of thought. I'll call this rich white man Pat, short for Patriarchy.

Pat's novel predictive financial model is seen by many as the source of the remarkable investment returns he has replicated for decades. While clearly a capitalist, Pat has also started writing and speaking about the importance of reforming capitalism and reducing inequality, since he believes changes must be made to protect America's standing in the world.

I had thought that Pat and I might see many of the issues similarly, yet our interview took a turn when I asked Pat a question he seemed to have never been asked before: If he had been born a Black woman, how wealthy would he be today?

As a multibillionaire, he may have found this to be a complex question. After all, he is richer than Oprah, America's wealthiest Black woman. There is no precedent in America for a Black woman accumulating as much wealth as he has.

At first, Pat sidestepped the question, emphasizing there were "some positives" to being a Black woman in America. His example? "It's probably easier," he told me, "to get on a corporate board if you're a talented Black woman."

The numbers tell a very different story. Of the 5,670 board seats in the Fortune 500, just 154 are held by Black women. That's 2.7 percent. By comparison, white men hold 66 percent of the seats.[1] Clearly, Pat must believe there is a shortage of talented Black women.

When our discussion shifted to patriarchy more broadly, this otherwise-articulate man became almost incomprehensible. "Society, at the top tends to be more, uh, more male in that society," Pat told me. "So, they tend to have more of, uh, oh, you know, I don't know, a little bit of a, boy, fraternity, kind of, you know, okay, you know, that can be that way."

I felt as if I had encountered a bug in Pat's computing system. He had agreed to an on-the-record interview. He knew in advance that the topic was inequality, but he still seemed caught by surprise. In his mind, inequality was about class—not race, gender, or anything else.

All his "you knows" were telling. It seemed he presumed that because I am also a wealthy white man, there was a kinship between the two of us, that I knew how it all worked.

As he went on, the conversation took a turn for the worse, devolving into a proclamation about his views on the biological differences between men and women. "There are things that have to do with... hormones... the difference between having estrogen and testosterone," Pat told me. "A man in an argument can recover from an argument in a half hour," he proclaimed confidently. "For a woman it might actually take a day to recover for those things, having to do with... our makeups and things like that."

It was a disturbing exchange. Pat was willing to acknowledge that men ran the world, but ultimately, he relied on differences in talent and biology to explain why.

The biases of rich white men at the top matter. Every day, Pat has dozens of opportunities to exercise his judgment and shape the opportunities of those around them. When rich white men like Pat decide whom to select as the next board member or chief executive, which up-and-coming leaders to sponsor and mentor, which politicians to back, which philanthropic initiatives to fund, or even whom to interrupt in a meeting, these biases—implicit and explicit—shape trajectories. When there's a bias at the top, that bias typically ripples through the culture of the organization. "An institution," American poet Ralph Waldo Emerson once said, "is the lengthened shadow of one man." And when that bias is embedded in leading national institutions—like it is in the United States Supreme Court, where male justices interrupt female justices three times as often as they do each other[2]—its effects ripple through entire societies.

When bias is institutionalized within an organization's culture, opportunities for compounding unearned advantages abound. During a stint at McKinsey, I noticed how compounding unearned advantages accrue to male employees at another powerful institution.

While my colleagues and I were being onboarded as summer associates, one of my female colleagues asked some of the firm's white male leaders about its plans to foster gender equality. She was concerned about the fact that just six of the fifty individuals promoted to senior partner that year were women.

The white male partners emphasized that equality was just around the corner. Nearly half of the company's new hires were women. So, if she committed a decade or two to the firm and rose up the ranks alongside these other recently hired women, she could expect to be part of a gender-equal partnership later in her career. They made achieving equality sound easy, and inevitable.

Yet in my very first days on the job, I encountered cracks in this argument.

"I *really* appreciate your ordering lunch for us," Andrea—one of my peers on the project—told me in my first week.

Andrea is sharp as a tack. In college, she was top of her class. Though just twenty-three, Andrea had already developed outstanding analytical and interpersonal skills.

I didn't think spending five minutes ordering lunch for the team was a big deal, so I found her enthusiastic gratitude surprising.

"Usually," she added softly, "it's the female business analysts who do stuff like that."

Just a year out of college, she had already learned one of corporate America's infamous unwritten rules: unpaid, undervalued work is a woman's responsibility.

That reality ran counter to what I had heard in the firm's recruiting and onboarding pitch. Over and over, the company had professed its ostensible commitment to promoting gender equality and fostering a workplace environment that was inclusive for women. On my interview day, the cover of the recruitment brochure featured a smiling white woman.

Yet considering what I had learned of how unearned advantages compound, my colleague's offhand comment suggested a lot about the culture and who might be expected to advance. That's particularly true at a company known for its up-or-out policies, since marginal variations in performance ratings can determine who is promoted and who is pushed out. In such an environment, every moment on task counts, both for meeting deadlines and for producing the breakthrough ideas for which the firm charges its clients millions. In that way, it is similar to other professional service firms that adhere to a pattern identified by scholar Linda Babcock and others: women are disproportionately saddled with "nonpromotable work." Such tasks lead to recurring losses in work time that cost women advancement and other professional benefits.[3] And despite all the talk about gender parity, the age-old practice of men doing the "real work" while women ensure the men are well fed and comfortable is alive and well.[4]

A few weeks later, I learned that lunch responsibilities were just the tip of the iceberg. Young female associates also had to deal with sexual harassment, often in the guise of corporate hijinks.

One friend of mine remembers being warned by an experienced McKinsey colleague to "watch out for" a certain partner at the firm. "He *really* likes South Asian business analysts," she was told. "You're *exactly* his type."

The partner was a man tasked with mingling with hundreds of summer interns at a ritzy hotel conference. But I watched him spend the entire evening at the poolside bar in close quarters with a South Asian summer analyst, a junior in college who was not yet legally old enough to drink.

I considered reporting the incident, but my friend suggested that would be pointless. "This kind of thing happens all the time," she said. "Besides, if you are going to report someone, there are a bunch of other people who are *much* worse than him." (I did report the incident. As of this writing, the man is still at the firm.)

Nowhere in the McKinsey employee handbook does it say that female employees are responsible for undervalued, administrative work. Nor does it say that male employees are entitled to the bodies of their female colleagues, or that female employees must band together to protect themselves from perpetrators. McKinsey boasts about its "caring meritocracy," but many of the white men in charge seem reluctant to acknowledge the ways that the organization struggles to be caring and meritocratic with respect to how it treats its female employees. My impression is that McKinsey is more interested in landing seven-figure contracts to advise other companies on diversity and inclusion than it is in cleaning up its own shop internally.

Such inaction perpetuates disparities that produce compounding unearned advantages for men. Over the past fifteen years, the gender pay gap hasn't budged: in 2020, women earned 84 percent of what men earned, according to a Pew Research Center analysis of median hourly earnings of both full- and part-time workers.[5] Some of that gap is due to direct gender discrimination—different pay for the same work—but there are other factors, too.

One significant issue is occupational segregation, since women remain underrepresented in positions that offer access to wealth and power. And the more wealth and power an occupation offers, the more women are typically underrepresented. For example, venture capitalists have backed America's seven richest people.[6] All seven are white male technology entrepreneurs, and their combined wealth exceeds $1 trillion. Yet there is a particularly large gender disparity in how capital is allocated: in 2021, Bloomberg reported, just 2 percent of venture capital dollars went to women founders.[7] That figure inched upward to 3 percent in 2019, at the height of the #MeToo movement, but it's back down again.[8] While women are gaining more access to historically prestigious fields perhaps in decline—like medicine, which is becoming less lucrative[9]—they remain locked out of the richest and most powerful industries. Other factors contribute to the gender wage gap, too, like the fact that women continue to be routinely punished professionally for having children while men receive a "fatherhood bonus."[10]

The environment inside these money-making fields reflects the influence of a male-dominated culture that mirrors wider societal norms, where masculinity is permitted, or even encouraged, to be toxic. Most

toxic masculinity

of the wealthy white men I've discussed this topic with seem to have only a superficial grasp of the concept of toxic masculinity. Often, when the phrase comes up, men I know have started laughing.

Toxic masculinity underpins a legacy of violence that is no laughing matter. And it is a cultural choice; alternatives have existed in other cultures and throughout history. Before Europeans colonized Turtle Island—a name that refers to the totality of the Indigenous territories claimed by the United States—gender-equal societies flourished.[11] In the Haudenosaunee Confederacy—the nations that French colonizers called the Iroquois—women enjoyed equality long before colonizers arrived in 1492.[12] Unlike colonial women, Haudenosaunee women had significant political authority and influence. Women participated in all major decisions, and checks and balances ensured power was shared across genders. While men served as chiefs, women held the power to nominate, select, and remove chiefs; they also held veto power over any act of war and were the principal arbiters of justice. If the United States were to adopt such a model for its context, the approximate equivalent might be something like a male president whose power is balanced out by an entirely female Supreme Court and Congress. Women were powerful at home, too: unlike colonial women, Haudenosaunee women were the principal landowners and were free to divorce their husbands. In their quest for power, European male colonizers diminished or extinguished gender-egalitarian societies that had thrived for millennia all around the world. Some colonizers went as far as to claim that the presence of gender equality was part of what made Indigenous communities "uncivilized."[13] It's a lesser-known history that the toxic masculinity of white male colonizers extinguished not only Indigenous Peoples but also gender equality.

In part because this history remains hidden, many wealthy white men struggle to grasp how the term relates to our current context. My sense is that when they hear the phrase "toxic masculinity," many rich white men imagine a man who is physically abusive. As a result, men who don't behave that way—or behave that way only occasionally—don't think the label applies to them. Similar to how they describe racism as being

[handwritten marginalia: toxic masculinity embedded in the culture]

[handwritten marginalia: gaslighting, emotional abuse]

perpetuated by bigots, many rich white men claim that toxic masculinity is perpetuated by a few "bad apples" and not embedded in the wider culture. Many even mock the phrase, suggesting they have found what they believe to be another example of women "exaggerating" or "being too sensitive." That is a sexist idea and a type of gaslighting, which itself is a form of emotional abuse.

Green Hill Recovery—a nonprofit in Raleigh, North Carolina that helps young men recover from substance addictions—defines toxic masculinity as "the need to aggressively compete with and dominate others." By contrast, they define healthy masculinity as "the idea that men can be emotionally expressive, have female friends or mentors, and express their emotions without feeling emasculated."[14] What I have come to realize is that toxic behavior is simply any behavior where a person takes an action to get their needs or wants met at the expense of others. And when we rich white men prioritize our desires above other people's needs, that reflects a high degree of entitlement.

The predatory behavior of the McKinsey partner at the intern conference was toxic. Given the power he held relative to summer interns, his advances were buoyed by some degree of coercion, which is an abuse of power. Feeling entitled to flirtation, or more, at a work event is toxic behavior. No psychologist would say it's appropriate to meet our desires in this way.

Perhaps no heterosexual male behavior is more toxic than having unhealthy expectations about sex without requiring consent. My sense is that most men take their sexual autonomy for granted. Even male police officers and military personnel are less likely to encounter violence on the job than female nurses.[15] "We don't report sexual violence," one nurse emphasized, "because it happens so often." Unequal treatment at work also leads women to be less safe during their commute: women are more likely to be required to work odd hours and face greater risks of sexual assault when they commute to and from their workplace at these times.[16] *[handwritten marginalia: work hours.]*

Men are safer in many other ways as well. At home, men are half as likely as women to experience severe physical violence such as beating,

Violence as a deliberate mechanism

burning, or strangling. Half of all women murdered are killed by a husband, boyfriend, or ex-partner.[17] Online, men receive fewer digital threats, and the threats they receive are less severe.[18] As a result, men are also largely shielded from the aftereffects of sexual violence and other forms of physical violence. Like all systems of oppression, patriarchy leverages violence as a deliberate mechanism to maintain control.

Part of why sexual terror is so pervasive is that most of the time, men are not held accountable for their behavior. One rigorous study estimated that in New York City, 96 percent of sexual harassment incidents and 86 percent of sexual assaults are not reported.[19] Other studies have found that over 90 percent of sexual assault on college campuses and 88 percent of child sexual abuse is not reported.[20] Even when women report sexual assault, men are rarely held accountable. In her *Atlantic* article "An Epidemic of Disbelief," journalist Barbara Bradley Hagerty describes the process that enables most perpetrators of sexual assault to get away with their abusive behaviors.[21] A victim files a report, then officials assign a detective, then the detective decides whether to make an arrest, then a prosecutor decides whether to bring the charges to trial, and finally a jury decides whether to convict the accused. Justice routinely falls short somewhere among those steps, and 98 percent of the time, men accused of rape go free.[22]

The process of how male rapists avoid accountability is an example of how repeated unearned advantage produces compound effects. Reporter Brandon Stahl calls this pattern a "reverse domino effect." Prosecutors consider that juries are older than the general population, more conservative, and more skeptical of rape allegations, so they don't prosecute as often as they could.[23] When detectives see that prosecutors are declining most cases, they conclude a case isn't worth investigating unless they're confident that it will see a courtroom. And when police or prosecutors decline to move forward, victims have effectively no recourse. Similar to how men's odds of being promoted at work are bolstered by unearned advantage at each level, the process for holding men accountable for sexual assault is a repeated game in which subtle biases at each stage chip away at the likelihood of securing justice. Until men see sex as requiring consent and not an entitlement, many of us will continue to weaponize sex as a toxic tool for upholding power.

While women face gender-based terror at home, at work, and in their communities, men benefit from a peace of mind that helps enable us to maintain power. Men are significantly less likely to report experiencing public incivility, which means we typically experience public spaces as less threatening.[24] Men are safer from threats from people we know, too: men are a third as likely to be aggressively stalked by an intimate partner during their lifetime.[25] In public, while women are eyeing their surroundings for possible threats, men are relaxing, refining their ideas, or listening to podcasts. Every minute we aren't worrying about our safety offers opportunities for the unearned advantages of patriarchy to compound. *safety*

An increased sense of safety is one of the countless ways that we have more autonomy over our time as men, which translates into having more time that is productive or rejuvenating. Regardless of class status, leisure time is an unearned advantage that is largely available only to men. Men do less of what many of us consider to be women's work, taking on just a third of childcare responsibilities and a quarter of housework. Each week, the typical man creates seven hours of housework that women clean up. Even when a man is unemployed and his female partner is working, he typically does less than half of the housework. Later in life, when their parents age and their children have babies, men spend less time caring for aging relatives and their grandchildren.[26] Over his lifetime, the typical man does four years less of unpaid work than the typical woman, a greater amount of time than it took me to get two graduate degrees.[27] *Time*

Even America's social aesthetic offers unearned time advantages to men. Popular magazine *Glamour* found that men save 362 hours each year by spending less time on basic grooming tasks: doing their hair, shaving, applying and removing makeup, manicuring their nails, selecting outfits, shopping for clothes, waiting in fitting room lines, and waiting in restroom lines.[28] These 362 hours represent forty-five workdays—or 2.3 work months—every year. Over a lifetime, these activities are equivalent to fourteen years of work.

And all these activities aren't just about vanity or entertainment. Women who wear makeup earn more than women who don't, although such women still earn less than men.[29]

While men sometimes trivialize unearned advantages like these, the male backlash that occurs when even the smallest advantages are withdrawn offers a glimpse into how deeply men value them. When Soldier Field, home of the Chicago Bears football team, added more women's restrooms to reduce the amount of time women spent in restroom lines, men complained until five women's restrooms were converted back into men's restrooms.[30] This reversion doubled the time women spent in line waiting to enter the restrooms. Compounding unearned advantage also includes the power to make small tweaks for convenience.

After all, leisure time *matters*. It is how human beings relax, recharge, explore ideas, and plan for the future. I used to think of leisure as a luxury afforded primarily to the rich. That is true, to an extent. But what I eventually came to see is that by leveraging our collective power, men have engineered a world where—much of the time—even working-class men get more leisure time than wealthy, powerful women.

The world is optimized for men in other ways, too. In her book *Invisible Women*, Caroline Criado Perez chronicles how men tally unearned advantages because we are seen by society as "the default." Car safety is one example: cars are designed for male bodies and tested on crash dummies modeled after men. As a result, in a car crash, women are 73 percent more likely to be seriously injured than men and 17 percent more likely to die.[31] Health care is another arena: male diseases are better studied, and medical textbooks offer photos of male body parts three times as often as female body parts.[32] That may be part of why women are more likely to die from heart attacks: their experience is less studied and their symptoms are more likely to be overlooked by doctors.[33]

Even nearly ubiquitous products are designed with men in mind. Everything from bricks to wrenches are sized for male hands, which is one among the many reasons why men are seen as a better fit for many construction jobs.[34] So are iPhones, which ensures men are more productive during the 5.4 hours Americans spend on their phones each day.[35] And thermostats are usually set to accommodate male metabolic rates, resulting in room temperatures five degrees too cold for women.[36] Researchers have found that when women take standardized tests with room temperatures that better align with their metabolic rates, gender gaps in test scores disappear.[37] The modern world is designed for men—and the unearned advantages compound.

One of the ways we men abuse our power is that we often don't listen to women, which is disrespectful and oppressive. I learned this lesson the hard way. If my spouse had not gone to great lengths to get my attention, this chapter wouldn't even be in the book.

"You know that book you're writing about racial justice?" Pooja asked me on a sunny scenic drive in Cape Town, South Africa, in 2019 on our way to visit the city's famous vineyards.

"Uh-huh," I said.

"You need to write about gender, too," she said, in a tone that signaled this was not merely a suggestion. "Think about me, your sister, your mom, the daughter we may have. What world do you want us to live in?

"I wrote something on the plane," Pooja added. She pulled out her phone and read a letter she'd composed on her flight. Her declaration included a long list of things she felt I didn't understand about sexism and books she felt I needed to read. Usually Pooja finds me smart, but on this topic, she clearly felt I wouldn't figure it out on my own and needed a lot of direction. Just days after I had made a self-righteous call to Pooja, where I had expressed my shock at Cecil's ignorance, the tables had turned in my direction.

As I listened, memories of a prior conversation with Pooja rushed back. "You know, if you really cared about social justice," she'd said, "you would consider being a stay-at-home dad so I can better keep up with all the male surgeons who have stay-at-home spouses."

She was joking, but I was so consumed by anger and fear that I didn't realize it. *Maybe I have made a mistake encouraging such open conversation at home about sexism*, I remember thinking. *How could I allow this to happen?*

"Allow"—as if I was the one who gave permission. We had always talked about intellectual ideas and ambitious career pursuits. We'd always supported each other's professional goals. We'd talked openly about our commitment to an equitable world and an equitable marriage. Suddenly I was questioning the wisdom of all of that. It felt like I'd opened a Pandora's box I could never close.

Before I could even open my mouth to respond, though, I was consumed with shame. Was that really who I wanted to be—a man who pushed back on his wife's career ambitions the moment he had to compromise? We'd talked many times about our shared desire for a fifty-fifty marriage. I'd actually thought we had one. But I hadn't considered that in a world where most men don't pull their weight, gender equity can only be achieved if many other men—including and perhaps especially some of us with grand professional ambitions—shoulder the majority of responsibilities at home. The mere suggestion that an equitable contribution might be needed from me was overwhelming.

Throughout our relationship, I had used my own identity-based advantages to claim the lion's share of our collective attention, shortchanging her in ways that I didn't see. She called me out on these behaviors and forced me to see how my attitudes had hobbled me as a partner, a future parent, and a change agent. And, if I'm honest, an equitable partnership still doesn't come easily to me. I've done the easier parts—like stepping up my chores game—but we still spend more time on my professional priorities and spend more money on things I want. As much as I believe in the benefits of a truly equal marriage, contributing equitably is still difficult for me.

As the father of a young son, I'm also struggling to be an equal partner as a parent. While she was breastfeeding, Pooja was on call twenty-four seven in ways I wasn't. Yet I still found the transition to being a parent more exhausting and a bigger adjustment than she did. After talking to other new dads, my impression is that this is a common experience. I think this is because parenting is the first event that significantly impacts our autonomy as men. This is in contrast to women, who are routinely expected to defer to the needs of others and whose autonomy is often diminished and questioned. My wife has had a lifetime to acquire resilience in ways that I'm still developing. While we men like to imagine ourselves as omnipotent and unbreakable, I've found value in acknowledging the ways that Pooja is stronger than me and worthy of emulation.

When rich white men don't listen, there are often ripple effects that impact people around the world. If that sounds fantastical, consider Melinda Gates, who opens up in her book *The Moment of Lift* about her decades-long struggle to get her husband, Bill, to see her as an equal partner.[38] Although the Bill & Melinda Gates Foundation bears both of their names, Melinda did not have equal decision rights, which kept a $1 billion initiative to advance gender equality on the back burner. It was only after Melinda convinced Bill to capitalize Pivotal Ventures, a separate fund that she oversees, that she was able to launch the initiative. Apparently Bill saw advancing gender equality as women's work that was unfit for the foundation that bears his name.

In 2019, a World Economic Forum study estimated that it will take the United States another 268 years to reach gender equality.[39] How much time did America lose because one rich white man didn't see his wife as an equal and treat her as a full partner? How much could this country gain if even a few powerful white men took that step?

After Pooja convinced me to bring an intersectional lens to this book, I came across a letter that Abigail Adams wrote in 1776 to her husband, John, who would go on to serve as the second president of the United States a couple of decades later.

"And by the way in the new Code of Laws which I suppose it will be necessary for you to make," Abigail wrote, "I desire you would Remember the Ladies, and be more generous and favorable to them than your ancestors. Do not put such unlimited power into the hands of the Husbands. Remember all Men would be tyrants if they could."[40]

She may have been thinking in part of Napoleon Bonaparte, who, across the Atlantic, had proclaimed that "nature intended women to be our slaves. They are our property."[41]

I felt a lump in my throat. I saw myself and Pooja in the interactions between John and Abigail. Here was a rich white man who, I imagine, felt he was doing something extraordinary, even radical: he was trying to build a new, more egalitarian country.

Yet two and a half centuries later, wives like mine are still pleading with rich white men like me to see their lives and perspectives as equally valuable. America has made real progress, but in important ways, little has changed. As much as I like to think of myself as an advocate for Black Lives Matter and other social justice movements, I'm embarrassed to say that, in some ways, I am still struggling to value even my own spouse's life equally.

Enough is enough. Change can be scary, but it's time for us men to chart a new path.

CHAPTER 5

INTERSECTIONAL ADVANTAGE

We're throwing down a fat party THIS SUNDAY. In honor of Valentine's and President's Day, celebrate the legacies of our two-timing forefathers—Clinton and Lewinsky, Kennedy and Marilyn, Jefferson and Sally Hemings (get some, Jefferson).

—EVAN SPIEGEL, COFOUNDER OF SNAPCHAT AND ALUMNUS OF STANFORD UNIVERSITY'S KAPPA SIGMA FRATERNITY

MYTH:

The wealthiest 1 percent of Americans are the most advantaged.

The world can be a brutal place for a girl with a penis.

—JANET MOCK, AMERICAN TELEVISION HOST AND TRANSGENDER RIGHTS ACTIVIST

REALITY:

The intersectionally advantaged benefit from unearned advantages that no amount of money can buy.

The retired academic I was meeting with had just finished an impactful decade as the president of his institution. He's a biologist, so I'll call him Charles after Charles Darwin, known for his theory of evolution. While at the helm of one of America's most prestigious private universities, Charles had shattered his institution's fundraising records. The endowment had grown dramatically, which had fueled major expansions of research in a variety of fields and new scholarships for socioeconomically disadvantaged students.

Charles has access to a remarkable range of knowledge. Whether the subject is cancer, climate change, the COVID-19 pandemic, criminal justice reform, or social mobility, he opines with expert-level eloquence. Several years earlier, he had shared with me one of his secrets to success: every week he invited a different faculty member over to his office for lunch, which gave him opportunities to soak up knowledge from their field of expertise.

So when I interviewed him for this book, I was surprised to find that my topic stumped him. "In your own words," I asked, "how would you define 'intersectionality'?"

There was a long pause. For a moment, he fumbled with his words. Then he sighed. "I can't. I can't define it."

Admitting that he couldn't answer a question seemed to have been an uncommon experience for him. I sensed that he was embarrassed. "That's okay," I reassured him. "It's a complicated topic. We can move on."

Coddling white people

Looking back later, I was surprised by my instinctual desire to comfort him—what I've heard people of color describe as the coddling white people sometimes desire to soothe their ignorance. Charles is a powerful white man who had served on the boards of several large and influential companies. But in that moment, I found him to be resigned, and exposed.

I wasn't shocked that intersectionality was among the few topics that hadn't reached his radar. In 2018, just 3 percent of his university's full-time professors were Black or Latinx women. Other elite universities are no better: as of 2020, Harvard reported the same figure.[1]

American lawyer and UCLA law professor Kimberlé Crenshaw is credited with coining the term "intersectionality," which she describes as "a metaphor for understanding the ways that multiple forms of inequality or disadvantage sometimes compound themselves."[2] The obstacles that can create "are often not understood within conventional ways of thinking about antiracism or feminism or whatever social justice advocacy structures we have," she explains. It's a way to understand the complex interactions between interlocking dimensions of identity.

Intersectionality first entered the lexicon as a legal concept. In a 1989 paper published in a legal journal, Crenshaw develops the metaphor of a crossroads of two avenues—one denoting race, the other gender—to illustrate how certain types of discrimination can manifest at the intersection of two identities.[3] She argues that those who focus on each individual road ignore the way that intersecting traits can amplify the discrimination that occurs.

In her paper, Crenshaw cites a 1976 discrimination lawsuit against General Motors. Emma DeGraffenreid and several other Black women argued that Black women were excluded from the General Motors workforce. Women were invited to apply for jobs held exclusively by white people, and Black people were invited to apply for jobs exclusively held by men. As a result, even though some women and some Black people secured jobs at General Motors, no Black women were hired. The court dismissed the claim because General Motors was not entirely excluding Black people or women. Crenshaw conceptualized intersectionality as a legal framework so DeGraffenreid and millions of other women of color would not continue to fall through the cracks.

But it's not only in the courts where women of color are overlooked. In 2014, business school professors at Wharton, Columbia, and NYU conducted an audit study that looked at the impact of intersectionality.[4] They sent emails to 6,500 professors at top American universities from eighty-nine disciplines and 259 institutions. The emails came from fictitious prospective students requesting a ten-minute meeting to discuss research opportunities before applying to a doctoral program. The messages were identical; the only difference was that student names were randomly assigned to signal gender and race. For example, Brad Anderson was a name used for white men; Keisha Thomas for Black women; Raj Singh for Indian men; Mei Chen for Chinese women; and Juanita Martinez for Latinx women.

Whom did professors agree to meet with? The fictitious white men got more invitations than white women, and white women got more invitations than women of color. And the more monied an institution was, the more biased it was: business school professors were 40 percent more likely to offer to connect with white men than women of color, and private university professors also demonstrated atypical favoritism for white men. The study confirmed Crenshaw's observation that multiple sources of disadvantage can produce compound effects.

Within most institutions, white women and people of color—and especially women of color—face growing marginalization as they climb the ladder. For example, consider a company that has an entry-level workforce that is 40 percent white men, 30 percent white women, 20 percent men of color, and 10 percent women of color. What happens if, at each level, 50 percent of white men are promoted, 40 percent of white women are promoted, 30 percent of men of color are promoted, and 20 percent of women of color are promoted? (Such patterns are typical at many companies.) As this repeated game is played over and over, women of color disappear quickly, men of color disappear eventually, and white women remain only in small numbers. By the fifth level, the makeup is 78 percent white men, 19 percent white women, 3 percent men of color, and 0 percent women of color. And by the executive level—the tenth level—white male power becomes unalterably dominant: 92 percent are white men, 7 percent are white women, 1 percent are men of color, and 0 percent are women of color. Subtle biases, repeated over and over, reproduce compounding unearned advantage.

These dynamics may also help to explain why many white women often do not feel they are harmed by discrimination early in their careers, only to find later that it gets in their way. That is, the deeply held biases that limit opportunity for people of color initially help to create the *illusion* that the playing field is level for white women. But as white women move up the ladder and people of color disappear, white women increasingly become the primary targets of white male bias. By the time many white women realize what is happening, their numbers have dwindled and they lack the critical mass they need to fight effectively for equal treatment.

When Rinku Sen, Indian American author and former executive director of Race Forward, a racial justice organization based in Oakland, California, talks about intersectionality, she emphasizes that it is an analysis of identity, not an identity in itself.[5] "We wouldn't say that someone had a complicated, intersectional identity," Sen writes in a blog post for Narrative Initiative—the nonprofit she currently runs—entitled "How to Do Intersectionality," "because we all have that. There is nothing more complicated about my identity than that of a white, middle-class, straight man." That said, "some of these identities give us a leg up," she says, "while others push us a rung down the ladder. The combination of identities can compound (or diminish) advantage or compound (or relieve) harm."

Height is one such example. In 2004, psychologists Timothy Judge and Daniel Cable found that those who are at least six feet tall earn, on average, nearly $166,000 more during a 30-year career than someone who is five feet five inches, even when controlling for gender, age, and weight.[6] Height seems to be especially useful for climbing the ladder: in his 2005 book *Blink*, Malcolm Gladwell documented that 58 percent of Fortune 500 CEOs are at least six feet tall, even though only 15 percent of American men and 1 percent of American women cross that threshold. And over half of those CEOs were at least six feet two, even though just a quarter of six footers have those extra inches.

From what I've observed, the next generation of tall elites seems eager to maintain these advantages. In fact, the only time I personally felt excluded at Harvard because of my appearance was when—at a school formal—one of my taller male classmates suggested that a class photo be taken that only included those who are at least six feet tall. The other tall guys were happy to oblige. All of my female classmates were excluded, as were shorter guys like me. I clock in at five foot eleven—and in that moment, I really wished I'd had that one extra inch.

Like other sources of identity-based unearned advantages, height intersects with other identity characteristics. Since women are rarely six feet tall, gender height differences may be among the reasons why women are underrepresented in leadership positions. Anecdotal evidence seems to bear this out, since many well-known female leaders are atypically tall: former Hewlett Packard CEO Meg Whitman is six foot one; First Lady Michelle Obama is five foot eleven; U.S. Senator Elizabeth Warren, former Yahoo CEO Marissa Mayer, and former Facebook COO Sheryl Sandberg are all five foot eight; and Urusla Burns, who became the first Black woman to lead a Fortune 500 company in 2009, is six feet tall. Sometimes, it appears, part of what it takes to break glass ceilings is being tall enough to reach the glass.

At the same time, though, I don't want to imply that height carries the equivalent weight of other identity-based hundred advantages like socioeconomic status, gender, and race. I couldn't find a specific study that analyzes these intersections explicitly, but I find it telling that there are more short white men worth at least $50 billion—Jeff Bezos, Sergey Brin, Michael Bloomberg, Michael Dell, Charles Koch, Jim Walton, Mark Zuckerberg are all at most five foot seven—than there are Black people of *any* height who are CEOs of Fortune 500 companies. Nor do I want to suggest that gender inequities specifically would be resolved if American society had more tall women, since height is also another prism through which women face a double bind: tall women are perceived to be more masculine,[7] which may help to explain why they can sometimes access additional leadership opportunities, but that same perception also leads some men to conclude that they are less likable and less fit for promotions.

What intersectional analysis enables us to do, Sen argues, is "to look at all these possible combinations of privilege and vulnerability." Some people—like me—are intersectionally advantaged. Some people—such as Black women—are intersectionally disadvantaged. Still others—such as queer white men raised in poverty—are *both*.

Many identity combinations exist. Commonly discussed identity markers include physical ability, age, citizenship, class, gender, native language, nationality, race, religion, and sexuality. Using just these ten dimensions of identity, 3,628,800 unique intersectional identities can be constructed. Even that calculation understates the diversity of identity because the same identity marker can be experienced in different geographical and cultural contexts, and some dimensions of identity—such as gender and sexuality—are better represented as a spectrum, with infinite possibilities occurring along that spectrum.[8] As a result, every one of us has a unique lived experience that is shaped by our unique combination of identities.

Like all people, I have a complex intersectional identity that has many components. Among the more salient aspects of my identity and lived experiences are these:

- My socialization, which includes being treated for most of my life as able bodied, above average in height but not tall enough to be seen as a tall man, cis male, heterosexual, a member of the elite, a millennial, overweight, a US citizen, and white
- My roots, which include having European ancestry, eating meat, being raised Jewish, being born and raised in California, and being born and raised in the United States
- My relationships, which include brother to biological and adopted siblings, dad to a person of color, colleague and friend to people from many different backgrounds, grandson to my grandparents, who are now deceased, husband to my high school sweetheart, participant in a multicultural marriage, and son to my parents
- My personality, which is shaped by my socialization but seems to lean toward sensitive, introverted, agreeable, conscientious, and curious
- My academic roles, which include K–12 public school student, economics major at Stanford, and MPP-MBA student at Harvard
- My professional roles, which include board member, CEO of a college access nonprofit, cocreator of a Black-led racial justice

organization, donor organizer, fundraiser, manager, McDonald's cashier, McKinsey consultant, philanthropic adviser, philanthropist, recovering serial entrepreneur, researcher, Resource Generation member, SAT tutor, support facilitator for a rich white men's social justice circle, and writer

- My lived experiences, which include being a patient for anxiety, chronic pain, and trauma; causing harm and being harmed; being raised in a family that is wealthier than nearly all Black, Indigenous, and Latinx American families but also not in the top 1 percent of American wealth holders; living in California, the Midwest, and New England; and visiting many countries but never living outside of the United States

And experiences I haven't had have shaped me as much as those I've had. Some of my limitations that are particularly relevant for this book include the fact that I've had relatively few experiences grappling with how systems of oppression function outside of the United States, interacting with America's criminal justice system, learning from the wisdom of Indigenous leaders, living under the weight of systems of oppression, serving in professional roles where I am not a founder or leader, working in the government, working in the private sector, and working on climate change and justice. Other authors are better equipped to speak to those experiences and perspectives than I am, and I'm sure my limitations are apparent in this book to readers who have had more of those experiences.

When American society attempts to metabolize our complex and intersecting identity-based identities, it can generate some bizarre outcomes. Through his research, Harvard Kennedy School psychologist Robert Livingston has found that while having a "baby face"—a round face, large forehead, and small nose—is negatively correlated with success among white males, Black male CEOs were significantly more babyfaced than white male CEOs. Livingston's research also showed that, while Black people are typically rated as less warm than white people, Black CEOs are judged as warmer than white CEOs. He also found that baby-faced Black CEOs lead more prestigious corporations and earn higher salaries than mature-faced Black CEOs, a pattern that did not emerge for white CEOs. Livingston posits that having a baby face is a disarming mechanism that tempers stereotypical perceptions that Black people are threatening, thereby enabling biased elites to be more accepting of their leadership.[9] When a concoction of different types of biases are blended, the results can be quite peculiar.

And when intersecting advantages intersect, the advantages that result can be quite extreme. For example, men are uniquely positioned to perpetrate sexual violence; the wealthy can purchase a more convincing legal defense; and white people typically secure more lenient sentencing. The ultimate result is that for rich white men, rape continues to usually be permitted. That's a disturbing callback to Antebellum American policy, which stated that it was legal for rich white men to rape the people whom they enslaved.[10]

Recent examples of sanctioned sexual violence illustrate how this particular form of intersectional advantage manifests. In 2015, Stanford undergraduate and Varsity swimmer Brock Turner—a white man raised in a wealthy, 93% white suburb—sexually assaulted an unconscious woman after a college party.[11] A year later, Turner was convicted of three charges of felony sexual assault. While many states have mandatory minimums for violent crimes and Brock's convictions in California carried a potential fourteen-year prison sentence, Santa Clara County Superior Court judge Aaron Persky—himself a wealthy white man, Stanford graduate, and college athlete—sentenced Turner to six months at county jail and three years of probation. Turner's toxic entitlement may have been nurtured in part by his father Dan, who told the court that the verdicts were a "a steep price to pay for twenty minutes of action."[12]

Jeffrey Epstein was similarly successful at evading accountability for the extreme sexual violence he perpetrated. In 2008, after years of orchestrating a sex ring composed of underage girls, Epstein avoided federal charges and served just thirteen months in jail.[13] During his time in jail, Epstein was permitted to leave the jail for twelve hours a day, six days a week, to work at his office in Florida.[14] Only wealthy white men can access such extreme leniency.

I think that one of the reasons why some rich white men are threatened by the idea of intersectional identity is that systems of oppression can only function when the entire population is divided into a small number of categories. Similar to how a company may have quality-control issues if it offers too many products or services, systems of advantage and oppression must be constrained to a limited number of categories or else the population will become confused about who deserves to benefit from unearned advantages. If these differences in treatment are not applied somewhat universally with a high degree of consistency, the system breaks down. It is no accident that the Western world relies on the gender binary, South Africa relies on three racial categories, India relies on four primary castes, and the United States relies on five primary racial categories. Acknowledging that every one of us brings a complex and unique set of identities is a step toward seeing every one of us as individuals. While denying difference erases uniqueness, acknowledging and celebrating differences honors our unique lived experiences.

In some ways, this book is about how a small subset of us with a particular combination of advantaged identity markers—those of us who are rich, white, and male—wield extraordinary power in America. Yet this book is also about celebrating and honoring our human individuality; how every one of us brings a unique combination of identities and lived experiences.

Because the problem is not just that women and people of color are undervalued by the status quo but that wealthy white men are oblivious to how overvalued our own contributions tend to be, in a culture that has put us on a pedestal since this nation's founding.

One of our collective challenges in America is to transcend that culture, which requires honest self-examination and a willingness to pull the blinders off. Acknowledging our own individual blessings and ignorance is a critical early step toward building a movement that dismantles the deep-seated inequities that are hollowing out American democracy.

CHAPTER 6

THE EXCEPTION FACTORY

[Obama] is postracial by all appearances. You know, I forgot he was Black tonight for an hour.

—CHRIS MATTHEWS, MSNBC HOST

MYTH:

Systemic discrimination cannot exist if any marginalized people succeed in that system.

What gains? All you have gotten is tokenism—one or two Negroes in a job, or at a lunch counter, so the rest of you will be quiet.

—MALCOLM X, AFRICAN AMERICAN MUSLIM MINISTER AND
HUMAN RIGHTS ACTIVIST

REALITY:

The elite generate and showcase exceptions that fuel an illusion of equality.

On a sunny winter day in Los Angeles in early 2018, Alfredo Vasquez, a son of Mexican immigrants and rising star at one of the world's largest financial management institutions, woke up to a slew of unexpected congratulatory emails from his colleagues. As he flipped through the messages on his iPhone, he learned he had just become the brown face of a very white firm: his likeness covered his company's annual report, which was at that moment being transmitted to thousands of stakeholders around the globe.

Being selected for the cover was a big deal. With a trillion dollars in assets under management, the company had a high profile, and Alfredo had compiled a decade-long list of stellar achievements. The annual report cover photo reflected how Alfredo's career was taking off. But was it also meant to signify something else about the company and Alfredo?

Alfredo was flattered by the recognition, but he had mixed feelings about being showcased. He had never been one to seek the limelight, so why, among thousands of capable professionals in dozens of offices around the world, had he been chosen for this particular spotlight? And why had no one asked for his permission, or even notified him? Would that not have been a reasonable courtesy to expect?

Alfredo had legitimate reasons to be skeptical about his employer's motivations. As of January 2021, less than 10 percent of the firm's leadership was Black or Latinx. Of the ten most senior executives highlighted on the company's website, all but a few were white men; none were Latinx. His spot on the cover implied a degree of parity that didn't really exist.

Alfredo had also seen how powerful white men employ tokenism to mask our hegemony. Through tokenism—the practice of elevating a few members of a minority group in a perfunctory and largely symbolic way—an organization can convey a false sense of diversity in its ranks. The concept took hold in the United States in the late 1960s as white Americans grappled with how they might give ground grudgingly toward racial integration.[1] As a result, tokenism emerged as a means to minimally accept Black people in American society. In his 1964 book *Why We Can't Wait*, Dr. Martin Luther King Jr. explained how tokenism falls short of equality: "But he who sells you the token instead of the coin always retains the power to revoke its worth. . . . Tokenism is a promise to pay. Democracy, in its finest sense, is payment."[2]

Some people I know bristle at the suggestion that highly successful people from marginalized backgrounds are "tokens." The fear is that labeling people in this way diminishes their achievements by suggesting that they were chosen not because of their merit but because of their identity. However, as I understand it, the premise behind tokenism isn't that the few marginalized people who secure lofty posts are not deserving; rather, it's about how rich white men laud those they tokenize in public and then undercut them in private.

The interaction that crystallized this reality for me was a conversation I had in 2017 with a man who had served in a recent Democratic president's cabinet. I'll call this rich white man Thomas, after Thomas Jefferson, who served as secretary of state before becoming president.

When I told Thomas that I was planning to dedicate my career to advancing diversity, equity, and inclusion—I thought he'd prefer the phrase to "social justice"—I was taken aback by his knee-jerk negative reaction. I reminded him that his President's cabinet was more diverse than that of his predecessors. Didn't that diversity help the President make better decisions for the country? What about all the studies that have shown that diverse teams perform better?[3] "Those people," Thomas said curtly, "were B and C players selected for political reasons."

I found his dismissiveness unsettling. The women and people of color he had just disparaged were an extraordinary bunch. There was no reason why Thomas couldn't have seen these people as equals; people who brought unique lived and professional experience that our country needed to prosper and progress. Instead, his condescension was overwhelming. Even when people from marginalized backgrounds reach the summit of the mountain, they still aren't valued fairly for their accomplishments. Powerful white men like Thomas make sure of that.

While tokenism can rear its ugly head in many ways, its most common manifestation—as Thomas pointed out—involves recruiting small numbers of people from underrepresented groups to create the appearance of equality at an institution dominated by rich white men. Harvard Business School professor Rosabeth Moss Kanter writes that token employees are usually part of a group that represents less than 15 percent of the total workforce.[4] Such employees face an array of burdens, such as being expected to represent their entire group, educate colleagues, or spend time away from promotable work to serve—usually unpaid—on diversity, equity, and inclusion committees.

The Burden

Tokenism shows up in different ways depending on the industry. In Hollywood, women and people of color are often depicted in stereotypical roles and storylines, which eerily includes Black characters often being the first to die in horror movies.[5] In politics, political parties sometimes put forward candidates from underrepresented groups, even if they are unlikely to win, to create the impression that the party is committed to a diverse slate of candidates.

Tokenism can also be practiced collectively as a society. Eager to imagine an America that had transcended racism, countless white Americans—including many elected officials and members of the media—tokenized President Obama's election, claiming the ascent of a single individual offered proof that America had become a postracial society.[6]

Through tokenism, rich white men have learned it is possible to move some pieces around on the board without jeopardizing white male power—and earn diversity points in the process. "Tokenism does not change stereotypes or social systems but works to preserve them," feminist Mary Daly has noted, "since it dulls the revolutionary impulse."[7]

The tendency of rich white men to sometimes rely on tokenism as a first line of defense against perceptions of bias substantiates Daly's thesis. As long as we can point to one person in leadership who is not a white man, the theory goes, we can feel entitled to proclaim that bigotry has no place in our organizations. That relieves us of the responsibility to embrace real diversity, which could dilute our power and upend the status quo.

Those tokenized are often discouraged from challenging existing biases and power structures. In fact, a common condition of their rise is that they don't make white male leadership uncomfortable. Such people face pressure to be palatable to white men; to diminish differences between themselves and their white male colleagues; to stay silent when white men insult or ignore them; and to be patient when they are passed over for promotions.

In a 2018 study, sociologist Ted Thornhill quantified how this bias can impact Black people as soon as they express interest in joining an institution.[8] Thornhill sent inquiry emails from fictitious Black high school students to white admissions counselors from 517 historically and predominantly white institutions. The inquiry emails were modified only to present some students as deracialized and racially apolitical, and other students as professing a commitment to antiracism and racial justice. White admissions officers responded 18 percent more often to Black applicants whose letters suggested they were apolitical.

To squeeze as much propaganda value as possible from those they tokenize, powerful white men have also gone to great lengths to exaggerate the diversity present within their ranks. In 2000, University of Wisconsin undergraduate Diallo Shabazz discovered he had been photoshopped onto the cover of the admissions brochure: although he'd never attended a football game, Shabazz was depicted cheering alongside white students.[9] Despite public outrage over the subterfuge, that practice continues: in 2019, Pennsylvania's York University—which is 78 percent white—circulated doctored photos that artificially enhanced diversity.[10]

When Ausburg College sociologist Tim Pippert and his researchers reviewed ten thousand images from college brochures in 2013 in order to compare the racial breakdown of students in the pictures to the colleges' actual demographics, he found that the whitest schools were the least honest in their brochures.[11] While African Americans represented just 5 percent of the student body at predominantly white universities, they were 15 percent of those photographed. It seems to me that these institutions were more interested in *appearing* to have Black students than they were in actually having them.

Historically and predominantly white institutions, such as Ivy League universities, also exaggerate the extent to which racially marginalized populations are represented in their student bodies. Elite universities do acknowledge Black and Latinx underrepresentation: while the United States is 13 percent Black and 18 percent Latinx, the student bodies at most elite universities are in the 5–10 percent range for these groups.[12] However, they also typically leave out that most of the Black and Latinx students they admit are from wealthy immigrant and international families. While 90 percent of Black Americans are descendants of enslaved people, these individuals are rarely offered slots.[13] Since many universities do not disclose sub demographics and deploy tokenistic practices to amplify their institution's rare "rags-to-riches" stories, many advantaged students and alumni assume their institutions are more diverse and representative than they actually are. That approach perpetuates elite ignorance, and reproduces inequality.

My Harvard Business School cohort followed this pattern. In my section of ninety-three students, two-thirds were American and six identified as Black. Of these six students, three were international students from Africa, one was an American descendant of Caribbean immigrants, and two identified as African American with long histories in the United States. While Harvard Business School describes my section as 6 percent Black, African Americans represented just 3 percent of that cohort. The school's representation claims appear even more outrageous through a global lens: global parity would require that my section have sixteen students of African descent. So it is not that African students are overrepresented but rather that African American *and* African students are underrepresented.

Sometimes, rich white men intentionally groom tokens. Known as *exceptionalism*, this practice relies on a belief that only a small subset of the population that is not rich, white, and male warrants investment. In return, rich white men expect individuals from marginalized backgrounds to assimilate, adjusting their appearance and behavior to create the impression they are "worthy" of the tokenization that eventually allows them to fraternize with rich white men.

Scholars call this practice "respectability politics," and politics is

Respectable politics

where it has been most visible.[14] Would Barack Obama have been electable as president if he had been dark-skinned and had grown up in concentrated poverty, with all the baggage that brings? Even the white man he would ultimately choose as his vice president, Joe Biden, seeded that perspective during the 2008 campaign by lauding Obama as a strong contender because he was "articulate and bright and clean and a nice-looking guy."[15] Author and journalist Ta-Nehisi Coates perhaps said it best in his 2012 essay in *The Atlantic*, "Fear of a Black President": Obama had to be "twice as good" and "half as Black" to meet the presidential standard.[16] The same might be said for token employees.

Through philanthropy, mentorship programs, and related activities, rich white men seek to identify "diamonds in the rough" whom we perceive to be exceptions to negative stereotypes of the populations they represent. One Black female CEO, who leads a national nonprofit organization, shared how she has experienced rich white men's obsession with cultivating exceptions:

> Donors only want to fund the high achievers. The exceptional students who made it and go on to prestigious universities. They want those poverty porn stories—stories where students overcame amazingly tremendous barriers. Kids whose parents are strung out on drugs. Kids who saw their friend shot to death in front of them. Kids who overcame all that, went to an Ivy League college, graduated, and are now working in a STEM field. The dominant mindset is unless a student fits that profile, they are not worthy of support.

She also emphasized the pressure she feels to showcase extreme stories at fundraising events:

> The barometer is, "Is the story bad enough?" The more people cry, the more they open their checkbooks. The students we highlight can't be ordinary people—just everyday poor kids from a loving family who start at City College, transfer to [California

State University] East Bay, and are now working. That isn't "good enough" to inspire philanthropic dollars. To get the money, we have to amplify the extreme cases.

The focus on exceptionalism is hardly about dismantling systems of oppression. In many cases, it's about helping rich white men wash away any guilt we have about our advantages. It can also be a strategic process to preserve wealth and power. Consider, for example, the glass cliff, in which those from marginalized backgrounds are offered leadership roles during periods of crisis when the chance of failure is highest, such as when a company is facing poor share price performance, a scandal, or reputational risk. Prominent examples include Jill Abramson's appointment as executive editor of the *New York Times* in 2011 when the newspaper business was in free fall, and Marissa Mayer's appointment as CEO of Yahoo in 2012 after Google had pillaged Yahoo's market share.[17] Those from marginalized backgrounds may also be more likely to take risky positions, because they know they are rarely invited to lead.

Scholars have confirmed the systemic nature of the glass cliff. In 2005, University of Exeter researchers found that companies that recruited female board members were more likely to have experienced poor financial performance in the preceding five months than those who brought on men.[18] Utah State University researchers followed up with a study of Fortune 500 companies over a fifteen-year period and found that white women and people of color were more likely than white men to be promoted to CEO at weakly performing firms.[19]

When leaders from marginalized backgrounds take on these difficult roles, the additional risks they assume often go unacknowledged. A 2013 PwC report found that over a ten-year period, female CEOs were 41 percent more likely than men to be pushed out.[20] And once female CEOs are pushed out, they are less likely than men to be granted another CEO opportunity.

The glass cliff phenomenon may also apply to entire fields. In 2017, the Association of American Medical Colleges found that, for the first time, women represented the majority of medical school matriculants.[21]

The finding was rightly heralded as a win for gender equality. However, there are also some confounding variables. The medical profession is not as lucrative as it used to be: the pay is still good, but the increase in expenses associated with becoming a doctor—like medical school tuition and malpractice insurance—is far outpacing inflation.[22] What finally tipped the scale was not only that female applications grew by 10 percent but also that male applications dropped by 2 percent. These trends have continued: between 2017 and 2021, female applications grew by another 16 percent while male applications dropped by another 2.5 percent.[23] It may be the case that emerging equality in the medical profession might be less about a shift in power and more about men becoming less interested in becoming doctors.

Particularly telling is that the broader trend does not apply to coveted physician specialties like neurosurgery, which is medicine's most prestigious and highest paid.[24] Women represent just 12 percent of neurosurgery residents, 5 percent of practicing neurosurgeons, and 1 percent of department chairs.[25] Dr. Karin Muraszko, a University of Michigan scholar, became the first woman to head a neurosurgery department in 2005; she's still the only one.[26] When researchers studied neurosurgery residency enrollment patterns in the 2010's, they found that there was no statistically significant change in the percentage of women matriculants; those findings held up for Asian American, Black, Indigenous, and Latinx matriculants, too.[27] To track where the wealth and power lies—and how it is shifting, if at all—just follow the white male elites.

In an earlier era, the glass ceiling prevented women and people of color from breaking through to leadership positions. Today the glass ceiling is made out of tokens, which rich white men produce in the exception factory. It's not the first time that rich white men have used marginalized people as human shields, and unless things change, it probably won't be the last.

CHAPTER 7

THE PEOPLE OF COLOR RANKING SYSTEM

The mingling of Asiatic blood with European or American blood produces, in nine cases out of ten, the most unfortunate results.

———FRANKLIN D. ROOSEVELT, THIRTY-SECOND PRESIDENT OF THE UNITED STATES WHO IS REGARDED BY MANY HISTORIANS AS AMERICA'S MOST PROGRESSIVE PRESIDENT

MYTH:

Systemic discrimination cannot exist if any marginalized *groups* succeed in that system.

Already before we get out of train, army machine guns lined up toward us—not toward other side to protect us, but like enemy, pointed machine guns toward us.

———HENRY SUGIMOTO, ARTIST AND SURVIVOR OF THE JAPANESE AMERICAN INTERNMENT CAMPS

REALITY:

Rich white men rank people of color using oversimplified categories to fuel an illusion of equality.

After winding through rolling green hills into a tucked-away neigh-borhood, I found myself at the estate of a retired venture capitalist I'll call Don, after Don Valentine, a founder of Sequoia Capital who has been called "the grandfather of Silicon Valley venture capital."

When the conversation turned to my work focused on racial justice, I could tell he was eager to ask me something. "So, other groups have it figured out," Don said. "Jews are doing well. Asians are doing well. Why can't Black people get it together?"

The question struck a nerve with me. Don had chaired the boards of multiple public companies, through which he had overseen the recruit-ment and selection of countless board members and CEOs. Most of those he selected were wealthy white men. Now I couldn't help but won-der how his attitudes toward racial and ethnic groups might have col-ored his thinking about whom to recruit and which causes to support.

While the question troubled me, I wasn't surprised. Within business and philanthropic elites, such views about perceived cultural differences between minority groups are common. Across America, many people believe that certain ethnic groups are culturally superior to others.

Two prominent leaders promoting that view are Jed Rubenfeld and Amy Chua, a married couple who teach at Yale Law School and iden-tify as Jewish and Asian American, respectfully. In their 2014 bestselling book *The Triple Package*, Chua and Rubenfeld highlight the successes of various American immigrant groups.[1] They emphasize that Mormons, Jews, Indians, Chinese, Nigerians, and other ethnic groups attend elite educational institutions, earn high incomes, and obtain other positive outcomes more often than the typical American. According to Ruben-feld and Chua, these immigrant groups outperform other groups because they see themselves as superior, hold deeply rooted insecurities they seek to disprove, and have impulse control that other groups lack.

These ideas are dangerous. Any claim that an ethnic group's superior outcomes are the result of having superior qualities other groups lack must be evaluated as a racist claim.

Asian Americans *do* have higher median incomes than white Americans, but they are still less economically secure than the median white American. White Americans are far more likely to own a home: while 73 percent of white Americans owned a home in 2019, just 59 percent of Asian Americans did.[2] Meanwhile, Asian Americans have twice as much debt: from 2010 to 2013, the typical mortgage held by Asian Americans was $236,011, whereas it was just $118,515 for white homeowners during the same period.[3] As a result, white Americans spend less of their income on housing, rely less on housing as the principal source of their wealth, and are less vulnerable to shocks in housing prices. By erasing wealth and, in particular, inherited wealth from discussions about inequality, rich white men mask not only economic disparities between white and Black Americans but also disparities between white Americans and other groups of color.

Moreover, the many ethnic groups that are arbitrarily slotted into the singular racial category "Asian American" cannot be characterized as a monolith. That practice is itself racist because it generalizes about subpopulations that have little in common, like the descendants of Hmong subsistence farmers and Chinese magnates. When someone like the CEO I met claims that "Asians are doing well," he is implicitly referring to specific Asian-origin subgroups that are thriving economically. These subgroups include Indian American households, which—with average incomes of $119,000 and poverty rates of just 6 percent—have the best economic outcomes of any Asian-origin subgroup.[4] On the other end of the spectrum are Burmese Americans, whose incomes average just $44,000.[5] One-quarter of Burmese American families live below the poverty line, compared with 20 percent of Black families and 8 percent of white families.[6]

The subgroups that earn the most typically come to the United States with relatively advantaged positioning. While most Burmese Americans are refugees from Myanmar's bloody civil war,[7] the Indian American community is composed predominantly of highly educated people with white-collar occupations. For example, those who secure H-1B visas—which allow foreign workers employed by American companies to work in the United States in specialized occupations—are better educated than the typical American and have valuable technical skills such as computer programming abilities. In 2018, Indian immigrants submitted over one hundred thousand visa petitions, reflecting a significant portion of the Indian immigrant population; by contrast, only fifty-one Burmese immigrants submitted a petition.[8]

Yet even the most advantaged immigrant groups face significant discrimination in American society. Yes, highly educated and elite immigrants of color—particularly Chinese Americans, Indian Americans, and Nigerian Americans—have had considerable success building their own American dream: they are disproportionately likely to enroll at elite colleges, earn white-collar incomes, and own homes in affluent communities.[9] But while members of these high-achieving immigrant groups can access the American dream, they rarely access the levers of American power, which is concentrated in the hands of rich white men in influential industries such as finance, media, politics, and technology.

Despite being more likely to be highly educated, Asian Americans have the lowest chance of rising to management or political office. Asian Americans represent 5.6 percent of the total population in the United States but hold just 0.3 percent of corporate officer positions and 2.6 percent of seats in the United States House of Representatives.[10] In New York City, Asian Americans represent the largest group of associates at New York law firms but are least likely to make partner.[11] At the National Institutes of Health, where 21.5 percent of scientists are Asian American, just 4.7 percent of lab and branch directors are Asian American.[12]

There are exceptions, of course—like Sundar Pichai, an Indian American who serves as the CEO of Alphabet, Google's parent company.[13] But even in this exceptional case, Pichai's white male bosses, Larry Page and Sergey Brin—Alphabet's founders who oversee Pichai on the board—are each one hundred times wealthier than he is.[14] Similar to how the few everyday citizens who became wealthy in Old Europe brought special skills that further enriched patrons like the Medici family, it is difficult to get rich in America without rich white male sponsors, who become exponentially richer when their investments in the leadership of people of color pay off.

Asian Americans experience discrimination so frequently in their efforts to climb the corporate ladder that there is a term for it: the *bamboo* ceiling. A derivative of the "glass ceiling" coined by Jane Hyun in her 2005 book *Breaking the Bamboo Ceiling*, the term refers to cultural and organizational characteristics of businesses that limit the career progress of Asian Americans. Barriers include subjective factors that block promotions, such as a perceived "lack of leadership potential" and "lack of communication skills," characterizations often rooted in stereotypes that seldom link to job performance or qualifications.

Asian Americans face discrimination outside of the workplace as well. A recent national housing audit found that one in four Asian Americans experience systematic discrimination in home buying, a rate similar to that experienced by Black Americans. And one in four American residents hold the racist views that Chinese Americans are taking away "American" jobs.[15] Perhaps due to the Trump Administration's rhetoric linking the COVID-19 pandemic to China, the FBI reported that anti-Asian hate crimes increased 73 percent in 2020.[16]

Anti–Asian American discrimination is rooted in a long history of racist propaganda and policy in this country. Throughout the nineteenth century, Asian immigrants were characterized as illiterate, disease ridden, and unassimilable.[17] They were also denied citizenship and segregated into ethnic enclaves. In the Chinese Massacre of 1871 in Los Angeles, eighteen Chinese immigrants in Old Chinatown were murdered by a mostly white mob of five hundred.[18] The Immigration Act of 1924 limited the number of Asian immigrants, labeling them an "undesirable" race. In 1942, while Franklin D. Roosevelt was shoring up the white middle class through an array of wealth-building policies that excluded people of color, he issued Executive Order 9066, incarcerating 122,000 Japanese Americans in internment camps. Seen in the white gaze as perpetual foreigners, Asian Americans continue to be asked "Where are you really from?" regardless of their family's longevity in America.

In 1965, United States immigration law changed to give preference to highly educated and skilled applicants.[19] Today, Chinese immigrants to the United States are twelve times as likely to have graduated from college than the average Chinese citizen and nearly twice as likely as other Americans.[20] As immigration policy shifted and the makeup of Asian American immigrant groups evolved, new stereotypes emerged to characterize the new arrivals. In a 1966 *New York Times Magazine* article, Columbia University sociologist and white man William Petersen introduced the idea of the model minority, the notion that certain Asian American groups achieve economic and social success—and lower rates of poverty, crime, welfare dependency, and divorce—because of positive group qualities.[21] "This is a minority that has risen above even prejudiced criticism," Petersen wrote, referring to Japanese Americans. According to Petersen, Japanese Americans were law abiding, hardworking, well educated, and well dressed—unlike Black Americans, a "problem minority" deserving of prejudice.

Even positive stereotypes can perpetuate and sanction racism. The model minority concept suggests that wide generalizations can be made about individuals and subgroups that are vastly different, which is denigrating and dehumanizing. It also suggests that other minority groups—such as Black, Indigenous, and Latinx populations—are inferior to the supreme minority group. And it props up white supremacy because it assumes that white people are entitled to sit atop a racial hierarchy and rank everyone else below them.

When wealthy white men like Petersen claim a racial hierarchy exists, people of color face pressure to demonstrate their own group's worthiness. Such an environment ensures that every marginalized group must work harder for less; it also fosters competition among marginalized groups already disenfranchised and fighting for leftovers. These divide-and-rule tactics make it easier for rich white men to hoard resources.

The model minority concept isn't a compliment. As is often the case with rich white men, there is a catch. In his work, Petersen praised the "obedience" of Asian Americans, which fueled myths that Asian Americans are quiet, docile, and easy to boss around. These stereotypes persist and have wide-ranging implications that can stall careers and stifle social mobility. White supremacy has always been about dominance and control, so submissiveness is a prerequisite for "acceptance" as a model minority.

Divide + Rule

The cocktail of positive and negative stereotypes that rich white men advance about Asian Americans ensures that even the most advantaged Asian American subgroups are stuck in the middle of America's hierarchy. In a growing number of American companies, Asian Americans occupy the majority of entry-level positions, yet they remain locked out of the C-suite.[22] The dual stereotypes that sustain these apartheid-like structures are exploitative: rich white men extract value from Asian American labor, delegating tedious white-collar grunt work without sharing the firm's power and profits. As a result, the model minority myth is merely another opportunity for rich white men to tap into compounding unearned advantage.

White Americans were not the first to advance the idea of a model minority. In Nazi Germany, Hitler described his Japanese military allies as "honorary Aryans."[23] In apartheid South Africa, Prime Minister Hendrik Verwoerd offered "honorary whiteness" to the Japanese because trade with Japan was necessary for the regime's survival.[24] That "honor" wasn't extended to the Chinese, which South Africa didn't have ties with.

Like Asian American immigrants, Black immigrants are not a monolith; they arrive in the United States from many different contexts. Similar to Chinese and Indian immigrants, Nigerian immigrants are more educated than the typical American. In fact, according to the United States Census Bureau, Nigerian Americans are the most educated immigrants in the United States: Nigerian Americans are twice as likely as white Americans to obtain a graduate degree; they are also well represented at elite institutions: while Nigerian Americans represent less than 1 percent of America's Black population, they represent a quarter of Harvard Business School's Black students.[25]

Nigerian American success is sometimes cited as evidence that anti-Black racism is not severe, but the data suggests the opposite. Among highly educated and skilled immigrant groups, Nigerian Americans have the lowest incomes. Similar to how the median household income of white Americans is 71 percent higher than that of Black Americans, Indian immigrants earn 85 percent more than Nigerian immigrants. South African immigrants to the United States—87 percent of whom are white—also earn 43 percent more on average than Nigerian immigrants. In fact, despite their educational advantages, the typical Nigerian American's income is no higher than the typical American's.[26] These data suggest Nigerian Americans receive the lowest returns on education of any American immigrant group. In America, not even education can overcome the negative labeling of those with Black skin.

Other African immigrants face discrimination, too. In 2015, the Pew Research Center found that while African immigrants are 25 percent more likely to be college educated than the typical immigrant, they earn 10 percent less.[27] Pew also found that African immigrants have lower homeownership rates than other, similarly educated immigrant populations, which suggests that their average household wealth is likely lower, too. And the Black Alliance for Just Immigration has found that while only 7 percent of noncitizens in the United States are Black, Black noncitizens represent 20 percent of those facing deportation on criminal grounds.[28] While detained by ICE, many Black immigrants are treated with extreme cruelty: one study found that African and Caribbean immigrants were just 4 percent of those detained by ICE but 24 percent of those locked up in solitary confinement.[29] Ultimately, Black immigrants are more likely to be deported for minor offenses. While anti-Blackness impacts Black immigrants differently than it does descendants of enslaved people, white supremacy nevertheless permeates every dimension of American society.

Some ethnic groups have secured access to American power. Jewish Americans are one example. Half of Jewish Americans report annual household incomes above $100,000, and one-quarter report incomes above $200,000.[30] While Jewish Americans are less than 2 percent of the American population, they make up 9 percent of US senators and a third of America's billionaires.[31] Jewish billionaires Mark Zuckerberg, Larry Page, Sergey Brin, Larry Ellison, and Michael Bloomberg—whose combined wealth exceeds $500 billion—are five of America's ten wealthiest people.[32]

But every ethnic group that has accessed American power has one thing in common: rich white men eventually deemed their light skin as assimilable into whiteness. In his 1995 book *How the Irish Became White*, Noel Ignatiev describes how oppressed immigrants became American oppressors. Much like the European indentured servants who became the frontline enforcers of chattel slavery, Irish immigrants achieved acceptance among an initially hostile white population by proving they could be even more brutal to African Americans than the pre-existing white population. For many Jewish, Italian, Irish, Mormon, and other light-skinned Americans—especially immigrant families like my great grandparents who were desperate to make ends meet—the advantages offered by whiteness have been too attractive to resist.

Such assimilation brings a cultural cost. American Jews like me are less religious than the typical American adult, and Jewish Americans with several generations of history in the United States, like me, are more disconnected from their Jewish heritage. The decline in cultural connection maps directly to embracing whiteness: while most Jewish immigrants don't identify as white, nearly all of those who have been in America for three or more generations do.[33]

Even for groups that have been assimilated into whiteness, a long-standing history of discrimination leaves traces. In 2017, the Anti-Defamation League documented 1,015 instances of antisemitic harassment, 952 incidents of vandalism, 163 bomb threats against Jewish institutions, and 19 physical assaults.[34] In its 2021 report titled *The State of Antisemitism in America*, the American Jewish Committee found that one in four American Jews says they have been a target of antisemitism in the last twelve months. While 90 percent of American Jews say antisemitism is on the rise, just 60 percent of the general public agrees.[35]

And even for these relatively advantaged subgroups, glass ceilings remain. In a Gallup poll leading up to the 2008 presidential election, 4 percent of Americans said they wouldn't vote for a Catholic presidential candidate, 7 percent said they wouldn't vote for a Jewish candidate, and 24 percent said they wouldn't vote for a Mormon candidate.[36] Such percentages directly follow the extent to which these groups have been assimilated into whiteness and are corroborated by the reality that just two Catholics—the closest cousin to America's founding Protestant tradition—and no Jews or Mormons have been elected president of the United States.[37]

And who are these fringe populations that are withholding support for Jews and Mormons? Primarily, white supremacists who contend that Jews aren't white and Protestants who claim Mormons aren't "real Christians."

Even within ethnic groups of color, proximity to whiteness is materially rewarded. Colorism is a form of bigotry that occurs when light-skinned people of color are treated better than those in the same racial group who have darker skin. Such bigotry has a material impact on opportunities and outcomes in the United States. One study found that light-skinned Latinx Americans make $5,000 more annually than darker-skinned Latinx Americans.[38] Other studies found that light-skinned African Americans receive better treatment from teachers than dark-skinned African Americans,[39] and that—in capital punishment cases with Black defendants and white victims—light-skinned African Americans are half as likely as their darker-skinned counterparts to receive the death penalty when they are accused of similar offenses.[40] When I attended Harvard Business School, I couldn't help but notice that the students of color on campus were disproportionately light skinned. America's only Black president and only Black vice president both have light skin that reflects their mixed racial heritage. By preferencing lighter skin, colorism reinforces white supremacy.

Some people of color with sufficiently light skin can "pass" as white. "Passing" refers to the ability to be regarded as a member of an identity group or category different from one's own, which can offer advantages in situations when expressing one's true identity may be dangerous. As a Jewish American, I have personally exercised passing. When a person in my presence made antisemitic remarks, assuming I was Christian, I chose not to rebuke him because I did not feel it was safe to do so. While passing kept me safe in that moment, I was still harmed because I was pressured to hide my identity.

Given the benefits, many of those who can pass choose to do so. For example, in the 2004 census, 86 percent of Cuban Americans—typically lighter skinned than some other Latinx populations—identified as white compared to just 60 percent of Mexican Americans, 53 percent of Americans of Central and South American descent, and 50 percent of Puerto Ricans.[41] Those who can pass as white are disproportionately rewarded access to American power: while Cuban Americans represent less than 1 percent of the American population, half of Latinx US senators have Cuban roots.[42]

Increasingly, light-skinned Latinx subgroups are being assimilated into whiteness, a process that includes being courted by rich white men to participate in anti-Blackness and xenophobia. That includes Cuban American state senator Frank Artiles, who sought to diminish the legitimacy of the Florida State Senate president when he told two of his Black colleagues in the Florida State Senate that the leader had only risen to power because "six n——" in the caucus had elected him.[43] It also includes the popular 2018 Miami play *Tres Viudas en un Crucero*, a commercial success buoyed by a promotional video that shows a fair-skinned Cuban American actress in blackface pounding her chest and joking about having fun like gorillas.[44]

Meanwhile, dark-skinned Latinx subgroups—which represent most of America's Latinx population—are encountering obstacles similar to Black and Indigenous populations. In its 2017 population survey, the US Census found that Afro-Latinx people are 26 percent more likely to live in poverty than the general Latinx population.[45] Mexican Americans—who often have Indigenous ancestors who stewarded land since annexed by American colonizers—live in poverty nearly as often as Black Americans.[46] Discrimination against Black and Latinx populations is so severe that a 2017 Institute for Policy Studies report predicts that median Black household wealth will zero out by 2053, and that Latinx wealth will follow suit a couple of decades later.[47]

While I was a student at Harvard Business School, I had an interaction that led me to feel concerned that the next generation of rich white men might be vulnerable to embracing its predecessors' racist views.

After I helped to lead a discussion focused on racial justice, one of my white male classmates pulled me aside and suggested we have lunch so we could discuss the issues further. Since this white man was far wealthier than even the typical Harvard Business School student, I'll call him Anderson, after Vanderbilt dynasty heir Anderson Cooper. This Anderson's great-grandfather founded a company a century ago that remains a major force today. The company is a source of pride—and riches—for his entire family.

At lunch, on a sunny spring day, we sat outside in Harvard Business School's grassy courtyard. Surrounded by a cadre of coordinated brick buildings, manicured landscapes, and well-fed squirrels, Anderson and I found our way through some small talk and then dug in.

His first question for me was a familiar one. "So, my [European immigrant] family figured it out," he said. "Asians are doing great. Don't Black people need to finally take responsibility for the situation they find themselves in?"

My heart sank. Unlike Bob—the retired venture capitalist I'd heard from previously—this rich white man was born in the 1990s and raised in a liberal suburb. Anderson was squarely a millennial; had he been born a few years later, he'd have been considered Gen Z. Already, he'd donated several thousand dollars to a variety of Democratic political candidates.

And yet it was as if an invisible baton had been passed between the two men. My classmate in his twenties asked the same burning question as the retired venture capitalist in his sixties. They approached the issue with an eerily similar ignorance.

CHAPTER 8

BLAMING THE VICTIM

The rich invest in time, the poor invest in money.

—WARREN BUFFETT, CEO OF BERKSHIRE HATHAWAY
AND BILLIONAIRE PHILANTHROPIST

MYTH:

To succeed, marginalized people just need to behave like rich white men.

It is cruel jest to say to a bootless man that he ought to lift himself by his own bootstraps.

—DR. MARTIN LUTHER KING JR., AMERICAN BAPTIST MINISTER
AND CIVIL RIGHTS ACTIVIST

REALITY:

Since many elites hoard power, no degree of assimilation is ever enough.

nside the mahogany walls of the faculty lounge at the Harvard Kennedy School in 2018, a cadre of faculty members had gathered to discuss Harvard economist Raj Chetty's latest research about race and social mobility.

The study had made waves in part because it tracked the lives of millions of children and found that Black men raised in even the wealthiest families and living in some of the most well-to-do neighborhoods earn much less and are far more likely to end up in prison than white men with similar backgrounds.

The research was highlighted in a March 2018 *New York Times* profile titled "Extensive Data Shows Punishing Reach of Racism for Black Boys."[1] Three days later, the *Times* published an op-ed by Stanford law professor Ralph Richard Banks titled "An End to the Class vs. Race Debate." "[Chetty's] study," Banks writes, "rebuts a widely shared view that racial disparities in social mobility are economic inequalities in disguise—the belief that if we address class issues, we can fix racism."[2]

Part of the reason the study attracted so much interest at the Kennedy School is that the majority of the school's tenured faculty are—like their Harvard colleague Chetty—economists. Perhaps because of the close relationship between economics and business, economists are the darlings of many billionaire philanthropists. Following a series of major gifts endowing new faculty positions, the field of economics has had many breakthroughs. As economic tools have become more capable of isolating the causal impacts of social phenomena, economists have become the most powerful players in the social sciences.

There's another reason, too. More than the rest of the social sciences, economics is dominated by white men, who leverage their collective power to assert that their contributions are superior to those in other fields like history, psychology, and sociology.[3] Since its founding in 1958, the Kennedy School had been led by white men. And since a white male economist was selected as dean in 2004, it has been led by white male economists.[4]

One of those white male economists decided to host a meeting on

Chetty's research in 2018. I'll call him John, after John Maynard Keynes, the economist. This John has dedicated his career to the issue of American poverty and welfare. He's a nationally recognized expert on the topic, and his books have helped to shape national policy.

Perhaps due to his perceived status on the topic, John was dominating the conversation in the faculty lounge. Even though the Kennedy School of Government is a public policy school that has the word "government" in its name, the idea he unveiled for combating the issues that Chetty's research identified sidestepped government policy solutions. Instead, he promoted a private sector high-tech proposition.

"Maybe there could be a smartphone app that helps Black kids stay on track," John proposed. "What if they had a checklist of all the things they needed to do to achieve the American dream and then got push notifications whenever they started to go off the rails?"

The other Harvard faculty members got excited. Soon everyone was spitballing about how this technology could keep Black kids on the straight and narrow, and how they, as academics, could enlist their networks to help enable this vision to become reality.

Everyone, that is, except their lone Black colleague in the room. He barely could get a word in because his white colleagues were repeatedly interrupting and talking over him. Even though he'd spent his entire career studying anti-Black racism, the institution's leading white male economists made clear that neither his lived nor his professional experience was valued, because they could solve the problem with checklists and apps.

These were the leaders of America's most prestigious public policy school, which gets a bad rap from political conservatives for being "too liberal." And given their posts and career choices, these men clearly believe in the power of government to advance social change. Yet even when they were presented with the most robust quantitative evidence of systemic racism to date—from a colleague in their own field—they continued to discount the systemic barriers that limited Black success. Instead of addressing the ways Black people are locked into intergenerational poverty, they thought the best approach would be to nag Black people to behave better. By ignoring the ways in which white people might need to change, these white male elites recast compelling evidence of discrimination as yet another opportunity to explore how to correct Black people's deficiencies. While many of the white male economists I know like to describe themselves as objective, they, too, can be vulnerable to racist ideologies.

Such approaches are not only offensive and paternalistic; they are also rooted in notions of superiority. When rich white men imagine creating an app that helps keep Black kids on course, they are expressing a belief that the path to equality runs through getting more people from marginalized backgrounds to behave more like them. While we wealthy white men do have valuable lived experience and professional skills that we have developed through our unique access and opportunities, we also—like all human beings—have gaps in our lived experience and skill set. When we seek emulation without considering our own limitations, we are living out a narcissistic fantasy, not engaging fellow human beings from a place of equality.

Rich white men have a long history of pathologizing anyone we see as different. We've justified genocide and colonialism by calling Indigenous Peoples "savages." We've justified slavery by claiming that Black people were more like cattle than human beings. In the early twentieth century, we described Mexican Americans as "greasers," which implied they were dirty.[5] In the 1990s, Bill and Hillary Clinton described Black youth as "super predators."[6] And of course, America recently transitioned from a president who is now infamous for resurrecting the longstanding tradition of using racist and xenophobic tropes on the campaign trail and in the Oval Office.[7]

Groups now recognized as white have been pathologized, too. For example, cop cars are still sometimes referred to as "paddy wagons," which reflects the legacy of an earlier era in which Irish Americans were condemned into poverty and frequently hauled off to prison. While researching this topic, I was surprised to learn that in the early 1900s, Jewish immigrants—who were then mostly poor and not seen as white—dominated professional basketball.[8] Why? I suspect it was because, like today's Black Americans, they had few other opportunities. However, according to a *New York Daily News* journalist in the 1930s, it was because "the game places a premium on an alert, scheming mind, flashy trickiness, artful dodging, and general smart aleckness."[9] Stereotypes are not fixed; historically, rich white men have twisted and contorted them to meet our current interests.

Up until the mid-twentieth century, rich white men pathologized other people primarily by claiming that they were biologically inferior. It was during this era that eugenics and social Darwinism went mainstream. Gilded Age robber barons like John D. Rockefeller and Andrew Carnegie helped popularize these racist theories by bankrolling research into them, as they found the ideology aligned with their "survival of the fittest" worldview.[10]

Adolf Hitler drew inspiration from America's eugenicists and Jim Crow segregation laws. When I read James Whitman's 2017 book *Hitler's American model*, I was disturbed to learn that the Nazis discussed America's one-drop rule—by which a person with any Black ancestry was labeled Black[11]—and decided the American approach was too severe, which is how they arrived at the one-quarter cutoff for identifying Jews.[12] The whole world knows what happened next: a genocide that extinguished six million Jews and five million other people, and a world war that killed another seventy to eighty-five million.

After the horrors of the Holocaust became visible to the world, it became uncouth to say that groups of people were biologically inferior. That made the apartheid system in the Jim Crow South harder to justify, which helped to fuel for America's civil rights movement.[13]

After the civil rights movement reshaped the landscape, rich white men needed a different way to justify inequality. That inspired ideologies that emphasized that people of color were culturally and behaviorally inferior. In his 1971 book *Blaming the Victim*, psychologist William Ryan describes this practice as "savage discovery," which is rooted in an ideology that imagines everyone other than rich white men as "uncivilized" and involves searching within marginalized groups for "pathologies" that might be "fixed." "Victim blaming" has since become widely used jargon in the psychological field, and today the term describes any instance when the victim of a crime or any wrongful act is held entirely or partially at fault for the harm that befell them.[14] In his book, Ryan argues that victim blaming is a rationalization that justifies social injustice in the United States.[15] He wrote the book in part as a rebuke to United States senator Daniel Patrick Moynihan's influential 1965 Moynihan Report, which claimed that racial disparities were caused at least in part by cultural deficiencies within the Black community.[16]

People of color are not the only people in America whose cultures and behaviors are pathologized. Americans in poverty are also blamed for their condition. "I've always resented the smug statements of politicians, media commentators, corporate executives who talked of how, in America, if you worked hard you would become rich," historian Howard Zinn wrote.[17] "The meaning of that was if you were poor it was because you hadn't worked hard enough. I knew this was a lie, about my father and millions of others, men and women who worked harder than anyone, harder than financiers and politicians, harder than anybody if you accept that when you work at an unpleasant job that makes it very hard work indeed."

Women are also blamed for the ways they are oppressed. When a woman who was sexually assaulted is questioned about the length of her skirt, her decision to walk home alone, or how much she drank, that's victim blaming. White men often claim objectivity, but white male judges sometimes bring their victim-blaming biases into their courtrooms—like Judge John Russo, Jr., a New Jersey judge who was removed from the bench in 2020 after condescending remarks that included asking an alleged rape victim in 2018 whether she had tried closing her legs to prevent the assault.

Jackson Katz, a white male activist, offers an alternative to the victim-blaming approach. In a TEDx Talk, Katz encourages men to take responsibility for rape culture and then dismantle it. "We talk about how many women were raped last year," Katz emphasizes, "not how many men raped women."[18]

Since rich white men understand that there can be backlash if we engage in victim blaming personally, many instead amplify fringe voices within a marginalized group that aligns with our worldview. That includes people like Candace Owens, a conservative Black activist whose platform has been amplified by rich white men who deny that anti-Black racism exists. These rich white men relish Owens's claims that Black

Owens
Kirk

culture is "broken," Black people are "pretending to be oppressed," and Black Lives Matter activists are "domestic terrorists."[19]

Owens is a spokesperson for Turning Point USA, a conservative nonprofit organization led by Charlie Kirk, a wealthy white man who has called George Floyd a "scumbag" and characterized Democratic immigration policies as "diminishing and decreasing white demographics in America."[20] Turning Point's board of directors is composed exclusively of rich white men. Its major backers include members of the Koch Network—which has hosted semiannual meetings for wealthy right-wing donors since at least 2006[21]—like Richard Uihlein, a billionaire who backed Roy Moore's candidacy for one of Alabama's US Senate seats even after he was accused of sexual misconduct with underage girls.[22] Rich white men like Uihlein stay out of the public eye while funding people like Owens and Kirk to do their dirty work.

Even liberal philanthropy typically reproduces inequality. While I've often heard rich white men claim that philanthropy is an adequate substitute for government, that is hardly at all true. Americans donated $449 billion in 2019[23]—a substantial sum, to be sure—but that's still just 2 percent of US GDP. And a significant portion of those funds are earmarked for universities, hospitals, museums, and other large institutions that predominantly serve the wealthy, especially rich white men. For example, while many rich white men I know claim that education reform is the best way to advance equal opportunity, 73 percent of philanthropic giving within education goes to colleges and universities, which half of those who grew up in poverty do not attend.[24] Philanthropists also disproportionately prioritize wealthy universities that serve primarily wealthy students: while UC Berkeley enrolls nearly as many Pell Grant students as the entire Ivy League combined, Ivy League universities received ten times the donations in 2021.[25] In fact, since the wealthiest 1 percent get a tax refund worth 29 percent of their charitable contributions,[26] they actually *take* more from government coffers with their education donations than they give to K–12 education reform. Focusing on giving totals draws attention away from how little is donated to address poverty.

Even if the entire $449 billion reached those with incomes below the official poverty line—a long way from the current reality—poverty wouldn't be eliminated. Since thirty-seven million Americans live below this threshold, only $12,000 in philanthropic giving would reach these individuals. If workers in the twenty states where the minimum wage is $7.25 instead got a bump to $15 per hour—the rate demanded by political movements like Fight for $15—more money would end up their pockets than if they were granted a slice of the philanthropic pie.

While such a view of philanthropy may sound cynical, it is generous, since the Kochs and other major philanthropists prioritize philanthropic investments that seek to dismantle the social safety net and weaken democracy. After I read Jane Mayer's 2016 book *Dark Money* and Nancy MacLean's 2017 book *Democracy in Chains*, I concluded that politically conservative philanthropists have been far more successful at gutting public services than liberal philanthropists have been at backfilling those same services via their charitable contributions. That led me to consider an alarming possibility: even if many philanthropic initiatives are having a positive impact, the philanthropic sector—on the whole—might be having a net negative impact.

There's another problem. Historically, many of the organizations dedicated to fighting poverty take a paternalistic, "blame the victim" approach. For example, my impression is that KIPP—the nation's largest network of charter schools—was founded with a presumption that children in poverty need alternative schools that enforce high standards, not communities and schools that are as well resourced as those found in white affluent communities. Similarly, my impression is that Teach for America, which recruits young teachers into high-poverty communities of color, was founded with a belief that what children in poverty need are teachers with elite pedigrees, not access to community wealth and power. Nonprofits like these do have a positive impact on many children's lives, but they do not offer America a way out of extreme inequality.

Richard Barth and Wendy Kopp—a married couple who were KIPP's and Teach For America's longest tenured CEOs—are themselves quite well off. In the 2010s, Kopp and Barth each had salaries above $400,000, earning a combined income that is easily within America's 1 percent.[27] Yet instead of sending their own children to KIPP high schools—frequently staffed by Teach for America teachers—Barth and Kopp sent their three sons to Regis High School, a private high school on New York's Upper East Side. Regis was chartered in 1914 to provide a free education for Catholic boys and especially those who could not otherwise afford a Catholic education,[28] but a century later, Regis sends 13 percent of its mostly well-heeled graduates to Ivy League universities; another 15 percent go on to Boston College, Georgetown University, and the University of Notre Dame, America's three wealthiest private Catholic universities.[29] When wealthy white people champion public school reform efforts yet prioritize separate and unequal educations for their own rich white boys, inequality is reproduced into subsequent generations.

Corporate diversity and inclusion initiatives—increasingly called diversity, equity, and inclusion initiatives—often have similar shortcomings. There are exceptions, but for the most part, these programs train people from marginalized backgrounds to mimic the behaviors of rich white men and make few demands that rich white men share power more substantively or change our attitudes and behaviors. These are among the many reasons why such initiatives are struggling to produce transformative change—or even, in many instances, incremental change.

Within institutions, a common refrain from those in power is that it isn't possible to achieve equal representation because the problems are "too big." When I participated in efforts to advance equity at Harvard Business School, I asked administrators why the student population did not reflect the demographics of the American population. I was told that wasn't possible because of a "pipeline problem": that is, HBS couldn't achieve equal representation because of widespread systemic factors that HBS couldn't control, like the quality of our nation's K–12 system and the hiring practices of influential corporations. If HBS were to achieve equal representation, they argued, these massive systems would need to be transformed first.

There is an allure to this framing, since significant systemic reforms are indeed needed. However, recategorizing what might very well be a manageable problem into a massive, unaddressable one can be a strategy to defend an inequitable status quo. For Harvard Business School to have equal representation of women and Black students, all the school needs to do is enroll about fifty more women and about sixty more Black students. Enrolling fifty more Black women, who are particularly underrepresented at HBS, would address two needs with one deed. Such students who are nearly admitted to HBS are already extremely qualified: these are students who end up enrolling at Stanford, Wharton, and other prestigious business schools. The whole world doesn't need to be upended for HBS to increase its appreciation for the value these students would bring.

In 1969, the year after Dr. Martin Luther King Jr. was murdered, the number of Black students enrolled at HBS grew tenfold, to about sixty students.[30] Over the past fifty years, Black enrollment has stayed around that same level. Then, after the uprisings following George Floyd's murder, HBS immediately enrolled dramatically more Black students.[31] Neither of these changes occurred because the K–12 system or corporate America was reformed overnight. They happened because those in power—the people who decided which students were worthy—altered their perspectives, or at least felt external pressure to walk back inequitable policies.

On the other hand, when those in power are asked about whether they support significant reforms to society—like significantly changing the tax system so that more resources can be invested in high-poverty communities of color—I've noticed that they often retreat into emphasizing that the answer is fixing a single pipe in the pipeline. For example, when I asked a white male president of an elite university what America could do as a society to foster equity, he stressed that what would make the biggest difference are programs that prepare Black people for their first board seats. Other rich white men have told me that early childhood programs are the highest-leverage solution. Still others have told me that the magical elixir may be programs that help underrepresented students access college, succeed in college, get their first jobs, access graduate school, or climb the corporate ladder. It reminds me of how Christopher Columbus "discovered" North America: rich white men often arrive at these approaches by "discovering" a place in the pipeline where a pipe is broken; they then focus their energies on that one pipe.

Fixing individual pipes is a good thing, but such approaches often

Ground water ignore the reality that *every* pipe in the pipeline is broken. And unless all of the pipes are fixed—which requires major resources—the pipes will keep leaking.

The Racial Equity Institute discusses these systemic realities through what they call the groundwater approach. I think the groundwater approach is too important for me to try to paraphrase, so here is how REI summarizes its metaphor:

If you have a lake in front of your house and one fish is floating belly-up dead, it makes sense to analyze the fish. What is wrong with it? Imagine the fish is one student failing in the education system. We'd ask: Did it study hard enough? Is it getting the support it needs at home?

But if you come out to that same lake and half the fish are floating belly-up dead, what should you do? This time you've got to analyze the lake. Imagine the lake is the education system and half the students are failing. This time we'd ask: Might the system itself be causing such consistent, unacceptable outcomes for students? If so, how?

Now...picture five lakes around your house, and in each and every lake half the fish are floating belly-up dead! What is it time to do? We say it's time to analyze the groundwater. How did the water in all these lakes end up with the same contamination? On the surface the lakes don't appear to be connected, but it's possible—even likely—that they are. In fact, over 95% of the freshwater on the planet is *not* above ground where we can see it; it is below the surface in the groundwater.

This time we can imagine half the kids in a given region are failing in the education system, half the kids suffer from ill health, half are performing poorly in the criminal justice system, half are struggling in and out of the child welfare system, and it's often the same kids in each system!...

Our groundwater metaphor is designed to help practitioners at all levels internalize the reality that *we live in a racially structured society, and that that is what causes racial inequity.* The metaphor is based on three observations: racial inequity looks the same across systems; socioeconomic difference does not explain the racial inequity; and inequities are caused by systems, regardless of people's culture or behavior. Embracing these truths forces leaders to confront the reality that all our systems, institutions, and outcomes emanate from the racial hierarchy on which the United States was built. In other words, we have a "groundwater" problem, and we need "groundwater" solutions.[32]

In the United States, racism is a groundwater issue. So are sexism, classism, and other forms of bigotry. Shielding a few fish from their demise is a good thing, but it's not sufficient for building an equitable society. Treating the groundwater requires a different set of solutions.

But what about personal responsibility? If the poison isn't killing all of the fish, why not just try to figure out what's different about the fish that survive and train the other fish to be like them? There is value to the idea that we need to be responsible for the actions we take. Every human being has some level of agency, and—to an extent—the choices we make do matter.

That's true at an individual level, but it becomes problematic when that logic is applied to groups. If it is said that Black people as a group are more likely to make poor choices than white people in the same circumstances, that's a racist idea. If it's said that women are more likely to make poor choices than men, that's a sexist idea. And if it's said that people in poverty are more likely to make poor choices than wealthy people, that's a classist idea.

It is also the case that when there is a significant power differential, the powerful party holds the responsibility. If a parent abuses their child or a boss sexually assaults their subordinate, the responsibility lies with the abuser, not the abused. Since us rich white men hold most of the power, we hold most of the responsibility.

America needs to treat its groundwater. That starts with rich white men taking responsibility for the inequitable structure of our society. If we accepted that responsibility, I believe marginalized people's increased trust in the system would do more to inspire people to make the most of the agency they do have than any fish-fixing program in contaminated waters ever could.

One way we can take responsibility is to divest from inequitable structures. Chuck Collins, an activist and policy researcher, has done more than most rich white men on this front. In his 2016 book *Born on Third Base*, Chuck explains why he chose to donate the inheritance he received as an heir to the Oscar Meyer fortune. Chuck wasn't just motivated to support good causes; he was also divesting from a system that reproduces inequality at other people's expense.

Yet divesting is not enough. We also need to invest in the creation of an equitable America. We can still invest in programs that support individuals—those efforts are crucially needed to create pathways for Gen Z to access opportunity in a vastly unequal America—but we also need to take a longer-run view. Historically, the efforts that have moved the needle on inequality most have been social movements and political campaigns.[33] To accelerate progress, there needs to be more investment in social movements that are building the people power necessary to challenge plutocracy, such as the Movement for Black Lives, Poor People's Campaign, and the Sunrise Movement, which has catalyzed momentum for the Green New Deal. Citizens can also do well by supporting elected officials like The Squad—Congresspeople Alexandria Ocasio-Cortez, Ilhan Omar, Ayanna Pressley, Rashida Tlaib, Jamaal Bowman, and Cori Bush—who are shaking things up politically. Funding efforts like the Movement Voter Project, Way to Win, and The Working Families Party—which build electoral power by investing in local grassroots organizations—are a way to bolster social movements *and* progressive politics.

How us wealthy people invest is as important as where we invest. Restricted, short-term grants are paternalistic and communicate a lack of trust. When the rich white men I know invest in for-profit entrepreneurs, they typically provide long-term, flexible capital; nonprofits deserve the same. My wife and I tried to model this approach by making an unrestricted, ten-year financial commitment to the Movement for Black Lives, which represented a significant portion of our present assets. Over time, I hope more rich white men will make more major, unrestricted, and long-term commitments to social justice movements. I can't begin to describe how significant the impact would be if a white male billionaire made an unrestricted billion-dollar commitment to any of the leading movements promoting systemic change. And MacKenzie Scott (America's wealthiest woman) and Robert F. Smith (America's wealthiest Black person): if no white men step up first, maybe a few of them will follow your lead if you show them the way.

A growing number of organizations are offering support and community for donors who aspire to have a different type of relationship with intergenerational wealth. In earlier chapters, I mentioned my involvements with Liberation Ventures and Resource Generation. Other efforts that inspire me include Emergent Fund, Grantmakers for Girls of Color, Groundswell Fund, Justice Funders, Liberated Capital, NDN Collective, Patriotic Millionaires, Solidaire Network, Third Wave Fund, and many others.

Within institutions, some organizations are launching "reverse mentoring" programs, which call for junior employees to mentor executive team members on various topics of strategic and cultural relevance. I don't love the name—it suggests there is something abnormal about junior employees mentoring executives when the reality is that anyone can learn from anyone—but it's nevertheless a promising idea. While reverse mentoring is just starting to pick up steam, it's been around at least since the 1990s, when General Electric CEO Jack Welch enlisted recent recruits to equip his senior executives with more expertise about the internet.[34]

In their 2019 *Harvard Business Review* article "Why Reverse Mentoring Works and How to Do It Right," Jennifer Jordan and Michael Sorell profile some of these efforts.[35] At BNY Mellon and Estée Lauder, millennial staffers mentor executives, which has increased millennial retention and also improved executives' digital and cultural competencies. At global law firm Linklaters and global accounting firm Pricewaterhouse-Coopers, staffers from marginalized backgrounds mentor partners. These two-way programs enable executives to obtain valuable information and learn new skills while giving younger hires—particularly those from marginalized backgrounds—greater proximity to those who hold power at those institutions.

Parents can engage in reverse mentoring, too. In elite circles, one of the least commonly questioned mentalities seems to be the notion that parents—and dads in particular—are superior to their children, which is a characteristic of patriarchy. There are good reasons why parents have authority over children: parents have wisdom that children do not, and it is helpful for parents to set expectations and boundaries that help their children stay healthy and develop over time. That said, children have wisdom that their parents may have forgotten. For example, every time my toddler son Ayan looks at a flower or leaf with wonder, he is helping me to restore my beginner's mind; he also modeled for me, as an infant, the restorative value of a full-body stretch after I wake up, which I've since embedded within my morning routine. It is possible to be in a position of authority while honoring that everyone, even infants, has valuable intuition we can learn from and follow. I have great appreciation for Claire Saunders, Georgia Amson-Bradshaw, Minna Salami, Mik Scarlet, and Hazel Songhurst, whose 2019 children's book *The Power Book* helped me grasp how power looks and feels through the eyes of a child. As the father of a young son, I have found this book's teachings invaluable.

In my view, the fundamental principle these various efforts share is a deep conviction—a *really* deep conviction—that every human being is unique and equally valuable. It sounds obvious, but I am surprised by— now that I am paying attention to it—how often I judge people because of how they look, dress, or talk. Sometimes those judgments rely, implicitly or explicitly, on identity markers, and those judgments also affect who I think is charismatic, interesting, smart, and worth spending more time with. If I find myself getting bored in a conversation or questioning whether a first interaction with a person is a good use of my time, I push myself to check my biases and dig deeper, because every person has a unique life story, something unique to contribute, and wisdom they uniquely hold. Even if I don't anticipate a future conversation, no one deserves the dehumanizing experience of being dismissed.

For centuries, rich white men have blamed the people we've oppressed

for their circumstances. It's time that we rich white men take responsibility for America's inequitable system and build deep relationships across
differences, relationships that aren't rooted in paternalism or narcissism
but in equality. Only then will we have the foundation necessary to truly
learn from one another—and to foster equitable change together.

CHAPTER 9

THE LUCK DEFENSE

Some people, through luck and skill, end up with a lot of assets. If you're good at kicking a ball, writing software, investing in stocks, it pays extremely well.

——BILL GATES, COFOUNDER OF MICROSOFT AND BILLIONAIRE
PHILANTHROPIST

MYTH:

Rich white men are successful because of hard work, talent, and luck—and nothing else.

The system wants you to occupy a jail cell, not a college dorm.

——RAYMOND SANTANA, A MEMBER OF THE EXONERATED
FIVE WHO SERVED FIVE YEARS IN PRISON FOR A CRIME HE
DID NOT COMMIT

REALITY:

Hiding behind luck enables rich white men to cloak our unique access to structural power.

On a sunny spring day in Palo Alto, California, in 2008, I left my sophomore dorm room at Stanford, hopped on my bike, and started peddling toward the Coupa Café.

I was excited because I was about to meet one of my classmates, but not just any classmate—someone who had a larger-than-life presence on Stanford's campus because he was a real-life *social entrepreneur.* I'll call him Scott, after Scott Harrison, the founding CEO of Charity: Water, which funds solutions that get clean water to rural communities in the developing world.

After Scott volunteered abroad and saw international poverty first-hand, he decided to start his own nonprofit. By the time we'd met, Scott had already raised several million dollars for his enterprise. I wanted to learn his secret.

"We got really lucky," Scott told me. According to Scott, his non-profit launch had coincided with a burst of interest in the specific aspect of global poverty that he was working on.

Throughout our conversation, he stuck with the luck narrative. The closest I got to a practical suggestion was his advice that I meet very rich people and ask them for money. I didn't know anyone like that, though, and I had no idea whether that would work.

But I did start to keep an eye out for opportunities to meet very rich people, taking advantage of the environment I'd landed in. Stanford is America's third-wealthiest university—as of 2021, its $29 billion endowment lags behind only Harvard and Yale[1]—so tapping Cardinal alums seemed like the best place to start. A few months later, I stumbled into a resource called Honor Rolls, a database available to Stanford students and alumni that lists all of Stanford's benefactors by donation level. I still hadn't figured out how to meet them, but at least I now knew who they were.

Near the very top of the list, I found a familiar last name. This woman was on a short list of the institution's multi-million-dollar benefactors.

There's no way this could be Scott's mother, I remember thinking. But, sure enough, a quick Google search confirmed that she was.

I felt a surge of resentment. Why hadn't Scott mentioned that he'd grown up in an extremely affluent family? How could he have left out that his mother was a philanthropist who mingled with the fabulously rich all the time? No wonder his main advice was to just go meet very rich people. I envied his powerful connections and became worried that—without a similar inheritance—I wouldn't be able to get my own organization off the ground.

Shortly after, my mom told me about Matt Dalio, who had cofounded a successful nonprofit when he was just sixteen. She'd read an article about Matt online and thought his nonprofit—the China Care Foundation, which serves children in China's orphanages—would interest me because our family had adopted my younger sister Gracie from China.

Like Scott, Matt had raised millions of dollars to launch his nonprofit. Inspired by Matt's success, I googled him to learn more. I was just about to email him for advice when I learned that his father was Ray Dalio, the founder of Bridgewater, the world's largest hedge fund. At that time, Ray was worth several billion dollars; his net is $22 billion today.[2] *Was every successful nonprofit started by a super-rich person?* I remember thinking. I was starting to feel like the nonprofit game was rigged, and that there was nothing I could do to succeed.

I considered giving up but instead decided to see if I could transform myself. Almost overnight, I became an eager networker. I'm in the middle of the introvert–extrovert personality spectrum, so I've never been super gregarious. And until meeting Scott I'd seen networking as sleazy and insincere. But after learning more about Scott's and Matt's success, I started to see networking as the ticket to making a positive difference in the world. At a Stanford friend's suggestion, I gobbled up networking guru Keith Ferrazzi's 2014 book *Never Eat Alone* and Dale Carnegie's 1936 classic *How to Win Friends and Influence People.* I started applying for every scholarship and fellowship I could find so that I could build my credibility and network, and I began signing up for conferences. I bunked with two Navy SEALs in training during a leadership conference hosted by the US Naval Academy, mingled with young progressives at Young People For in Washington, DC, and attended Northwestern University's Global Engagement Summit, which offers training for student social entrepreneurs.

My big breakthrough, though, was attending the 2008 Business Today International Conference, an all-expenses-paid event organized by Princeton undergraduates that convenes 150 college students from around the world and business leaders to discuss management and societal issues. It blew my mind that college students had organized the event: it was held at the swanky Marriott Marquis in the heart of Manhattan; we even received gift cards to dine out on the town.

The lifeblood of this student organization is *Business Today*, a student-led business magazine that was cofounded at Princeton in 1968 by then student and now billionaire Steve Forbes.[3] Over time, the organization built an extraordinary network. Every year, dozens of entrepreneurs, financiers, and CEOs fly in to make keynote speeches and mingle with students.

I had hoped one of these titans of industry would bankroll the nonprofit I was starting, but I ended up leaving the conference with something even more valuable: the secret of how most elite-led nonprofits get off the ground. One student staffer of *Business Today* told me that every spring, *Business Today* buys lists of corporate executives using sales databases like those offered by D&B Hoovers. They then send thousands of cold emails asking to learn more about their businesses. Students spend the entire summer meeting with those executives and pitching sponsorships for the annual Business Today Conference. That approach has allowed *Business Today* to send out a dozen pairs of students each summer, build an influential network of corporate executives, and raise over a million dollars annually.

One of *Business Today*'s most famous alumni is Teach For America founder Wendy Kopp. In 1988, as a Princeton college student, Kopp became president of *Business Today*. That enabled her to spend the summer meeting with high-profile contacts in the *Business Today* network and gave her the authority to decide the topic of the annual conference.

She chose education reform, aligning the conference with her interests and drawing benefactors who might support her start-up nonprofit, which had been the topic of her senior thesis. After Kopp graduated, she flew around the country asking philanthropists who had a relationship with *Business Today* to support Teach for America. Kopp pulled so heavily from the organization's contacts for her own aims that, according to one student staffer, many Business Today alums were still angry with her.

Out of desperation, I decided to take a page from Kopp's playbook, even though it felt disingenuous to—as she had done—send cold emails that were personalized to suggest that I valued more than their financial resources. I found lists of Stanford's major donors on the Honor Rolls website and used the alumni database to find their email addresses. At one point, a handful of student interns and I were all logged in to my Stanford alumni account at the same time so we could pull a couple of hundred email addresses from the database every hour. I contacted so many of Stanford's major donors that at one point Stanford's fundraising office ordered me to stop. But eventually, it paid off. Coleman Fung, a successful entrepreneur and Stanford alum who was passionate about education, contributed $510,000 in seed funding for CollegeSpring. Coleman's support is the reason why cofounder Jessica Perez and I were able to lead the organization full-time, which was the catalyst for building what is now a national organization.

It may not be the story they put on their websites, but many of the social entrepreneurs I've met over the years have origin stories like mine: either we hit up our very wealthy family and friends, or we attended an elite university and found a way to get the ear of our alma mater's biggest philanthropists. Now I've seen the process from both sides. One nonprofit entrepreneur I mentored emailed all of CollegeSpring's major donors without my knowledge, saying I had suggested they connect with him. I didn't want to torpedo his effort, so I didn't tell our donors what he had done. Several of them went on to fund his fledgling effort, which is now a nationally acclaimed nonprofit with an eight-figure annual budget.

I am still sorting out which behaviors I see as ethical in such a corrupt system. While I don't believe in the idea that the ends justify the means, I also know that many social-change efforts wouldn't exist were it not for devious behaviors that unlock access to rich white men. And there's something distasteful about powerful institutions like Stanford hoarding their wealthy alumni, who have told me that it leaves a bad taste in their mouth when they sense that their alma mater is treating them as if they are university property. What I know for sure is that for many nonprofits, what most enables their success is their relationships with rich white men, not their relationships with the people and communities they claim to serve.

Many philanthropists prioritize the interests of these well-connected leaders. The Robin Hood Foundation has a reputation for making grants to organizations where its billionaire board members are already involved. When I first heard about New Profit—a venture philanthropy bankrolled by some of Boston's richest white men that makes $1 million capacity grants to help social entrepreneurs scale their ventures—back in 2010, I noticed that their official criteria mentioned prioritizing leaders who are magnets for resources. Such criteria elevate those who already have significant access to rich white men and marginalize those who don't. To their credit, New Profit and some other funders are selecting more social innovators from outside of elite networks. However, since many of these organizations have boards that are dominated by rich white men who don't see a need for a significant or rapid change, shifting those norms is often a slow and arduous process.

In my first few years as a social entrepreneur, I didn't fully grasp the many ways that the nonprofit sector reproduces unearned advantage. My strategies were proving useful for accessing opportunities—like the connection to Coleman Fung—that enabled CollegeSpring to get off the ground and grow. Over time, I developed savvy at getting into the right rooms, in front of the right people, and making a pitch the ultra wealthy found compelling. Once I had built an organization that outperformed some efforts founded by even wealthier peers, I started to attribute my successes to my own capabilities and a few serendipitous moments.

Increasingly, I saw myself as an unusually capable fundraiser who had engineered my own good fortune.

That was true to an extent, but the full truth is more complicated. I am grateful to Dr. Robert Livingston, a professor of mine at Harvard Kennedy School and sociologist who studies the science underneath bias, for helping me see reality more clearly.

"When I started CollegeSpring," I told him, "I didn't have a network." Robert responded with an incredulous look.

What I meant was that I had a different story than rich white men like Scott, who had been networking with philanthropists since they were in diapers. But like many people who wield some degree of power, I focused more on the power I didn't have than on the power I had leveraged.

"What are you talking about?" Robert asked me. "Stanford was your network."

It took a little while for his feedback to sink in, but eventually I saw the light. While Scott benefited from wealth advantages far greater than mine, Stanford still offered access to rare resources—controlled by rich white men—that aren't available to most people. And even within Stanford, access is unequal: wealthy white male students like me have more access than anyone else.

After talking to Robert, I began to see my "luck" differently. I had been quick to give myself full credit for opportunities I had helped to generate. Now, I still feel proud of my resourcefulness, but I also acknowledge that 99 percent of the population didn't have access to the rooms that I did, and that my "serendipitous" wins relied on that access.

What I eventually realized is that when elites say we got lucky, what we are often saying is that we interacted with a powerful person—usually a rich white man—who treated us favorably. In this sense, luck is often a bestowing of power. Much of what I've heard described as luck—good or bad—occurs when a rich white man makes a decision that impacts our lives, whether through public policy or private grace.

One important experience for my nonprofit felt like more good luck at first. When I got an email from an Obama administration staffer inviting CollegeSpring to a college opportunity event at the White House, it seemed to come out of the blue. That invitation was invaluable for CollegeSpring's credibility, and it unlocked future opportunities. It felt serendipitous—but it wasn't random chance. John Hennessy, a wealthy white man who was then the president of Stanford University, had mentioned CollegeSpring during a call with Obama administration staffers. Yes, building and maintaining a relationship with John took skill and resourcefulness on my part. However, if I hadn't gone to Stanford, I doubt I'd have ever met anyone whose endorsement could secure CollegeSpring an invitation to the White House. And had John not been comfortable with me and my aims, even a Stanford diploma might not have been enough.

Another way that rich white men deploy the luck defense is to credit our own excellent timing. When I started getting invitations to exclusive conferences, I saw how white male elites rely on personal relationships with those who pull the strings to plan for the future. That is, those with access to powerful white men have exclusive access to information about which visions of the future to bet on. When you know which ideas and issues rich white men favor, you can make a fairly safe wager on where the tides of investment will be heading. Too often, society conflates rich white men's anticompetitive access to informational power with prescience and brilliance.

Rich white men also have unique access to other types of power. When social psychologists John R. P. French and Bertram Raven studied power in the 1950s, they identified six types: positional power, which refers to formal authority; referent power, which refers to reputation; expert power, which refers to skills and expertise; reward power, the ability to give material rewards; informational power, the ability to share insights; and coercive power, the ability to force someone to do something against their will.[4] Leveraging all these sources of power enable rich white men to preserve our hegemony.

Despite its ubiquity, power is not well understood. So what is power? Dr. Martin Luther King Jr. defined power as "the ability to achieve purpose."[5] In his 2010 book *Power* Stanford professor Jeffrey Pfeffer defines power as "the ability to get things done the way one wants them to be done."[6] And in their 2021 book *Power, for All*, Harvard scholars Julie Battilana and Tiziana Casciaro define power as "control over access to resources that people value."[7] What these definitions share is the idea that power reflects an ability to impact other people's lives. Similar to how people with identity-based advantages I've met often underestimate those advantages, powerful people I've met often underestimate their power, focusing more attention on what lies outside of their influence than on what they already affect.

Those of us with identity-based advantages have power our entire lives. In her 2015 *New York Times* article "How Hospitals Coddle the Rich," Dr. Shoa Clarke describes how, at one major hospital, wealthy white couples arriving to give birth are covered in scarlet blankets—instead of the typical white—to signify their status.[8] At another hospital, rich patients receiving any treatment are labeled "pavilion patients." Even from the womb, rich white babies are influencing the behavior of doctors and other influential people, who bend over backward to ensure they receive the best possible treatment. While these parents and babies are being pampered, Black newborns are three times as likely to die as white newborns.[9] In fact, newborns born into poverty from any racial background are substantially more likely to die.[10] Trust fund babies aren't "lucky" to make it out of birthing rooms alive; their better treatment relies on unique access to structural power that could be made available to all newborns.

The first time I realized I had power was in summer 2008, after my sophomore year of college. On a hot summer night in Orange County, California, I arrived at the University of California, Irvine. I was there to teach SAT preparation at Upward Bound, a federally funded educational program enshrined into law in the 1960s under the Economic Opportunity Act and the Higher Education Act that empowers students from low-income families to become the first in their families to obtain a bachelor's degree.

Yet despite its focus on college access, the satellite at the University of California, Irvine, did not offer SAT preparation programming. Tony, the director, had spent years searching for reliable free or low-cost alternatives that his site could afford but had always come up empty. Perhaps out of sheer desperation, Tony was willing to take a chance on me, a college sophomore who had provided SAT tutoring to wealthy students but had never spent time in low-wealth communities of color. After Tony agreed to a partnership, I was deemed to have the necessary community buy-in to be eligible for a summer fellowship from Stanford University's Haas Center for Public Service. This program, funded by a white male venture capitalist, offered undergraduates a $4,000 stipend and $1,000 for supplies to design and implement a public service initiative within the United States.

The pilot program I led was impactful. Students improved their scores on the SAT—then on a 2,400 scale—by an average of 237 points, as measured by pre- and postprogram diagnostic tests. Every student improved their scores, and every student went on to college. Half went to selective University of California colleges, and two were awarded Gates Millennium Scholars scholarships, enabling them to attend prestigious universities on a full ride. My CollegeSpring cofounder Jessica Perez taught a similarly successful program at her alma mater in working-class South El Monte, California. So had Amy Truong, one of our first volunteers, at a site in East Palo Alto, a primarily Black and Latinx community around the corner from Stanford.

I didn't have the words for it back then, but teaching at Upward Bound was the first time I felt powerful. Throughout that summer and afterward, I felt as if electricity were running through my veins. People I barely knew were going to have better lives because of *me*.

But power is easy to abuse. It turns out that this feeling I had—the rush of power—is what experts call a "white savior complex," in which white people see people of color as passive recipients of white benevolence.[11] Because I was steeped in an environment where many of my Stanford classmates were doing less with their advantages—the more common paths were lucrative roles at technology start-ups, consulting firms, and investment banks—other white elites were flooding me with encouragement and praise for my "good works."

I prioritized those encouraging white voices over more skeptical voices of color, who asked more critical questions, like whether the pilot program's success justified the creation of a new nonprofit and whether I might have more impact if I first dedicated a number of years to working in the communities I aimed to serve. Those voices were also more critical about the SAT itself, which, from their vantage point, walled off opportunity more than enabled it. If high test scores can be bought, some community members had asked me, wasn't it inherently a classist and racist tool?

While I remember thinking at the time that these were good questions, I underestimated how crucial they were. At the time, I hadn't had any exposure to systems analysis. And at nineteen, I didn't think there was much I could do to change those systems. Yet instead of figuring out how I could best contribute to transforming those systems, I was overwhelmed by the urgency—and, if I'm honest, the thrill—of helping more children access opportunities. As a result, I didn't slow down and consider other possible approaches. For all the business planning I did when I started CollegeSpring—primarily in Stanford courses on social entrepreneurship led by white faculty members—I never analyzed why I had access to valuable resources that high-poverty communities of color had been denied. Instead, I focused on the downside of not using my power and advantages for good. I was so invested in growing my personal power that several years went by before I stepped back to investigate the power I held and whether I was wielding it appropriately.

Most American schools don't teach their students about power: what it is, who has it, and why. So, for the most part, neither my classmates at Stanford nor my students at Upward Bound had language to describe the power dynamics between elite and marginalized communities. In this country, rich white men gaslight Black and Brown kids about how power works; they, too, are taught that America is a meritocracy, hard work will make them rich, and if they end up in poverty, it's because of their laziness and poor decision-making.

The Upward Bound students considered themselves lucky. Several of the students told me how fortunate they felt that the SAT preparation program I was leading had happened to arrive during the year when they needed to prepare for the SATs. Had the program arrived even a year later, they would have lacked crucial resources to secure admission to universities that served as gateways to further opportunities.

Many rich white men credit luck with enabling at least some of their success, too. There are exceptions—like Elon Musk, who tweeted "Working 16 hours a day, 7 days a week, 52 weeks in year and people still calling me lucky"[12]—but most rich men I know factor in luck. When I reviewed the two hundred letters written by billionaires who signed the Giving Pledge—an initiative started by Bill Gates and Warren Buffett that asks the world's wealthiest individuals and families to dedicate at least half of their wealth to charitable causes—participants reference how luck contributed to their success more than sixty times. "My wealth," Warren Buffett writes in his Giving Pledge letter, "has come from a combination of living in America, some lucky genes, and compound interest."[13]

Other billionaires echo similar sentiments. "Through hard work, luck at the right times, and a determination to succeed," businessman Jon Huntsman Sr., concludes, "we filled our coffers."[14] "I recognized early on," oil tycoon George Kaiser emphasizes, "that my good fortune was not due to superior personal character or initiative so much as it was to dumb luck. . . . I had the advantage of both genetics (winning the 'ovarian lottery') and upbringing."[15] "Outliers happen," financier Jonathan Nelson observes, "and my number came up."[16] "No amount of business acumen," real estate developers John and Susan Sobrato note, "could have offset the luck of place and time as our region transformed from the orchards of the Santa Clara Valley into Silicon Valley."[17]

When rich white men I know have emphasized the role of luck in their success, I've found it disarming. It can feel difficult to criticize someone who is, or at least appears to be, humble about their own success. Sometimes the humility is genuine, but other times I've sensed there's a strategic element to it. When rich white men talk about benefiting from luck as if it is distributed randomly, we obscure the structural advantages that underpin our success. Across the hundreds of Giving Pledge letters, almost none mention privilege, unearned advantage, systems that favor some people over others, or government policies that make extreme wealth accumulation possible.

I think that plutocratic talk about luck is an adaptation of how Old Europe's aristocrats discussed their standing in society. Aristocrats typically said they were "blessed," a reference to the divine right that they claimed underpinned their political legitimacy. The rich white men spearheading America's settler colonialism also described themselves as blessed; such ostensible blessings legitimized manifest destiny, the nineteenth-century concept that claimed that the United States' dominion over North America was ordained by God. When rich white men claim their success is due to hard work, talent, and luck alone, they suggest their monopoly on power is legitimate, in the same way that aristocrats used divine right to legitimize their rule.

There remains a close connection between how yesterday's aristocrats and today's meritocrats view their sense of *noblesse oblige*, a French expression from the days of European aristocracy that suggests that the elite had a responsibility to be generous to commoners. In their Giving Pledge letters, forty of the two hundred signers mentioned feeling "blessed."

"We have been blessed," Bill and Melinda Gates write in their letter, "with good fortune beyond our wildest expectations."[18] In his letter, philanthropist Eli Broad offers his view that "those who have been blessed with extraordinary wealth have an opportunity, some would say a responsibility . . . to give back to their communities."[19]

Yes, it is better that elites feel noblesse oblige than feel no responsibility at all. But that is a centuries-old idea, which has now been proven inadequate. On the margin, noblesse oblige can prove useful for those who find themselves on the receiving end of rich white men's "blessings." After all, it was crucial that the resources the students at Upward Bound needed arrived right as they needed them. But the noblesse oblige lens ignores the reality that the reason they didn't have the necessary resources already was that rich white men had decided to withhold investment from their communities. As rich white men, we need to transcend the notion that we are "blessed" and sharing a portion of our "good fortune," which reproduces inequality.

Robust community investment is expensive, and many of the rich white men who bankroll political campaigns consider it *too* expensive, which is among the reasons why resources arrived through the back door of a charitable initiative. Charity offers rich white men a way to do some good at a fraction of the cost of community investment, cleansing our consciences and names without diminishing our wealth or power. My sense is that impact investing is all the rage in part because it is a way for rich white men to feel and claim to be doing good while still getting richer, just less quickly.

Part of the reason why such a competitive culture permeates throughout the nonprofit sector is that nonprofit organizations fight for scraps thrown to them by rich white men. When rich white men bestow good luck, we often prioritize those whose activities preserve our monopoly on power and resources, make us money, advance our political agendas, and—often our absolute favorite—those who claim to do all three.

While many of those bankrolled by white male plutocrats have some power and impact, we are also beholden to the agendas of the investors and benefactors who sustain us. And as long as I did not question rich white men's power and led initiatives that aligned with their worldviews, resources flowed in.

While fundraising is never easy, many elites shared my goal of expanding charitable education programs, so funding opportunities at least existed for CollegeSpring. But when I shifted my focus to supporting the Black-led reparations movement in the United States, rich white men were much more reluctant to offer resources. And those who eventually did support the initiative watched from the sidelines until Josh Mailman—an unusually progressive rich white man who takes uncommon risks with his philanthropy—made a $100,000 donation, which signaled to other wealthy white men that the effort deserved investment. It's a common tale: historically, grassroots initiatives led by people of color that are working to advance systemic change have been the least likely to attract rich white men's support.

People don't happen upon good luck; it is only accessible to a select few. It's like that scene in the TV adaptation of *Little Fires Everywhere* when Elena, played by Reese Witherspoon, says, "I made good choices," and Mia, played by Kerry Washington, replies, "You had good choices."

Such good fortune interacts with other sources of compounding unearned advantage, which further amplifies rich white men's success. Because of the structure of our networks and personal biases, we rich white men disproportionately bestow "luck" on the next generation of guys like us, which reproduces inequality into the next generation.

Building an equitable America requires disrupting these cycles. That means rewarding leaders for their proximity to marginalized communities, not their proximity to rich white men. It means major investments in marginalized people and communities with no strings attached. And it also means more rich white men finding a different role to play in society, so that those who bring different lived experience and wisdom can lead.

When rich white men hold up their winning lottery tickets and say they got lucky, society needs to call bullshit—because whenever any of us buy in to that, we forget that tens of millions of people have to suffer in poverty, dilapidated schools, and overcrowded prisons so that guys like me could draw that card.

PART II

BECOMING EQUITABLE

CHAPTER 10

INTERSECTIONAL EQUITY

I want my fair share, and that's all of it.

—CHARLES KOCH, AMERICAN BILLIONAIRE AND FOUNDER OF
KOCH INDUSTRIES, WHICH HAS SETTLED HUNDREDS OF ENVI-
RONMENTAL VIOLATIONS FOR PENNIES ON THE DOLLAR AT A
TOTAL COST OF $880 MILLION

MYTH:
Equality can be achieved without addressing disparities
in wealth and power.

*They say that the United States is one of the wealthiest coun-
tries in the world. Why are citizens still living with no access
to clean water?*

—AMANDA L., A MOTHER OF FIVE IN NEW MEXICO WHO IS
AMONG THE 30 PERCENT OF NAVAJO NATION FAMILIES WHO
LACK ACCESS TO CLEAN RUNNING WATER IN 2022

REALITY:
Equality requires that each person has the resources they uniquely
need to thrive.

I hope I have made clear by now how rich white men are often insulated by ignorance, underestimate other people's suffering, and promote myths that justify our hoarding of wealth and power. I also hope I have made clear that the structural changes needed to disrupt our monopoly on power won't occur unless other perspectives are valued and heard.

In part 1, we examined how, for centuries, rich white men have been taught to see the world through an egocentric lens, in ways that disenfranchise, stereotype, and silence marginalized groups. Now, in part 2, we'll explore how guys like me can share the stage, access the leadership and capabilities of all Americans, and repair the damage inflicted by history, in ways that honor the humanity in all of us. I chose to name this part of the book "*becoming* equitable" because of how Michelle Obama describes the word in her 2018 book *Becoming*: the term, as Obama describes it, reflects a process and practice; it's a lifelong journey toward an aspiration, an ideal that rests on the horizon of human potential.

One of the many places that would benefit from more intentional efforts to become equitable is Aldrich Hall at Harvard Business School, which is where I found myself on a cold yet sunny spring day in 2019. A gorgeous brick building with emerald-green doors, Aldrich is an institution within an institution. In 1953, John D. Rockefeller donated the building and named it after his father-in-law. For decades, Aldrich has been the academic home of first-year MBA students.

Aldrich's ninety student classrooms are arranged in a U shape. The professor is like an orchestra conductor: every class session at HBS covers a different business case study, and the professor's role is not to lecture but to draw out analysis, questions, and ideas from students.

On this day we were studying leadership and corporate accountability, known on campus as LCA. LCA is a more recent addition to the required curriculum: it was added after HBS was embarrassed in 2001 by the Enron scandal, which had been spearheaded by one of its alums.[1] Jeffrey Skilling, a rich white man from the class of 1979, was CEO when the public learned of Enron's egregious wrongdoing, which included hiding billions of dollars in debt from investors and regulators. Skilling's rise to CEO was greased by a stint at McKinsey, where he joined the energy and chemical practice after business school.

I was my section's community values representative, meaning I was responsible for fostering a culture of mutual respect within our ninety-student cohort. Like LCA, community values was another recent, reactionary addition: the need for the position was identified, I was told, after second-year male students sent sexually explicit letters to incoming female students.

After class, several students approached me because Paul, one of our white male classmates, had dominated the class discussion again. They urged me to intervene because they wanted to hear from everyone in our class, which included people who came from around the world and had worked in many different industries prior to business school. Some students were also concerned about their academic performance, since student grades are determined largely by class participation and it was more difficult to get a word in because of students like Paul.

After that intervention, I informally started tallying how often Paul interjected. While the typical student speaks in every other class session, Paul averaged five comments every class. That was ten times as often as the typical student, and thirty times as often as less vocal students.

The desire to hear from everyone is about more than an appetite for novelty. In his 2014 book *Social Physics*, MIT data scientist Alex Pentland studies teams and groups. In his research, Pentland found that groups where a few people dominate the conversation are less collectively intelligent than groups where more people contribute. "The largest factor in predicting group intelligence," Pentland writes, "was the equality of conversational turn taking."[2] Why? Groups that share airtime generate more ideas, a wider range of ideas, and a wider range of feedback on ideas, all of which build collective intelligence and ultimately enhance decision-making.

HBS could have facilitated more equitable access to class airtime, but they took a different approach. Historically, many of the predominantly white male faculty have insisted that it isn't their responsibility to manage the speaking time in their classes. Yet HBS isn't just nonchalant

about balancing speaking time; it often celebrates students who monopolize class discussions. Every year, HBS gives a cash award to the student
with the best academic record—and, at least in the year I graduated, that
was a student who hogged the floor in class, depriving other students of
a chance to speak. To me, that suggests that the institution teaches rich
white men how to climb to the top of an inequitable system, instead of
teaching us how we can build organizations and societies that maximize
human potential.

HBS also punishes students if they can't get a word in among the
domineering big talkers. Such students are described colloquially as having "hit the screen," meaning they must appeal to an academic committee at the end of their first year to plead for the right to return to HBS
for their second year of business school. Every year, several students are
required to take a year off before returning to the MBA program—a gap
that can have long-lasting consequences. These students, many of whom
come from low-wealth families, must scramble at the last minute to find
temporary full-time jobs. They also lose significant social capital, which
is among the main reasons why students shell out $200,000 for an HBS
degree: in addition to not being able to build relationships with their
first-year classmates, who graduate before they return, such students
face stigma from peers and faculty who connect the dots and realize that
person was at the bottom of the class.

Since rich white men rarely hit the screen, I didn't sense that any of
my white male classmates were concerned about failing out. However,
underrepresented populations—including white female students, American students of color, and international students for whom English isn't
their first language—are much more likely to be flagged by the predominantly white male faculty. "When I graduated from HBS in 1990," HBS
alum Steve Perry wrote in the comments section of a *Boston Globe* article about diversity at HBS, "somewhere between a third and half of the
students who 'hit the screen'... were Black."[3] Three decades later, students from marginalized backgrounds still complain about how HBS's
screening process disproportionately jettisons students from already
underrepresented groups.

The HBS example suggests how while access to an institution is a sign of equality, it doesn't guarantee equal access to that institution's resources—and not having equal access to those resources can reproduce compounding unearned advantage. For example, in its annual MBA student survey, Harvard Business School asks students about the quality of their experience and the extent to which they can access opportunities such as friendships with their wealthy and powerful classmates, research positions with distinguished faculty, and prestigious internships and jobs. During my time at HBS, white male students reported the most positive experiences; on the other hand, Black female and queer students reported having the most negative experiences. When a group of us recommended that the administration share its findings publicly and develop a plan to eliminate disparities, the administration declined. Since HBS grooms its future alumni to hold powerful positions—its alumni include George W. Bush, Jared Kushner, Mitt Romney, and countless white male CEOs and financiers—such inaction helps to preserve intersectional hierarchy, not only at HBS but also nationally and globally.

Throughout the time I've participated in social justice efforts, a commonly discussed issue is who is taking up space. A frequent complaint I've heard from marginalized populations is that many white men feel entitled to dominate conversations. When I've asked rich white men to consider participating equally, they often feel insulted. Many see the request as an affront to their individual freedom. "It's not my responsibility to hold back," one white male classmate told me. "Each person is responsible for ensuring their own voice is heard."

For advantaged people like me who are used to having our voices dominate, unequal airtime may feel like a relatively minor issue. In fact, many rich white men have told me that they don't understand why marginalized populations bring so much attention to it.

I used to be someone who unwittingly dominated many conversations. What I eventually came to see is that sharing space is among the most essential ways for me to express that I see other people as equals. If I feel I deserve more than my share of the airtime, then I must also feel other people deserve less. That means I see myself as superior and other people as inferior. While there are times when my lived experience or expertise warrants an atypically vocal moment, I've realized that behaving that way all the time, regardless of the insight I bring to a particular conversation, can be harmful.

I learned this lesson the hard way as a student a few years back, when I alienated classmates and my own prospective allies with my white male ignorance.

I could hear the frustration in the voice of Charlene Wang, my classmate who took a risk by challenging me publicly. "Inside of my head, I was like, 'Fuck you, Garrett,'" Charlene announced to the class. She was tired of listening to me drone on in the Harvard class we shared. "You know that you're privileged, and then you take up space like this anyway," she said. "I get frustrated when I see white men of privilege who, in wanting to be allies—and it's genuine—end up taking all the space in social justice....I judge [you] a bit for trying to be the savior."

I needed time to process her feedback. After all, it was a jarring experience: she had cursed me out in front of 140 of my peers. But after I thought more about it, I realized she was right. I had rationalized that it was okay for me to dominate the conversation if I was doing so in the name of social justice. But the reality was that I was still speaking for people fully capable of speaking for themselves. I overestimated how much I had to contribute and underestimated how much my classmates—and I—could learn from everyone else.

And it wasn't just about how much I talked. I also communicated in a way that undermined my ability to build trust across differences: in the way of rich white men, I was forceful, argumentative, and conveyed every remark as if I were certain I was correct; I also listened poorly and was long-winded. While these behaviors are often rewarded at places like Harvard Business School, I've come to see how they can be harmful in diverse groups where there are significant identity-based differences and complex power dynamics.

I eventually came to see that dominating conversations isn't just unfair or unkind; it's dehumanizing. Among the central characteristics that distinguishes human beings from all of Earth's other creatures is the complexity of our communication. In fact, the origin of the word "intelligent" has roots that mean "to speak." When a person is denied the opportunity to contribute their voice, it implies they're less than human.

I think part of why marginalized populations find the speaking imbalance so frustrating is that rich white men have a long history of taking things that don't belong to us. That includes the land we live on in the United States, the labor of African populations, and power over women's bodies. In this context, dominating conversations isn't just taking up space; it's reinforcing inequality. For this reason, I've come to see dominating conversations as *colonizing airtime.* We rich white men have taken almost everything from marginalized communities; do we really need to take marginalized people's voices as well?

There's another problem. Many of the rich white men I know leverage the status they gain through unearned advantages to justify disrespectful behavior. For example, many fathers talk over their families during family dinners, and many bosses talk over their employees during team meetings. Such behaviors are harmful to children, whose brain development, language development, and well-being relies on kind, active listening from adults. And those behaviors aren't good for organizations either: studies show that managers who listen to their employees gain better information, have more engaged teams and less turnover, and obtain better long-term results.[4]

From what I've observed, these behaviors seem to stem from a scarcity mindset. Us rich white men seem to be afraid that if we allow someone else's voice to be heard, our own voice will be diminished. Eventually, I realized that there are ways to express my opinions and needs that also enable other voices to be heard. For example, when I invite more people to the table, invite other people's voices into a conversation, or ask questions with an open mind, I can convey my preferences without dominating the conversation. The goal, as I've come to see it, is not to avoid taking up any space at all, but to create more space than I take.

One place where I've seen rich white men sometimes get this right is when they serve on boards. The most effective board members I've met understand that they have a fiduciary responsibility to offer guidance and direction, while still respecting the CEO's autonomy to manage the organization. I think that if more rich white men treated everyone they interact with as the CEOs of their own lives—instead of people whom we are entitled to control directly—it would have a life-changing impact.

Still, I must also confess that I still often struggle to share space. While I wish I could say I flipped a switch and have gotten it right ever since, there are many times when my spouse, family, and friends need to rein me in. I've been so deeply socialized to think of myself as the arbiter of things that just listening can still be a challenge. As much as I believe in the benefits, giving other people the respect they deserve can still be difficult for me.

I suppose I ought not be surprised. I've developed these patterns of behavior over decades—and the institutions that educated me have reinforced those habits. So it's taken me a lot of effort to try to unlearn them. I wish that as a boy I had been given the advice that human beings have two ears and one mouth for a reason, that being a good listener is every bit as important as being a good talker. But that wasn't part of the rubric for parenting or schooling wealthy white boys in the 1990s. As far as I can tell, it still isn't.

Many of the rich white men I know move through the world as if it were possible to achieve equality without addressing disparities in wealth and power. However, to achieve equality, every person must have the resources they uniquely need to thrive. *Equality* is giving everyone the same thing; *equity* is about balancing the playing field by providing resources according to need, so that historical and contemporary disadvantage can be remedied.

When I was in high school, my family adopted my younger sister Gracie from China. She'd wound up, as an infant, in an orphanage where a single worker tried to care for thirty infants. Eventually babies just stopped crying because there wasn't capacity to address their calls for help. Gracie was nonverbal when she joined our family as a two-year-old, and she needed a lot of support. To help meet her needs, our mom talked to her often, spent countless hours helping her with her schoolwork, and made sure she had access to resources like speech therapy and special education courses for speech-delayed students. Today Gracie is thriving as a college student with a broad range of interests and a great group of friends. Most importantly, Gracie is the kindest person I know. She has developed such a generous spirit that in middle school, she was chosen for the All-Around Good Kid Award, her school's sterling character award.

I didn't have the words for it at the time, but my mom treated Gracie equitably. Gracie wasn't given the same thing as everyone else; she was given something different because that's what she needed. My family and community had more resources than we needed, so we repurposed some of that surplus so Gracie could thrive. I know an equitable world can be built because I've seen it constructed with my own eyes.

I don't mean to suggest that I have a superior family or superior parents; like all families, ours has its strengths and shortcomings. *Every* parent I know tries to treat their children equitably, providing their children the same thing when possible and different things when need be. The many parents I've crossed paths with seem to know that favoring one child is problematic and can build resentment, so they try to offer equal spending treatment, like similar amounts on each of their children's clothes and birthday gifts. But they also know that treating all their children exactly the same all the time isn't necessarily what's best for them. Since every child has different capabilities and interests, parents strive to nurture each of their children's unique strengths, mitigate their unique weaknesses, and help them discover and pursue their passions. The rule most of the parents I know seem to follow is: treat every child equally when possible but equitably when need be, so they can reach toward their full potential.

For a long time, I thought I understood what equity meant. But then, in 2017, I had a conversation that helped me understand that, for all my high-minded thinking, I still harbored racist views. "Part of being anti-racist," Harvard historian Dr. Khalil Gibran Muhammad told me in a meeting at his office, "is believing there is absolutely nothing wrong with Black people."

It was a simple statement, a truism really, but having that truth expressed to me directly shook me. My mind flashed back to College-Spring's first pilot programs in 2008, after I had graded the first set of practice SAT exams for the high-poverty students of color I was teaching. The scores were low, often in the 300s and 400s for the math and verbal sections. Some of the high achievers had scores in the 500s, which were comparable to the scores obtained by some of the most academically disengaged students I'd met at my own high school.

The conclusion I drew at the time, I'm embarrassed to admit, was that the students I had been teaching were less intelligent than the well-to-do white kids I grew up with. Of course, I knew that the students I was teaching had far fewer resources—in school and at home—than my classmates and I had benefited from growing up. But since I didn't understand at the time the severity of systemic injustice in the United States and how unearned advantages compound, it didn't feel possible that systemic injustice could alone explain the enormous gap between the students I was teaching and the classmates I grew up with.

The realization that I had internalized racial ideology hit me hard. After all, I'd dedicated my life to creating opportunities for Black and brown youth to go to college and improve their lives. And yet, I held racist views.

Once I acknowledged that reality, I realized I had much more to confess. I've felt my body stiffen when I pass a group of Black men. I've doubted a Black person's intelligence when they made a math error or misremembered a detail. And I've given racist advice, too—as when I told a Black Stanford classmate, who just a few years later gave an acclaimed talk at a TED conference, after a mock job interview that he ought to overhaul his communications style, which I had perceived to be inadequate.

Growing up, I was taught that only bad people had racist thoughts. I was told to never reveal prejudice, not because stereotypes were untrue, but because it was disrespectful. At the time, I thought it was rare to have racist thoughts. I was afraid to ask other white people if they had similar thoughts. What if no one else did? What if something was wrong with *me*?

It turns out that racist thinking is common among white people.[5] It's a topic that few white people discuss publicly, but privately, many white people have told me that they've had these types of thoughts. Throughout my K–12 and college education, no one told me where these ideas came from. I wasn't taught that absorbing racist ideas about Black people and other marginalized groups—through the media, our education system, other people, and even elected officials—was part of my socialization as a white American. Over time, my relationships across differences chipped away at these negative stereotypes. But it wasn't until Dr. Muhammad pushed me to confront my biases directly that the foundation of my bigoted views began to crumble.

I have to admit that I've harbored many other types of discriminatory views, too. I've misinterpreted assertive women as aggressive. I displayed my arrogance when I tried to teach one of my friends from a low-wealth family how to better manage his finances, even though I've never been successful at managing a budget and I spend money frivolously in ways he'd never dream of doing. And during my freshman year of college, I remember one of my classmates giving me a horrified look when I expressed doubt that queer couples could effectively raise children. Even now, for reasons I'm still trying to unravel, I am often drawn to books that are written by other white men. And these are just a few of many examples.

Underlying these bigoted thoughts and actions is an implicit belief that negative stereotypes about marginalized groups hold validity. That mindset ultimately fuels a self-fulfilling prophecy: if I believe in group stereotypes, I will treat advantaged and marginalized people accordingly, which reproduces disparities. By contrast, a true belief in equality requires conviction that negative stereotypes about groups are not just exaggerated but false, that disparities—like identity-based gaps in wealth, education, health, incarceration, housing, and more—are the result of systemic injustices, not behavioral, cultural, or genetic deficiencies.

For those who believe marginalized groups have these deficiencies, the societal yardstick doesn't need to be parity. To some white people, the passage of civil rights legislation and Barack Obama's election as president proved that America had become a post-racial society. According to some men, women achieved equality once they secured the right to vote or the right to attend elite universities. These may be signs of progress, but they are arbitrary markers set by rich white men who claim, as most have historically, that discrimination is a relic of the past, not something woven into every dimension of our American society.

If I believe negative stereotypes about a marginalized group, by definition I believe in positive stereotypes about the advantaged group. In the context of advantage, scholars call this phenomenon "internalized supremacy." With whiteness, it's called white supremacy. With gender, it's called misogyny. With social class, it's classism.

These are seemingly radioactive phrases. From what I've seen, rich white men like me seem reluctant to even say them out loud. But if we can't acknowledge them, we can't address them.

"White supremacy," the poet Guante reminds us, "is not a shark; it is the water."[6]

The same is true for sexism and classism.

Building a fair society requires acknowledging that, in the current system, people begin life at different starting lines and experience life on different trajectories. In an equitable America, identity characteristics would not predict where individuals start or where they end up.

Building an equitable America requires equitable policies. In his book *How to Be an Antiracist*, Ibram X. Kendi describes equitable policies when it comes to race:

> A racist policy is any measure that produces or sustains racial inequity between racial groups. An antiracist policy is any measure that produces or sustains racial equity between racial groups. By policy, I mean written and unwritten laws, rules, procedures, processes, regulations, and guidelines that govern people. There is no such thing as a nonracist or race-neutral policy. Every policy in every institution in every community in every nation is producing or sustaining either racial inequity or equity between racial groups.[7]

Kendi's ideas can be generalized to equity more broadly. An inequitable policy, as I understand it, is any measure that produces or sustains inequity between groups. An equitable policy is any measure that produces or sustains equity between groups. Equitable policies can be as large as a multi-trillion-dollar federal program or as small as hiring more people of color or adding resources to an organization's diversity, equity, and inclusion budget. If a policy moves our society closer to equity, it is equitable.

Centering equity for the most marginalized requires acknowledging the uncomfortable reality that not all people who face discrimination are equally oppressed. For example, as a wealthy Jewish man, I have experienced antisemitism personally, and I know that work remains to stamp out antisemitism in America. I am careful not to minimize the additional societal burdens I carry as a Jew, but I also strive to admit honestly that, most of the time, I benefit from compounding unearned advantages that are quite similar to those that are available to other wealthy white men in America. I've learned that it's possible for me to acknowledge that, overall, the American system favors me greatly, even if it doesn't favor me absolutely.

Achieving equity for the most marginalized is a significant task. In an equitable society, disparities between what I think of as the *Advantaged 1 Percent* (heterosexual, cis-gender, able-bodied, wealthy white men) and the *Marginalized 1 Percent* (queer, transgender, differently abled, low-wealth Black and Indigenous women) wouldn't exist. It's difficult to say exactly how wide the disparities between these populations are because, to my knowledge, no attempt has been made to calculate them. The lack of data itself reflects compounding advantage and disadvantage: it's more challenging to confront the unearned advantages of the Advantaged 1 Percent when it isn't known how great our advantages are, and it's more difficult for the advantaged among us to have compassion for the Marginalized 1 Percent when we lack information about what their lives are like.

Some research hints at the scale of inequity. Harvard economist Raj Chetty's research revealed that Black boys raised in the lowest-income families are one hundred times as likely to be incarcerated as white boys raised in the highest-income families.[8] The National LGBTQ Task

Force found that 34 percent of Black transgender people report living in extreme poverty, with household incomes of less than $10,000 per year; that's four times the rate of the general Black population (9 percent) and eight times the rate of the general US population (4 percent).[9] The National Disability Institute found that 37 percent of Black Americans with disabilities live in poverty.[10]

Intersectionally disadvantaged Indigenous people fare no better. A 2016 study by the National Institute of Justice estimated that 56 percent of Indigenous women have experienced sexual violence and that 88 percent of crimes committed against Indigenous women are interracial.[11] According to the Centers for Disease Control and Prevention, murder is the third-leading cause of death for Indigenous women, who are murdered at ten times the national average.[12] Indigenous women face so much violence while receiving so little state protection and support that Indigenous activists created the MMIWG2S—Missing and Murdered Indigenous Women, Girls, and Two Spirit—grassroots movement to bring attention to the issue.

While the Marginalized 1 Percent are fighting for their lives, the Advantaged 1 Percent dominate powerful positions. No person in the Marginalized 1 Percent has ever been a congressperson, senator, president, Fortune 500 CEO, or billionaire; in this sense, the historical data indicates that the Advantaged 1 Percent are *infinitely* more likely to reach America's most influential posts than the Marginalized 1 Percent. In January 2017, while Georgia resident Jon Ossoff was counting down the days until his thirtieth birthday would unlock his eligibility to run for a seat in the United States Senate, Jamie Lee Wounded Arrow—a twenty-eight-year-old Indigenous woman who identified as transgender and two spirit—was being stabbed to death in her home in Sioux Falls. That degree of inequity is more the norm than the exception.

I hope that researchers eventually provide better data about the disparities between the Advantaged 1 Percent and Marginalized 1 Percent. If America is going to become an equitable nation, an early step will be illuminating how far it has to go. At the same time, though, I hope that the advantaged among us don't lose sight of the fact that no quantitative

measures can adequately represent the psychological impact of being destitute in the richest country in the world, or grappling with the hypocrisy
of being terrorized in a country that claims life, liberty, and the pursuit
of happiness are unalienable rights.

I also hope that someday more rich white men will understand that,
when it comes to our political preferences, our own material interests
and biases sometimes come into play. For example, voting patterns map
directly to intersectional hierarchy. Embedded in the word "conservative"
is the word "conserve," which means protecting things the way things currently are; the word "progressive," on the other hand, contains the word
"progress," which is about breaking from the past in order to create something new. That observation is not a judgment about which approach is
inherently better—any successful society must conserve some of its heritage and practices while also embracing change—but it is telling that those
who align themselves with progressive change are disproportionately
those who are currently at the bottom of the hierarchy: during the 2020
presidential election, 95 percent of Black women, 87 percent of Black men,
61 percent of Hispanic women, 57 percent of Hispanic men, 46 percent of
white women, and 40 percent of white men voted for the liberal candidate
(I couldn't find precise figures for Indigenous Peoples, which is part of the
erasure and inequity).[13]

It doesn't surprise me that the Marginalized 1 Percent—whose experience is often that the system doesn't meet their most basic of needs—
are often among the most consistent advocates for a significant overhaul
of society. Nor does it surprise me the Advantaged 1 Percent, who accrue
enormous benefits from the status quo, are often among the most resis-
tant to change. And the fact that voting preferences vary greatly by race
and only slightly by gender suggests that most people feel their lives are
more affected by their race than by their gender, even if us white people
don't always acknowledge how our association with whiteness shapes
our political preferences.

However, all of that can change. Increasingly, I've heard dialogue in
elite spaces about "centering Black and Indigenous women." Taking that
seriously, as I understand it, requires that the Advantaged 1 Percent put

our wealth and power behind the leadership of the Marginalized 1 Percent and those working in close solidarity with them. That includes efforts like the Movement for Black Lives—which from the beginning has had transgender Black women in its leadership and been reminding the public that trans Black lives matter—and the Missing and Murdered Indigenous Women, Girls, and Two Spirit movement. If even a small percentage of rich white men supported institutions, campaigns, and movements led by such people—with our time, skills, financial resources, and full collaboration as unpaternalistic partners—I'm confident that progress toward equity in the United States would greatly accelerate.

America has a long way to go on its path to becoming equitable. Given the tremendous distance we must travel, America needs leaders who are willing to take responsibility for dismantling disparities and reimagining how society functions. I hope that more rich white men will provide that kind of leadership themselves, yet I also hope that more rich white men will have the courage and humility to acknowledge that at times the best way to acclerate progress is to step aside so that others can lead.

It's long past time for rich white men to drop the microphone and stop pretending our collective success rests on our individual insights alone, and to start listening to the perspectives of other people with humility and an open mind. The paternal role that many rich white men claim is merely socialized and not actually necessary for society to function. After four centuries of inequity, rich white men need to create room for every American to contribute their wisdom and ideas. Only then can America become a nation that offers liberty and justice for all.

CHAPTER 11

ANTIMONOPOLY

Big business in America is a ... meritocracy.

—STEVE JOBS, APPLE COFOUNDER

MYTH:

Reducing inequality will damage the economy and ultimately hurt everyone.

We all too often have socialism for the rich and rugged free enterprise capitalism for the poor.

—DR. MARTIN LUTHER KING JR., AMERICAN BAPTIST MINISTER
AND CIVIL RIGHTS ACTIVIST

REALITY:

Reducing inequality will strengthen democracy and unlock shared prosperity.

nside a Harvard classroom, I was seated with twenty-two of my classmates for a seminar focused on income inequality. This particular session was led by two white male professors who are known as card-carrying liberals; one serves on the board of a civil rights nonprofit, while the other is a leader in the university's efforts to foster diversity and inclusion.

Professors had dubbed this particular cohort of students as "the best of the best" because we were all dual-degree students, admitted independently to Harvard's business and public policy schools. Harvard was grooming us to become "triathletes" who could hold leadership roles in three different arenas: business, government, and nonprofits.

The program's principal benefactor is David Rubenstein, a white male billionaire who made his fortune as the cofounder and CEO of Carlyle Group, the private equity giant. Rubenstein is known for his charitable giving but also for his fierce resistance to closing the carried interest loophole, which enables Rubenstein and other finance moguls to avoid $180 billion in taxes every decade. Bernie Sanders, Hillary Clinton, and Donald Trump all campaigned against the loophole, but efforts to close it were defeated by the American Investment Council, a lobbying organization that was chaired at the time by one of Rubenstein's lieutenants.[1] The measure died three votes short of the majority it needed in 2010—and the loophole advantage hasn't been seriously challenged since then.

I wasn't surprised that the faculty members had chosen to frame our discussion that day as being about income inequality, not wealth inequality. That is the norm in elite spaces, and Harvard faculty in particular have reasons to leave wealth off the table. For the world's wealthiest university, rampant wealth inequality had been a boon: Harvard's endowment swelled from $4.8 billion in 1990 to $53.2 billion in 2021.[2] The university's largest gift to date—a whopping $400 million—was a direct product of rising inequality: hedge fund manager and rich white man John Paulson made the donation after pocketing $4 billion from shorting the housing market during the 2008 subprime mortgage crisis.[3]

While millions of Americans were losing their homes and tumbling into poverty, Paulson—and Harvard—were getting richer.

And yet, despite their liberal leanings, the professors leading our inequality seminar perpetuated a myth also echoed by their more politically conservative colleagues. "Let's start by discussing the efficiency-equity trade-off," the first professor announced to our class.

An efficiency-equity trade-off is a concept in economics that suggests there can be a trade-off between economic output and societal fairness. If a trade-off exists, policy makers are tasked with assessing whether it's worth sacrificing some economic output to achieve a more just society.

Drawing on the blackboard, one professor charted the prospect. "On the vertical axis, we have efficiency," he said. "On the horizontal axis, we have—what should we call it—social justice." Between the two axes, the professor drew a straight, downward-sloping line. Harvard's message to its students was clear: economic output and social justice are inversely related.

The efficiency-equity trade-off underpins many of rich white men's perspectives about inequality. Prioritize social justice, the argument goes, and the overall economy will suffer. And as a result, it is often claimed, those at the bottom economically will end up even worse off.

The professor's pat acceptance of that theory made me and other classmates uneasy. What about research that has shown that more-inclusive companies perform better financially? And how can a society perform optimally when a significant portion of the population lacks the most basic of resources, can't reach their potential, and can't contribute their gifts to society?

The truth is that my professor's diagram was wrong. Some people might consider that a partisan claim, but it's not. A society with extreme inequality cannot function. At its most extreme, that configuration wouldn't even be recognized as a society. If a society were perfectly unequal, one individual would hold all the resources while the rest of the people would have none. In this scenario, everyone except the keeper of the resources would starve and die. And those resources would be socially meaningless, since the hoarder would have no one to share them with. Nor would they be able to use their resources productively, since no one else would be able to add value to them. Such a world is neither just nor efficient. When rich white men claim that no ceiling for inequality is too high, we are spreading a falsehood that protects our economic interests.

It seems to be a well-kept secret that high marginal tax rates are not only part of America's recent history but also active during the decades when America built its middle class and cemented its status as a superpower. From 1944 to 1963, the highest marginal tax rate for individuals exceeded 90 percent. While the top bracket was lowered in the 1960s, it was still pegged at 70 percent for two decades, until Reagan slashed it to 50 percent in 1982 and 28 percent in 1988. Reagan's trickle-down economics has been the law of the land ever since, regardless of whether Republicans or Democrats control the executive branch: since 1988, the top bracket has hovered between 28 percent and 43 percent.[4] Currently it stands at 37 percent.[5]

No one can say for certain that economic growth rates would have been higher if Reagan cut taxes. However, a few things are clear. First, the American economy has grown more slowly in every decade since the shift in tax policy: American GDP grew by 166 percent in the 1970s, 109 percent in the 1980s, 72 percent in the 1990s, 47 percent in the 2000s, and 39 percent in the 2010s. Second, over the past few decades, the rich have gotten richer while the poor have suffered: between 1989 and 2018, the top 1 percent increased its wealth by $21 trillion while the bottom 50 percent lost $900 billion.[6] Third, inequality got worse during the COVID-19 pandemic, which drove millions more Americans into poverty while stuffing the pockets of the four hundred wealthiest Americans with another $4.5 trillion.[7] And finally, the 1930s Great Depression came after an explosion in wealth inequality now known as the Gilded Age.

Many of the rich white men I know like to say that our country functions best when the free market reigns, but those same men seem to prefer an economic system that is tilted heavily in their favor. In his 2019 book *People, Power, and Profits*, Nobel Prize–winning economist Joseph Stiglitz describes how corporate profits are higher than they have been in nearly a century.[8] A central reason why is that many companies act more like monopolies than competitors. Presently, most major industries are at best weakly competitive, with two to five players dominating most of the market. That includes powerhouse industries such as banking and technology, as well as industries that directly shape public opinion, such as media and publishing. Stiglitz is especially critical of the technology giants, which preserve their near-monopoly status by engaging in an array of anticompetitive behaviors, such as acquiring new companies and then shelving their innovations so they aren't threatened by upstarts. As a result of practices like these, corporate power—and profits—are becoming increasingly concentrated.

Winner-take-all economic systems sometimes produce profitable innovations that benefit society, but they also encourage freeloading. When the American Investment Council aligns otherwise-competing private equity firms to protect the carried interest loophole, that's anticompetitive—and antidemocratic, since the public's desire to close the loophole is suppressed. Extractive actions like these enabled Amazon and Tesla—the companies led by Jeff Bezos and Elon Musk, the world's two richest men—to pay zero income taxes in 2018.[9] When rich white guys deplete public infrastructure—such as the public universities that educate our workforces and the roads that get employees to our offices—without renewing it, we are engaging unsustainably, enriching ourselves at the expense of the public good.

It's not an accident that the most profitable companies behave monop-olistically. When they don't think the public and government regulators are listening, many rich white men talk openly about how they aspire to hold monopolies. "Monopoly," technology investor Peter Thiel writes in his 2014 bestseller *Zero to One: Notes on Startups, or How to Build the Future*, "is the condition of every successful business."[10]

Thiel also advises highly profitable companies on how to disguise their monopolies. "Anyone that has a monopoly will pretend that they're in incredible competition," Thiel writes. "If you have a monopoly, you will describe [your market] as super big, and there is lots of competition in it." Thiel offers Google as an example: while Google owned less than

3 percent of the global advertising market and less than 0.24 percent of the global consumer technology market when Thiel wrote his book, it owned about two-thirds of the global internet search market. "It's not enough to have a monopoly for just a moment," Thiel emphasizes.

Famed investor Warren Buffett communicates the same concept using different language. "In business," Buffett wrote in his 1995 shareholder letter, "I look for economic castles protected by unbreachable moats."[11] Buffett is credited with coining the concept of the "economic moat." Just as water-filled moats surrounding castles protected kings and queens from rival armies, economic moats protect companies—and the rich white men who own them—from competitors.

Monopolies are harmful to society. When a company behaves monopolistically, it maximizes its own profits at the public's expense. Compared with companies that face more competition, monopolies produce less and charge more. At a societal level, that means a smaller economic pie coupled with higher prices, which reduces what consumers can afford to buy.

As monopolistic firms gain power, they dedicate a growing share of their attention to rent-seeking activities, like tax evasion. While the IRS has 15,000 staffers, large corporations employ a combined 250,000 accountants.[12] These armies of financial wizards enable companies to manipulate their tax bills. For example, in a recent year, Google claimed that it made $23 billion in Bermuda—which doesn't have a corporate income tax—and nothing in the United States, even though most of its revenue comes from American consumers.[13]

A principal reason why corporate profits are at a seventy-year high is that corporations are covering a smaller share of the federal tax bill than they have in decades. In 2019, the corporate income tax raised $230 billion, 6.5 percent of total federal revenue.[14] That's a much smaller percentage than in the 1950s, when corporate income tax covered 30 percent of federal revenue. If corporations paid the same share they did then, the federal government would receive an extra $750 billion annually.[15] That figure is more than the government currently spends on education, training, employment, social, and veterans' services combined.

Large companies exercise power over their workers, too. Amazon is a prominent example: in 2020, Vox gained access to internal documents that outlined Amazon's plans to spend hundreds of thousands of dollars to analyze data on unions around the world, so it could better track—and thwart—employee efforts to secure higher wages and protections.[16] Thanks to initiatives like these, a significant percentage of Amazon employees are paid so little that they qualify for federal welfare programs like food stamps. In some recent years, Amazon didn't pay any income taxes *and* taxpayers subsidized workers to whom Amazon didn't pay a living wage.[17] Many other companies follow a similar strategy: for example, Walmart's low-wage workers qualify for $6 billion in public assistance, for benefits like food stamps and Medicaid.

Sometimes, companies coordinate with their "competitors" behind the backs of their employees. In a 2010 United States Department of Justice antitrust action and a 2013 civil class action suit that involved sixty-four thousand computer programmers, Apple, Google, Intel, Intuit, and Adobe were accused of orchestrating "no cold call" agreements. Such agreements are illegal because they prevent high-tech employees from obtaining the jobs—and salaries—they are qualified for.

The complaint offered damning evidence that Apple CEO Steve Jobs orchestrated the effort directly through private conversations with other chief executives. For example, in 2007, when a Google recruiter solicited an Apple engineer, Jobs complained directly to Google CEO Eric Schmidt. "I would be very pleased," Jobs told Schmidt, "if your recruiting department would stop doing this." Schmidt immediately forwarded Jobs' email to HR leader Arnnon Geshuri, asking him to "get this stopped." Geshuri assured Schmidt that the recruiter "will be terminated within the hour." Three days later, Shona Brown—Google's Senior Vice President for Business Operations—praised Geshuri's action and requested that he "make a public example of this termination with the group." Schmidt seemed to know that at least some of these activities were legally dubious: for example, he instructed an executive to only discuss the company's no-call list verbally "since I don't want to create a paper trail over which we can be sued later." While the companies never admitted to any wrongdoing, they did agree to a massive $415 million settlement.[18] It's difficult to assess how much these practices buoyed Apple's path to becoming a multitrillion-dollar company. Still, I expect many investors see a slap on the wrist equivalent to 0.01 percent of Apple's current market cap as offering an outstanding return on investment.

Those who are part of an advantaged identity group can engage in anticompetitive behavior, too. University of Southern California law professor Daria Roithmayr studies racial cartels, the all-white or predominantly white groups—such as homeowners' associations, school districts, trade unions, real estate boards, and political parties—that have coordinated throughout American history to exclude people based on race.[19] Racial cartels are profitable because they are anticompetitive. Like all monopolistic behaviors, racial cartels enrich themselves but shrink the overall pie by ignoring the talents of those who have far more to contribute.

White people are not the only ones who at times function in groups as identity-based cartels. Many men collude in similar ways, and so do many wealthy people. Effectively an alliance of identity-based cartels, rich white men are the primary beneficiaries of such monopolistic behavior.

Every act of identity-based collusion is principally a way to coerce the oppressed into accepting lower wages than they would in a fair economy. Slavery is perhaps the most extreme example of identity-based collusion: the rich white men who oversaw southern plantations did not find an open labor market sufficiently lucrative, so they colluded to avoid paying any wages at all. Rich white men's resistance to women's suffrage, child labor laws, and minimum wage increases have a similar throughline. When investors learn that minimum wage increases are struck down, employees are prevented from unionizing, corporate taxes are reduced, or labor laws are relaxed, stock prices increase. "The stock market is not the economy," Existential Comics tweeted. "It's an estimate of how much wealth can be extracted from workers."[20]

I don't mean to suggest that such collusion is always conscious and explicit. From the many conversations I've had with rich white men, I don't think it usually is. But since America is working toward equity from an anticompetitive and antidemocratic starting point, efforts to protect the status quo reproduce inequality.

Study after study has shown that rich white men's monopolistic behavior shrinks the overall economic pie. In 2020, a Citigroup study found that at least $16 trillion has been erased from United States GDP over the last two decades because of racial discrimination.[21] In 2015, the McKinsey Global Institute reported that advancing women's equality could add $12 trillion to global GDP by 2025, a figure equivalent to the combined economies of Japan, Germany, and the United Kingdom.[22] These studies and others confirm that both high and low wealth countries would see major gains from increased equality. When only a small percentage of a population is allowed to fully participate in the economy, the overall economy doesn't produce as much.[23] That is, when rich white men hoard resources for ourselves, the overall economy suffers.

Rich white men like to boast about the size of the economic pie our leadership has created, but the reality is that global resources are insufficient to meet global needs. Total global wealth is $431 trillion, which sounds like an enormous sum, but that computes to about $50,000 per person.[24] When a pie this size is accompanied by high inequality, the inevitable result is that most people effectively have no resources. Such a society is not only unjust but also inefficient, since no one can benefit from the gifts and talents of those whose energies are allocated to simply fighting for their lives.

When I studied economics at Stanford, I was taught that discrimination is economically irrational behavior. That was the consensus among white male economists at the time. As far as I know, it still is. The theory goes like this: If I discriminate against a potential customer or a potential employee, I lose out on a money-making opportunity. Another enterprising company will scoop up those customers and talented employees, and I won't be unable to compete successfully with those who don't discriminate.

But what about slavery? Within Stanford's economics department, I was taught that slavery is an aberration. However, if it was a one-off exception, why did it last 250 years in America—longer than nearly every major corporation, not to mention longer than the United States has been a country? The reality is that while slavery was—obviously—not the best approach for producing shared prosperity, it was highly profitable for the white male plantation owners who fought hard to protect their anticompetitive abuses.

Roithmayr's analysis of identity-based cartels sheds light on how identity-based collusion can be economically rational for the advantaged population, as long as a critical mass of the advantaged population is willing to collude. Such dynamics remain relevant in the present. For example, if corporate America shares a view that white men are more competent, then firms that sell products or services to those companies— such as Goldman Sachs, McKinsey, and Microsoft—are incentivized to prioritize white men in their hiring and promotions. But if more rich white men reject this notion, it will become increasingly costly for those who dig in their heels to protect the status quo.

The antidote to monopolistic practices is antimonopoly policies. That means breaking up companies that wield coercive levels of power, like many of the technology giants. It means fostering competition in the many industries that are only weakly competitive. And it means taking on corporate tax evasion, including leveraging America's soft power to prevent other countries from serving as tax havens for rich white American men and their companies.

On an individual level, it means overhauling a tax system that indulges the wealthy. To level the playing field, America must close loopholes like the carried interest loophole, abolish the $1 trillion-per-year tax deductions program, implement robust inheritance taxes to combat the literal reinvention of aristocracy, and tax capital gains as ordinary income because, in a capitalist system, few things are more ordinary than growing one's capital. It must also reinstitute a highly progressive tax system that accounts for the fact that it is expensive to be poor and the fact that rich white men's monopoly on power is unjust—and inefficient.

In their 2019 book *The Triumph of Injustice: How the Rich Dodge Taxes and How to Make Them Pay*, UC Berkeley economists Emmanuel

Saez and Gabriel Zucman provide robust evidence that the elite have vanquished progressive taxation in America. Today, most Americans pay similar tax rates, regardless of their socioeconomic status. And billionaires pay lower tax rates than America's firefighters, nurses, and teachers.

Saez has given more thought than most to what a just taxation system might look like. Now a household name in the economics field, Saez got his start by collaborating with Thomas Piketty, who made waves with his 2013 book *Capital in the Twenty-First Century*. Later, Saez was awarded a MacArthur "genius grant" and the John Bates Clark Medal, which the American Economic Association bestows on a rising star in the field under the age of forty.[25]

One question Saez has asked is, What is the tax system that maximizes tax revenue—which can then be reinvested in public services? That would be a sharp shift from the current system, which maximizes rich white men's wealth at everyone else's expense. Saez's economic modeling revealed that, to maximize federal tax revenue, the wealthiest 1 percent must pay 60 percent of their income in taxes—double what they pay now—including a top marginal tax bracket of 75 percent.[26] If such a tax program were implemented, it would significantly reduce economic inequality without eliminating the possibility of becoming rich. For example, if Saez's program had been implemented in 1990, most of today's billionaires would still be billionaires; they would just have fewer billions.

To produce such a system, Saez favors a wealth tax, which is a direct path to reducing wealth inequality. In his book, Saez proposes a wealth tax of 2 percent on wealth above $50 million and 3.5 percent on wealth above $1 billion. While Warren Buffett paid just $1.8 million in taxes during a recent year, he would have paid $1.8 billion—billion with a *b*—if the wealth tax had been implemented.[27] Such a policy would multiply Buffett's tax burden by one thousand times, so it is no wonder that many billionaires bristle at such proposals. Still, it's the least the extremely wealthy can do to renew the infrastructure that made it possible for them to build their fortunes.

Many ultrawealthy white men have told me that their peers will leave the United States if America adopts a wealth tax. Here is how I see it: if some billionaires leave because they don't want to pay more taxes, let them. I don't say this cavalierly. Tax policy reflects America's culture and values, and instead of letting them hold this nation hostage, those who care more about having a few extra billions than our country's well-being can go. And politicians can call their bluff: some millennial techies might relocate, but most boomer billionaires aren't about to leave their grandchildren behind so they can set up shop in Singapore. My prediction is that the additional revenue that America would then be able to invest in millions of Americans will unlock so much brilliance and do so much to strengthen democracy that the few oligarchs who relinquish their citizenship won't be missed. It seems to be a largely forgotten history that Franklin D. Roosevelt—the first president to heavily tax the wealthy—advocated for near-confiscatory tax rates on the wealthiest Americans, not because those policies maximized tax revenue but because they were a safeguard for democracy.[28]

All that said, a wealth tax does have some drawbacks. Wealth can be challenging to measure, and much of America's wealth is held in the stock market, which means that wealthy people would often need to sell securities to pay their wealth taxes. In some cases, it could create undesirable outcomes, like requiring entrepreneurs to sell so many shares that they lose control of their companies. For these reasons, it may be better to simply have a much more progressive tax system that incorporates capital gains as ordinary income rather than introduce the complexities associated with a new type of tax.

Even from a utilitarian perspective—the preferred moral framework of many white male economists—high taxes on the wealthy are morally justified. A key concept within utilitarianism is diminishing marginal utility, the idea that everything becomes less valuable as someone acquires more of it. For example, while eating a slice of chocolate cake might bring me joy, I most certainly won't enjoy a second slice nearly as much, and past a certain point, even the thought of eating any more chocolate cake will make me sick to my stomach. Diminishing marginal utility applies to economic inequality, too: an incremental $100 can be life changing for a person in poverty who is starving, whereas many of the wealthy people I know might not even notice an erroneous $100 charge on their credit card statement.

Contributive justice is another important consideration. Emphasized by Harvard philosopher Michael Sandel in his 2020 book *The Tyranny of Merit*, contributive justice is the idea that human beings long to feel needed, that they are contributing to society.[29] When rich white men swallow up all the glory—and leverage their considerable public-relations budgets to brand themselves as saviors—it diminishes everyone else's contributions. When elites like me claim to deserve our monopoly on resources, those who are struggling sense our condescension and prejudice. Building an equitable society requires not only an equitable distribution of resources but also an equitable distribution of credit and honor. "One day our society will come to respect the sanitation worker if it is to survive," Dr. Martin Luther King Jr. famously said in a speech in support of the Memphis sanitation workers' strike two weeks before his assassination, "for the person who picks up our garbage, in the final analysis, is as significant as the physician, for if he doesn't do his job, diseases are rampant. All labor has dignity."[30]

Contributive justice also requires recognizing currently unpaid labor. The countless mothers doing thankless work for their households deserve greater acknowledgment, and the countless fathers doing less than their share need to participate in the home equitably. Companies take strides toward closing the expectations gap when it comes to who is the primary parent and who is the primary earner by normalizing having fathers participate equally in parental leave.

Whenever a proposal is made to level the distribution of resources, though, a common refrain among rich white men is that such a program is socialist. It's a centuries-old tactic: before the Civil War, pro-slavery advocates labeled abolitionist newspaper editor Horace Greeley a socialist.[31] Minimum wage and child labor laws faced a similar onslaught. So did Roosevelt's New Deal, Johnson's Medicare, Obama's Affordable Care Act, and Biden's Build Back Better.[32] In 2008, John McCain characterized Barack Obama's tax proposals as "socialism," declaring in a radio address that Obama "believes in redistributing wealth, not in policies that help us all make more of it."[33]

But the reality is that none of these initiatives are socialist. Fundamentally, the distinction between capitalism and socialism is about who owns the means of production, not the level of economic inequality within that society. The idea that America's only options are extreme inequality or socialism is a false binary. Many capitalist countries—such as most Nordic and Central European countries—have far less inequality than the United States.[34]

That said, America doesn't need to succumb to rich white men's false binary between capitalism and socialism either. The choice, as I see it, is not whether government manages nothing or everything: every successful society does some centralized planning while empowering its citizens with some level of individual agency. If most rich white men swear by centralized planning in their businesses—CEOs have centralized power—can we then go on to deny that some degree of centralized planning is beneficial in our governments? When Dr. King called for a third way between capitalism and socialism, he was urging America to grapple with such complexity and access the best from both of these models.

The truth of the matter is that there already is a significant redistribution of resources in America. It's just that presently that redistribution flows upward. Rich white men often claim reducing inequality damages the economy, moves resources into less-capable hands, and ultimately hurts everyone. However, the reality is that reducing inequality will more likely accelerate economic growth, strengthen the economy, and unlock shared prosperity.

Deep down, I think most rich white men know this is true. After all, even the white male billionaires who own America's NFL teams concluded in 1994 that the league would benefit from a salary cap.[35] Owners, players, and fans know that when inequality is too high, the game is too close to rigged and no fun for anyone. And since the cap was introduced, the NFL has flourished economically: adjusted for inflation, NFL annual TV revenues increased sixfold.[36]

For the first time in decades, America's economic preeminence is under threat. Further stuffing America's fat cats will do little to prevent the American experiment from disintegrating. Instead, this nation must find a way to unlock the potential of all its people. That means dismantling the monopolistic practices of rich white men that preserve our power over wealth and democracy.

It's difficult to contribute your gifts to society if you're starving. That's why a crucial step is fulfilling Dr. King's final wish of abolishing poverty, absolutely and in perpetuity.

CHAPTER 12

ABOLISHING POVERTY

*The only way to beat poverty in America is to completely,
totally transform our public education system.*

—PAUL TUDOR JONES II, AMERICAN HEDGE FUND BILLIONAIRE
AND FOUNDER OF THE ROBIN HOOD FOUNDATION

MYTH:

Poverty is caused by the inadequacy of individual systems.

*I am now convinced that…the solution to poverty is to
abolish it directly.…We are likely to find that the problems
of housing and education, instead of preceding the elimination of poverty, will themselves be affected if poverty is first
abolished.*

—DR. MARTIN LUTHER KING JR., AMERICAN BAPTIST MINISTER
AND CIVIL RIGHTS ACTIVIST

REALITY:

Poverty causes individual systems to fail.

When I started to shift my social change focus from education reform to inequality more broadly, some rich white men tried to talk me out of it.

One of these men is a retired American businessman who is among America's leading education philanthropists. He's the former CEO of an investment bank, so I'll call him Morgan, like Morgan Stanley (that's not the bank he ran).

No matter where he puts his energy, Morgan gives it 110 percent. He's known for his affable personality and ruthless approach to business. Now in his seventies, he still exercises like a fiend. When I asked Morgan the question about how wealthy he would be today if he had been born a Black woman, he said he wished he could test that out. "I'd love the challenge," he told me.

Now that he's retired from banking, Morgan brings the same hard-charging approach to his philanthropy. He's a national advocate for education reform and supports a growing network of charter schools, and understood my commitment to CollegeSpring. "I hope you don't give up on education," Morgan told me. "Education is the key to addressing inequality and advancing equal opportunity in America."

Many elites share that view. Of America's fifty largest family foundations—which, as of 2019, managed a combined $144 billion in assets—forty consider education a priority for support.[1] However, many of them are also frustrated about their inability to have the impact they desire. Some endeavors—like Mark Zuckerberg's $100 million gift to Newark Public Schools—have been so disastrous that entire books chronicle their failings. "If there's one lesson we've learned about education after twenty years," Bill Gates told CNBC in 2020, "it's that scaling solutions is difficult. Much of our early work in education seemed to hit a ceiling. Once projects expanded to reach hundreds of thousands of students, we stopped seeing the results we hoped for."[2]

Gates follows a long line of plutocrats who have attempted to reduce inequality via education reform. John D. Rockefeller and Andrew

Carnegie, who established the first iterations of what is often described as modern philanthropy in the early 1900s, kicked things off with a focus on education. Rockefeller bankrolled the General Education Board, which—among other activities—built more than nine hundred high schools and developed programs to modernize farming practices in the American South.[3] Carnegie built 2,509 libraries.[4] A century later, many rich white men still see school reform and expanded extracurricular options as the primary paths for children from marginalized backgrounds to secure opportunities and experience mobility.

I saw the dominance of this viewpoint at the annual Milken Institute Global Conference, an event hosted by billionaire and convicted white-collar criminal Michael Milken that attracts four thousand business and political leaders to Los Angeles. At the conference, a white male philanthropist had invited me to attend—as his guest—a private lunch meeting with financial elites and education leaders. Much of our discussion focused on the Los Angeles Unified School District, America's second-largest school district and one that has struggled for decades, through several waves of well-meaning reforms. The audience of mostly rich white men desperately wanted reform, but they were also jaded. They referenced many past failures and seemed overwhelmed with despair about how to reform the district. Since these were among the world's wealthiest and most powerful people, I was surprised by their collective exasperation and sense of powerlessness. They believed fixing America's public schools would unlock shared prosperity but felt they lacked the resources and influence necessary to accomplish that.

Morgan and other rich white male philanthropists are right that America needs a high-quality education system. Its success is essential for individuals as well as for American economic competitiveness, national security, and democracy. They are also correct that many of America's public schools, particularly in high-poverty communities of color, aren't providing students with the skills and opportunities they need.

What first started to shift my perspective was seeing how many of my Stanford friends from marginalized backgrounds were struggling financially in the years after we'd graduated. One of those friends is Luis

Chavez, who grew up in a one-stoplight farm town of Mexican American immigrants in California's Central Valley. After graduating from Stanford, Luis earned a solidly middle-class income. Yet class and racial barriers blocked him from growing that into the kinds of massive financial payoffs that more advantaged alumni like me had enjoyed. He aspired to live a middle-class lifestyle, but a big chunk of his income went to paying down his student loan and supporting family members living in poverty. Now, saving enough money to buy a home feels like a pipe dream. Many of my Stanford classmates who grew up in low-wealth communities of color find themselves in similar situations. If the American dream remains inaccessible to this demographic, even after they earn prestigious degrees—with all the cachet and access those degrees offer—how can education possibly be a silver bullet for all Americans?

What I eventually concluded is that rich white men like Morgan have the causation mostly backwards. While the conventional wisdom among rich white men is that poverty is caused by the inadequacy of individual systems, I now believe that poverty causes individual systems to fail.

After all, plenty of American schools and communities still offer opportunity. But these communities have unusual resources, and resource-starved communities cannot possibly "innovate" enough to offset the $1.4 million that wealthy parents spend on each of their children from age zero to eighteen. When education reform and extreme inequality duel, extreme inequality tends to win, since well-heeled parents ensure well-resourced schools. Yet philanthropists like Morgan continue to be surprised that it is so difficult to reform schools in low-wealth communities of color, even when those communities lack resources.

When historian Rutger Bregman attended the World Economic Forum at Davos, he made a similar observation. Like Milken attendees, Davos participants were also searching for ways to drive systemic change without addressing wealth inequality. "It feels as if I'm at a firefighters' conference," Bregman remarked, "and no one is allowed to speak about water."[5]

The view that education reform is the linchpin to fighting poverty is so commonly held among wealthy philanthropists that there is now a term for it. In his 2019 *Atlantic* article "Better Schools Won't Fix America," philanthropist Nick Hanauer describes how he came to shift his own focus from education reform to inequality. Hanauer coins the term "educationalism," which he describes as an ideology that claims America's middle class is crumbling because its public schools are inadequate. The truth, Hanauer argues, is that great public schools typically result from a thriving middle class. Nearly all of America's high-achieving public school districts, Hanauer emphasizes, "are united by a thriving community of economically secure middle-class families with sufficient political power to demand great schools, the time and resources to participate in those schools, and the tax money to amply fund them . . . Pay people enough to afford dignified middle-class lives, and high-quality public schools will follow. But allow economic inequality to grow, and educational inequality will inevitably grow with it."[6]

Over the past half century, Americans have become significantly more educated. Since 1970, high school graduation rates have increased from 49 percent to 90 percent and college graduation rates have risen from 11 percent to 35 percent.[7] However, over that same time period, real wages for all but the wealthiest Americans have hardly changed. "Income inequality has exploded [since 1970] not because of our country's educational failings," Hanauer argues, "but despite its educational progress."

Even when social-change advocates have different priorities, rich white men push them to prioritize education reform. In a 2021 paper, political scientist Megan Ming Francis chronicles how, in the early twentieth century, the NAACP's focus was getting antilynching legislation passed. Then, after urgings from white philanthropists, the NAACP pivoted to education reform, which remains its central focus a century later. Francis calls this phenomenon, in which funders pressure activists to change course, "movement capture."[8] "I'm concerned that sometimes even with the best of intentions," Francis told Vox, "the priorities of the poorest and marginalized get replaced by the priorities of the rich and powerful."[9]

Still, many Americans see poverty as a central issue in the United States. In 2018, thirty-eight million Americans—12 percent of the total population—lived below the official poverty line, which in 2018 was $25,100 for a family of four.[10] Children and women are more likely to live in poverty.[11] So are people of color: while 9 percent of white people live in poverty, 10 percent of Asian Americans, 21 percent of Black Americans, and 17 percent of the Latinx population do.[12]

Thanks to dated methodology, the official poverty rate drastically understates the actual level of American poverty. Overseen by the Census Bureau, the official poverty measure compares pre-tax income against a threshold that is set at three times the cost of a minimum food diet in 1963.[13] "The official poverty line is a joke," a friend whose family grew up on welfare told me. "Another hundred million people in this country are struggling to make ends meet who don't show up in the official figures." I'm inclined to agree with her: after all, the amount Pooja and I spent annually on Ayan's day care in Boston is higher than the poverty line for a family of four.

There is some evidence that the extreme poverty experienced by those who fall below the official poverty line became less widespread in the twentieth century. Research on poverty rates before the 1960s is spotty, but a 1993 paper titled "Inequality and Poverty in the United States: 1900 to 1990" estimates that in 1900 as many as 80 percent of Americans lived in poverty.[14] The authors also estimate that poverty rates fell to 50 percent in the decades leading up to the Great Depression, increased to 70 percent during the Great Depression, and then dropped to 25 percent during the 1930s following the implementation of New Deal policies. Between the 1940s and 1960s, poverty rates stayed relatively flat. Then they dropped again after the 1960s' War on Poverty, which introduced new programs and reduced poverty rates to their current levels. The state of poverty hasn't changed much since: as many Americans live in poverty today as in the 1960s.

If there is one thing America ought to have learned about eradicating poverty over the past century, it is that government transfers are the only proven way to significantly reduce poverty rates. Substantial drops in poverty rates followed the New Deal and War on Poverty, both of which were major government-led initiatives that put more money in impoverished people's pockets. Otherwise, poverty rates have been stable or increasing, even in eras when GDP and productivity have been growing quickly. So-called poverty reduction efforts such as education reform barely moved the needle. To solve a problem, it's often best to tackle it directly.

Even in America—whose citizens hold more wealth than those in any other country—poverty operates at a genocidal scale. In a 2021 study, Columbia University researchers estimated that 874,000 people died the previous year from poverty-related causes in America. That makes poverty more deadly than cancer. Since most violence is concentrated in impoverished neighborhoods suffering from discriminatory policies like redlining, Brookings Institution scholar Andre Perry calls such conditions "policy violence."[15] "The idea of freedom is inspiring," Angela Davis has written. "But what does it mean? If you are free in a political sense but have no food, what's that? The freedom to starve?"[16]

Every thirty-six seconds, an American dies from poverty-related causes. After I learned that statistic, I started reflecting on the fact that a hundred Americans die from poverty during every hour-long meeting I attend. In meetings since, I've strived to summon the sense of urgency that comes with knowing people are unnecessarily meeting death in this moment. I've also strived to feel connected to the thousands of family and community members who are grieving those they've lost. Every hour that America maintains the status quo condemns more people to death. "Poverty," Mahatma Gandhi once said, "is the worst form of violence."[17]

One of the ways that poverty is different than cancer is that there is already a known cure. In his final book, *Where Do We Go from Here*, Dr. Martin Luther King Jr. called for the government to provide every American a guaranteed, middle-class income. The reverend believed that a guaranteed income ought to be "pegged to the median of society" and rise automatically with the US standard of living.[18] He argued that such a plan was feasible at the time, citing an estimate by economist John Galbraith that a generous guaranteed income could have been created at a cost of $20 billion per year, a figure similar to what the United States was spending at the time on the Vietnam War. King suggested that given the vast economic resources available in 1960s America—a fraction of America's present resources—poverty had become as barbaric as cannibalism.

In the period after King's death in 1968, there was some bipartisan interest in addressing poverty via a guaranteed income. In fact, the moment when the idea had the most traction—until perhaps recently—was when President Nixon proposed the Family Assistance Plan, which would have guaranteed every family of four $1,600 per year, at a time when the median household income was $7,400.[19] It never came to pass, but yes, just a few decades ago, Republicans were advocating for a universal basic income—as well as reparations for the forced internment of Japanese Americans.[20]

Still, reducing poverty is not the same as abolishing the condition. While a variety of efforts in education, housing, economic development, health care, and other systems assist those in poverty, no program exists that formally puts an end to poverty. Abolishing poverty would require a federal mandate guaranteeing everyone the income necessary to support basic needs. Such a mandate would be more robust than the hodgepodge of local, state, and federal programs that America currently relies on. I've come to think of America's patchwork approach to addressing inequality as "trickle-down-programnomics," which—like tax cuts for the rich—never quite seem to deliver relief for those in poverty.

America didn't reform slavery; it abolished it. The same can be done with poverty. If this nation followed Dr. King's prescription, many community issues would resolve themselves.

Other countries are reaching a similar conclusion. When UK police chief Andy Cooke retired, he was asked what he'd do if he were given five billion pounds to cut crime. He said he'd put four billion pounds into reducing poverty and increasing opportunity. According to Cooke, most low-wealth families are eager to earn money legally; they just lack opportunity. "We need to reduce...the scale of deprivation that we see in some of our communities," Cooke said, "because if you give people a viable alternative, not all but a lot will take it."[21]

Research substantiates Cooke's claim. In a 2020 meta study looking at sixteen diverse countries between 1990 and 2014, researchers found that greater income inequality resulted in more crime.[22] In 2014, World Bank researchers analyzed more than two thousand municipalities in Mexico and arrived at the same conclusion.[23] They also found that greater inequality led to increased crime even when they compared municipalities with similar poverty rates, which demonstrated that more homicides occur in places where the rich are getting richer even if the poor aren't getting poorer. A follow-up World Bank study in 2020 found that even when controlling for economic inequality, racial and gender inequalities are connected to greater community violence.[24] Inequality, the evidence seems to suggest, is among the central reasons why many American cities are among the most violent in the world.

The idea that reducing inequality addresses other social ills is hardly new. Roman emperor Marcus Aurelius—heralded for his wisdom before his successors drove the Roman Empire to collapse—had a strong view on the subject. "Poverty," he said 1,900 years ago, "is the parent of crime and revolution."[25]

The idea of an income floor isn't new, either. In 1795, Thomas Paine, one of the intellectual architects of the American Revolution, proposed that a "groundrent" of fifteen pounds be paid to every individual upon turning twenty-one and ten pounds be paid every year after turning fifty. "Every person, rich or poor," Paine argued, should receive the payments "to prevent invidious distinctions."[26]

I first became interested in the idea of a universal basic income back in 2008 while I was a student at Stanford. Alex Berger, one of my classmates, had gotten involved in effective altruism, a philosophical and social movement that advocates for "using evidence and reason to figure out how to benefit others as much as possible, and taking action on that basis."[27]

Alex told me about GiveDirectly, a nonprofit organization operating in East Africa—primarily Kenya, Uganda, and Rwanda—that helps families living in extreme poverty by making unconditional cash transfers to them via mobile phone.[28] The program has expanded significantly: in 2019, GiveDirectly provided a total of $33 million to forty thousand households.[29] Part of what has enabled GiveDirectly's growth is that the organization measures its impact using randomized control trials. Studies have shown that when households receive a grant from GiveDirectly, they buy more food and do not increase spending on vices like alcohol or tobacco.[30] There is also evidence that recipients can invest cash transfers at high rates of return—about 20 percent per year—which enables long-term increases in individual and community wealth.[31] Transfer recipients also see major improvements in their psychological well-being, including reductions in the stress hormone cortisol, which is associated with improved quality of life and longevity.

Similar approaches are starting to bear fruit in the United States. The Stockton Economic Empowerment Demonstration (SEED)—the first mayor-led guaranteed income demonstration—showed the power of providing people in poverty with more resources to meet their basic needs. Launched in 2019 by then mayor Michael Tubbs, SEED gave 125 residents in Stockton, California, $500 per month for twenty-four months with no strings attached.[32] Like GiveDirectly's cash transfers, SEED was found in a randomized control trial to be beneficial. Recipients were more likely to find full-time employment; were healthier, with less depression and anxiety and enhanced well-being; and were able to pursue new opportunities for self-determination, goal setting, and risk taking. Individuals spent most of the money on basic needs, including food, clothing, utilities, and automobile expenses; less than 1 percent was spent on alcohol or tobacco. The study also had positive ripple effects: stabilizing food security for one household lessened strain on other family and community members whom impoverished families had previously relied on for food and other basic needs. "Before SEED came along, I was paying a lot of bills and didn't know how I was gonna eat," Laura, one of the participants, said. "It's like being able to breathe."[33]

"The five hundred dollars didn't make people stop working," Mayor Tubbs informed PBS. "Actually people worked harder. People were able to take time off, particularly from jobs that don't offer paid time off, to interview for better jobs."[34]

Inspired by the pilot's success, Tubbs created Mayors for a Guaranteed

Income, a network of mayors advocating for a guaranteed income to ensure that all Americans have an income floor. Since its founding in 2020, more than fifty mayors have joined the network, and many more guaranteed-income experiments are now underway.

"But isn't abolishing poverty too expensive?" rich white men often ask me. "How does the math work?"

The math is pretty straightforward. In 2020, median per capita income was $31,133 (median household income was $67,521).[35] Multiplied by the thirty-seven million people living in poverty, the total annual cost of providing this $31,133 to every impoverished American would be $1.1 trillion. That's about 5 percent of the United States GDP—the monetary value of all goods and services produced. That percentage is similar to what the United States allocated to the Marshall Plan in 1948 to support the recovery of Western Europe after World War II. It would be expensive, but it's a commitment that I believe is not only decent but also would pay long-term dividends for America's democracy and economy.

San Francisco would be a great place to experiment with abolishing poverty at a significant scale. Thanks to its proximity to Silicon Valley and the welcome mat the city has thrown out to the tech industry, San Francisco has the most billionaires per capita of any city in the world. San Francisco has seventy-seven billionaires, yet ninety thousand people—about 10 percent of its residents—live in poverty.[36]

One of San Francisco's tech titans could singlehandedly abolish poverty in San Francisco and still have tens of billions of dollars left over. For example, it would cost about $60 billion to create a permanent endowment that provides $100,000 annually in perpetuity to the 30,000 San Francisco families who live below the poverty line. As of October 2022, Google co-founder Larry Page's net worth is $87 billion. Page could lift every one of San Francisco's poorest residents out of poverty and still have $27 billion to spare. Jeff Bezos could afford a similar arrangement in Seattle, as could Warren Buffett in Omaha. In heavily populated cities like New York City or Los Angeles, a small cadre of billionaires could team up to close the gap.

There is also, of course, the encouraging possibility that such a program may cost far less than what I outline above. As formerly impoverished families secure sustainable sources of income and find their footing, I expect that poverty rates will decline, which will decrease the program's cost and enable newly empowered residents to provide more tax revenue to the city.

Cities might also be able to pare back their municipal budgets. San Francisco, for example, has an annual budget of $13 billion. Since citizens would be more self-sufficient, the community would be safer, and many complex programs—which have high administrative costs—could be eliminated or scaled back.

If the American citizenry can unlock some of the capital that rich white men currently tuck away in vaults, other approaches to abolishing poverty could also be considered. The most robust evidence about the impact of relatively large unconditional cash transfers comes out of Kenya: when researchers Johannes Haushofer and Jeremy Shapiro gave low-income Kenyan households cash transfers that were enough to cover household expenses for two years, they found significant impacts on economic outcomes and psychological well-being.[37]

One approach that America could try is a universal basic capital. Economist Joseph Stiglitz suggests establishing a sovereign wealth fund, or national endowment, that distributes regular dividends to all citizens.[38] Models for this approach already exist: Alaska has a fund that pays dividends to citizens from the state's oil revenues; a Norway fund, also from oil revenues, pays into the general pension system; and citizens can draw from Singapore's Central Provident Fund to pay for health and housing needs.

Baby bonds are another idea cut from the same cloth. Effectively a trust fund for low-wealth families, a baby bond funded by the US Treasury would be given to each child at birth and managed by the federal government until the child reaches adulthood. Every year, the government would add more money to the account, the amount varying based on family income.[39] As the child reaches adulthood, they can access the resources to invest in ways that enable them to increase their wealth, like going to college or buying a home.

Another solution is to simply introduce a wealth floor. America could top off its forty-three million citizens who currently have less than $50,000 in household wealth by making a one-time investment of $2.2 trillion, which would contribute varying amounts to families depending on their current assets. This investment would broaden access to the American dream by enabling low-wealth people to pursue additional education and training, relocate to regions that offer greater economic opportunity, buy homes, and start new businesses, among other benefits.

A similar program could make the American dream more accessible for immigrants. A $60 billion annual program could write a $50,000 check to the 1.2 million immigrants who arrive in the United States each year, amplifying their ability to immediately contribute their gifts—including their entrepreneurialism—to American society.

Or investment could be channeled into low-wealth communities. A one-time allotment of $700 billion—3% of GDP—would invest $50,000 in each of the fourteen million Americans who live in concentrated poverty. Such a program would help to revitalize communities that suffer from chronic disinvestment.

I am not claiming that any of these approaches is perfect or that no unintended consequences would occur if they were attempted. Each of these proposals has some drawbacks, and—as megainvestors have told me—unexpected things happen anytime billions of dollars are invested anywhere. What I'm trying to emphasize with these examples is that it *is* possible to end poverty in America; that if addressing wealth inequality became a priority, this nation has more than enough resources to launch a war on poverty that actually wins.

One reason why I feel so much urgency about abolishing poverty is that countless impoverished Americans ultimately end up somewhere even more inhumane than a high-poverty neighborhood: *prison*. Instead of investing in abolishing poverty, America's leaders have invested in the prison industrial complex, which is plagued by brutal conditions that normalize sexual assault and murder. Even wrongly convicted and non-violent offenders sometimes find themselves sentenced to death by guard brutality, inmate violence, or unsanitary conditions. The COVID-19 pandemic has compounded the health crisis in American prisons: as of April 2021, three thousand incarcerated people died of COVID-19.[40]

In today's era of mass incarceration, both liberals and conservatives are questioning the massive resources that the United States is allocating to maintain its role as the incarceration capital of the world. According to the American Action Forum, the United States spends nearly $300 billion annually policing communities and incarcerating 2.2 million people.[41] The societal costs—lost earnings, adverse health effects, and damage to families—are triple the direct costs, bringing the total annual burden of America's criminal justice system to $1.2 trillion. That's as much as the federal government currently spends on Medicare, Medicaid, the Children's Health Insurance Program, and veteran medical care combined—and it's more than what is needed to implement Dr. King's guaranteed income proposal.[42]

Given the economic and moral benefits, why haven't rich white men replaced the prison industrial complex with a guaranteed income? It's complicated, but a shorthand answer is that, at least historically, it has cost elites less money to maintain the prison industrial complex than to reduce inequality. Similar to how corporate lobbyists advocate for policies that increase profits at the public's expense, the prison industrial complex enables rich white men to further enrich themselves. As we did during slavery, rich white men have manufactured a system of social control that trades millions of bodies—mostly Black and brown bodies, but white bodies too—for trillions of dollars.

Poverty has become so absurdly expensive for America that the economic case alone may provide sufficient reason to abolish it. If poverty were abolished, the $1.2 trillion that America currently sends down the drain to sustain the prison industrial complex could be dramatically reduced, if not eliminated. And if America made direct transfers to individuals, many of the convoluted poverty reduction programs—and the massive bureaucracies that administer them—could be phased out. And investing in our citizens would fuel innovation and shared prosperity: if such investments yielded millions of additional knowledge workers and even a few more innovations—like three-light traffic signals, refrigerated trucks, automatic elevator doors, electret microphones, carbon light bulb filaments, IBM PC monitors, and Gigahertz chips, all invented by Black Americans—how much would this country gain?

Most of the rich white men I know act as if poverty is a necessary, insurmountable evil. On countless occasions, they've told me it is impossible to end poverty. However, this is a myth. "Like slavery and apartheid," Nelson Mandela once said, "poverty is not natural. It is manmade and it can be overcome and eradicated by the action of human beings."[43]

We rich white men have the power and resources to abolish poverty if we take it on directly. And if we don't take that initiative, I hope the rest of America will demand that those in power take action.

CHAPTER 13

A CULTURE OF REPAIR

I am not, nor ever have been in favor of bringing about in any way the social and political equality of the white and black races.

—ABRAHAM LINCOLN, SIXTEENTH PRESIDENT OF THE UNITED STATES, WHOSE PROCLAMATION FREED AMERICA'S ENSLAVED BLACK PEOPLE

MYTH:

The past is the past, so forward-facing policies that give the same thing to everyone are sufficient.

If you stick a knife in my back nine inches and pull it out six inches, there's no progress. If you pull it all the way out, that's not progress. The progress is healing the wound that the blow made.

—MALCOLM X, AFRICAN AMERICAN MUSLIM MINISTER AND HUMAN RIGHTS ACTIVIST

REALITY:

The past impacts the present. Every past harm is unique and needs a unique remedy.

In 2019, from my bedroom in Boston, I put in a call to a billionaire philanthropist who had made his money in the oil and gas industry. Since he had ties to Enron earlier in his career, I'll call him Ernie.

I first met Ernie at a gathering for entrepreneurs and financiers back in 2015, where we talked for hours over drinks about education reform. The event was held in rural Georgia at the Ritz-Carlton Lodge Reynolds Plantation, then named for a local family that made its fortune by developing a process to solidify cottonseed oil.[1] Nearly all the conference participants were white, and most were men. And nearly all the resort's employees were Black and had deep southern drawls. Part of what drew guests to Reynolds Plantation, it appeared to me, was that it offered wealthy white people an opportunity to be transported back in time to the "good old days" and the comfort of a particularly extreme form of racial hierarchy.

This time around, our conversation was focused on inequality. Ernie agreed to be interviewed for this book because he felt the topic was important. Inequality "is potentially the number one issue of our time," Ernie told me.

Why? Ernie was concerned about political polarization, declines in social mobility, and a hollowed-out middle class. When I asked him what had caused those issues, Ernie—like many of the Davos regulars I've met—pointed the finger at technology and globalization. When I asked whether there were any other significant factors, he was quiet for so long that I wrote "crickets" in my notes.

I knew Ernie's foundation was bankrolling efforts to reform the criminal justice system, which is known for its particularly egregious racial disparities. So I was curious to get his perspective about the role of race in American inequality. I thought we'd have a lively exchange. However, he seemed taken aback when I asked, as if the question didn't even warrant discussion. "I don't think race is the divider today," Ernie told me. "It's socioeconomic. I agree with Charles Murray's argument that it's a wealthy-versus-middle-class divide."

I was surprised, and disturbed, that Ernie had relied on Murray's analysis. Murray is an academic sociologist whom the Southern Poverty Law Center has labeled a white nationalist for wielding racist pseudoscience and misleading statistics to argue that genetic inferiority explains the plight of marginalized communities.[2] According to Murray, wealth and social power naturally accrue to a "cognitive elite" made up of high-IQ individuals—who are overwhelmingly rich, white, and male—while those on the lower end of the bell curve form an "underclass" crippled by their low intelligence. "The United States is on a trend to becoming more race blind in its policies," Ernie insisted. "I think that's the right thing."

It was a troubling exchange. While I had presumed that most white people drawn to criminal justice reform aimed to combat racial injustice, Ernie didn't seem to think systemic racism was a problem. He had chosen to align with Murray, a wealthy white man who has spent decades trying to rehabilitate long-discredited theories of IQ to justify his aspiration to demolish the welfare state.

Ernie was right that wealth inequality is a crucial issue. He was also correct that universalist policies do help to level the playing field, not only because they reduce wealth inequality but also because they often disproportionately benefit marginalized populations impacted by racial injustice. Still, even ambitious initiatives like antimonopoly policies and a guaranteed livable income are not silver bullets; they don't address every societal ill, and they fall short in important ways. Even if these policies were in place, white supremacy, patriarchy, and other oppressive systems would remain intact. In this sense, abolishing poverty is akin to abolishing slavery: abolishing slavery weakened white supremacy but it did not fully eradicate the underlying cultural, economic, and political forces that made it so difficult to abolish slavery in the first place. Since further reparative measures were not taken, wealth and power remained primarily in white male hands, a trend that persists into the present. Universalist policies are necessary, but they are not sufficient.

The person who most helped me wrap my head around this idea is Ed Whitfield, an activist in Greensboro, North Carolina, who has been working to advance racial justice since he organized protests at Cornell in the 1960s.[3] For decades, Ed has been a force for social change within philanthropy: as the head of the Fund for Democratic Communities from 1997 to 2020, Ed oversaw a spend-down approach that depleted the fund's endowment by investing significant capital into marginalized communities.[4] In recent years, Ed has also been a leader within the Black Land and Power Coalition, a strategic alignment of organizations focused on keeping Black-owned land in Black hands.[5] As part of his involvement in that effort, he coaches philanthropists participating in Reparations Summer, a program that supports white donors in giving to BIPOC-led food and land initiatives without strings attached, so organizations can decide for themselves where and how to use those resources to have the most impact.[6]

When Ed teaches about the need for repair, he often relays a story he was first told by Reverend Bugani Finca, who was involved in South Africa's truth and reconciliation work:

A Black South African, Tabo, confronted a white man, Mr. Smith, who had disrespected him and stolen his prize cow. With the prospect of amnesty for telling the truth, the white man admitted to having done what he was accused of, recognized how horribly wrong it was and he asked for forgiveness, saying that he was truly sorry. Tabo was visibly relieved for having an opportunity to confront his oppressor and get an apology. They shook hands and embraced. As Mr. Smith stood to leave, free, with his amnesty, the Black man called out to stop him. The white man turned back with a questioning look on his face, not sure why he was being stopped. Tabo, the Black South African, asked him: "But what about the cow?" Mr. Smith was visibly angry: "You are ruining our Reconciliation," he shouted, "This has nothing to do with a cow."

That is the question we must ask to all those who say that the past is long gone but still retain ownership of the herd produced by that old cow. We won't forgive and forget until we get the cow back. But just suppose that the Mr. Smiths in the world make a counteroffer: "I'll tell you what, why don't I just give you a supply of butter?" "The hell," Tabo might reply. "If you give me back my cow, I can give you butter!"[7]

The "what about the cow" dilemma sheds light on the limitations of universalist policies. Certainly, the parable includes a financial dimension: it's more difficult to survive and build wealth without your cash cow. But also, what does it say about a society that it allows resources to be stolen without acknowledgment, apology, or consequence? What can be said about a culture that not only sweeps its history under the rug but also tells those negatively impacted that the theft of people's resources has nothing to do with their current poverty?

Perhaps no statistic better captures the longevity and scale of racial injustice than the racial wealth gap, which clocks in at $11 trillion—meaning Black and Indigenous people are $11 trillion short of their share of American wealth.[8] And, like a runaway train headed downhill, the racial wealth gap continues to accelerate. It has expanded during both Democratic and Republican administrations, and some experts argue that Black people are more economically destitute than they were before the civil rights movement. Such data doesn't necessarily prove that America is becoming more racist—it could be becoming economically oppressive for all low-wealth Americans faster than it is becoming antiracist—but nevertheless, most Black and Indigenous Americans remain unable to accumulate wealth in America.

I first became drawn to reparations as a potential solution to racial injustice back in 2017, after I studied the racial wealth gap. Until every racial group begins life at the same financial starting line—which requires that the wealth gap be closed—I don't see how a claim can be made that America offers any semblance of equal opportunity across racial lines. And because the racial wealth gap is so large—and growing—I don't see a path to closing it that doesn't involve a significant transfer of resources. Whether those resources are granted to individuals, communities, institutions, or some combination thereof is a reasonable and complex question. However, the alternatives—indirect approaches, like education reform—have had limited impact. As Dr. Martin Luther King Jr. discovered in his efforts to abolish poverty, rich white men often favor indirect solutions, not because those solutions are more effective, but because those solutions threaten our wealth and power less.

Financial reparations are a meaningful way to advance racial equity. In a capitalist system, capital is an advantage and a source of power, and whoever has less capital is disadvantaged. It must be asked whether a capitalist system can function equitably, particularly in America, where capitalism is rooted in slavery, but until that question is resolved, the very least this nation can do is ensure that race does not predict a person's starting financial allotment.

The question of who ought to receive reparations is complex. When rich white men ask me that question, my experience has often been that they are less interested in figuring out the answer than they are interested in using that complexity to justify setting the issue aside. Some Black reparations advocates argue that Black people who are descendants of enslaved people ought to be prioritized for reparations—for historical, legal, and strategic reasons that have merit—but ultimately, I hope that this country will offer reparative resources to every population of color that is harmed by systemic racism. I would personally go as far as to say that even white people living in intergenerational poverty—like Connor, whose story I told in Chapter 3—deserve an apology and some level of restitution, for being told lies so that rich white men could more easily extract resources from their labor and communities.

Like abolishing poverty, making cash reparations on the scale of the racial wealth gap is expensive yet feasible. In his 2020 book *From Here to Equality*, Duke economist William Darity Jr. and consultant A. Kirsten Mullen suggest that one possible path forward could be for the Federal Reserve to pay out reparations over ten years.[9] Such a program would function as an economic stimulus, helping to grow the economy. While some critics express doubt that such a program would actually be economically energizing, such critiques rely on the racist idea that even if Black and Indigenous Americans had more resources, they still wouldn't have much to contribute.

The money for reparations could come from either federal coffers or the wealthiest 1 percent—a group that is 91 percent white and worth $25 trillion.[10] The COVID-19 pandemic has shown that fortunes of the ultra-wealthy are skyrocketing.[11] Even assuming a very conservative annual investment return of 5 percent, the top 1 percent is becoming $1.25 trillion richer every year. Darity estimates that the racial wealth gap could be closed by 2030 with a ten-year investment of $1 trillion per year. If the top 1 percent were just willing to get richer less quickly, America could close its racial wealth gap within a decade.

If reparations make sense, why haven't they been provided? I now realize that America's racial wealth gap can be understood as both a structural and a cultural problem. It is structural in that the racial wealth gap, if not directly addressed, will reproduce and compound inequality in perpetuity, even if anti-Black and anti-Indigenous bias is eliminated. And it is cultural in that a critical mass of white Americans buy into "blame the victim" narratives that claim that Black and Indigenous people lack capital due to their own deficiencies.

America's sexual assault epidemic is a structural and cultural issue, too. It is structural in that women and gender-nonconforming people—the populations most impacted by sexual assault—are underrepresented in positions of power and have less ability to influence policies that affect their lives.[12] And it is a cultural issue in that sexual assault is sufficiently normalized that men continue to perpetrate it, even when it is widely acknowledged that assault is immoral.

Whenever harm is caused, a unique wound is created that requires a unique path to repair. If one patient comes into the emergency room with a broken arm and another comes in with a third-degree burn, doctors don't say, "Oh, the only treatment we offer patients is chemotherapy. But don't worry, that will solve your problem." So why would universalist policies, which provide everyone with the same thing, cure all of a nation's ills?

That analysis led me to cofound Liberation Ventures with Aria Florant and allen kwabena frimpong in 2019. Liberation Ventures is supporting the "ecosystem of organizations working on truth, reconciliation, and reparations in order to build public will for a comprehensive, federal, financial and non-financial reparations program."[13] Among its other successes, Liberation Ventures was one of the first philanthropic efforts to make grants to grassroots, Black-led organizations focused on reparations and repair in the United States. Since I transitioned out of my role in 2021, the organization continues to grow under Aria's leadership.

Among the many things I learned at Liberation Ventures is that a society's unwillingness to repair harm breathes life into systems of oppression. That is, a "culture of disrepair" emerges when unrepaired harms compound. Over time, harms become normalized, inferiority becomes internalized, and social norms become embedded in interpersonal, institutional, and structural relationships as systems of oppression. That culture of disrepair can be seen in America's lackluster response to harm caused by genocide, settler colonialism, slavery, Jim Crow, and mass incarceration.

That paradigm also applies to other systems of oppression. For example, my colleague Allen helped me understand that a rape culture developed in the United States less because of the actions of individual rapists and more because of the way institutions responded when such harms were perpetrated. When perpetrators were not held accountable, that behavior became normalized, and that normalization allowed for systemic misogyny to emerge. Ultimately, societies can degrade into a culture of abuse, complete with narratives that rationalize abusive behavior. If the first perpetrators of sexual assault in America had been held accountable and encouraged to engage in repair, such abuses might have never become embedded in the culture.

The antidote to a culture of disrepair is a culture of repair. Reparative actions can be taken interpersonally, institutionally, and societally—and at any scale. Repair happens when a parent apologizes to their child for yelling at them and promises to take a kinder approach going forward. It materializes when an institution fires a predatory misogynistic leader and commits to equitable policies that ensure such behavior is costly, not rewarded, in the future. And it will be realized when the United States commits to a comprehensive reparations program, negotiating a new and equitable social contract with Black and Indigenous Americans.

While I was at Liberation Ventures, Aria—with support from Basund-hara Mukherjee and Asrat Alemu, who helped us out pro bono—led the development of a framework that describes how a society can nurture a culture of repair. The framework describes repair as a cycle that includes four elements: (1) reckoning, or grappling with actions that contributed to the harm that occurred; (2) acknowledgment, or admitting harm was done; (3) accountability, or taking responsibility for the harmful actions; and (4) redress, or acts of restitution that heal the wound and prevent further wounds. The notion that the repair process can be seen as a cycle clarifies that over time, momentum builds to embed a commitment to repair into the culture.

Every reparative action accelerates the flywheel of repair. When Pooja and I decided to pledge $50,000—a figure that was symbolic to us because it was equivalent to the inheritance I received from my grand-mother, to the Movement for Black Lives, we chose to shift resources that had been accumulated during an era when Black people were locked out of opportunity into Black control. Instead of using those unearned resources to further enrich ourselves, we invested in a more equitable America. It wasn't an easy decision: we could have used those resources to stock up our rainy day fund in a country that lacks an adequate safety net, but instead, we took what was for us a modest risk.

Repair begets repair. After we made our commitment, I was sur-prised to hear that friends collectively committed another $300,000 to Black liberation causes—not because I asked them to but because mak-ing a similar commitment felt right to them, too. Every reparative action nudges culture in the direction of repair. And a culture of repair benefits all of us.

But while individual reparative actions are important, no individual can, on their own, repair harms caused by an institution or society. Whoever caused harm—whether an institution, society, individual, or some combination thereof—is uniquely responsible for making repairs.

In the 1970s and 1980s, Chicago police commander Jon Burge over-saw the torture of at least 118 people in police custody to coerce false confessions.[14] It was necessary for Burge to be held accountable as an individual who abused his power. But the Chicago Police Department, which had institutionalized a culture of violence that predated Burge, was also responsible. So was the City of Chicago, which appointed Burge. In 2015, after decades of Burge's victims demanding justice, Chicago took a first step toward a culture of repair by pledging a reparations package to survivors of police torture. The $5.5 million package included a formal apology from former Chicago mayor Rahm Emanuel, compensation to survivors and their families, waived tuition to City Colleges of Chicago, a mandatory Chicago Public Schools curriculum to educate students about police torture under Burge, and the creation of a permanent memorial. Critics are right to argue that the package is too small, and trust that the project would deliver repair has eroded over the years as the city has failed to deliver on its commitments (as of this writing, the city still hasn't broken ground on the memorial that was promised).[15] Still, while far from perfect, attempts at repair like this one offer a glimpse into what might be possible if institutions accepted responsibility for the harm they cause.

When the state itself causes harm, the federal government has a unique responsibility to repair it. If done correctly, federal repair programs can supercharge societal repair by challenging the chronic denial, lack of accountability, and extraction that institutionalize atrocity and injustice. Such initiatives shock the system, establish a new social contract with marginalized populations, and weaken the systems that perpetuate injustice. That approach can bring America closer to achieving democracy.

Some attempts have been made around the world to build a culture of repair at scale. Germany paid reparations to Israel after the Holocaust.[16] Canada paid reparations to its Indigenous population for harms related to educational segregation that stripped generations of their culture and traditions.[17] South Africa conducted a national truth and reconciliation process to support the country's healing from the collective trauma of apartheid, and also paid reparations.[18] In 2005, the United Nations adopted a multilateral approach to reparations outlined in a document called "Basic Principles and Guidelines on the Right to a Remedy and

Reparation for Victims of Gross Violations of International Human Rights Law and Serious Violations of International Humanitarian Law." This document lays out when a reparations study ought to be commissioned and when reparations payments ought to be made.[19] The United States is a textbook case for owing reparations; it is only because of America's power on the world stage that there has been no enforcement in response to the United States' human rights violations.

What happens after an atrocity matters. In Germany, a memorial consisting of nearly three thousand stone blocks helped to instill a memory culture, acknowledging the six million Jewish people murdered by the Nazi Party. That's a sharp contrast to the United States, which still maintains over 1,500 monuments memorializing leaders of the Confederacy as heroes.[20] And Confederate monuments are not America's only racist monuments: many hospitals still line their walls with portraits of James Marion Sims, a medical doctor whose breakthroughs in gynecology relied on risky and excruciating medical experiments on enslaved Black women;[21] approximately three hundred schools in twenty states currently bear the names of men with ties to the Confederacy; and many sports teams—including the Atlanta Braves, Chicago Blackhawks, and Kansas City Chiefs—valorize Indigenous caricatures, reproducing a culture of disrepair in their stadiums. The problem is "the imagery that gets associated with those names," activist Crystal Echo Hawk told NPR.[22] "It's the racist fan behavior. When a fan paints their face red, right? That is blackface. Blackface is wrong. I think most people in this country get that now."

And for all its foot-dragging about issuing reparations to Black and Indigenous Peoples, the United States has paid reparations to its citizens before. In 1988, Ronald Reagan signed off on the bipartisan, $1.2 billion Civil Liberties Act, which authorized reparations for Japanese Americans who were ordered into internment camps during World War II. Four years later, George H. W. Bush expanded the program with a $400 million amendment. The act provided $20,000—$40,000 in today's dollars—for each former internee still alive when the act was passed.

Those internment camp victims ought not to have had to wait four decades for redress; a four-century wait is despicable.

There is also the uncomfortable fact that white Americans received reparations for slavery. When President Abraham Lincoln signed the District of Columbia Emancipation Act in 1862, white people loyal to the Union were paid up to $300 for every enslaved person freed. At the time, land sold for three to five dollars per acre.[23] Black people never got their promised forty acres and a mule, but white enslavers got that and then some.[24]

Genocide, settler colonialism, and slavery are not the only places where the United States can repair harm through reparations. Other transgressions include Jim Crow restrictions, mass incarceration, and Puerto Rico's continued treatment as an American colony, which is a glaring example of how colonialism is not a relic of America's past but very much part of its present.

Some of the rich white men I know see reparations as a bridge too far, favoring instead a national truth and reconciliation process they hope would bring the country together. That process was used perhaps most famously in postapartheid South Africa, where the Truth and Reconciliation Commission was created to investigate gross human rights violations—including abductions, killings, and torture—that were perpetrated during the apartheid regime's 1960 to 1994 reign.[25] Since then, similar processes have been used across Africa and Latin America.[26] But while truth and reconciliation processes can be necessary and address a specific atrocity, they struggle to uproot deeply institutionalized cultures of disrepair. For example, even after its process, South Africa's racial inequities continue to be among the largest in the world.[27]

What distinguishes successful reconciliation is *full* collaboration. Those harmed deserve to define what they consider to be reparative. If their voices aren't shaping the terms of the healing process, the process becomes a reenactment of how their consent was violated during prior atrocities.

A crucial aspect of this process is for those of us who didn't experience the harm to refrain from making assumptions about what the harmed party wants. I've realized that I may have been guilty of that when I engaged early on with the reparations movement. While many activists see reparations as about so much more than a financial remedy, I initially saw reparations primarily as a solution to the racial wealth gap. Looking back on it, I think I initially honed in on the financial benefits of a reparations program because I was taught growing up that money can be a cure-all solution for many different types of problems. Now I understand that some harmed parties might not want financial restitution, or they might want money in addition to something else. For example, Honor Keeler of the Cherokee Nation is leading the International Repatriation Project, whose priorities include getting stolen ancestral burial items returned to Indigenous communities around the world.[28]

I've also acquired a greater appreciation of the need to shift culture. To create an America where all people—including and especially Black and Indigenous Peoples—can thrive, societal norms must change, interpersonally, institutionally, and nationally. Yes, closing the racial wealth gap is important. However, if America doesn't also address the fact that its culture treats white people better throughout our lives, the gap will immediately reopen.

Part of that cultural shift is about helping white people understand how we would benefit if this nation provded reparations to Black and Indigenous Peoples. For white Americans in poverty, that means building awareness that they would benefit materially from a system that lowered overall wealth inequality. For middle-class white Americans, that means increasing understanding that repair isn't about taking anything from them but rather making the security and opportunity they benefit from in their suburbs accessible to all Americans. And for wealthy white Americans like me, that means emphasizing how any potential material losses are outweighed by the benefits of investing in this country's healing, democracy, and economy.

While a federal reparations program is a way to directly counteract racial injustice, achieving and sustaining racial equity across systems is a more difficult task. Negative stereotypes, unconscious bias, overt bigotry, and institutional racism cemented over centuries will not disappear overnight. Even if the racial wealth gap were closed directly, rich white men would still monopolize economic and political power in the United States. An $11 trillion reparations program would do little in the short term to change the reality that most powerful billionaires and politicians are wealthy white men. And every historical precedent suggests that white people—especially rich white men—will abuse our remaining power to roll back reforms. Major milestones, including abolition, civil rights, and Barack Obama's election, have always inspired backlash. For racial justice to become a durable reality, white people and predominantly white institutions with an exclusionary past or present must reckon with the entirety of the ideological, institutional, interpersonal, and internalized harm that our racism has caused. Repair requires some large-scale policy changes, but it also requires millions of smaller reparative actions.

As a Jew, I have thought a lot about the Holocaust—how it came to occur, and how Germany sought to repair the harm afterward. One of the things we say as Jews is "Never again"—an affirmation that we will be vocal when the conditions that make genocide possible arise anywhere in the world. If we are serious about "never again," we need to look further upstream. It's not enough to raise the alarm after an authoritarian leader bans interracial marriages, relocates marginalized populations into ghettos, or labels Mexican immigrants rapists. There is also a need to dismantle the underlying structural and cultural conditions that normalize monstrous behavior and enable manipulators to use bigotry as a resource for acquiring political power.

Every one of us has a responsibility to nurture a culture of repair. Ed Whitfield, the activist I mentioned earlier, puts it this way:

> I know that...there are counterexamples that have to do with people saying, "Well, you know, my folks came here from wherever and they were poor when they got here and they worked really hard, saved money, and they've accumulated this and that." I would want to tell them that this is like somebody who comes

into the room, a really good gambler, and he's gambling at a table that's loaded down with stolen money.

I'm not arguing that the person is not a good gambler, nor am I arguing that they didn't bring their own stake to stake themselves in the game initially. Nor am I arguing that they didn't actually win at this table. I am arguing, though, that if the table were not already loaded down with stolen money . . . their gains would not have led to them walking out of the room with very much.

So that as they go out of the room it's like, "You can't keep that. That was stolen money." "But I won it fair and square." "Well of course you did, but it was still stolen money the whole time you were playing for it."[29]

Societal repair can feel like an overwhelming task, but there is a role for each of us. And there are concrete steps we all can take—particularly those of us who benefit from white advantage—to build a culture of repair. White people can join the Fund for Reparations NOW!, an intergenerational community of white people started by activist David Gardinier that is working in solidarity with the National African American Reparations Commission.[30] White people who have inherited significant land and wealth can participate in the Black Land and Power initiative's Reparations Summer program, which creates opportunities for wealthy white people to return inherited land and wealth to Black and Indigenous communities.[31] Those whose ancestry includes enslavers can also join Reparations 4 Slavery, a network started by activist Lotte Dula that helps descendants of enslavers process that experience and make amends.[32]

Many institutions are also starting to move toward a reparative lens. In 2019, Georgetown University announced it would raise $400,000 a year to benefit the descendants of the 272 enslaved people who were sold to raise money to help keep the college afloat nearly two centuries ago.[33] In 2020, the *Los Angeles Times* denounced its own racist reporting in a sensationalized 1981 series that demonized Black men living in high-poverty communities, and apologized for harm the project caused.[34] In 2022, Harvard University pledged $100 million to make amends for its historical reliance on slavery.[35] Within philanthropy, several efforts—including Justice Funders, Kataly Foundation, Liberated Capital, Liberation Ventures, Omidyar Network, NDN Collective, New Media Ventures, Resource Generation, and Solidaire—have embedded aspects of a reparative frame into their grant making. Over time, I hope more institutions elevate repair as a core priority, as part of a wider commitment to equity.

Elected leaders are also working to advance societal repair. In January 2022, Evanston, Illinois, became the first American city to pay cash reparations to residents.[36] In 2022, California became the first state to study reparations.[37] As of May 2022, 45 percent of the House of Representatives have cosponsored H.R.40: The Commission to Study and Develop Reparation Proposals for African Americans Act.[38] An equivalent bill in the US Senate is also building momentum: as of May 2022, S.1083, first championed by Senator Cory Booker, has twenty cosponsors.[39]

And on the ground, many grassroots Black and Indigenous organizations are building momentum for a culture of repair. These organizations include the National African American Reparations Commission and its sister organization N'COBRA, which have been fighting for reparatory justice for decades. It also includes newer efforts like FirstRepair, a national nonprofit that is equipping leaders, stakeholders, and allies who are advancing local reparations policies; Media 2070, which is taking steps to transform the media from a bullhorn for white supremacy into a lever for racial justice; and Project Truth, Reconciliation, and Reparations, an emerging Black-and-Indigenous-women-led mass movement to demand reparations.[40]

A culture of repair is the gateway to a *healing society*, a concept I first heard about from social justice consultant Jenn Wynn that refers to a society that is committed to ongoing interpersonal, institutional, and societal repair. To cultivate a healing society, us rich white men need to value healing for ourselves. That's where we'll go next.

CHAPTER 14

A HEALING SOCIETY

You feel like you're staggering around—you've been in a fifteen-round prizefight that was extended to thirty rounds, and here's something that'll take your mind off it for a while.

—BILL CLINTON, FORTY-SECOND PRESIDENT OF THE UNITED STATES, SPEAKING IN 2020 ABOUT HIS 1995–97 AFFAIR WITH WHITE HOUSE INTERN MONICA LEWINSKY

MYTH:
All rich white men are thriving.

He who controls others may be powerful, but he who has mastered himself is mightier still.

—LAOZI, ANCIENT CHINESE PHILOSOPHER

REALITY:
Many rich white men are in pain, which spills onto those we have power over.

In the last four chapters, I have argued that it is in America's national interest to significantly reduce inequality; that for myriad reasons related to our democracy, economy, and collective morality, America would benefit from major structural and cultural changes that shift this nation toward equity. While many of these changes may result in material losses for rich white men, I don't believe that—overall—rich white men would be worse off if this nation became equitable. In the final chapters, I will share how I've arrived at the conclusion that an equitable America benefits *all* of us, including rich white men.

For me, the long and windy path to that perspective began on New Year's Day in 1995, when I awoke with my heart racing. I'd just had a nightmare—a really bad one. As a six-year-old, I was shaken.

I ran into my parents' bedroom. I knew that they could comfort me, hold me tight, and repeat that it was just a dream until the horrible feelings went away.

I recounted my nightmare to them: There had been an accident at home. An ambulance had come, and we'd gone to the hospital. At the end of the night, a relative had pulled me aside to tell me that my toddler brother, Gaven, had died.

Then I paused and my eyes darted around my parents' room. Gaven wasn't there. Why wasn't he there? I focused on my parents' eyes and saw an emptiness I'd never seen before.

"It wasn't a dream," my mom told me, her voice somber and low. "Gaven is gone."

I was stunned. For the next several days, I woke up disbelieving, certain that today would finally be the day I found out that Gaven was home and his death was indeed only a dream. It took a long time for reality to set in.

When my parents decided to keep me home from school for a week, I remember feeling scared that I would get in trouble with my first-grade teacher and then feeling surprised—and relieved—that she was instead so forgiving. I was too innocent to grasp the magnitude of what was unfolding in my life.

But even at that young age, I felt intimately that my family was in pain. Relentless, excruciating pain. Experts call the shared experience we went through collective trauma. It hurt us individually, and together. Many marriages don't survive the death of a child. I learned a lot from my parents' resilience and their determination to support each other and their grieving children.

My childhood was still blissful in many ways; there was baseball, school field trips, video games with friends, happy birthdays and holidays with family. However, in other ways, my childhood ended before it started. The memories I have from before Gaven's death will be forever blurred. I think life is different after you've seen death, especially when it takes someone before they've gotten their fair share of time on earth. For me, the experience conferred an enduring sense of vulnerability. From a young age, I was aware that I could die suddenly, that life is fragile and any moment could be my last.

As an adult now, I understand that the tragedy of Gaven's death granted me wisdom in ways that only adversity can. But I am still struggling to grasp the full effect that experience had on my six-year-old self. Recently, my mom reminded me that she'd saved a journal I kept in the weeks after Gaven's death. I'd hoped it would help fill the gaps in my memories, but I mostly came up empty. In each journal entry, I repeated the same thought over and over—that I didn't understand why Gaven had been taken from us. The entry that pained me the most was one where I was grappling with childish anger I had toward Gaven. In the journal, I'd called him a "little stinker" because he'd done something to annoy me shortly before he died. Looking back on the journal as an adult, I could tell that—even though I didn't have the words for it at the time—I felt discomfort about being angry at my baby brother, who Mom told me was now an angel in heaven. My unresolved feelings had no place to go.

My parents went to a trauma therapist just once. The one thing my mom remembers from their session is listening to the therapist callously compare losing a child to losing money in the stock market. After that, they never went back.

As I came into adulthood, I didn't think I needed therapy to process Gaven's death either. Since many of my classmates knew Gaven, it was a topic of conversation with my childhood friends more than it might have been otherwise. I ended up talking about how my family's loss impacted me in my college and graduate school admissions essays and later in some public settings, which gave me further moments to process the tragedy. Eventually, I thought I had unearthed all there was to be aware of about how Gaven's death shaped my life.

It wasn't until I enrolled in graduate school after nine years running CollegeSpring that I realized how wrong I was. While I was CEO of CollegeSpring, my body gave me signs that I was very stressed: I had two stomach ulcers and my hair started falling out, even though there was no history of hair loss in my family. I was terribly afraid to fail and ignored the signs my body gave me, since I had assumed that extreme stress was just part of the job.

After I was no longer responsible for running a national nonprofit, I thought the stress would melt away. It did, to an extent; at least my hair grew back. However, I found myself getting as worried about completing graduate school assignments as I'd been about meeting payroll for CollegeSpring's two-dozen staffers and hundreds of part-time employees. That observation was a wake-up call. No one in my family had ever relied on therapy, but I decided to give it a try. When I did, I was diagnosed with anxiety.

Three years of weekly therapy gave me knowledge and strategies that helped me manage my anxiety. I learned that I was prone to catastrophizing, which occurs when a person misdiagnoses an unlikely worst case scenario as probable. I made a more consistent commitment to running, which I'd realized was important for not just my physical health but also my mental health. I began journaling regularly, which enabled me to process my experiences and make better decisions. I started saying no more often, which reduced how often I felt overwhelmed. By the time the COVID-19 pandemic rolled around, I thought I'd conquered my anxiety, or at least had it well under my control.

Then, in early 2021, after my anxiety crossed a new threshold, I again was forced to confront the reality that I was mistaken. This time, I started feeling physically sick; the scariest symptoms were trembling and chest pain. The rise in my anxiety was the result of multiple factors: I had a demanding job, my wife was pregnant with our first child, and—like everyone else—I was challenged by the isolation and uncertainty of the pandemic. I don't think it's possible to pull apart the relative impact of each factor, but ultimately, I decided I needed to leave my job to prioritize my mental health.

I agonized over the decision to leave my job. I cared deeply about the mission of the organization I worked for, and knew that my sudden exit would impact my Black colleagues tremendously, given the societal power I hold. I also knew that job and income insecurity would put more pressure on me and our expanding family. Ultimately though, I concluded that I needed to get myself to a stronger place so I could be the husband and father that my wife and newborn son needed. Looking back on it, I feel confident that I made the right decision for me and my family, *and* that there are many things I could have done differently which might have enabled better outcomes for me personally and those whose lives were impacted by the decline in my mental health.

One of the surprise gifts of this painful experience was rediscovering trauma therapy, which I had never seriously considered, given my parents' experience with it. I decided to see a trauma counselor at the suggestion of a white male friend who told me that trauma therapy had helped him recover from the residual effects of growing up with an abusive father. It took me awhile to find the right counselor, but once I did, the experience illuminated some of the missing pieces in my life. For the first time, I had the opportunity to work fully through the emotions I had when Gaven died. I acquired new compassion for my six-year-old self, and that has enabled me to heal. Through this process, I've been able to reclaim parts of myself that I had buried for decades. I've also been able to challenge my own faulty thinking, like the idea that it's useful to suppress feelings of joy so that I can feel more prepared when something bad happens.

As I learned more about trauma, I came to see that much of what

I thought I knew about trauma was wrong. I had thought that trauma occurred only after a terrible event, like an accident, rape, or natural disaster. However, trauma actually refers to any situation that triggers a feeling of danger in a person's body, beyond what that person can physically tolerate at the time. During their lifetimes, 60 percent of men and 50 percent of women in America experience at least one traumatic event.[1]

In his 2014 book *The Body Keeps the Score*, Dr. Bessel van der Kolk describes trauma as a "hidden epidemic" that is among the leading public health crises of our time.[2] According to the Centers for Disease Control and Prevention, at least one in seven American children—about ten million children—experienced child abuse or neglect in the past year.[3] That figure is five times higher for children in poverty, and it's likely an underestimate because many cases are unreported. In 2018, the CDC estimated the lifetime economic burden associated with child abuse and neglect at $592 billion, on par with public health problems like heart disease and diabetes.

Many people romanticize the home as the epitome of safety, but for many children, the home is where they are first introduced to trauma. One in five girls and one in twenty boys are sexually assaulted or otherwise abused at home.[4] One in twenty children have experienced physically violent abuse like hitting, kicking, shaking, burning, and other forms of force.[5] Verbal abuse is even more common: a University of New Hampshire study of three thousand parents reported that 63 percent of parents were at times verbally aggressive toward their children.[6] And in romantic relationships, a third of women and a quarter of men experience rape, physical violence, and/or stalking by an intimate partner.[7]

Those who are abusive in one way are more likely to be abusive in other ways, too. For example, 95 percent of physically abusive men also abuse their intimate partners psychologically—making threats, manipulating behavior, projecting blame, or invalidating emotions.[8] Such physical and emotional abuse is literally toxic: those who have experienced abuse have higher rates of anxiety, depression, and suicide.[9] According to one study, those who report six or more adverse childhood events typically live to just sixty years old, two decades less than the typical

American.[10] Since countless instances of abuse are never reported and alternative paths to accountability remain scarce, most interpersonal trauma is never repaired.

And while the armor of intersectional advantage is strong, it is not a force field that blocks all pain. I'm pretty sure that every one of us, even the most powerful white men I know, has interacted with people who exercised some level of power over us. Parents are particularly influential: when a parent abuses their power by hitting, yelling, or manipulating their child, it leaves a deep imprint with a lifelong impact.[11] That's as true for white boys who grew up eating from a silver spoon as it is for anyone else.

It's true, statistically, that marginalized populations have it worse than rich white men when it comes to trauma. Those from marginalized backgrounds generally experience more traumas, and their traumas are typically more severe.[12] It's also true that us rich white men have more resources to help us heal our childhood traumas, including health insurance that covers psychotherapy, a larger pool of therapists who share our background and lived experience, and more control over our time, including flexible work schedules and fewer responsibilities at home.

That said, trauma is a physical experience that takes hold in a person's body. That's especially true for children: when a child feels under attack and overwhelmed, they can't reason their way out of it. And when those attacks come from caregivers who are supposed to protect them, children often conclude that they themselves are defective. Since the world home environment that caregivers create is a child's "normal," abusive caregivers create the false sense that abuse is normal, and that way of thinking is difficult to unravel.

In fact, rich white boys are disproportionately subject to certain types of abusive parenting styles that teach guys like me to see the world through an egocentric lens. According to research by Simon Croom, a professor at the Knauss School of Business at the University of San Diego, 12 percent of corporate senior leaders—most of whom are white men—display psychopathic traits, compared with just 1 percent of the general population.[13] Who do these psychopathic men wind up parenting? Rich white children. And their sons are often rewarded throughout their lives—materially and otherwise—when they mimic their father's toxic tendencies, like egocentricity, aggression, recklessness, lack of empathy, and a propensity for manipulation and exploitation.

However, thanks to cultural stigma and other factors, most of the rich white men I know are reluctant to address the root causes of their psychological pain. Instead, the dominant approach is to try to numb and ignore it. While the war on drugs was sending millions of Black people to prison, the percentage of teens and adults taking antidepressant drugs—mostly white people—increased by 400 percent between 1988 and 1994 and again from 2005 to 2008.[14] Such medications numb pain and may halt further declines in mental health—I personally found an antianxiety medication to be helpful at a particularly challenging period in my life—but they minimally impact the root causes of mental health issues. For example, a 2022 study—in which 90 percent of participants were white—found that those who took antidepressants for two years reported feeling no better physically or mentally than those who did not.[15]

Even taking medication is stigmatized. Many rich white men I've met medicate their pain in other ways, relying on, for example, alcohol, drugs, unhealthy foods, lavish spending, and other vices. The only time I've heard some white male acquaintances express how they really feel is when they're drunk. A night of bottle service in Las Vegas can be an exhilarating escape—I enjoyed a few of those nights myself in my twenties—but it can also indicate that a person lacks the support to face traumas that shadow their lives.

When I was the high-flying CEO of CollegeSpring, I didn't take my mental or physical health seriously. And, to some extent, I'm still struggling to establish that new intention. I pop an unhealthy amount of Tylenol to dull my chronic neck and shoulder pain, even after previously doing the same with Advil led me to two stomach ulcers. When I feel anxious or overwhelmed, I rely on unhealthy foods to help regulate my emotions, to the point that I am overweight. And instead of getting the sleep my body craves, I down highly caffeinated cold brew coffee from Starbucks to help me power through my days.

However, I'm starting to turn a corner. I have a ways to go, but I am happier and less anxious today than I was at the start of the pandemic. My trauma therapist has told me that anxiety is the human body's way of communicating something needs to be resolved. As I've worked through my trauma—and become more confident I can get my needs met without anxiety—I've had less reason to be anxious.

Part of the reason I feel strongly that there's a particular need for rich white men to heal from our traumas is that taking those steps have been invaluable for my interactions across differences. Since leaving College-Spring, where I was in charge, I've sought to intentionally share power with those whose backgrounds are different from mine. That means doing my best not to lean on my identity-based advantages to control my environment or the people in it.

As an intersectionally advantaged person, I have additional responsibility to heal my trauma, because the greatest harms result when a person's unresolved pain seeds a hunger for power. Instead of using my unearned advantages as a cudgel, I am discovering alternative ways to get my needs met. I'm starting to understand what healthy relationships look like and how to maintain them. I have realized that to reduce the harm I cause across differences—with my spouse, family, friends, and colleagues—I needed to face my own trauma.

Through my interactions across differences, I learned that my anxiety can lead me to fall short, since seeking the comfort that comes from certainty and control is a common—and unhealthy—coping mechanism for anxiety. Sometimes my desire for control seems to be rooted in the hypervigilance following the trauma of childhood loss. At other times, it seems to be rooted in the entitlement I've been socialized to feel as a wealthy white man. And, surprisingly, I've found it can be challenging to differentiate between the two.

In her at-times controversial 2016 book *Conflict Is Not Abuse*, novelist and activist Sarah Schulman emphasizes that traumatized behaviors are often difficult to distinguish from oppressive behaviors.[16] Both tend to be rooted in a person's desire to gain control of their environment, which can manifest as a desire to control other people. For example, when I'm in conflict with someone and the dialogue gets heated, my tendency is to freeze. For a long time, my wife thought that in these moments I wasn't listening, which is a stereotypically masculine oppressive behavior. But the reality was that, when I froze, she was encountering my trauma response, not an entitled oppressive response. That said, my socialized entitlement does show up at other times, when my trauma isn't activated yet I struggle to listen effectively. It's been important for me to learn to tell the difference, and it's been important for my spouse to be able to tell the difference, too, so she knows when I need support and when I ought to be challenged, I understand that asking those from marginalized backgrounds to be sympathetic to wealthy white men's traumatic experiences is a big ask, and that not everyone has the capacity to take on that work. I'm immensely grateful that my spouse has been willing to work with me on this sometimes-painful path, because it has enabled me to heal and show up better in everything that I do.

The journey I've been on to process my trauma while also seeking to uproot my socialized feelings of entitlement has led me to try to separate healthy entitlement from toxic entitlement. I anticipate that learning to make that distinction will be a lifelong endeavor, but the way I understand it currently is that healthy entitlement means being proactive about getting my own needs met, but not in a way that harms me or other people. By contrast, prioritizing my wants over other people's needs is particularly toxic and rooted in notions of superiority. When I've exhibited toxic entitlement, the implication has been that I deserve more than other people do and that it's okay for me to exploit others in order to get what I think I deserve. Toxic entitlement.

Part of my search for healthy entitlement has included realizing that, even with the structural advantages I have, the system does not fully support me getting my needs met. As a man, I'm discouraged from sharing emotions other than anger, and when I share my emotions, it can be challenging to receive emotional validation because gender norms suggest men don't deserve that kind of support. In a capitalist system, I am encouraged to see myself and other people as human capital, which encourages me to neglect my own mental and physical health to accomplish work objectives. In a society that demands that those of European descent assimilate into whiteness, I'm encouraged to neglect my ancestry and spirituality in exchange for material advantages. While there is a tendency to think of entitlement as a negative thing, I now believe it is healthy to feel entitled to things that support my well-being, as long as I don't secure that well-being at other people's expense.

There are also ways that I am different from other people and deserve accommodation. Perhaps because of my previously undiagnosed anxiety and longstanding overwork habits, I have had chronic neck and shoulder pain since college. I've needed to spend significant time in physical therapy, and I now complete a stretching and exercise regimen every morning, which has made the pain much more manageable; I also take short breaks throughout the day to help keep my muscles from tightening up. In America's winner-take-all-economy, I've experienced how my physical ailments can sometimes be characterized as weaknesses and used to justify that I deserve less in a "survival of the fittest" culture. And as I went deeper into equity work, I initially minimized my chronic pain, thinking it was trivial in comparison to what marginalized populations endured and that it would seem entitled for me to request anything more for myself. What I've since realized is that even the most advantaged deserve accommodations that serve their mental and physical health, and that when the most advantaged request equitable treatment, it can help to pave the way for other people to receive equitable treatment, too.

I've also learned that I have personality characteristics that are marginalized in the dominant culture. In 2021, I realized that I am what psychologist Dr. Elaine Aron describes as a "highly sensitive person," which refers to the 15–20 percent of the population who respond more strongly to physical, emotional, or social stimuli.[17] In my case, being an HSP means that I process everything deeply whether I want to or not; that's a gift in many ways, but it's also meant that I'm more prone to feeling overwhelmed and need more downtime to recover than most other people. Accommodations for such differences ought not to be considered luxuries. If rich white men, given the power we hold, reimagine forms of healthy entitlement as human rights, that could help to create space for everyone to be their true selves.

I'm working on amplifying healthy entitlement and purging unhealthy entitlement with my spouse, too. I've started requesting validation for all my emotions, which is healthy. But I'm also paring back the share of time we spend discussing my problems, which is inequitable and a demonstration of unhealthy entitlement. What's been most interesting about this process is how interconnected these two things are: now that I feel more emotionally supported, I feel less need to vent to my spouse about my frustrations. And I feel less frustrated in general.

One of my biggest insights in working through my trauma is that, in some areas of my life, I had weak *boundaries,* which in her 2021 book *Set Boundaries, Find Peace*—therapist Nedra Glover Tawwab defines as "expectations and needs that help you feel safe and comfortable in your relationships."[18] People who struggle to set boundaries often find themselves neglecting self-care, feeling overwhelmed and resentful, and engaging in avoidance instead of addressing conflicts directly.

When I haven't protected my boundaries, I've found that—even as a person who benefits from robust unearned advantages—I can still find myself on the receiving end of unkind treatment. For example, if someone is yelling at me and I don't insist that they stop before we continue the conversation, I'm implicitly communicating that I don't deserve respect. And if I calmly assert my boundaries instead of retaliating by yelling back, I also avoid tumbling into power-seeking behaviors that can be destructive, given the societal power I hold.

In the past, when I haven't felt empowered to set those types of boundaries, I've found myself feeling powerless, even with my identity-based advantages. Over time, I've become wary of that sense of victimhood, which I've sensed is often what nudges the advantaged toward unhealthy coping mechanisms—such as anxiety, manipulation, or violence—to get our needs met. I've also seen how that sense of victimhood can lead advantaged people like me to project blame onto other people or groups, instead of taking responsibility for our lack of self-expression.

I think those of us with identity-based advantages may be especially prone to boundary issues because the power we hold in society can make it difficult for other people to set boundaries with us. For example, when I exhibited controlling behavior as CEO, my employees often put up with it, not because they thought it was right but because of the positional power I held. When we rich white guys aren't held accountable for our toxic behavior, we continue to lean on unhealthy behaviors instead of figuring out how to get our needs met in healthier ways.

As I've started setting boundaries, my needs and limitations have become more visible. When need be, my boundaries serve as a source of protection so other people don't harm me. But most of the time, they're simply a way for other people to understand who I am and what I value.

Boundaries don't just matter in interpersonal relationships; they shape and define the culture of institutions, too, in both healthy and toxic ways. For example, cultures that minimize the experiences of those from marginalized backgrounds are also toxic. In his 2019 book *How to Be an Antiracist*, historian Ibram X. Kendi recasts what are often described as "microaggressions" as racial abuse. "Abuse accurately describes the action," Kendi writes, "and its effects on people: distress, anger, worry, depression, anxiety, pain, fatigue, and suicide."[19] When I read that initially, I thought that Kendi was communicating with a hyperbolic flair to make a point. But as I learned more about what verbal abuse looks like and how perpetrators justify it, I came to see that Kendi was right. Just as some people who perpetrate generic verbal abuse redirect blame to avoid accountability, advantaged people who exhibit racial or other  forms of identity-based abuse often deflect by gaslighting, creating a false narrative that leads the target to question their own reality.[20] When an advantaged person tells a marginalized person that they are being too sensitive, overreacting, or that what they feel happened is a figment of their imagination, that's gaslighting. Yes, there is room for differing interpretations about what occurred. However, there is a big difference between saying "That didn't happen" and saying "I understand you experienced my actions as hurtful, and I'd like to understand why you feel that way." A healthy response starts with validating a person's emotions and bringing curiosity about why a statement or act had the impact that it did. By contrast, denying someone's emotions and experience ought to be considered abusive.

Societies can be abusive, too. America has been shaped and corrupted by collective and interlocking historical traumas. The United States has never reckoned with its settler colonialism, genocide of Indigenous Peoples, chattel slavery, racial terror, or institutional apartheid. Nor has it reckoned with a rape culture and other symptoms of misogynistic disrepair. Or the violence of homelessness, starvation, and poverty. When violence is normalized, dropping bombs on Afghan children and torturing Iraqis can be rationalized as a defense of democracy. In such a culture, I'm not surprised that interpersonal violence is common and has escalated into atrocity.

The stolen land and labor that America is built on are products of profound boundary violations. Imagine if, instead, European arrivals had engaged Indigenous populations as equals, worked together to produce greater abundance than either population could have on their own, and then collaborated with African populations as equals to unlock even greater abundance.

I believe that much of the world's trauma is rooted in boundary violations, instances when people are mistreated in ways that devalue their humanity. Those interpersonal, institutional, and collective traumas live on in our bodies intergenerationally. In his 2017 book *My Grandmother's Hands*, therapist Resmaa Menakem describes how our body houses our instincts—like our fight, flight, or freeze response—and how those instincts vary depending on the specific ills that plague a society.[21] Systems of oppression, Menakem argues, are literally embedded in our blood and nervous system. And the advantaged are impacted negatively, too. When systems of oppression cause the advantaged to fear "the other," the guilt, shame, and anxiety attendant to that lingers, absent any threat. In this sense, systems of oppression are a violation of our bodily autonomy, injecting trauma without our consent. The trauma that lives on in our bodies keeps subsequent generations fearful and helps to normalize an abusive culture.

As a Jew, I've also started thinking about how Menakem's work might relate to the Jewish American experience, following the Holocaust. When I was a kid, my grandparents told me about how American Jews are often characterized as neurotic. Sometimes we can laugh about it—like when we watch Larry David's *Curb Your Enthusiasm*—but I now suspect that a deeper pain lies beneath that laughter. Similar to how racist stereotypes about Black people that were generated to justify slavery continue to justify anti-Black discrimination today, I now think the impact of the trauma that Jews experienced during the Holocaust may now be used to justify antisemitism today. Instead of seeing the intergenerational trauma we experienced as an excuse to once again suggest that Jews are abnormal and less than, I wish more Americans would see our full humanity and value every American getting the mental health support we need, so every one of us can navigate the environment we find ourselves in without restlessness or fear.

To build a healing society, America—and the world—needs to heal from its collective traumas. I believe that the absence of healing is why those of us with unearned advantages—such as white people—sometimes feel negative feelings, like guilt and shame, about the advantages we hold. If healing occurred, I suspect that these negative feelings would dissipate.

Through my work at Liberation Ventures, I've come to see how a culture of repair is essential for nurturing a healing society. Repair is part of our earliest practices as social beings: on the playground, even the youngest children are habitually encouraged to try to make amends when they hurt someone. In our intimate relationships, adults practice repair, too. John Gottman, founder of the Gottman Institute and author of *The Seven Principles for Making Marriage Work*, has found that conflict is not a problem in marriage if couples repair and restore their emotional connection.[22] Marriages fail, Gottman finds, when repair is chronically unsuccessful. Put differently, marriages fail when they exhibit a culture of disrepair.

It's time to retire the "an eye for an eye" approach. When violence is addressed punitively with more violence—as it is today in America's prison system—it recycles a culture of violence. Restorative justice offers an alternative way to address harms. When perpetrators of harm come to the table and accept accountability, it can lift a great burden and be a powerful step toward healing. Building such a culture requires not only holding those who cause harm accountable, but also helping those who cause harm to feel remorse, commit to not repeating harmful actions, and return to their communities as advocates for a culture of repair, with their own humanity intact. Punitive justice systems, like the American system, encourage unaccountable behavior because it incentivizes perpetrators to deny that they've caused harm.

At the same time, though, healing is not something that happens instantly. Like the experiences of other people I've talked to, my healing journey has been long, intensely personal, and riddled with ups and downs. Healing requires significant, long-term mental health resources, which I believe to be a human right, alongside resources that protect physical health. In the long run, that's a crucial societal investment: whenever a person heals, they stop trauma in its tracks and prevent it from being passed down to the next generation. And for those of us who wield societal power, healing our own trauma reduces the harm we inflict on people who are impacted by our actions.

A commitment to America's collective mental health is particularly important now, in a country that is still living in the shadow of the COVID-19 pandemic, which raised our collective anxiety and depression dramatically. According to a Kaiser Family Foundation study, the share of American adults reporting symptoms of anxiety disorder and/or depressive disorder increased from 11 percent in 2019 to 41 percent in 2021.[23] That's a perhaps never-before-seen 273 percent increase. I've found that when I'm feeling anxious, I crave certainty. And that when I've felt depressed, I crave hope. The pandemic produced the opposite of that; the rules about how to avoid contracting the virus shifted as the virus mutated, and the science wasn't always clear. And the negligence of the Trump administration fueled the illusion that Americans were in competition with one another and must operate from a place of scarcity. When a society is overwhelmed by a scarcity mindset, its citizens lose

 *Scarcity mindset* (handwritten)

sight of their interdependence, squander goodwill, and hoard resources. When societal inequality is high—as it is right now—the rungs between individuals and groups are further apart. That fuels anxiety because those of us at the top are scared that we or our children will fall to lower rungs, and those at the bottom are scared because they know that even their most basic needs may be out of reach.

There is something empowering about the idea of *self-determination*, the belief that a person can control their own destiny. However, what I think many rich white men don't realize is that trying to achieve self-determination by controlling other people is counterproductive. Absolute control is an illusion; it's unattainable. Being shackled to the fantasy of absolute control offers far less freedom than healing our trauma, which I believe for many of us is the linchpin to liberating ourselves from that unattainable yearning.

One of the things that I've observed that holds us rich white guys back is that we try to meet our emotional needs by buying material wants. This approach can generate a temporary high, but in the long run, none of the things money can buy deliver lasting happiness. It's also wasteful: when we spend lavishly to numb our pain, we are depleting resources that other people could use to survive. "Live simply," Gandhi is often credited as saying, "so that others may simply live."

I'm not saying we need to say no to all our wants. I suspect that's unrealistic in a society that pumps $298 billion worth of advertisements into our brains to encourage us to want things.[24] And fulfilling at least some of our wants brings us joy, which engages our humanity. However, when Jeff Bezos spends $500 million to build a superyacht—so big that it requires a support yacht and knocking down a historical bridge to get it out of the harbor[25]—that is toxic entitlement. I mean this quite literally: Amazon workers are starving, trying to get by on food stamps, because Bezos would rather buy a superyacht than pay his employees a living wage.

I think many rich white men are unusually tempted by the allure of absolute control because we are closer than anyone else in American society to being able to obtain it. While I wasn't able to find data on the anxiety rates of rich white men specifically, the data available about white people suggests that advantaged populations may be more anxious. In an analysis of over one million mental health screens in 2020, the Mental Health Alliance found that fifty-one percent of white people experienced anxiety or depression, compared to just twelve percent of people of color. While I expect that part of the gap is due to racially unequal access to mental health services, I also suspect that many white people are anxious because we have less control over our lives than we feel they deserve. In therapy, I learned that human beings experience anxiety when we overestimate danger, or underestimate our ability to cope. If more of us white people sought out mental health support, I believe that we would be better equipped to assess the dangers in our lives and manage any adversities that come our way.

It seems to me that one of the dangers of highly individualistic societies is that anxiety can reign, since such cultures—inaccurately—imply that a person's outcomes result from their own actions alone. And as societies become more anxious, authoritarian heads of state begin to look more appealing; bosses ratchet up the overwork of their employees because the hours their employees work is one of the few things they feel they can control; and men act more dominant over their spouses and children so they can have a semblance of control in a world where their leaders and bosses are trying to control their lives.

To build a healing society, us rich white men need to confront our pain head-on. If we find the time—and courage—to heal, we can gain confidence that we can get our needs met without exerting dominance. Learning to build healthy relationships—particularly with those who are different from us—would be life-changing, not only for ourselves, but also for all of those who are suffocating under the weight of the gold plated boots we have on their necks.

CHAPTER 15

EMBRACING FEMININE LEADERSHIP

Everybody pities the weak. Jealousy you have to earn.

—ARNOLD SCHWARZENEGGER, AUSTRIAN AMERICAN
ACTOR, FORMER BODYBUILDER, AND FORMER GOVERNOR
OF CALIFORNIA

MYTH:
Stereotypically masculine leadership qualities are superior.

In an antipatriarchal culture males do not have to prove their value and worth. They know from birth that simply being gives them value, the right to be cherished and loved.

—BELL HOOKS, AMERICAN FEMINIST AND WRITER

REALITY:
Stereotypically feminine leadership qualities are equally valuable.

In the final episode of the second season of the Emmy Award–winning television show *Succession*, Kendall Roy is having a private conversation with his father, Logan, aboard the family yacht off the coast of Monaco.[1]

On the show, Logan is the patriarch of a dynastic American family. The story is fictional, but the Roy family is modeled on prominent American families like the Murdochs and Trumps.

In this pivotal scene, Logan informs Kendall that he will have to take the fall for crimes committed by the family business. Most notably, the company is at fault for its negligence in responding to accusations of sexual assault by company executives, which ultimately drove some of the abused women to suicide. It is a disturbing interaction: Logan takes no responsibility for the company's actions and decides to sacrifice his son to save himself.

Kendall is a tortured character. Like many rich white men who have narcissistic, psychopathic, or sociopathic fathers, Kendall is frequently wounded and bewildered by his father, who is abusive, callous, deceitful, and manipulative. Logan keeps Kendall off-balance by occasionally feigning care with intermittent positive reinforcement. And while it's difficult to be sympathetic to Kendall and his three siblings—they are all selfish and lack moral compasses—they have also obviously been shaped by their father's abuse.

At the end of the scene, Kendall asks his father if he ever thought Kendall had what it would take to succeed his father as the CEO of the family business. His father vacillates before offering a telling rebuke of Kendall's lifelong dream to run the company. Logan sighs and then says, "You're good, you're smart.... But you're not a killer. You have to be a killer."

The great irony is that Kendall is indeed a killer. In an earlier episode, Kendall took an employee on a run to get illicit drugs, and when the car went off the road and into a lake, he left the employee to drown. After Logan learns what happens, he covers it up on his son's behalf.

When Logan says "killer," he doesn't literally mean someone who has killed, although I'm not sure he'd have a problem with that. He means someone who operates without emotion or remorse. That's not Kendall, who feels guilty about the young man who died. But in a single word, Logan Roy captures what is perhaps the most pervasive and harmful myth about what effective leadership looks like: the idea that only men who are "killers" are equipped to lead.

That concept is embedded in everything from how mercenary leaders treat employees to how they dress. Some modern corporate practices originated in the horribly violent slave plantation, which introduced sophisticated bookkeeping and labor optimization practices that factories borrowed during the Industrial Revolution.[2] Men's business suits can trace their lineage back to military dress: during the Napoleonic era, French soldiers wore open, single-breasted blue-and-white coats, white waistcoats, white breeches or trousers, and either boots or shoes with gaiters; Russian soldiers wore dark-green double-breasted coats with standing collars, white breeches or trousers, and boots in the winter and gaiters and shoes in the summer. By the twentieth century, these two setups had formed the model for three-piece and double-breasted suits.[3]

The business world is rife with battle metaphors: Capture market share. Rally the troops. Establish a beachhead. Pursue target markets. Pull the trigger. "Execute or be executed—that's my mantra," a famous tech titan told me when we met at an entreprenuership conference.

And the business world isn't the only context that rich white men reimagine as a battlefield. A neurosurgery resident at one of California's most prestigious hospitals shared an experience with me that suggested to me that at least some of today's leading doctors believe that in order to be effective doctors, their physician trainees need to be—as Logan Roy might put it—killers.

That made Becca Sullivan's path to becoming a neurosurgeon an unlikely one, even though—in many other ways—the deck had been stacked in her favor: Becca is a straight, able-bodied white woman who had been raised in a wealthy family. And when she decided to pursue a career in medicine after graduating summa cum laude and guiding the

Brown University soccer team to back-to-back Ivy League champion-
ships, she had a leg up there as well, since her mom was a doctor and
could help her navigate the profession.

Yet Becca had also experienced how lacking even a single advantaged
identity had been enough to leave her vulnerable to white male aggresion:
as a teenager and college student, Becca was sexually assaulted by two
different white men whom she had thought she could call friends. It
had taken a lot of strength—and therapy—for Becca to heal from those
experiences without allowing them to completely overrun her life. After
she graduated at the top of her class from Yale's School of Medicine,
where she published research on the brain that had an immediate impact
on the field, leading neurosurgery residency programs sought her out as
a star recruit.

Neurosurgery continues to be medicine's most male dominated field,
so Becca was surprised to find that—for the first time in her program's
storied history—all three of the residents in her class were women. These
women had a lot to feel good about: they would soon be brain surgeons.
After spending a year learning the ropes, they felt ready to take on the
world.

But in the middle of their second year, the three women sat ner-
vously, crowded around a small conference table in a sterile hospital
office. Apparently a few of the senior attending surgeons—all white
men—had convened informally and concluded the women needed help.
Deeming themselves too busy to meet with the residents themselves, they
had tasked a female colleague to deliver their assessment: all three of
the women—and none of the residents in the all-male classes above and
below them—needed coaching to bolster their confidence. They were
good, they were smart, but they weren't—at least according to the white
men in charge—"killers." Right when she was beginning to feel that
toxic masculinity could no longer hurt her, male bias and entitlement
was reigning over the life she deserved yet again.

The trope that women lack the bravado to lead is a familiar one. Much
has been written about the confidence gap, the idea that part of what
catapults men forward in their careers is that they are more self-assured

than women.[4] Some evidence supports this analysis. When researchers Linda Babcock, Sara Laschever, Michele Gelfand, and Deborah Small studied MBA students, they found that men initiate salary negotiations more often and ask for more money.[5] Another study found that men typically apply for promotions when they meet some of the criteria whereas more women apply only if they meet all the criteria.[6]

And while adopting stereotypically masculine traits can help some women get ahead, systemic barriers ensure that these strategies do not work as well for women, even as they offer compounding unearned advantages to men. In her research, Hannah Riley Bowles, codirector of the Women and Public Policy Program at Harvard Kennedy School, found that when women negotiate, their future colleagues are more likely to develop a lasting negative impression of them.[7] While the social cost of negotiating pay is not significant for men, it is for women. Studies like these embody the double bind of "likability," in which gentle and caring women are seen as lacking the gravitas for leadership, while ambitious and confident women are labeled unfeminine, aggressive, and unlikable. In all cases, women are less likely to be promoted. Since men do not face the same problem, access to compounding unearned advantages abound.

No matter how hard women may try, they never quite become "one of the guys." After all, no matter how much they curse or talk about sports, they don't *look* like guys. Or, if they do, they may be treated even worse. For all their talk of wanting female executives to behave more like them, male leaders tend to pay female employees who don't wear makeup less.[8] My observation has been that the women who reach executive positions are often those who the men in charge deem pretty enough to enjoy having around, but not so stereotypically gorgeous that men find them threatening or make the ungrounded assumption that they aren't intelligent.

The second—and perhaps even bigger—problem is that many of today's leaders are ineffective and hardly worth emulating. In his 2019 book *Why Do So Many Incompetent Men Become Leaders?*, leadership psychologist Tomas Chamorro-Premuzic starts with the observations that most leaders are ineffective and most leaders are male. His book explores whether these two variables are causally linked and whether the prevalence of bad leadership would decrease if fewer men and more women were in charge.

Chamorro-Premuzic's primary call to action is elevating the standards of leadership, regardless of the gender makeup of leaders. He encourages readers to type "my boss is" into Google and see what comes up. When I followed his advice, Google offered these autofill options: toxic, exhausting, a micromanager, causing me anxiety, gaslighting me, and incompetent. Chamorro-Premuzic then cites a series of studies that demonstrate people's dissatisfaction with their leaders: 75 percent of people leave their jobs because of their direct line manager and 70 percent of employees aren't engaged at work—a reality that costs an estimated $500 billion in annual productivity loss. Only 4 percent of those unengaged employees had good things to say about their bosses.[9]

Do leaders really need to be more confident? Chamorro-Premuzic emphasizes that high confidence is good for our self-esteem and is a tool for persuading others, but being overconfident has major downsides. For example, when competent individuals lack confidence, they prepare more; when incompetent individuals are overconfident, they hide their shortcomings from their colleagues. If there is a time in my life when my life is on the line, I do want my doctor to be skilled and decisive, but I don't want them to be arrogant or reckless.

For all their sexist talk of women being "hormonal," male leaders often struggle to manage their testosterone levels, which can lead to excessive risk-taking. When Cambridge University researchers used saliva samples to track the testosterone levels of high-rolling London hedge fund managers (every participant had an annual bonus above $5 million), they found that traders who started the day with higher levels of testosterone made riskier trades.[10] If the trades paid off, their testosterone levels surged further. One trader saw his testosterone level rise 74 percent over a six-day winning streak. Excessively high testosterone levels bring other problems, too—such as aggressiveness, irritability, acne, oily skin, and sleep apnea; it also reduces sperm counts, shrinks testicles, diminishes fertility, and raises bad cholesterol to unhealthy levels, putting men with high testosterone at greater risk for heart attacks, cardiovascular disease, and strokes.[11]

A particularly significant risk of prioritizing overconfident leaders is that it often elevates those who have malevolent personalities. On average, men score higher than women on the "dark triad" personality traits: narcissism, Machiavellianism, and psychopathy.[12] While leaders with these traits sometimes seem charismatic and perform well in interviews and early on in their tenures, they often cause damage in the long run. After such leaders climb the ladder, they are more prone to counterproductive and antisocial work behaviors, including bullying, fraud, white-collar crime, harassment, and sexual harassment, all of which produce toxic cultures in their teams. They also often prioritize their own compensation and influence above company performance: for example, after self-centered leaders become CEO, they are more likely to be attracted to extravagant acquisitions that put themselves in the spotlight but don't pay off for shareholders.

Outside of work, men are responsible for much of the world's toxic behavior and violence. In America, the firearm homicide rate is twenty-six times higher than that of other high-income countries, and men are responsible for 77 percent of homicides.[13] Male political leaders are also more inclined to kill: the twentieth century's ten most deadly genocides—which historians estimate killed upwards of one hundred million people—were all driven and led by men.[14]

Some evidence suggests that women are increasingly adopting stereotypically male traits, for reasons that I suspect at least partially have to do with attempting to survive in a patriarchal system. For example, while historically men have tended to be more narcissistic than women, rates of narcissism in young women are increasing.[15] Such self-centeredness can help individual women get ahead, but it also perpetuates the toxicity sustained by patriarchal norms. Similar to how the pigs in George Orwell's *Animal Farm* became the new authoritarians after they banished the humans from their farm, I fear that gender "parity" might only be achieved when feminine leadership qualities are erased. That's not to say I'm judging those who are navigating patriarchal structures however they can. The responsibility for redefining leadership lies with America's current leaders—mostly rich white men—who offer the contemporary archetype for what leadership looks like and are poised to dispropor-tionately influence who the next generation of leaders will be.

For reasons researchers are just beginning to unpack and under-stand, female leaders are outperforming male leaders on many leader-ship measures. New research suggests that direct reports, on average, perceive their female managers to be better leaders. In a 2019 *Harvard Business Review* article, leadership consultants Jack Zenger and Joseph Folkman highlight a longitudinal analysis of 360-degree assessments that found that women are rated by those who work with them as more effective: women were rated more positively on thirteen of the nineteen leadership effectiveness competencies, and female leaders also received higher employee engagement scores from direct reports, who described themselves as more satisfied and committed.[16]

"Perhaps the most valuable part of the data we're collecting through-out the [COVID-19] crisis is hearing from thousands of direct reports about what they value and need from leaders now," Zenger and Folkman write. "Based on our data they want leaders who are able to pivot and learn new skills; who emphasize employee development even when times are tough; who display honesty and integrity; and who are sensitive and understanding of the stress, anxiety, and frustration that people are feel-ing. Our analysis shows that these are traits that are more often being displayed by women."[17]

New evidence suggests that female leaders have been especially effective during the COVID-19 pandemic. When Zenger and Folkman conducted 360-degree assessments again during the pandemic, the gap between male and female leaders had widened.[18] In another study, Uni-versity of Wisconsin researchers found that states with female governors issued earlier stay-at-home orders and ultimately had fewer COVID-19 deaths.[19] That study reviewed hundreds of governor briefings, totaling 1.2 million words, that took place between April 1, 2020, and May 5, 2020, and found that female governors were more confident *and* empa-thetic. In a global analysis, using a constructed data set for 194 countries,

British researchers found that COVID-19 outcomes were systematically better in countries led by women, who were more proactive and coordinated in their policy responses.[20]

Former president Barack Obama also offered his anecdotal impressions of women leaders from his time in the Oval Office. "I'm absolutely confident that for two years if every nation on Earth was run by women," Obama said in a 2019 speech in Singapore, "you would see a significant improvement across the board on just about everything—living standards and outcomes."[21]

All that said, no evidence has found that women are biologically superior leaders to men. Rather, the socialization of men and women in a patriarchal system deems different sets of behaviors as acceptable for men and for women. When men and women are socialized differently in a world dominated by rich white men, the leadership qualities exhibited by rich white men are overvalued while the leadership qualities exhibited by everyone else are undervalued. To convey that men, women, and nonbinary people hold equal value and make equally valuable contributions, I believe that we must structure our institutions so that all genders are fully represented in the halls of power.

But while achieving equal representation is itself a substantial challenge, it is not sufficient. The more daunting task is building an America where stereotypically feminine leadership qualities—such as empathy, vulnerability, humility, inclusiveness, generosity, flexibility, balance, and patience—are equally represented in positions of power. In my view, gender equity requires that every leader—male, female, and nonbinary—be free to pursue the leadership style that fits them personally *and* meets the needs of all affected stakeholders, unshackled from gender norms.

When the neurosurgery residency program I mentioned earlier enrolled its first all-female class, it had an opportunity to embrace feminine leadership qualities it had neglected since rich white men had founded the institution decades earlier. But instead of tapping the potential of promising new leaders, the incumbent white male bosses turned up the volume on excuses about why anyone outside their circle was undeserving of power.

Before I became interested in ending patriarchy, I was a leadership book enthusiast. During my first years as CollegeSpring's CEO, I devoured everything I could that might help me become a better leader, which I felt was especially important given my lack of real-world experience. Just to name a few, I read Jim Collins's *Good to Great*, where I learned about "Level 5" leaders who are mission driven, display a powerful mixture of personal humility and indomitable will, and are often self-effacing, quiet, reserved, and even shy; Travis Bradberry and Jean Greaves's *Emotional Intelligence 2.0*, which guides leaders toward improving their self-awareness, self-management, social awareness, and relationship management; and Bill George's *Authentic Leadership*, which advises leaders to lead with their hearts, cultivate long-term relationships, and demonstrate excellence through self-discipline.[22]

Looking back, I now believe that much of what I've heard rich white men describe to me as the "leadership canon" are books written by powerful white men who are trying to persuade other powerful white men to integrate stereotypically feminine leadership qualities into their leadership style. What has been missing in this dialogue is a directness about the fact that much of the other half of the population already has these qualities in spades, that organizations would improve if more women were invited into the leadership fold, and that male leaders could themselves improve if they were more open to the possibility that female leaders possess leadership qualities that they ought to emulate.

Women aren't the only people who would benefit from a more comprehensive set of leadership criteria. Plenty of men and gender nonconforming people have advanced levels of compassion, empathy, self-awareness, and other desirable qualities. However, many of these people are overlooked in a system that undervalues those traits and underestimates their charisma and strength. Prioritizing a more complete and balanced set of leadership criteria—instead of only those qualities valorized by rich white men—is not by any means a lowering of standards to make room for women, gender-nonconforming people, and more sensitive men; it's *raising* the bar so that the leaders selected actually have the capabilities to effectively serve all their stakeholders.

A commitment to gender equity also means caring about the ways that men are harmed by the current system. One white male activist who helped secure a right for men that I value deeply is Dale Clark, who—in the 1940s—ignored hospital policies that kept fathers out of delivery rooms so he could be next to his wife when his child was born. Clark went on to become an advocate for the issue, and his influential 1949 *Esquire* opinion piece "A Husband's Place Is Not in the Waiting Room" helped men to see how we were being denied an opportunity to support our spouses and bond with our newborn children. I am grateful to Clark, whose advocacy paved the way for me to have what is among my most cherished memories.

Yet there are still many ways that men don't receive equitable treatment. For example, compared with women, men are more likely to have traumatic experiences, half as likely to receive mental health treatment, and four times as likely to kill ourselves.[23] That unresolved pain produces spillover effects that also harm people of all gender backgrounds; a particularly grisly example is that men are five times as likely as women to murder their spouses.[24] I believe such disparities are driven by patriarchal norms, since men are more likely to be shamed or punished when we are vulnerable and seek out the support we need to thrive, or even to survive.

In his book *The Mask of Masculinity*, All-American athlete and entrepreneur Lewis Howes unpacks some of these patriarchal norms by identifying nine masks that men are called to wear: the stoic, athlete, material, sexual, aggressive, joker, invincible, know-it-all, and alpha masks.[25] These masks distance us men from our true selves and our needs, and fuel anxiety, since no mortal man can juggle all these masks simultaneously. Just as the quest for absolute control is an illusion, the masculine ideal is an unattainable, anxiety-inducing aspiration, too.

I suspect that Howes starts with the "stoic" mask because what I believe most distinguishes the way men and women are socialized is the differing guidance we receive about expressing our emotions. While girls and women are typically encouraged to share the full range of their emotions, many boys and men only feel permitted to express anger. What that means in practice is that many boys and men struggle to express that they are sad or scared. While men sometimes perpetuate the sexist trope that women have "daddy issues," men are by definition every bit as likely as women to have disappointing or scary fathers. The difference is that men are often discouraged from acknowledging that pain and harnessing its lessons in healthy ways.

Anger is often understood as an expression of strength—and it is, in the sense that it can be used as a coercive display of force—but underneath anger are usually feelings of powerlessness. In fact, psychologists have found that when people get angry, they feel a rush of power that temporarily mutes feelings of helplessness.[26] For those who feel sad or scared but lack the capacity to express those feelings or doubt that anyone in their life would care if they did, anger provides temporary relief. Like drugs and other addictive substances, anger offers a fleeting, chemically induced hit that boosts adrenaline and numbs pain.[27] My sense is that those who violently harm themselves or others are often those who are most overwhelmed by their own pain, a population that is disproportionately men because it is mainly men who are told to keep their pain bottled up inside, like a powder keg.

As a boy and man who grew up nerdy and sensitive, unpacking my masculinity has been complex. There have been times when I felt like I wasn't a real man, as when I struggled as a kid with certain sports. But I now know that even in these moments, I was wearing certain masks to perform a socially acceptable version of masculinity. Like many men, I once believed that my worth could be measured by my professional success. Even though my brother's death dimmed my daredevil tendencies, I have still fallen prey to the mask of invincibility, letting my health deteriorate to a breaking point on multiple occasions before taking action. I've also worn the know-it-all mask, communicating with ostensible certainty about topics I knew little about and offering unsolicited advice on far too many occasions.

One of the great ironies is that when a man deviates from gender norms—and thereby moves closer to accessing his full humanity—he is often criticized for being less of a man. I think the underlying assumption is that men are godlike, as if suggesting that men are merely human is an insult. After all, the patriarchs of Noble households in Old Europe called themselves "Lord," the same honorific they ascribed to Christ. But the reality is, men are as flawed, fallible, and mortal as anyone else. So, even if the intention of patriarchy is to glorify men, the result is that countless men are treated as unlovable in life and disposable in death.

"To create loving men, we must love males," bell hooks wrote in *The Will to Change*, which offers her enduring feminist take on masculinity. "In an antipatriarchal culture," she says, "males do not have to prove their value and worth. They know from birth that simply being gives them value, the right to be cherished and loved."[28]

Many men I know are taking steps to reclaim their full humanity and partnering with the gender-oppressed people in their lives toward the same aspiration. Some men—like Marlo Pedroso, who runs the Emergence Project in Boston—facilitate men's groups, which create space for men to develop healthy and emotionally deep relationships with other men.[29] The ManKind Project offers weekend retreats with similar aims.[30] Many therapists and support groups specialize in assisting those raised by a narcissistic parent, and trauma therapists can be an invaluable resource for those seeking healing from a variety of traumatic experiences. Most cities offer anger management classes. Al-Anon supports family and friends of alcoholics, two-thirds of whom are men. These are just a few of the many resources available to men seeking a different relationship with themselves and others.

Rich white men's bias in favor of stereotypically masculine leadership qualities helps to sustain a culture of violence. To counteract that, American society ought to attach equal value to men, women, and nonbinary people and offer everyone access to "feminine" qualities like empathy, flexibility, collaboration, and emotional expressiveness.

Reconciling differences can be challenging. But I've found few things more rewarding than reclaiming shared humanity in ways that patriarchal norms didn't intend for me.

CHAPTER 16

RESTORING CONNECTION

Money is a scoreboard where you can rank how you're doing against other people.

—MARK CUBAN, BILLIONAIRE ENTREPRENEUR AND TELEVISION PERSONALITY

MYTH:
Power and control offer the surest path to belonging.

If your dream is just to be the head and winner of a rat race, then you can do that. But when you win, you're still a rat. It's still moral and spiritual impoverishment [and] that person is successful in an empire that's disintegrating.

—CORNEL WEST, AMERICAN PHILOSOPHER AND POLITICAL ACTIVIST

REALITY:
Power and control fuel loneliness and disconnection.

What my spouse and I found most difficult about living in Michigan were the gray skies. After three Boston winters, we thought we'd be ready for anything. But we had taken for granted that in Boston we could at least usually count on a sunny blue sky, regardless of the temperature. The Michigan gray was another beast entirely.

When I think about what the pandemic's isolation felt like to me, Michigan's dark gray clouds shroud my memories. We had relocated to Ann Arbor in June 2020—shortly after the first COVID-19 shutdown—so my spouse could pursue a research fellowship at the University of Michigan. We didn't know many people there and hoped the world would open back up so we could make new friends. We attended a few outdoor gatherings that summer, but after it got cold around Halloween, no one felt safe convening inside, and the outdoor meetups dried up.

Pooja and I spent most of the next twelve months holed up in our apartment. We were fortunate to have each other, and had some joyful times—the most significant was discovering that we were pregnant—but mostly it was lonely, and a poor excuse to work more than ever.

On a classically gray Saturday morning, I found myself staring at a couple of dozen faces on my laptop, trying to adjust to the disappointing reality that a Zoom gathering was my best chance to feel a sense of community. But had I known how that gathering would change my life forever, perhaps I could have looked past the gray skies.

I was participating in a seminar led by Relational Uprising, a training and coaching institute that builds a "resilient, interdependent, and relational culture within organizations and communities working for social change."[1] According to RU, relational culture is characterized by a deep feeling of interdependence, connection, and sustained inclusion. Their relational culture training—which historically had been a series of three-day in-person retreats but was being held virtually because of the pandemic—emphasizes bonding, embodying, and bridging.

Their approach to building relationships across differences relies on political scientist Robert Putnam's ideas of two types of social capital:

"bonding capital," which occurs within a group or community; and "bridging capital," which occurs across differences.[2] RU also added an intermediate step they call embodying, a practice that offers a host of somatic exercises that reconnect participants with their embodied experiences nested in relationships. For years, RU has focused on one critical question: How can human beings build enduring relationships across differences?

One of RU's core exercises is "sharing resonance." Through this practice, community members share stories of connection with one another and after each story the other members identify those moments when they felt connected to the story they heard, without adding any interpretations or experiences of their own. Psychologists have found that when people choose to resonate with others, they move closer to matching their frequencies and signals, which strengthens rapport, intimacy, and communication.[3]

The first phrase we learned to help us express resonance was "I was right there with you when...." As I understand it, expressing resonance isn't about having had the same experience yourself: every human experience is unique, so conveying that the experience is shared can actually feel invalidating. Instead, the goal is to simply express that you were listening and felt connected.

What I've found most illuminating about sharing resonance is how it has enabled me to identify ways that my humanity is shared with people whose backgrounds are different from mine. For example, a woman of color in our group described a time when she didn't feel seen because of inaccurate assumptions white people had made about her. While I haven't had that particular experience, I still felt resonance: I know what it's like to feel misunderstood because of assumptions people make about me. When I expressed that resonance to her and the group, I could tell that the two of us—and the group—felt more connected. It's a powerful practice.

Part of how Relational Uprising solidifies that embodied feeling of our shared humanity is through "ceremony," which in the program refers to shared rituals that strengthen connection within a group. The most profound moment of the program for me occurred while preparing for a ceremony in which we'd been asked to sing a song that was meaningful to us with the full group.

When I first heard about the assignment, I was mortified. I couldn't remember the last time I'd sung publicly. My initial instinct was to opt out entirely. After I decided to give it a shot, the song that came to mind for me was "Kal Ho Naa Ho," the namesake and theme song of the 2003 Hindi film. Watching *Kal Ho Naa Ho*, a classic Bollywood love story, with Pooja is among my memories of how we fell in love.

Looking back on it, though, it troubles me that my knee-jerk reaction was to prioritize a song from my spouse's culture. Sure, selecting "Kal Ho Naa Ho" would have been a nice romantic gesture and meaningful in its own way, but there was something unsettling about approaching the invitation as if I did not have a culture of my own that was worth celebrating. When I prioritized my wife's culture, I was behaving as if I were painting on a blank canvas of white, American nothingness.

What had actually occurred is that white American culture had swallowed up my cultural roots. My dad grew up going to synagogue, and my mom grew up going to church. Eventually my mom lost interest in the church, so I was raised Jewish. I attended Hebrew school and was bar mitzvahed. However, after high school and especially after my Grandpa Moe and Grandma Anne passed away, I lost touch with Judaism. I continued to have a loose cultural identification to being Jewish, but I didn't think Judaism meant much to me.

As the date of the ceremony approached, I decided to sing the Mourner's Kaddish, which is a prayer that honors those who have passed away. It was the prayer I'd chosen to recite and opine on during my bar mitzvah ceremony. After Gaven died, I'd grown up chanting the Kaddish in his memory at our synagogue. For as long as I can remember, the Kaddish has been meaningful to our family.

As part of my preparation, I refreshed myself on the context behind the Mourner's Kaddish. One particular statement I uncovered as part of my online search struck me: the Kaddish is to be sung every year on the anniversary of the death of deceased loved ones. Perhaps because of my socialization as a man and lingering trauma and grief, I still don't cry easily. But in that moment, my eyes filled with tears. I was flooded with the memory that my grandparents' dying wish was for me to remain connected to Judaism and the recognition that for many years I'd told myself that I was too busy. Did I really not have the one minute a year it would have taken to honor their lives?

That was the moment that I realized the extent to which I, too, had accepted a racial bribe, that I had traded valuable ancestral wisdom for whiteness. Earlier in my life, I'd said that I had grown up without much of a culture of my own. It occurred to me then that I was implicitly saying that I felt whiteness was meeting my needs and no longer needed what my ancestors had gleaned across millennia. But in that moment, it was painfully clear that whiteness wasn't meeting all my needs: regardless of where I landed on the role of Judaism in my life, there was no reason why I couldn't dedicate at least one minute a year to honor my grandparents—and Gaven—in the way they wanted to be remembered. I felt guilty about being a disrespectful grandson, and brother. And I felt how the pressure of white supremacy had persuaded me to slowly become, at least in some moments, a person I didn't want to be. It was a disturbing revelation to see what had been hiding in plain sight all along: white advantage was so alluring that I was willing to discard the wisdom my ancestors had accumulated over millennia.

I'm hardly the only American Jew who has assimilated into whiteness. Most Israeli immigrants to the United States don't identify as white, some second-generation immigrants do, and by the time we reach the third generation, nearly all of us do. That transition is inversely related to our connection to Judaism: each generation is less connected to Judaism than the prior one, and a growing number don't identify as Jewish at all.[4] Some Jews are concerned that within a handful of generations, no one will identify as Jewish. Hitler's form of white supremacy began the contemporary erasure of the Jewish people, but America's form may finish us off.

For the past several years, I've been on a journey to reconnect with Judaism. It's been an uphill battle: my grandparents were the principal carriers of that culture in my family, and they are long gone. I am emerging from a fifteen-year hiatus from participating in any Jewish activities. Still, in fits and starts, I'm trying—and I'm starting to recover what I've lost.

The Relational Uprising gathering was the first time I really felt the pain of what I had lost by abandoning Judaism, but my connection to Judaism had been on the back of my mind since I'd gotten engaged in 2015. At the time, I'd sensed that it would be helpful for me to be able to help my children—who would be raised in a multicultural family—understand where they came from.

So, in 2018, I signed up for Birthright, a nonprofit educational organization that sponsors free ten-day heritage trips to Tel Aviv, Jerusalem, and the Golan Heights for young adults of Jewish heritage, aged eighteen to thirty-two. Most Jews go on Birthright in their early twenties. Even though I'd heard it could be quite a party, I hadn't been interested back then. Birthright has a mixed reputation: some Jews celebrate it as a pilgrimage to preserve the Jewish Diaspora; others denounce it as nationalist, Zionist propaganda. I found it to be both.

My most meaningful memory from the trip was visiting the Wailing Wall, known in Islam as the Buraq Wall. Resting my fingertips on the wall with my head bowed, I felt a connection to God. I had a sense that we were in dialogue: I made promises to God and felt my words were received. It was the most spiritual moment of my life. I didn't tell many people about the experience. Being religious isn't seen as "smart" in the elite spaces I inhabited, so I was scared I'd be labeled superstitious or maybe even a bit crazy. So I will be forever grateful to my friend Ahmed, who, when I recalled that memory to him, immediately validated that such feelings of spiritual connection are common in holy places. Given the historical context, I still find it remarkable that it was a Muslim friend whose single tiny action had perhaps the greatest impact on my reconnection to Judaism. If that isn't shared humanity, I don't know what is.

Birthright helped me see that, like all religions and creeds, Judaism is magnificent and beautiful. The Torah and Talmud contain countless ideas that were ahead of their time. Shabbat encourages us to unplug from the noise and work of doing to refocus on just being, offering a weekly opportunity to relate to family, friends, and our spirituality. Jewish values emphasize tikkun olam (repairing the world), tzedakah (justice), and chesed (taking action to help those in need).

And, like all institutions, Judaism has its flaws and is at risk of corruption by the powerful. Judaism is deeply patriarchal: many synagogues still do not allow women or gender nonconfirming people to serve as rabbis.[5] And in Palestine, anxiety about security has escalated into abuse.

When I participated in Birthright, I had a conversation with one of our trip's guides that continues to haunt me. I'll call him Ben, after Benjamin Netanyahu, who was Israel's prime minister during my visit.

When Ben was in the Israeli military, he trained Palestinians in Gaza. I asked him what the Palestinian recruits he worked with were like. "They were very poor, not very smart, and dirty," he told me.

I asked him what training he provided. "Mostly I trained them to snitch," Ben said. "We would offer them money and hospital treatments for their sick relatives. . . . I felt sorry for them, but what can you do."

Similar to how the United States contends that murderous cops, military prison torturers, and drone strike operators are vessels of democracy, here was an Israeli soldier who saw coercive abuses of power as justified under the pretense of safety and security. Hearing about the Palestinians who had been coerced into giving up their friends to save their loved ones horrified me.

And I felt sadness for the soldier. Ben's people—our people—had been oppressed by Adolf Hitler, annihilated by the Holocaust, and marked by the World War II era's culture of disrepair. He had so little hope that the culture could be transformed that he felt he had to be abusive to protect our people's safety. While abuse offers an illusion of safety and control, it does not provide actual safety. And it comes at an enormous cost, dehumanizing both the abuser and the abused.

When I visited the Palestinian territories a few months later with classmates from Harvard Kennedy School, I saw how coercion was the tip of the iceberg. Palestinian land is overrun by more than two hundred

Israeli settlements—most of which are approved by the government—that house six hundred thousand Israelis.[6] Unlike Israeli settlers, Palestinian residents are denied freedom of movement, having to pass through dozens of fully staffed military checkpoints in their own land. When we visited Hebron, Israeli soldiers threatened to arrest our tour guide—a Palestinian student from Harvard—and threw stun grenades at our group. At the refugee camp we visited, thirteen thousand people were packed into half a square kilometer with no electricity in the winter and a single doctor. When Palestinian businesspeople travel, they are required to carry ID cards, which reminded me of the ID cards that the Nazis issued to indicate that the cardholder was Jewish.[7]

I wondered how I had gotten here. Why had I never explored my mother's Christian heritage? Why had I abandoned Judaism after my grandparents spent thousands of hours encouraging me to honor our ancestry? What did being Jewish have to do with my commitment to social justice? In Palestine, how had the oppressed become the oppressors?

One of the people I credit for nudging me to reengage with my roots is Dr. Ron Heifetz, who teaches leadership courses at Harvard's Kennedy School of Government. A pioneer of adaptive leadership—which he defines as "the practice of mobilizing people to tackle tough challenges and thrive"—Heifetz emphasizes that nearly all social change builds on the preexisting culture in some way.[8] One of Heifetz's frameworks is "keep-discard-innovate," which is a way of thinking about which aspects of a culture ought to be preserved, abolished, or made anew.[9]

Before spending time with Ron, I had internalized the American assimilationist narrative that there was little harm in discarding everything my ancestry had to offer. After I realized how much I'd lost by replacing that millennia-old wisdom with white supremacy—which offers material benefits but is spiritually and morally bankrupt—I started to rethink that assumption. Now, whenever I encounter a cultural ritual that is hundreds or thousands of years old, I default to a notion that an ancestral tradition is worth keeping unless a compelling case can be made to discard it, instead of the other way around.

As I've gone deeper into that reexamination, I've also taken another

look at white American culture. I did so at the suggestion of Jean Willoughby, a trainer for the Racial Equity Institute, who was concerned
that I was starting to talk about white American culture with an overly
critical lens that she thought might be unhealthy. Jean helped me understand that, while white supremacy is evil because it positions white
American culture as *the* culture—as if all other cultures ought to wilt
in its presence—that doesn't necessarily mean that every aspect of white
American culture is harmful.

Like many cultures, white American culture includes cultural foods,
like hamburgers and hot dogs; cultural music, like country and rock and
roll; activities that build community, like baseball games and Sunday
church services; and so many other cultural characteristics. Other foun-
dational aspects of white American culture—such as its unusual emphasis on the written word, innovation, and scalability—have the potential,
if not taken to an unhealthy extreme, to support human resilience. Jean
helped me realize that when white progressives treat white American
culture as if every aspect of it ought to be discarded, there is a risk that we
may end up discarding some cultural elements that are actually valuable.
She also helped me understand that such an approach often alienates white
Americans who feel instinctively that aspects of that culture are valuable
and offer belonging and connection. Since white American culture is the
only culture that many white Americans know, I'm not surprised that so
many of us feel strongly about protecting it. For white Americans to give
up the aspects of white American culture that are harmful, it seems to me,
leaders must also assure white people that the aspects of white American
culture that aren't harmful can stay.

Part of what makes white supremacy so dangerous is the notion that
white American culture is beyond critique. In the cases when I've been
able to build trust across differences, people from communities different from my own—including Black and Indigenous communities in the
United States and other communities around the world—have been can-
did that there are ways their cultures might need to evolve, too. But I
don't think it's reasonable to expect marginalized communities to be
forthright and collaborative about those aims until those of us whom

the American system racializes as white express that we are committed to reforming our own cultural norms. In my view, that means being proactive about ensuring that other people's cultures aren't overrun by white supremacy and repairing damage that has already been done. That requires modesty that white American culture isn't superior to other cultures, but also the self-assuredness that white American culture isn't inferior either. "The key to global diversity," Esther Armah writes in her 2022 book *Emotional Justice*, "is cultural humility."

In part because my spouse and I come from different cultures, we have spent significant time as a couple thinking through the culture we aspire to create as a family. That's required that we try to develop a point of view about what we want to carry forward from our ancestral cultures, and reconcile conflicts in values like the relative importance of individualism and collectivism. To build a coherent family culture that is supportive of my son, Pooja and I both feel a responsibility to make sense of our pasts and the cultures that have influenced us. For me, that includes taking a hard look at my Western European roots, my Eastern European roots, *and* my white American roots.

Pooja and I have also sought to infuse cultural wisdom from cultures outside of our own ancestral heritages. I am particularly inspired by the fact that—before European invaders colonized what most of the world now recognizes as the United States—Indigenous communities stewarded this land for at least fifteen thousand years, and did so without prisons, homelessness, or other dehumanizing institutions. In lifting up these alternatives, I don't mean to disparage American innovation—which has helped to produce advances like cars, computers, and the internet—but rather to emphasize that I perceive a danger in putting innovation on a pedestal and sidestepping critical questions about what ought be preserved and left behind.

I think part of what drives America's obsession with "progress" is that innovation is seen as a path to acceptance in white American culture. Human beings often go to great lengths to fulfill their need to *belong*. Belonging can feel like an abstract concept, but I like the simple definition that it is a "human emotional need to affiliate with and be accepted by members of a group."[10]

john a. powell—who leads the Othering & Belonging Institute at the University of California, Berkeley—goes further. Ashley Gallegos, who works at powell's Center, describes belonging as "values and practices where no person is left out of our circle of concern." Belonging, Gallegos emphasizes, is about more than having access; it means having a voice and the ability to "participate in the design of political, social, and cultural structures." This includes "the right to both contribute and make demands upon society and political institutions."[11]

Belonging is an idea that is filled with paradox. "True belonging," author and researcher Brené Brown argues, "is the spiritual practice of believing in and belonging to yourself so deeply that you can share your most authentic self with the world and find sacredness in both being a part of something and standing alone in the wilderness."[12] Belonging, as I understand it, is something a person can only find in relation to others, but it is also something that a person must individually decide to feel.

Understandably, the most oppressed find it difficult to feel belonging. In 2019, Harvard conducted its first university-wide pulse survey.[13] It asked 20,572 students, staff, and faculty members how much they agreed with a series of statements, which were designed to measure levels of inclusion and belonging. For the statement "I feel I belong at Harvard," the survey found that those who felt the most belonging identified as white, male, heterosexual, and US citizens; they'd also grown up in families where parents held graduate degrees. Among all groups, Black, Middle Eastern, and genderqueer respondents were least likely to feel they belong.

Yet even the most advantaged struggle to feel belonging. While most Harvard students said they at least somewhat agreed with the statement "I feel like I belong at Harvard," only 13 percent strongly agreed. That 87 percent who don't feel a deep sense of belonging includes a whole lot of rich white men.

One of the reasons why I think this happens is because America's complex and often-oppressive structures make it difficult for everyone, including the most advantaged, to embrace their true selves. For example, whiteness separates those of us racialized as white from our roots;

patriarchy separates those of us labeled as men from our emotions; and wealth separates us from our pain, equipping us to numb it with drugs and money instead of facing it and healing from it. And the idea that some groups are superior to others separates us from each other. Many of the rich white men I know try to manufacture belonging by seeking control of the people in our lives, but "belonging" fostered by coercion isn't really belonging at all.

I suspect that human beings so deeply value belonging because it's a cornerstone of human resilience. In moments when I've felt alone or surrounded by people who don't accept me, I've found that even the smallest of challenges can feel insurmountable. But when I have a community that sees me, cares for me, and believes in me, even the most magnificent aspirations can feel attainable. "What makes a community or individual resilient is not self-mastery or will," insists Lucién Demaris, a somatic healer and codirector of the Relational Uprising program. "It is the quality, strength, intimacy, and inclusivity of our relational bonds."[14]

Research substantiates Demaris's thesis. In 2010, psychologist Julianne Holt-Lunstad and her colleagues Timothy Smith and J. Bradley Layton conducted a meta-analysis of 148 studies, including more than 308,000 participants, to determine the factors that predict longevity.[15] Least predictive were whether a person had access to clean air, was treated for high blood pressure, was overweight, exercised regularly, or was recovering from a heart attack. Drinking habits, smoking habits, and getting a flu vaccine were more predictive but were still not highest on the list.

What came out at the very top? Close relationships and social integration. Having at least three close relationships—family members and friends you can call on if you need money or help when you're sick—makes an enormous difference. So does social integration, which refers to how often a person interacts with other people in their community. I've started asking myself: Do I take the time to exchange pleasantries with my neighbors, cashiers, and baristas? Do I go to a book club or take exercise classes with friends? When I hop in a Lyft or Uber, do I converse with my driver? I've started asking myself these questions not only because they help me counter socialization I've received to devalue some people's humanity, but also because I've learned that daily inter-actions like these do more to boost longevity than the finest medicines, products, and services that money can buy. I've learned that, in the most primal sense, my well-being is tethered to the well-being of others.

In her 2017 TED Talk, psychologist and longevity researcher Susan Pinker describes the biological nature of these findings.[16] Face-to-face interactions—including things as small as making eye contact, shaking hands, or giving a high five—release neurotransmitters that lower corti-sol levels, release oxytocin, and generate dopamine. This natural cock-tail of positivity fosters trust, reduces stress, dampens pain, and induces pleasure. In-person interactions also light up many more areas of the brain than online interactions, which may be why the socially engaged have the lowest dementia rates. Women with strong social ties are four times as likely to survive breast cancer, and men with strong social ties are more protected from many life-threatening illnesses by social con-tact than we are by medication. "Building your village and sustaining it," Pinker argues, "is a matter of life and death."

Pinker has conducted much of her research in Sardinia. An island off the coast of Italy, Sardinia has six times as many centenarians as main-land Italy and ten times as many as North America. While in North America and Europe men live six to eight years less than women, Sar-dinian men live just as long as Sardinian women; it's the only place in the developed world where this is true. Their secret? All Sardinians, both men and women, are surrounded by family. Sardinians revere their elders, who rarely live on their own in retirement or nursing homes. Instead, elders live with their children, helping to maintain the home and watch grandchildren. "As [Sardinians] age...across their life spans, they're always surrounded by extended family, by friends, by neighbors, the priests, the barkeeper, the grocer people, [who] are always there or dropping by," Pinker explains. "They are never left to live solitary lives."

Pinker believes men elsewhere live shorter lives because traditional conceptions of masculinity discourage men from nurturing intimate relationships. That's one of the many examples that suggests that patriarchy is killing men—and helping to sustain a culture of disrepair that is reducing longevity around the world.

Something similar could be said for white supremacy. While Sardinians are surrounded by loved ones, many white people—and white men in particular—are living lonely lives. Such loneliness is what attracts some white men to white supremacist organizations, which prey on people's desperation to have their pain validated and healed. But instead of healing that pain, the "solution" these groups offer is encouraging members to project their pain onto people of color, rather than facing it directly.

Christian Picciolini is a former neo-Nazi who cofounded Life after Hate, which helps people leave the violent far-right, connect with humanity, and lead compassionate lives. When he was fourteen, Christian attended the first gathering of what would become the Hammerskin Nation, a violent, white-power skinhead group. Looking back, he described his introduction to the group as receiving a "lifeline of acceptance." "I felt a sort of energy flow through me that I had never felt before," Picciolini told NPR, "as if I was a part of something greater than myself."[17] Picciolini said that the man who recruited him into the organization "saw that I was lonely" and "knew that I was searching for three very important things: a sense of identity, a community, and a purpose." Picciolini believes he was vulnerable to being recruited because "it was the first time in my young life that I felt somebody had actually paid attention to me and empowered me in some way."[18]

And as I personally found when I was the CEO of an organization, positions of authority can feel isolating even when the institution revolves around you. Half of all CEOs report feeling lonely.[19] While 70 percent of employees say that work friendships are the most important element of a happy work life, CEOs struggle to build true workplace friendships thanks to the positional power they hold.[20] In fact, their experience is more likely to be the opposite: the typical employee has more negative feelings toward their boss than toward any other person in their life.[21] Bosses rightly get the impression that employees are often following their orders not because they want to but because they have to. More generally, many powerful people have told me that people in their lives—including, in some cases, their spouses, children, and friends—engage them less than authentically because those people desire access to the resources they control. These dynamics all conspire to reduce trust, altering not only powerful people's beliefs about others' intentions but also their own reactions.

Exercising dominance in our personal lives can fuel loneliness, too. Positions of authority are accompanied by entitlements that are legitimate—such as the responsibility to make certain decisions—but it also can corrupt people into feeling entitled to things they are not entitled to. Bill Gates' affair in 2000 with a young manager at one of Microsoft's offices abroad is one example.[22] Throughout his career, Gates regularly asked employees out, all while he was married. While such behavior is an obvious abuse of power, Gates also dehumanized himself. Instead of believing he was worthy of love and would receive it even if he treated women as equals, Gates felt his only path to intimacy was exercising power and control, which is not really love at all. When those abuses resulted in Melinda Gates deciding to divorce him, he lost his only opportunity to build a lifelong partnership with the person he had promised decades earlier to love and cherish.

I was drawn to Relational Uprising's programming in part because I felt something was missing from the various American subcultures I'd participated in over the years. Most of my college and graduate school friends were working sixty-, seventy-, eighty-hour weeks. They were paid well, but they were often treated more like commodities than human beings. Even, perhaps especially, when my friends had the autonomy that accompanies a business card that says "CEO," their personal lives took a backseat to their careers.

Among the obstacles that challenge our ability to find and preserve connection is the extent to which our society has become overrun by *neoliberalism*, which has become the dominant approach to governance and economics in America and much of the world. Ushered in by Margaret Thatcher and Ronald Reagan, neoliberalism elevates competition as the defining characteristic of human relations. It defines citizens as consumers who vote with their checkbooks and credit cards; the ballot box is secondary. Since neoliberalism argues that the market is superior to all centralized planning efforts, its supporters advocate for privatization, deregulation, free trade, austerity, and elimination of the 'public good.'

Neoliberalism is among the leading reasons why today even the most advantaged people are burning the midnight oil working on projects that deliver minimal value for society. Sure, executing a reorganization or an M&A deal improves "efficiency." But for *whom*?

In his 1930 essay "Economic Possibilities for our Grandchildren," John Maynard Keynes, the architect of Keynesian economics, speculated that productivity growth might enable humanity to someday work fifteen hours a week.[23] Keynes was correct about productivity growth: since 1948, productivity has tripled.[24] But Keynes did not anticipate neoliberalism: American workers today work just 10 percent fewer hours than we did in 1950, and hours have not decreased at all since neoliberalism took hold in the 1970s.[25] Productivity gains are not translating into much-higher wages either: while productivity grew 62 percent between 1920 and 1979, hourly pay only increased 17.5 percent.[26]

In Old Europe, leisure was a symbol of status. An aristocrat would never boast about working long hours because they'd sound like a peasant. Yet today, the "in" thing among many of the rich white men I know is being glued to PowerPoint, Excel, and Word while our bodies, relationships, hobbies, intellectual curiosities, morals, and spirituality wither.

I think that one of the reasons why even elites are getting walloped by neoliberalism is that plutocrats are running out of people to exploit. Today's captains of industry have squeezed nearly everything they can from the 99 percent, so now they're coming for the 1 percent, too. Yes, elites make good money at technology and professional service firms. But what good is that money if our personal lives are in the toilet, we're ignoring some of our basic needs, and our planet is being burned to a crisp? And even returns from optimizing elite productivity are running dry: I don't think it's a coincidence that, after decades mining the 99 percent *and* the 1 percent, the world's two richest men have become obsessed with colonizing new planets.

Some rich white men say that the neoliberal grind is necessary for

America's global competitiveness. In a 2018 *Financial Times* piece titled "Silicon Valley Would Be Wise to Follow China's Lead," billionaire venture capitalist Michael Moritz idealizes a work culture within the Chinese technology industry where executives work eighty-to-one-hundred-hour weeks. He laments how "the [California] blogosphere has been full of chatter about the inequity of life" and cites the prevalence of topics like "the appropriate length of paternity leave or work-life balances" as reflective of "the concerns of a society that is becoming unhinged." He celebrates how "these topics are absent in China's technology companies" and praises high-flying executives who only see their children a few minutes a day.[27]

But what rich white men like Moritz overlook is that for all of neoliberalism's promises, long hours aren't necessarily more productive. Research done by John Pencavel of Stanford University has shown that productivity decreases after fifty hours of work per week and is almost zero once a person's workweek increases to fifty-five hours.[28] When Iceland transitioned to a four-day workweek without a pay cut, researchers tracked 2,500 employees who worked at offices, preschools, and social service offices.[29] After these employees reduced their workweek to thirty-five or thirty-six hours, their well-being and productivity improved. Participants said the reduced hours allowed them to focus on exercising and socializing, which enhanced their work performance. From what I've observed, employees are often required to work grueling hours not to optimize results but to soothe the anxiety of their leaders and managers. And I've observed that anxiety often animates people who *choose* to work long hours, too. In my view, America's path to successfully competing economically with China runs through getting a handle on inequality, which is increasingly becoming a drag on the Chinese economy, much as it is here.

And human beings are more than human capital. In their book *Win at Work and Succeed at Life*, business owners Michael Hyatt and Megan Hyatt Miller break life down into ten domains: physical, vocational, avocational, emotional, financial, spiritual, parental, marital, social, and intellectual.[30] Like most wealthy white men I know, I've spent most of my life overindexed on work and underindexed on everything else. Most of the rich white men I know think we're making objective, rational choices about how to allocate our time, but the decision to shortchange most of life's domains requires ignoring feelings that beckon us toward them. I've realized that in the times when I've ignored these pieces of crucial data—yes, feelings are a form of data—I'm leaving valuable information on the table that I could use to make better decisions.

Sometimes I've ignored these other domains not because I think they're unimportant but because I've been so programmed for the world of work that I don't know what to do with myself in other environments. For example, I've been troubled by the times when I've struggled to be present with my infant son. More often than I'd like, my mind wanders to tasks I need to complete. At times I've felt restless, as if caring for my son is less important than an email I need to send or a document I need to write. While I'm embarrassed by these reactions, I take solace in the fact that I am not alone, that countless other people struggle in this way, too, and that as I grow more aware of my present limitations I'm gaining the capacity to change.

One of the more surprising aspects of my healing journey has been the benefits of learning to take my feelings and bodily responses seriously. If I'm feeling angry, what might I be so sad or scared about that I'm responding with anger? If I feel joy, how can I be intentional about savoring it as long as possible? If I feel lonely, perhaps I need to make more time for my family and friends. If I feel tired, perhaps I ought to take a nap, go to bed early, or sleep in. If I feel burned out, perhaps it's time to take a break, call it a night, or even call it a week.

I've also come to see that feelings are often fleeting, and that when I've allowed my emotional brain to dominate my logical brain, it can cause just as much harm as the opposite. When I first started naming my emotions, I felt rudderless, overwhelmed by the vast range of feelings that I wasn't used to consciously carrying. At first, getting in touch with my feelings and my body seemed to open a can of worms that was causing me to have less emotional stability. But as I've worked my way through these choppy waters—and as I've increasingly found a healthy balance—I've become less biased and more resilient than I was before.

When people are on their deathbeds, the things that they most regret are the very things that neoliberalism demands of them. In her 2012 book *The Top Five Regrets of the Dying*, Bronnie Ware—an Australian nurse who spent several years working in palliative care—lists the top five regrets of the dying:

1. I wish I'd had the courage to live a life true to myself, not the life others expected of me.
2. I wish I hadn't worked so hard.
3. I wish I'd had the courage to express my feelings.
4. I wish I had stayed in touch with my friends.
5. I wish that I had let myself be happier.[31]

There's a better world out there for all of us, and that includes rich white men. Power and possessions can be exhilarating, but they also depreciate in value over time, and on our deathbed, they are worthless. By contrast, relationships grow in value until, in our final moments, they are everything. And if we rich white men start demanding belonging and connection for ourselves, it will be that much easier for everyone else to find belonging and connection, too.

CHAPTER 17

TRANSFORMING THE POWER STRUCTURE

I promise you, you'll see the most diverse cabinet, representative of all folks—Asian Americans, African Americans, Latinos, LGBTQ—across the board.

—JOE BIDEN, FORTY-SIXTH PRESIDENT OF THE UNITED STATES

MYTH:

Equity can be achieved by diversifying the current power structure.

A new society cannot be created by reproducing the repugnant past, however refined or enticingly repackaged.

—NELSON MANDELA, SOUTH AFRICAN ANTIAPARTHEID REVOLUTIONARY AND FIRST BLACK PRESIDENT OF SOUTH AFRICA

REALITY:

Diversifying the current power structure is necessary but not sufficient.

On a Sunday evening in September 2018, Pooja and I arrived at the Dorothy and Charles Mosesian Center for the Arts. The theater is in Watertown, just outside of Boston. We were meeting a few friends to see the local production of *Straight White Men*. It was originally created by Young Jean Lee, the first Asian American woman to have her play produced on Broadway.

A satirical comedy, the show chronicles a man named Ed and his sons during Christmas Eve at home. The men are celebrating the holiday in their traditional style—eating Chinese takeout, playing games, and pranking each other—when it becomes apparent that Matt, the youngest son, is troubled.

Matt is less conventionally successful than his brothers. While Matt lives at home, Jake is a wealthy investment banker and Drew is a best-selling author. That's not to say that Matt couldn't have acquired similar accolades. After attending Harvard, Matt moved to Africa to pursue a prestigious role in international development. However, after he concluded that he was doing more harm than good, Matt returned home to serve his local community. He takes on a behind-the-scenes role at a local social justice nonprofit, where he spends most of his time making copies. Matt doesn't see himself as special or as a savior; he avoids the limelight and dutifully supports women of color in all he does. To make ends meet in his low-paying role, he moves back into his childhood home, where he lives rent-free with his father.

Matt's character was inspired by a workshop that Lee did with women, queer people, and people of color. She queried workshop participants about what they thought of straight white men and, after they responded critically, asked what they'd rather these men be like. The result was Matt, a character Lee created to try to bring to life the workshop participants' ideal straight white man. After Lee created the character, she brought her script to the group. "I thought they were just gonna love him," Lee recalled in an interview. "And they all hated him."[1]

What I eventually came to see is that Matt embodies the tension between the two dominant theories for how advantaged people can effectively engage in social justice issues: "listen and support" or "leverage your advantages." Matt follows the "listen and support" model to a T, which creates space for those from marginalized backgrounds to lead. But there is also something unsatisfying about the power Matt is leaving on the table. Why is he living at home and making copies instead of influencing his elite peers who are running the world into the ground?

In my experience, both the advantaged and marginalized can struggle to conceptualize the optimal role that elites ought to play in advancing social change. For example, it is often said that those who benefit from systems of oppression must take responsibility for dismantling them. However, when we do step up, we are sometimes criticized for centering ourselves at other people's expense.

I've observed that this confusion causes many advantaged people who are inclined to engage to freeze. Afraid to say or do the wrong thing, we often do nothing at all. The advantaged are right to be cautious—taking action can cause harm, and advantaged people are often prone to a bias toward action that perpetuates harm—but the status quo causes harm, too. I remember my initial steps down this path as scary: there were many unknown unknowns, and I was terrified I'd make mistakes. But once I made it through those anxiety-driven early steps, I started to feel that it was possible for me to contribute positively. Still, it's not an easy or straightforward path: I'm still learning, and—given rich white men's legacy of traumatizing individuals and communities—I've sometimes sensed that my mere presence in a space can bring unhealed trauma to the surface.

Since relatively few attempts have been made to codify how rich white men can constructively impact social change efforts in solidarity with marginalized peoples, the practice continues to be more of an art than a science. In my case, it's meant a lot of trial and error. That's required taking some risks and being committed to repairing harm I cause, so we can move forward together. But it also requires having the restraint to not charge ahead from a place of ignorance. I've learned that it's better to build together slowly than to follow Mark Zuckerberg's "Move fast and break things." (To his credit, Zuckerberg eventually decided to discard this core value at Facebook.)

Writer, activist, and facilitator adrienne maree brown describes this approach as "emergent strategy," which refers to "building complex patterns and systems of change through relatively small interactions."[2] Instead of embarking on a grand plan to fix everything that is wrong in the world, brown recommends starting with small experiments. For rich white men, that can include actions like reaching out to someone new, staying quiet, or speaking out—and then assessing the impact. The goal, as I see it, is not to be liked by everyone—that is never possible, and especially not in work as controversial and democratic as social justice— but to become attuned to how those who face oppression experience our actions. That attunement, which is enabled by deep and durable relationships across differences, is what enables us to use power accountably. "Small is all," brown has been known to say.

Still, I strive to be cognizant that my experiments—even the smallest of them—can cause harm. My friend, mentor, and fellow rich white man Abraham Lateiner—who has dedicated himself since 2014 to working in service of social justice movements—describes the sequence of harms he's perpetuated on his equity journey as his "trail of blood." In our conversations, Abraham shared with me how the growing pains of his learning journey often only came to him alongside the suffering of those he has partnered with. It's a graphic image, but the "trail of blood" notion resonated with me deeply. As soon as Abraham said it, it was as if it had been permanently imprinted on my brain. He gave language to pain I continue to feel about the many instances when my learning has come at the expense of my spouse, mother, sister, friends, and colleagues.

Over time, I've found that when I'm truly willing to listen and accept feedback about the impact of my actions—and to engage in repair when I cause harm—I've been able to nurture many trusting relationships across differences. These relationships have helped me to grasp the impact that interpersonal behaviors and institutional policies have on those marginalized in American society, and boosted my confidence that most of my activism will have a positive impact—and that when I do cause harm, I have the capacity to repair it.

The person who most inspires me in terms of his ability to navigate the tension between the "listen and support" and "leverage your advantages" approaches is Stanley Levison. In his 2014 book *Dangerous Friendship,* Ben Kamin describes how Levison, an American businessman and lawyer, became a lifelong activist for progressive causes.[3] In the 1960s, Levison was an adviser to and confidant to Dr. Martin Luther King, Jr. Many people have said that Levison was Dr. King's closest white friend.[4] Levison helped write speeches, raise funds, organize events, and hire staff. He brought insights about what white people thought and how their minds could be changed. He also brought experience building strong and stable institutions, which he had learned while mingling professionally with other rich and powerful white men. Levison didn't put himself at the center—he didn't run for president of the United States or ask to chair King's governing board—but he also didn't forfeit his power. He respected King's vision and supported it as an equal partner.

After I learned about Stanley Levison, I began discovering other elites who played similar roles in historical social movements. One of those men is Parsee Rustomjee, an Indian-South African philanthropist and businessman who was the largest South African contributor to the *satyagraha* (nonviolent resistance) and is known for his role as an adviser and financial sponsor of Mahatma Gandhi. Rustomjee was imprisoned on multiple occasions for his activism; he also endured threats, such as those from white South Africans who threatened to burn down his house and property while he was offering up his home to Gandhi and his sons for their protection. Like Levison, Rustomjee was willing to take significant risks in the name of justice.

Levison and Rustomjee's example suggests that what American society most needs from its elites are people who are willing to partner deeply across differences and ruffle feathers in the places where we have influence. Since marginalized people are fighting for their lives, they need lifelong partners who are willing to risk friendships, jobs, status, and resources in pursuit of a just future. The goal, as I see it, is not to try to become the planet's most socially conscious person—like absolute control, perfection is unattainable—but rather to participate meaningfully in efforts that shift culture and structures in ways that enable enduring progress toward achieving equity.

Some powerful white men have followed aspects of Levison's example. These men include former NBA player and United States senator Bill Bradley, the first white presidential candidate to talk about white advantage; Ron Heifetz, whose work on adaptive leadership includes teaching a course at Harvard Kennedy School focused on anti-Black racism and sexism; and Jeff Raikes, former CEO of the Gates Foundation, who speaks to foundation audiences about white advantage.[5] I've also found the examples included in the 2003 book edited by Cooper Thompson, Emmett Schaeffer, and Harry Brod *White Men Challenging Racism: 35 Personal Stories* to be instructive. While no one's leadership is beyond critique or accountability, what these men share is a commitment to shaking ground near the epicenter of American power.

Part of what I think is needed from us is playing a different role than most rich white men currently play in society. When I was at Harvard Business School, many students thought carefully about their prospective white-collar career choices, in particular whether to become an investor, operator, or adviser. In my view, we need more rich white men who are willing to be advisers: men who do not directly oversee resources or people but rather leverage our unique lived experience, professional skills, and social networks to empower marginalized people.

When I say "adviser," I don't mean someone who offers the sometimes arrogant, condescending, and unsolicited advice often found at places like McKinsey. I mean partnering across differences as equals, and serving as a sounding board to leaders from marginalized backgrounds without insisting that they follow our advice. Levison did this wonderfully: when he revised Dr. King's speeches, he leveraged his unique insight into the hearts and minds of white people to make edits that he felt were more likely to resonate with America's white majority. However, when King felt that Levison's changes watered things down in ways that unnecessarily prioritized white comfort, King knew he could decline his suggestions and that Levison would stand down.[6] To my knowledge, never once did Levison's support, financial or otherwise, waver because of disagreements he and King had over strategy or tactics. That's in sharp contrast to many of today's philanthropists, who contribute resources with strings attached, including an implicit or explicit expectation that the recipient will do what the donor says. By working together as equals who brought unique lived experience and expertise, King and Levison collectively created speeches—and a movement—that impacted the American public more than anything either of them could have produced on their own.

Abraham Lateiner, the rich white male activist I mentioned earlier, was the person who invited me to see *Straight White Men*. Abraham is part of several organizations, including Community Change Inc., Organizing White Men for Collective Liberation, Relational Uprising, and Solidaire Network.[7] Soon Abraham will launch Support Genius, a leadership development program that will train self-identified wealthy white men to become aware of how community support unlocks individual human genius and equip them to make decisions that enable them to live out their values in everything they do.

Abraham and I first collaborated in fall 2019, when he asked me if I would be his support facilitator for an inaugural pilot of a rich white men circle, a learning community for wealthy white men committed to advancing social justice. By tapping into his network, Abraham convened a dozen men from across the United States who met for two hours on Zoom twice a month for six months. The circle offered a space for rich white men to strengthen their practice across differences by sharing what they'd learned, reflecting on harm they had caused, and navigating dilemmas in their work. Throughout, Abraham modeled a culture of care that celebrated our unique value as human beings. It was okay and in fact encouraged for us to be vulnerable, share emotions, and be honest about our struggles. Participants shared airtime equally and listened deeply to everyone else. It was unlike any space I had ever been in with wealthy white men. I still haven't participated in an environment quite like it since.

One of the exciting aspects of participating in the rich white men circle is that I met other white men of means who defined success and contribution differently than the typical rich white man. Dariel Garner was well on his way to becoming a billionaire from his work as a real estate mogul when he decided to donate his entire fortune to nonprofit organizations; today, Dariel lives in a modest one-bedroom home in New Mexico and spends most of his time training people to participate in nonviolent resistance.[8] Chris Olin and his wife, Regan, established the Kataly Foundation, which is spending out its endowment over the next decade to support the economic, political, and cultural power of Black and Indigenous communities and all communities of color.[9] Otis Pitney quit his job in investment banking and now plans to become a financial adviser for rich white men who seek to repurpose their financial rewards toward social justice.[10] For me, getting to meet people like Dariel, Chris, and Otis was less about any one of them being the perfect role model for how to do things exactly right and more about having an awareness of how broad the alternatives can be. I'm like that young person whose world opens up when they meet someone working in a career that was previously unknown to them—I continue to discover new ways to contribute by interacting with those who are approaching life differently than most of the rich white men I'd met previously.

It was particularly interesting to see how these men had a different relationship with money than most of the rich white men I've met. While other rich white men see wealth as their property, these men see themselves more as stewards of resources than as owners. With their philanthropic giving, they think less about giving a percentage of their income and more about moving a percentage of their assets, particularly assets they inherited. They are all attuned to the power dynamics of money and mindful of how money influences their relationships.

The dilemma work we did in the group was particularly valuable. One philanthropist sought guidance about how to best share power with the staff members who run his family foundation. Another sought guidance about navigating the complex power dynamics of working for a woman of color within an organizational hierarchy. While such peer support is not by any means a substitute for relationships across differences, I've found it to be a way to improve my social justice practice without sapping the already overtaxed time and energy of marginalized people. In fact, I sought out affinity groups initially because a more experienced practitioner advised me that such spaces are a way to reduce the number of instances when I call on marginalized people without being able to compensate them for their contributions, which continues slavery's legacy by extracting even more unpaid labor from marginalized people.

One of my more significant lessons came from our dialogue about alternative models for governing institutions, models that reached beyond the conventional top-down hierarchies that many rich white men characterize as "best practice." In our work across differences, every one of us had made attempts to intentionally share power. In those endeavors, every one of us had had abused power *and* every one of us had gotten burned by others' misuse of power.

One participant—I'll call him Daniel to preserve his privacy—experienced recurring sexual abuse as a child. Because of his abusive past, Daniel is deeply bothered by any abuses of power he perceives, including instances when people from marginalized backgrounds have leveraged their institutional power at his expense. Rich white men have developed a reputation for causing harm, so marginalized people are right to be suspicious when people like me become involved in social change activities. Still, one of the ways I think guys like me are misunderstood is that many of us have also had traumatic experiences that led us to be unusually sensitive to how power is being wielded.

It's not often talked about in superficial conversations about diversity, but the truth is that anyone can abuse power. I suspect that is particularly true in hierarchical organizations. From what I've observed, unresolved trauma or insecurities can create a hunger for power and control in anyone. What my colleague Brian Stout—a white male activist who runs Building Belonging, an initiative that provides a figurative home for people who are committed to building a world where everyone belongs—helped crystalize for me is that while diversifying the power structure is important and necessary, achieving equity also requires transforming the power structure.

That is, there is an enormous need for the advantaged to follow the lead of marginalized people, but there is also a need for the advantaged to bring our lived experience, leadership, and resources to the table. That includes honoring everyone's contributions and humanity—including rich white men, who are sometimes treated as if all we have to offer are our checkbooks, which is yet another manifestation of the dehumanizing idea that all human beings can be reduced to dollar signs.

One of Daniel's contributions to our circle was that he introduced our group to a type of governance that I was unfamiliar with and later learned is embedded in the architecture of Brian Stout's Building Belonging initiative. *Sociocracy*, also called dynamic governance, seeks to create psychologically safe environments and productive organizations working in complex systems.[11] Unlike autocratic or majority rule, which ignore important feedback from the system and reasonable objections from stakeholders, sociocracy follows *consent-based decision-making*, which requires the consent of those who are affected by a decision.

Consent-based decision-making follows the consent principle, which means that "a decision has been made when none of the participants in the decision have any significant objections to it" and "no one can identify a risk that the group cannot afford to take."[12] Such risks might include a conflict with the group's stated purpose or strategy or more work being put on a person's plate than that person can realistically manage. Much of what I've learned about consent-based decision making I've gathered from Circle Forward, which equips organizations to embed the principle of consent into their governance systems.

I've noticed that consent-based decision-making is often confused with consensus, a different approach that requires that everyone agree with the decision being made. Building consensus can be exhausting because unanimous agreement is difficult if not possible to achieve, particularly in large groups. By contrast, consent-based decision making can be *very* efficient. There is no need to create an exhaustive pros-and-cons list and go through a deliberative process for every decision; all that needs to be asked is whether anyone has objections that fall outside their range of tolerance. As long as a culture is created where everyone feels safe to speak up, consent is more efficient in the short run than consensus *and* more efficient in the long run than centralized decision making— the norm in elite institutions—which erodes trust.

I didn't expect to find an example of consent-based decision-making from the Middle Ages—back when Europe was organized into absolute monarchies—so I was surprised to discover that the "speak now or forever hold your peace" custom practiced at Christian weddings is among the more famous examples of the consent-based decision model. The concept first appeared in the 1549 *Book of Common Prayer*, which provides guidelines for religious services, customs, and worship in the Anglican Church. Why did the church think it wise for the community to have consent-based decision rights to something as intimate as a union between husband and wife? It was for the community to bring its collective knowledge to bear in case there was alarming information that one party didn't know about, such as that a person's spouse-to-be was already married, underage, unbaptized, or coerced into the union. In these extreme instances, it was considered the duty of community members to object. That's different than consensus or democratic vote: when wedding attendees are asked whether they object, they aren't being asked to weigh in on whether they find the nuptials to be the ideal union; rather, they are being asked to speak up if, and only if, they are aware of a major issue that undermines the marriage's ability to be successful in the long term.

After I learned about consent-based decision-making, my spouse and I decided to give it a try. Sometimes, when one of us proposes an idea, the other person has an obvious and visceral negative reaction to it. In the past, we'd often debate the issue, trying to determine who was right. Now, the person who heard about the idea can simply express whether they consent or have objections. If we aren't able to resolve the other person's objections and secure their consent, we leave the idea behind and move on. That approach is more efficient than trying to arrive at consensus, which can be difficult to achieve. And, in the long run, it's more efficient than either of us making the decision autocratically; that's liable to foster unhealthy power dynamics and resentment that, if unaddressed, could destroy our marriage or encourage our child to develop an unhealthy perspective about how partners treat each other. The process was formal and clunky at first, but now that we've gotten the hang of it, we can usually determine whether the other party consents without the technical language.

When I've participated in environments where I have consent rights, I've felt much less anxious about where I sit in the hierarchy than I have when I've been part of top-down, command-and-control organizational structures. That's different from how I've felt under the current power structure. In contemporary America, there is some validity to rich white men's fears that their needs won't be met if they lose their place at the top of the pyramid. Even though power is not as zero-sum as rich white men often claim, it is still zero-sum to an extent because of the concentration of power in American society. For example, in major corporations, CEOs wield great power—and there is currently room for just one CEO at a company among the many thousands of employees. In many founder-led companies, the CEO often has a controlling stake of the company's voting shares, which means they can't be fired and aren't accountable to anyone. Many investors like to invest in companies that they describe as being led by a "benevolent dictator,"[13] but that approach only works until the dictators are no longer benevolent. And from what I've observed, the dictator often discards any benevolence after their power swells. Just ask Uber's board members how difficult it was to oust founder Travis Kalanick, even after chronic abuses of power.[14]

Sociocracy is part of a larger movement to transform the future of governance. Among the many pioneers in this emerging field is Ken Wilber, an American philosopher and writer. In his 2000 book *A Theory of Everything*, Wilber offers a conceptual model of the world. One of Wilber's frameworks is spiral dynamics, which is a way of understanding how the organization of human beings has evolved over the past 250,000 years and may evolve further in the future.[15]

Along the lines of Heifetz's keep-discard-innovate framework, Wilber proposes that human organization has followed a handful of major structures, each of which builds on the last. These major structures include the impulsive worldview, which introduced boss-led organizations that offered division of labor and top-down authority; the conformist worldview, which, through institutions like the Catholic Church, introduced societal standards and stable organization charts; the achievement worldview, which sees organizations as machines and introduced ideas like innovation, accountability, and meritocracy; and the pluralistic worldview, which sees organizations as families and introduced ideas like empowerment, values-driven cultures, and stakeholder value.

As I understand Wilber's analysis, much of the world's tension in the past century can be characterized as a conflict between the "achievement" (machine) and "pluralistic" (family) worldviews. That is, human beings have conflicting impulses: there is a hunger to optimize hierarchies so that they unlock human potential *and* there is a hunger to abolish them, given the harm that hierarchies often cause. It seems to me that this conflict connects to disputes about how to best protect individual freedom: some people—usually, I've found, the more powerful— argue for relatively few constraints on individual freedom; meanwhile, other people emphasize that individual freedom ought to be significantly constrained because those actions can sometimes harm other people. Whether the debate is capitalism and socialism, authoritarianism and democracy, or Western and Eastern ideals, I've noticed that these dynamics are at play. And they cast a shadow over more micro conflicts, too, like whether it was appropriate for the government to require citizens to be vaccinated or wear masks during the COVID-19 pandemic.

Wilber proposes that the reconciliation of this conflict is an evolutionary worldview, which sees organizations not as machines or families but as living systems. In a sense, it's a back-to-basics approach in that it recognizes that human beings, like other living beings, are organisms situated in Earth's natural ecosystem. That's an approach to systems design that many Indigenous cultures have followed for millennia. Such an approach acknowledges that the world is too complex for rigid hierarchies *and* too complex for there to be no types of authority at all.

I had thought that it was impossible for organizations to scale without rigid hierarchies, but it turns out that many large organizations use consent-based governance structures. In his 2014 book *Reinventing Organizations*, Frederic Laloux describes next generation organizations as "teal organizations"—he gives every organizational structure in the book a color—which are characterized by self-organization and self-management.[16] Instead of having a "predict and control" pyramid structure, teal organizations comprised small, decentralized teams that take responsibility for their own governance.

Teal organizations are distinguished by what Laloux describes as self-management, evolutionary purpose, and wholeness. Self-management refers to autonomous teams that have distributed decision-making, open information flow, and a robust conflict-resolution process; there are no fixed hierarchies of authority and no fixed job descriptions. Evolutionary purpose emphasizes societal impact above competition or profit, while wholeness acknowledges the human desire to belong and bring our full selves to our workplaces.

One example of a teal organization is Buurtzorg Nederland, a Dutch home-care organization that has attracted international attention for its ability to deliver low-cost and high-quality care via its innovative use of independent nurse teams.[17] Founded in 2006 by Jos de Blok and a small team of professional nurses who were dissatisfied with the delivery of health care by traditional home-care organizations in the Netherlands, Buurtzorg employs 10,000 nurses and 4,500 home help workers who all collaborate in a flat organizational structure facilitated by information technology.

At Buurtzorg, nurses work in teams of ten to twelve, with each team serving around fifty patients in a small, well-defined neighborhood. The team manages all tasks that were previously fragmented across different departments. Each team has a coach with no decision-making power who asks insightful questions that help teams find their own solutions. The team does its own intakes, planning, vacation scheduling, and administration. Since there is no singular authority figure and important decisions are made collectively, a problem-solving culture thrives. When things get tense, stressful, or unpleasant, there is no boss or structure to blame. That helps fuel a culture of responsibility, which is empowering because employees know they have the power and autonomy to solve their own problems. Buurtzorg employees find it liberating to not have a boss *and* they find it liberating to not be tasked with the awkward, autocratic responsibility of keeping subordinates in line.

Buurtzorg gets outstanding results. A 2009 Ernst & Young study found that Buurtzorg requires, on average, close to 40 percent fewer hours of care per client than other nursing organizations. While other nursing organizations tightly manage their nurses' time, Buurtzorg is ultimately more efficient, even though the nurses dedicate time to talk to their patients, families, and neighbors over coffee that other organizations in their industry do not. These deep personal relationships enable nurses to identify the root causes of problems, which results in patients staying in care half as long, healing faster, and becoming more autonomous.

An American example of a teal organization is RESIST, a public foundation in Boston that has provided grants to grassroots organizations since 1967. Today, RESIST describes itself as a worker-self-directed nonprofit organization, a framework introduced by the Sustainable Economies Law Center, which defines the structure as "an organization in which all workers have the power to influence the realms and programs in which they work, the conditions of their workplace, their own career paths, and the direction of the organization as a whole."[18]

RESIST is a wonderful example of what adrienne maree brown described in her 2017 book *Emergent Strategy* as a fractally aligned organization. Using the metaphor of the fractal—a pattern that appears in nature repetitively at different scales, like tree branches and snowflakes—brown argues that the culture within an organization reverberates outside of it.[19] That is, for organizations to produce equity and justice externally, they must also practice equity and justice internally. That is, to enable societies that disrupt dominance and empower human beings to live together as equals, organizations that have those aspirations must also walk the walk.

The evolutionary lens can be applied to America's overall economic system, too. When I was at Harvard Kennedy School, Khalil Gibran Muhammad—the professor I first mentioned in Chapter 10—facilitated a workshop with a group of students about American capitalism. The purpose of the activity was not to decide whether capitalism was good or bad but rather to break it into its many component parts and then discuss and debate which of those aspects were positively or negatively impacting humanity. In a couple of hours, we identified a couple dozen characteristics of American capitalism that most students thought had a positive impact, such as markets and a commitment to individual freedom; we also identified a couple dozen characteristics that most students thought had a negative impact, such as concentrated power and a boom-bust cycle that routinely endangers marginalized communities. By bringing the evolutionary lens to the question of American capitalism, Muhammad helped us understand that every system consists of many component parts and can be reconstructed to better meet people's needs.

A similar analysis can be conducted of twentieth-century socialism. While most rich white men I know are convinced that socialism is an obvious evil, I doubt many have studied it enough to have an opinion that is rooted in anything other than ideology. On the other hand, Left-Roots, a national formation of social movement organizers and activists, has assessed the last century's socialist experiments rigorously. According to LeftRoots' analysis, previous socialist experiments were valuable in that they offered visions of an egalitarian society, but those visions were thwarted by the creation of a coordinator class, which monopolized power and abused it in ways that are similar to how America's capitalist class has abused its power the past few centuries. "Previous socialist experiments employed the state as a proxy for the people," Left-Roots emphasizes. "This largely failed to produce emancipatory results. Instead, it gave rise to a coordinator class whose privilege grew from their exclusive roles within the state."[20]

In his final book, *Where Do We Go from Here*, Dr. Martin Luther King Jr. hoped that American society would dig itself out of the false binary of capitalism and socialism, terms that are too vague to carry precise practical meaning. Similar to the approach that Muhammad took with our class, Dr. King suggested that this nation use the two major systems that underpinned twentieth-century approaches as the basis for a "third way" that keeps, discards, and innovates as needed.

One organization that has made headway on this daunting task is Movement Generation. Founded in the early 2000s, Movement Generation got its start by convening dozens of young movement leaders in a series of strategy discussions. Later, in the aftermath of Hurricane Katrina, Movement Generation created the Justice & Ecology Project, which was rooted in a desire to better understand the connection between the opportunities and challenges facing working class communities of color and the global ecological crisis.

Among Movement Generation's many contributions is the *just transition framework*, which outlines an approach to building the necessary economic and political power to transform an extractive economy, which depletes resources, into a regenerative economy. The approach demands that harmful practices be stopped and new alternatives be built, in ways that block powerful interests from treating human beings and our planet as if they are disposable. Today, organizations like the Climate Justice Alliance offer training that equips participants to embed the principles behind the just transition framework into their work and lifestyles.

America needs more thinkers and doers who have the capacity to grapple with this complexity; it also needs more philanthropists and politicians who are willing to invest in the development of pluralistic alternatives that unlock new innovations that can be scaled up over time. For those who want to help build these alternatives, the hundreds of initiatives that are part of the New Economy Coalition—which includes amazing organizations like Seed Commons and United for a Fair Economy—offer many onramps to that work.

Part of why I think America needs to take this issue on is that capitalism, at least as it currently functions in the United States, isn't a consent-based model. I've heard many rich white men claim that workers provide their consent when they sign a labor contract, but power dynamics often shape whether an employee decides to accept an employment contract and the terms they are willing to accept.

That's part of the appeal of *cooperatives*, which are jointly owned and managed by their members; it's also part of the appeal of *market socialism*, an economic system that integrates cooperative ownership into the framework of a market economy. Similarly, *democratic socialism* addresses some of the shortcomings of authoritarian socialism by putting more checks on the power of the Coordinator Class. Even if the overall capitalist system remains intact, the principles behind cooperatives and democratic socialism can be used to produce a more just economy: for example, companies can share power by including workers on company boards.

When rich white men ask me whether I prefer capitalism or socialism, I emphasize that I find the question too complicated to provide a simple, absolute answer. Capitalism comes in many flavors; socialism does, too. The question, as I see it, is less about which system is superior and more about whether the system's various structures are configured to meet everyone's needs in ways that are sustainable for people and planet. By this measure, both twentieth-century capitalist *and* socialist systems have significant room for improvement. Facing this reality, I believe, is essential for unlocking possibilities that millions of Americans—and billions of people globally—desperately need.

Like all economic systems, capitalism is imperfect. A major limitation of capitalism is that it is unable to, in the strictest sense, offer equal opportunity: those who have more capital have more power, and, if the system were engineered so that every child started life with the same amount of capital, it would no longer be capitalism. The American version of capitalism has additional weaknesses, including the fact that it's racialized and tilted toward producing winner-take-all outcomes. At the very least, I'd like this country to acknowledge that American capitalism has its flaws and then take steps to mitigate them. For example, many of the capitalists and politicians I've met aren't honest about the fact that capital grows exponentially, regardless of whether the capital holder adds value to it themselves. That matters because—without robust redistribution mechanisms—capitalist systems naturally produce high wealth inequality, which in turn generates comorbidities like elite capture of the political system, civic unrest, and national vulnerability to authoritarian leaders who acquire power on the backs of subpopulations they scapegoat.

While I do believe that reforming capitalism could make a significant positive difference, I'm also compassionate when people on the bottom rungs of America's hierarchy have shared with me—often in confidence because critiquing capitalism can still be taboo in America—that they are pessimistic that capitalism will ever be reformed in ways that result in their basic needs being met. Over the years, many activists working in high-poverty communities of color have told me something like, "Four hundred years of racial monopoly capitalism hasn't worked for us, which is why we're experimenting with cooperatives, mutual aid networks, democratic socialism, and other approaches that center participatory governance and community wealth building." I've heard some rich white men describe such anticapitalists as "un-American," but I personally feel that—like other entrepreneurs and innovators that America cherishes—the pioneers behind these creative approaches ought to be celebrated, too. And since the communities most hungry for alternatives often lack capital, I believe that wealthy and powerful individuals and institutions have a responsibility not only to *allow* these approaches but also to *resource* them, with no strings attached. If the United States committed to something like a domestic Marshall Plan—pledging say 5 percent of GDP (about $1 trillion annually) to low-wealth communities over the next decade—I believe this nation would see tremendous leaps that support its racial healing, democracy, economy, global standing, and moral resiliency. Rich white men often tell me that America must choose between capitalism and socialism, but this nation has plenty of capacity to reform capitalism *and* experiment with potential alternatives simultaneously.

One of the things that excites me about attempts to produce nonviolent alternatives to some of America's major systems—such as capitalism, the police, and prisons—is that it is known that creativity thrives under constraints. When business school professors reviewed 145 empirical studies on the effects of constraints on creativity and innovation, they found that when the creative process is unconstrained, complacency sets in.[21] Constraints, on the other hand, provide focus and a creative challenge that motivates people to generate novel ideas. As many large companies have found after they launched largely independent innovation hubs, playing outside the sandbox of America's current systems unlocks possibilities that reforms do not.

Sometimes, building anew can be the faster path to progress. "Radical," Angela Davis reminds us, "simply means grasping things at the root."[22] When a society chooses to address the root causes of inequities, it avoids building inequitable, oppressive, and violent structures that eventually need to be torn down on the route to justice. While I don't know many rich white men who describe themselves as abolitionists, I've seen them acknowledge that there can be value in starting from scratch when they've initiated zero-based budgeting processes, demolished a building to make room for something new, or pivoted the focus of their start-up.

That said, even if efforts to build alternative systems were well resourced—which they currently are not—it takes time to develop confidence that a new structure is preferable to the legacy approach. America's present institutions offer some stability, meet a significant portion of its population's basic needs, and enable world-changing innovation, so many institutions will need to be sunsetted over a period of years before they can be put to rest without unintended consequences. Such a transition also gives America time to assess the strengths and weaknesses of its current institutions, so collectively a decision can be made about what to keep, discard, and build anew before any structures are retired for good.

I am intrigued by what my colleague allen kwabena frimpong has described as the "hospicing" of oppressive systems, phasing them out within a generation. For example, if America reduces its investment in the police and prisons each year and increases its investment in nonviolent alternatives—such as a guaranteed livable income and universal mental and physical health services—this nation may someday be able to keep everyone safe using a dramatically different approach.

As well-known self-help guru Tony Robbins tells individuals and organizations, many people overestimate what can be achieved in a year and underestimate what can be achieved in a decade.[23] Rich white men: What if, instead of saying it's impossible to deviate at all from the status quo because society will collapse if the police are abolished, we lent our support to politicians that launch initiatives that increasingly rely on nonviolent alternatives and incrementally shift budgets toward those alternatives over time? And what if more of us allocated major dollars to fund experiments that the government could later scale up, movements that build political will for these alternatives, and courageous politicians? It's difficult to outspend right-wing kingmakers like the Kochs, but the resource that plutocrats will never have access to is the millions of people who desperately want their voices to be heard in the name of justice. If those voices are empowered with resources, progressive social change can win.

One of the things that I've seen hold back rich white men who are considering backing social movements is that they think they need to agree with every bullet point of a social change effort's platform in order to support it. The reality is that social movements are likely to always have a more radical view than donors, because they are situated at a different place in the ecosystem. I hope more philanthropists will relinquish the fear that writing a $10,000 check—or even a $10 million check—will turn the entire world upside down in ways that make them too uncomfortable. It won't. But if the goal is to shift America toward equity and justice, robust movement infrastructure is essential.

In his 2018 book *Just Giving*, Stanford philosopher Rob Reich argues that philanthropy has an opportunity to mend its undemocratic legacy in favor of democracy. Reich argues that big philanthropies are well suited to fostering two democratic values: pluralism and discovery. If philanthropic foundations act as a counterweight to government orthodoxy by identifying and funding a diverse range of public goods and by being sources of innovation and experimentation, they can be supportive of democracy.[24] Funding social movements advances democracy because it amplifies currently marginalized voices; therefore, it serves as a counterweight to the existing power structure. Moreover, organizations like the

Movement for Black Lives operate more democratically than most other institutions I've encountered. Organizations like M4BL advance democracy because they embody a level of democracy that has not permeated nationally.

When we rich white men label human rights groups as threats, we are being influenced by societal programming that quells our natural prosociality. As a kid, I had a wild imagination and a sense of possibility, which I only recently realized I had lost on the path to adulthood.

My mom likes to tell the story of how, when I was five, I drew an amusement park that included a place for those without homes to stay. The idea was that the unhoused would receive food, water, and shelter while also enjoying roller coasters and other attractions. After I grew up, I'd though that this proposal was naïve and a bit silly. Now, I wonder if there are ways that children's ideas might provide a jumping-off point for creative solutions that enable this nation to meet the basic needs and some of the wants of all its people.

It saddens me that, until recently, much of my own creativity and imagination was buried. In my case, my true self was suppressed not by oppression but by advantage. Stanford and other elite institutions claim to be visionary, but much of the time, its graduates are encouraged to obsess over tiny problems and tiny solutions where there might be opportunities to make a buck, like how high-income urban millennials can get their laundry done without having to turn on their in-unit washing machines. My Harvard MBA advocated for a further narrowing of social possibilities, implying that being an executive, consultant, or financier was a sufficient aspiration. Is it enough, as Harvard Business School says in its mission statement, to "educate leaders who make a difference in the world"? Or does it matter if its alums make a *positive* difference?

We are all entitled to our imagination and dreams—to preserve our childish love for humanity and planet, to never settle for the world as it is but to revel in what it could someday be.

If we choose as a society to structure our interpersonal and institutional relationships to meet everyone's needs and are intentional about constraining and—when need be—repairing abuses of power, we can build a healthy society where everyone feels valued, supported, and able to be their true selves.

Collective liberation is the idea that we are all part of one human project. It acknowledges that our struggles are interconnected, that we must work together to create the kind of world we know is possible.

Someday, we can all be free.

CONCLUSION

My whole life is about winning.

—DONALD TRUMP, FORTY-FIFTH PRESIDENT OF THE
UNITED STATES

MYTH:
Plutocracy is good, and forever.

The planet does not need more successful people. The planet desperately needs more peacemakers, healers, restorers, story-tellers, and lovers of all kinds.

—DALAI LAMA, TIBETAN BUDDHIST LEADER

REALITY:
Each generation gets to decide how it will govern itself.

Few infants arrive from the womb with such grand expectations for leadership as Prince Harry. And his birthright leverages the compounding unearned advantages of wealth, whiteness, and patriarchy to nearly the very hilt.

Sixth in a line of succession to the British throne, the Duke of Sussex holds fortune and celebrity rooted in a thousand-year-old legacy that can claim some credit for the culture that produced inventions and innovations like Shakespeare's poetry, the steam engine, medical vaccinations, and Keynesian economics. However, that heritage also includes the unrepaired horrors of colonization and the conquerors' strategy of divide and rule, which continues to incite violence in many regions around the world.[1] Unlike many countries, Britain doesn't have an Independence Day: it has always been the ruler, never the ruled.

I don't know him personally, so my assessment could be off the mark, but what I've gathered from the outside suggests that Prince Harry embodies many of the principles espoused in this book. When Prince Harry decided to step away from the British royal family—to divest, if you will—for the sake of his new family, he exercised leadership that was in some ways more impactful than anything he could have done from within. He has built an intimate and enduring partnership across differences with his spouse, Meghan Markel, which has enabled him to be influenced by a Black woman in ways that few rich white men can claim. When Prince Harry eschewed his traditional role, he chose love over power. That's a big deal because, as Gandhi has said, "the day the power of love overrules the love of power, the world will know peace."

What most inspires me about Prince Harry's actions is that he sees his decision to step back from the power and prestige that was his birthright as being in his own self-interest. "[The British press] was destroying my mental health," Prince Harry told British talk show host James Corden in a February 2021 interview.[2] "I was like... 'This is toxic.' So I did what any husband and father would do—I needed to get my family out of here."

The castles that rich white men occupy, figuratively and literally, are only as strong as the heirs and soldiers who protect them. When rich white men decide to abandon our posts in favor of our own liberation and that of those we love, we shift structures and culture in ways that would never have been possible if we had stayed in the watchtower.

I don't mean to suggest that the answer is giving up on a person's family. I suspect Prince Harry will eventually find his way back into relationships with the other royals, and his actions at Queen Elizabeth II's funeral suggest that his familial relationships are on the mend. When Harry does re-engage his family, he will be doing so on his own terms, with degrees of freedom that would have been unimaginable under the old paradigm.

Many of the rich white men I know seem to sense that intersectional advantage can be used as powerful armor. We seem to be afraid that if we lay it down, we'll find swords in our chests before the armor hits the ground. And we seem to be especially afraid that those we have oppressed might want vengeance, given what we have inflicted on them. It feels like we have this siege mentality, as if existential threats are lurking behind every corner. But none of the people I know from marginalized backgrounds want us dead; they just want to live.

As Prince Harry has found, walking around in a suit of armor all the time can be burdensome, stifling, and exhausting. To become confident that we can shelve that armor, we need to nurture healthy ways to protect ourselves—tools that assure us that we can get our needs met, not at the expense of ourselves or others but in relation to others. That requires not just diversifying the power structure, and certainly not inverting it, but rather transforming it.

If Prince Harry can find the courage to step away from the royals, I have hope that other rich white men can find the courage to take the road less traveled. I believe that all human beings are innately good, and that even those impacted by trauma or corrupted by power are not beyond redemption. Therefore, I retain hope that billionaires with more money than they can ever spend can change their approach and use their vast power and resources to fight inequality instead of widening the gap.

That said, where most of my optimism lies is with our subsequent generations: the Millennials, Gen Z, and those who come after. What Prince Harry's example reminds us is that each generation gets to decide for itself what it means to be good, what it means to be successful, and what its relationship will be with the rest of humanity. Similar to how the British monarchy can only renew itself if the next generation embraces the role that its predecessors expect them to play, American plutocracy can only continue if subsequent generations accept that norm. The question for rich white men, as I see it, is not whether change is coming, but rather whether we can develop the will to change so that we can be at peace after American society no longer characterizes us as superior.

I am heartened by change agents like Chad Dyer, a rich white man who shifted his focus from venture capital to galvanizing other wealthy white people to join him in signing the Good Life Pledge, a philanthropic commitment to transfer one-third of their families' assets to Black, brown, and Indigenous communities; Jason Franklin, who advises a number of progressive donors and change agents; Justin Haas, who cofounded Men For Equity and Reproductive Justice, which invites men to move past guilt and shame and support womxn- and BIPOC-led reproductive health and abortion rights organizations; Mike Gast and Adam Roberts, who have helped to grow Resource Generation into a major force for progressive change; and Chris Westcott, who educates other donors through his staff position at the Solidaire Network.

And of course, I'm not only talking about rich white men as sources of inspiration. I'm inspired by people like Alicia Bell, whose Media 2070 initiative is holding the media accountable for repairing the harm biased reporting has caused throughout history; Honor Keeler, a citizen of the Cherokee Nation who is starting a new nonprofit to support Indigenous ceremonial leaders, Indigenous women, and Indigenous-led research; Takeo Rivera, who is reimagining the future of Asian American identity at Boston University; Jessica Salinas, who leads New Media Ventures' investing in progressive start-ups; Michael Tubbs, who pioneered the first mayor-led guaranteed income program and is now leading an initiative to end poverty in California; Erika Uyterhoeven, who is bringing the combined wisdom of her Harvard Business School degree and appreciation of Democratic Socialism to her elected seat in Massachusetts's House of Representatives; Jean Willoughby, a white woman from Arkansas who has trained thirty thousand people at the Racial Equity Institute and is a leader in recruiting low-wealth white people into class solidarity across racial lines; and so many other young people who are choosing to live and contribute differently.[3]

One of the things I learned from reading activist Mariame Kaba's 2021 book *We Do This 'Til We Free Us* is that hope is a discipline.[4] It's something we choose to believe in and need to practice day after day. "What gives me hope," scholar Ibram Kendi says in *How to Be an Antiracist*, "is a simple truism. Once we lose hope, we are guaranteed to lose. But if we ignore the odds...then we give humanity a chance to one day survive, a chance to live in communion, a chance to be forever free."[5]

When my brother Gaven died, it was a horrible and tragic loss. I won't call it a silver lining, because no one deserves to die for anyone else's benefit. Still, it's the truth that the adversity I experienced granted me the wisdom that life is precious at an unusually young age. Three decades after Gaven's death, I still think about how every life is precious and how my own life is too valuable to commit my waking hours toward other rich white men's quests for wealth and power.

I have seen other rich white men learn this lesson much later in life, like a mentor who was being groomed to become CEO of one of America's most influential companies, until cancer reoriented him toward his family and social change. For most of the rich white men I've met, the insight that wealth and power is not what matters most seems to come late in life, if at all. "I think everybody should get rich and famous and do everything they ever dreamed of," Jim Carrey is often credited with saying, "so they can see that it's not the answer."

In his 2021 book *4000 Weeks*, Robert Bosman reminds us that human beings—at least the advantaged and fortunate among us—arrive from the womb with about four thousand weeks on this planet.[6] As we progress through life, that figure quickly dwindles to three thousand, two thousand, one thousand. Wasting even one of those weeks is regrettable; wasting hundreds or thousands is a travesty. On their deathbeds, people rarely if ever say they wish they'd worked harder; instead, they wish they had been truer to themselves, had the courage to express their feelings, stayed in touch with friends, and let themselves be happier.[7]

In my efforts to reimagine what philosophers call "the good life," I have redefined what success and happiness look like for myself. As I've sought to shed toxic entitlement and nurture healthy entitlement, my relationships with my spouse and friends have deepened. I am closer to being at peace with my brother's death. My anxiety is melting away. I've learned things about my ancestors that my parents never planned to tell me, which would have been lost forever. I stand up for myself and what I believe more, but I also cause less harm. In short, I'm starting to feel *free*.

As a rich white man, I've only felt an enduring sense of imposter syndrome during my work to advance social justice. It was humbling, while I was putting the finishing touches on this manuscript, to receive feedback from a more seasoned white male activist that perhaps I didn't have the necessary experience to write this book. It was also humbling to receive feedback around the same time from Indigenous activists that Indigenous wisdom was underrepresented in this book. It's scary and disappointing to know that this book will inevitably fall short in important ways, but I am committed to repairing any harm I may cause and trust that this project is just one step in my own journey and a tiny speck in our collective journey toward justice.

During most of the time I've spent writing this book, I've been working alongside my pregnant wife and now our baby boy, Ayan. When I look at the world through Ayan's twenty-one-month-old eyes, I can tell he perceives the world as safe. He smiles at everyone he meets, seeming to believe that all people are good and that the society that surrounds him can be trusted. Ayan's optimism inspires me, but it also saddens me, because I know the world is not as safe or supportive as he imagines it to be. As he grows up, I could pour my energy into maximizing his unearned advantages, which would help to protect him in a violent world. However, I've come to believe that the world that is most likely to protect his safety, sense of self, and well-being is an equitable one.

A world with fewer bullies and manipulators and more people who nurture his true self, even and especially if the pronouns "he/him" get in the way of that. A world where there isn't so much inequality that he feels overwhelming pressure in school and work to sacrifice the many wonderful gifts of life, so he can cling to his rung on the ladder. A world where he doesn't become addicted to taking more than his share of the world's resources, because society tells him he deserves it and because marketers tell him that buying what he wants will meet his needs. A world where every purchase he makes is not complicated by the painful knowledge that his consumerism is subsidized by systems of oppression. A world where if he is harmed, individuals and institutions will make a sincere effort to repair his wounds instead of denying that the harm occurred. A world where he can express when he is sad or scared and, if need be, get the support he needs before that sadness or fear overwhelms him. A world where he can lead others in ways that feel authentic to him and embrace the humbling notion that every person—and every culture—brings leadership and wisdom he can learn from and follow. A world where, at work and home, he doesn't have to choose between being dominant or dominated.

Collective traumas like George Floyd's murder and the COVID-19 pandemic have horrified us, but they have also reminded us that we are interdependent, that we are all in this together. As we become sensitized to our collective vulnerabilities, many of us are just starting to feel the pain of millions of voices, including our own. Will those of us with sufficient advantages to have the choice keep medicating our fears, or will we replace toxic entitlement with healthy entitlement?

We rich white men are socialized to believe we're entitled to compounding unearned advantages and the bodies of countless human beings, none of which we deserve. But we are also taught that we aren't entitled to things we do deserve—like the ability to develop trusting and intimate relationships, prioritize our mental and physical health, heal from trauma, express our emotions and have them validated, maintain a connection with our ancestral and cultural roots beyond whiteness, and reclaim access to our true selves and the sense of belonging we seek.

In mysticism, a central idea is that every one of us already belongs.[8] If we feel we don't belong, the mystics have said, it is only because of the social constructs that envelop us. Like Michelangelo's *David*, which was carved from a single block of marble that Michelangelo had recovered after every other sculptor had rejected it, our true selves are inside of us; we just need to be committed to them and peel back all the layers.

As rich white men, we need to reclaim our humanity. To love ourselves enough to believe we deserve healing. To not be so numb that we feel we must rely on the spoils of extreme wealth and power to feel alive. To abandon our posts as the soldiers and generals of empire and reclaim our roles as husbands, dads, brothers, friends, and stewards of the collective good and our planet.

Power over others isn't freedom. Trying to play God can be exhilarating and cloak our insecurities, but the first step to freedom is acknowledging and accepting that we're human—that we have limits, which include the reality that we wither away when we feel isolated and alone. True freedom is being surrounded by a community of people who love you unconditionally, prioritize your needs, support your dreams, celebrate your uniqueness, and value your humanity.

After all, a unique and valuable human being is all each of us is— nothing more, nothing less.

ABOUT THIS BOOK'S RELATIONSHIP WITH WEALTH AND POWER

About This Book's Relationship with Wealth

I recognize that publishing a book is a commercial endeavor and that any profits from this book's sales could further consolidate wealth in white male hands. To guard against that, I'm transforming what would have been my ownership of author royalties into a royalties cooperative. By embedding community governance and ownership, I am attempting to align the book with its values (including abundance, accountability, interdependence, and reciprocity) and its aspirations (including collective liberation, fractal design, reparations, and a solidarity economy).

Author royalties beyond the advance, which financed my labor to write the book, are being divided into six equal shares. I hold one of those shares (16.7 percent of the total); the remaining six shares (83.3 percent of the total) are held by six activists, either personally or on behalf of organizations they are affiliated with. In addition to receiving a share of author royalties in perpetuity, each cooperative partner received a $5,000 honorarium—which was funded by Chad and Tenah Dyer as part of their commitment to the Good Life Pledge—and is acknowledged as a formal partner in the book and the book's website. I am excited to collaborate with these partners within the framework of democratic, relational governance, in light of the fact that publishing this book is an exercise of power and therefore needs accountability partners.

Cooperative partners include the following:

- Sandy Banks, a Black female journalist who has been involved in this project from its early stages and served as my writing coach throughout this process. I feel that Sandy's contributions warrant an equity stake in this project since it was only because of her that I was able to submit a book proposal of sufficient quality to attract backing from WME and Hachette; she also made countless positive contributions to the manuscript in the biggest and smallest of ways.

- allen kwabena frimpong, a cultural strategist, cooperative entrepreneur, and resource mobilizer who has advised my efforts to redistribute wealth and power including by serving as a cocreator of this book's royalties cooperative. Allen is representing ZEAL, a worker-owned creative agency and social-impact collaborative that develops emerging cultural strategies to build equity for community and has been active in the US reparations movement.

- Jasmine Gomez, an attorney, activist, and pioneer in the field of social-justice philanthropy who has helped to nurture my belief in the transformative power of worker-self-directed nonprofits. Jasmine is representing RESIST, a public foundation founded in 1967 that supports people's movements for justice and liberation.

- Erin Heaney and Ava Bynum, whose organizing has helped to inspire my activism and helped me gain clarity about what I might contribute given the advantages I hold. Erin and Ava are representing Showing Up for Racial Justice, which is a national network of groups and individuals organizing white people for racial and economic justice.

- Honor Keeler and Melody Talcott, activists and citizens of Cherokee Nation who supported this project with invaluable wisdom and guidance. Melody and Honor are representing Honor the Old Ways, an entity that supports Indigenous ceremonial leaders, Indigenous women, and Indigenous-led research, as well as the movement of land, wealth, and resources back to Indigenous communities.

- Chris Westcott, one of the donor organizers who inspired Pooja's and my ten-year commitment to the Movement for Black Lives. Chris is representing the Solidaire Network, a donor community that mobilizes critical resources to racial, gender, and climate justice movements.

About This Book's Relationship with Power

The writing and publishing of this book relies on the advantages and access I've had that are uniquely available to me as an elite-educated white man raised in a wealthy American family, which by definition makes this book an exercise of power. In choosing to exercise that power, my intention is to leverage my advantages and access to collaborate in solidarity with marginalized peoples toward the creation of an equitable America and world.

Since I believe that anyone who exercises power has a responsibility to be accountable to those who may be impacted, I have taken steps to ensure I am supported by many people and organizations who are holding me to my commitments. Those relationships include a diverse group of friends and colleagues who read drafts and provided feedback, including several Black and Indigenous activists who received honorariums for their contributions; allen kwabena frimpong, a pioneer in social justice philanthropy who is advising me on this project and has consent rights for major decisions related to the royalties collaborative; and my publisher, Krishan Trotman, one of the highest-ranking Black women in Big 5 publishing and the head of Legacy Lit, an imprint of Hachette that is focused on social justice and primarily publishes BIPOC authors. Throughout this process, Krishan has guided me to speak as much as possible from my own experience, not on behalf of activists who have their own stories to tell and can make many points far better than I ever could.

That said, I know that intentions don't always align with impact and that good intentions are often not enough. If my contributions or behaviors do not appear aligned with my stated goals, please share that feedback with me, privately or publicly. And if you feel that any of my actions or words—through this book or otherwise—have harmed you or communities you are part of, please encourage me to be accountable.

TEN ACTIONS THE ADVANTAGED CAN TAKE TO HELP CONSTRUCT AN EQUITABLE AMERICA

1. **Learn more about your ancestral roots,** both the hardships they endured so you could have a better life and how they may have been complicit in or directly involved in upholding an unjust system. If your ancestors enslaved people, reach out to Lotte Dula for guidance about processing that experience and making amends. If they had a connection to spirituality, learn more about why that connection was important to them and consider restoring any aspects of that connection that you've previously lost.

2. **Conduct a family equity audit.** Add up the hours that everyone spends on household responsibilities (e.g., childcare, animal care, chores, finances, planning, etc.); then discuss as a family whether responsibilities are allocated equitably and what changes might be made. Make a list of service providers (e.g., nanny, house cleaner, grocery delivery, Uber, etc.); pay them all significantly more, to try to account for the fact that the "market wage" is unlikely to be the wage such workers would accept if America's systems were not oppressive.

3. **Join an organization that equips advantaged people to work in collaborative solidarity toward social justice** (e.g., Liberated Capital, Liberation Ventures, Men for Equity and Reproductive Justice, Movement Voter Project, Patriotic Millionaires, Resource Generation, Showing Up for Racial Justice, Solidaire Network, Way to Win, Working Families Party). If you're a white man, also join an organization that supports that demographic (e.g., Breaking the Mold, Organizing White Men for Collective Liberation, Support Genius, White Men for Racial Justice).

4. **Join your institution's diversity, equity, and inclusion committee.** Build trusting relationships across differences, practice both the

"listen and support" and "leverage your advantages" approaches, and periodically ask colleagues from marginalized backgrounds whether you're striking that balance effectively. Encourage your institution to compensate individuals from marginalized backgrounds who are leading that work.

5. **Divest from wealth hoarding.** Think critically about the level of assets that your family truly needs; then, consider if it might be possible to halve that figure. If you already have more than you need, make a plan to give the rest away; relinquish control over how resources are allocated, too. If you are involved with any grant-making foundations, encourage those institutions to spend out their resources over a fixed period of time, instead of existing in perpetuity.

6. **Dramatically increase your personal philanthropic and political giving.** Ask yourself if you can afford to give away twice as much, or five times as much, or ten times as much money as you currently do; if you can, do it. Make long-term (5+ years) and unrestricted donations to organizations, or become a monthly donor who sustains organizations in perpetuity. Support Black and Indigenous organizations and politicians whose politics are more radical than your own, since they sit in a different place in the ecosystem, and don't shy away simply because you disagree with some details in their platform.

7. **Map your sphere of influence, then engage that sphere of influence intentionally.** Identify who you are uniquely well suited to influence (e.g., family members, friends, institutions you are affiliated with). Serve as a "bridge builder," meeting them where they are at. Learn to ask family and friends for money and other resources like other people's lives depend on it, because they do. Lead by example: influence more with your actions, and less with your words.

8. **Reconnect with your body and emotions.** Explore whether intergenerational trauma runs through your family, as well as whether you have been exposed to any toxic relationship styles (e.g., codependence, narcissism). Consider engaging a therapist, and a trauma therapist specifically if need be. Try self-care practices like journaling and mindfulness. If you're not sleeping enough, sleep more. If you're

not exercising regularly, make it a priority. Get clear on what healthy boundaries look like, and become attuned to your body as a source of wisdom for maintaining healthy boundaries.

9. **Complete Michael and Megan Hyatt's LifeScore Assessment (https:// assessments.fullfocus.co/lifescore/)**, which analyzes your satisfaction with ten professional and personal domains of your life. Then take what you learn and dedicate more time and energy to domains you value but are neglecting.

10. **Practice treating every human being as an equal.** Listen more and talk less. If you currently dominate some conversations, kick the habit. Work extra hard to share space with those who are "lower status" (e.g., children, direct reports, mentees, and people from marginalized backgrounds). Adopt consent-based decision making within your family and/or institutions you are affiliated with; if you need support with making the transition to consent-based decision making, take a sociocracy training or hire Circle Forward.

ACKNOWLEDGMENTS

This book reflects the wisdom and contributions of far more people to a far greater degree than I could have ever imagined when I started working on this project.

There are some obvious suspects who have influenced me and this book: My ancestors, who helped me understand that part of who I am is where I've come from. My parents, who bestowed the irreplaceable gift of unconditional love and encouraged me to pursue my passions. My sister, Gracie, whose early life experience gave me my first glimpse into how unequal our world is and what it means to practice equity. My brothers Dave, Gaven, Griffin, and Justin, who have taught me so much, including how different our lived experiences can be despite our shared upbringing and similar set of advantages and disadvantages. I love you all.

My spouse, Pooja, who changed the course of my life forever when we became friends in 2002. She gave me time and space to work on this book, even when that significantly increased her share of our familial duties. Her support and insight made this book possible, and infinitely better. Pooja, you have been my most important collaborator for defining, imagining, and practicing what equitable and lifelong partnership looks and feels like. I love you, Peezy.

My son, Ayan, who has already in his first two years in the world transformed my life for the better. Ayan, you inspire me with your love and trust, which has strengthened my resolve to participate in building a world that meets everyone's needs, including yours. I love you, AyMo.

I'd also like to thank my many teachers, who have supported my ability to see more clearly: Patrick Harnett, my high school AP US history teacher, who ignited my passion for history and restored my confidence that I had something to offer after I had veered off course academically. My Stanford friends, who helped me recognize the vast differences in our lived experiences. Tiq, I'm especially grateful to you for teaching me so much; you've changed the direction of my life for the better multiple times. My Harvard professor Dr. Khalil Gibran Muhammad, who was the first person to enable me to see with clarity how systems of oppression function in the United States. My Harvard professor Dr. Ron Heifetz, who encouraged me to reconnect with my ancestry and helped me understand what it really takes to advance social change. My friend and mentor Abraham Lateiner, who taught me the value of affinity spaces and was the first to inspire me to reconnect with my feelings and body. My colleagues at CollegeSpring and Liberation Ventures—especially my cofounders, Jessica Perez, Aria Florant, and allen kwabena frimpong—who taught me much of what I know about leadership, power, and working across differences. The activists, leaders, and experts I've met who are fighting for racial justice and repair, including Alicia Bell, Nicole Carty, Ron Daniels, Sandy Darity, Angela Glover Blackwell, Dreisen Heath, Michael McAfee, Andre Perry, Nkechi Taifa, Kavon Ward, and Ed Whitfield, among so many others. My therapists, who have helped me make sense of my past, heal from trauma, recover my sense of self, and correct distortions I had internalized. Countless authors I've never met whose brilliance, courage, and wisdom have influenced me. I am especially grateful to Kimberle Crenshaw, Angela Davis, bell hooks, and Peggy McIntosh—whose historical contributions greatly influenced my approach—as well as Robin DiAngelo, Anand Giridharadas, Ibram Kendi, Ijeoma Oluo, and Edgar Villanueva, whose recent contributions particularly inspired what I might be able to offer in this moment.

Then there are those who made direct contributions to this book: Those who saw the potential for what this book could become, back when my ideas were only seedlings, including Patti Bellinger, a Harvard professor who supervised an independent study so I could explore the compounding unearned advantage concept; Dr. Khalil Gibran Muhammad, who helped shape many of this book's ideas; Shirley Leung at the *Boston Globe*, who saw value in an early iteration of the compounding unearned advantages concept; Darren Walker at the Ford Foundation, who funded the background research that laid the analytical foundation for this book; my Harvard Business School professor Laura Huang, who shared her book proposal with me so I would have a road map; business executive and philanthropist Sheryl Sandberg, who introduced me to her literary agency, WME; journalist Sandy Banks, my incredible writing coach, who helped me craft the initial proposal and edit the book; and Robin DiAngelo and allen kwabena frimpong, who contributed a wonderful foreword and introduction, to this book.

I also want to thank those who were instrumental in this book becoming a reality: Mel Berger, my agent at WME, who has been an incredible advocate every step of the way, including taking seriously every silly first-time author question I've had; Krishan Trotman, publisher at Legacy Lit, who took a chance on this project and helped me see that this book was really about challenging myths generated in the halls of power; editor Emi Ikkanda, who made innumerable contributions to this book, including a vision for structuring this book in a way that made every page better; the entire team at Hachette Book Group and the publicity firm DEY., who have played an essential role toward getting this book into the hands of readers; Sandy Banks, who took me on "low-bono" as a writing coach client because of her belief in me and this project; and University of Michigan undergraduate student Irving Peña, who took on the crucial tasks of documenting the hundreds of sources that underpin this book and creating the accompanying resource list.

I appreciate those who took the time to read some or all of the manuscript and provide feedback. That includes many of the people I've listed above as well as Alicia Bell, Manoshi Datta, Stephanie Epps, Holly Fetter, Tom Friel, Avichal Garg, Honor Keeler, Larry Kubal, Abraham Lateiner, Ulysses Lateiner, Raffi Mardirosian, Martha Minow, Shazad Mohamed, Kaveh Navab, Chris Olin, Tia Oso, Bev Plass, Adam Roberts, Oren Robinson, Gene Sykes, Melody Talcott, Jean Willoughby, Liz Yates, and participants in the focus group that Jay Gilbert organized with members of the White Men for Racial Justice community. Every one of you made this manuscript better.

And finally, one last shoutout to Pooja. Thank you for everything!

RESOURCE LIST

Below is a partial list of books and organizations that have influenced how I think about inequality and how it might be addressed. I do not intend to convey that what I've included in this list is superior to what I haven't: many inspiring thinkers and organizations are outside my awareness, while in other cases my exposure has been too limited to claim they've influenced me.

Books

Alderman, Naomi. *The Power.* New York: Viking, 2016.

Armah, Esther A. *Emotional Justice: A Roadmap for Racial Healing.* Oakland, CA: Berrett-Koehler Publishers, 2022.

Aron, Elaine N. *The Highly Sensitive Person: How to Thrive When the World Overwhelms You.* New York: Kensington, 1997.

Banaji, Mahzarin R. and Anthony G. Greenwald. *Blindspot: Hidden Biases of Good People.* New York: Delacorte, 2013.

Bonilla-Silva, Eduardo. *Racism without Racists: Color-Blind Racism and the Persistence of Racial Inequality in America.* 6th ed. Lanham, MD: Rowman and Littlefield, 2022.

Brod, Harry, Emmett Schaeffer, and Cooper Thompson. *White Men Challenging Racism: 35 Personal Stories.* Durham: Duke University Press, 2003.

brown, adrienne m. *Emergent Strategy: Shaping Change, Changing Worlds.* Chico, CA: AK Press, 2017.

Cain, Susan. *Quiet: The Power of Introverts in a World That Can't Stop Talking.* New York: Broadway Paperbacks, 2013.

Chamorro-Premuzic, Tomas. *Why Do So Many Incompetent Men Become Leaders? (And How to Fix It).* Boston: Harvard Business Review Press, 2019.

Clayton, Philip et al. *The New Possible: Visions of Our World Beyond Crisis.* Eugene, Oregon: Cascade Press, 2021.

Collins, Chuck. *Born on Third Base: A One Percenter Makes the Case for Tackling Inequality, Bringing Wealth Home, and Committing to the Common Good.* White River Junction, VT: Chelsea Green, 2016.

Crass, Chris. *Towards Collective Liberation: Anti-Racist Organizing, Feminist Praxis, and Movement Building Strategy.* Oakland: PM Press, 2013.

Crenshaw, Kimberle. *Critical Race Theory: The Key Writings That Formed the Movement.* New York: The New Press, 1995.

Criado Perez, Caroline. *Invisible Women: Data Bias in a World Designed for Men.* New York: Abrams, 2019.

Darity, Sandy and Kirsten A. Mullen. *From Here to Equality: Reparations for Black Americans in the Twenty-First Century.* Chapel Hill: UNC Press, 2020.

Davis, Angela. *Women, Race and Class.* New York: Vintage Books, 1981.

DiAngelo, Robin. *White Fragility: Why It's So Hard for White People to Talk About Racism.* Boston: Beacon Press, 2018.

Giridharadas, Anand. *Winners Take All: The Elite Charade of Changing the World.* New York: Alfred A. Knopf, 2019.

hooks, bell. *The Will to Change: Men, Masculinity, and Love.* New York: Atria, 2005.

Howes, Lewis. *The Mask of Masculinity: How Men Can Embrace Vulnerability, Create Strong Relationships, and Live Their Fullest Lives.* New York: Rodale, 2017.

Ignatiev, Noel. *How the Irish Became White.* New York: Routledge, 2009.

Kendi, Ibram X. *How to Be an Antiracist.* New York: One World, 2019.

Kimmel, Michael. *Angry White Men: American Masculinity at the End of an Era.* New York: Nation Books, 2013.

King, Martin Luther, Jr. *Where Do We Go from Here: Chaos or Community?* Boston: Beacon, 2010.

Laloux, Frederic. *Reinventing Organizations: A Guide to Creating Organizations Inspired by the Next Stage of Human Consciousness.* Brussels: Nelson Parker, 2014.

Levine, Peter. *Waking the Tiger: Healing Trauma.* Berkeley: North Atlantic Books, 1997.

MacLean, Nancy. *Democracy in Chains: The Deep History of the Radical Right's Stealth Plan for America.* New York: Penguin, 2017.

Mayer, Jane. *Dark Money: The Hidden History of the Billionaires behind the Rise of the Radical Right.* New York: Anchor, 2017.

Menakem, Resmaa. *My Grandmother's Hands: Racialized Trauma and the Pathway to Mending Our Hearts and Bodies.* Las Vegas: Central Recovery Press, 2017.

Mock, Janet. *Redefining Realness: My Path to Womanhood, Identity, Love, and So Much More.* New York: Atria, 2014.

Muhammad, Khalil Gibran. *The Condemnation of Blackness: Race, Crime, and the Making of Modern Urban America.* Boston: Harvard University Press, 2019.

Oluo, Ijeoma. *Mediocre: The Dangerous Legacy of White Male America.* New York: Seal Press, 2020.

Pittelman, Karen. *Classified: How to Stop Hiding Your Privilege and Use It for Social Change!* New York: Soft Skull, 2006.

Saez, Emmanuel, and Gabriel Zucman. *The Triumph of Injustice: How the Rich Dodge Taxes and How to Make Them Pay.* New York: W. W. Norton, 2019.

Saunders, Claire, Hazel Songhurst, Georgia Amson-Bradshaw, Minna Salami, and Mik Scarlet. *The Power Book: What Is It, Who Has It, and Why?* Brooklyn, NY: Ivy Kids, 2019.

Schulman, Sarah. *Conflict Is Not Abuse: Overstating Harm, Community Responsibility, and the Duty of Repair.* Vancouver: Arsenal Pulp, 2016.

Shapiro, Thomas M. *Toxic Inequality: How America's Wealth Gap Destroys Mobility, Deepens the Racial Divide, and Threatens Our Future.* New York: Basic Books, 2017.

Stone, Douglas, Bruce Patton, and Sheila Heen, *Difficult Conversations: How to Discuss What Matters Most.* New York: Penguin, 2010.

Tawwab, Nedra Glover. *Set Boundaries, Find Peace: A Guide to Reclaiming Yourself.* New York: TarcherPerigee, 2021.

van der Kolk, Bessel. *The Body Keeps the Score: Brain, Mind, and Body in the Healing of Trauma.* New York: Penguin, 2015.

Villanueva, Edgar. *Decolonizing Wealth: Indigenous Wisdom to Heal Divides and Restore Balance.* Oakland, CA: Berrett-Koehler, 2018.

Organizations

Armah Institute of Emotional Justice. https://www.theaiej.com/.

Breaking the Mold. https://breakingthemold.community/.

Building Belonging. https://www.buildingbelonging.us/.

Circle Forward. https://circleforward.us/.

Critical Resistance. https://criticalresistance.org/.

Demos. https://www.demos.org/.

Economic Security Project. https://www.economicsecurityproject.org/.

Emergent Fund. https://emergentfund.net/.

Fight for IS. https://fightforIS.org/.

FirstRepair. https://firstrepair.org/.

Fund for Reparations NOW! https://www.fundforreparationsnow.org/.

Grantmakers for Girls of Color. https://grantmakersforgirlsofcolor.org/.

Groundswell Fund. https://groundswellfund.org/.

Institute for Policy Studies. https://ips-dc.org/.

Just Economy Institute. justeconomyinstitute.org/.

JustFund. https://justfund.us/.

Justice Funders. https://justicefunders.org/.

Kataly Foundation. https://www.katalyfoundation.org/.

Liberated Capital. https://decolonizingwealth.com/liberated-capital/.

Liberation Ventures. https://www.liberationventures.org/.

ManKind Project. https://mankindproject.org/.

Mayors for a Guaranteed Income. https://www.mayorsforagi.org/.

Media 2070. https://mediareparations.org/.

Movement for Black Lives. https://m4bl.org.

Movement Voter Project. https://movement.vote/.

National African American Reparations Commission. https://reparationscomm.org/.

National Black Food & Justice Alliance. https://www.blackfoodjustice.org/.

National Coalition of Blacks for Reparations in America. http://ncobra.org/.

New Media Ventures. https://www.newmediaventures.org/.

NDN Collective. https://ndncollective.org/.

Omidyar Network. https://omidyar.com/.

One Fair Wage. https://onefairwage.site/.

One for Democracy. https://onefordemocracy.org/.

One Project. https://oneproject.org/.

Opportunity Insights. https://opportunityinsights.org/.

Organizing White Men for Collective Liberation. https://www.owmcl.org/.

Othering & Belonging Institute. https://belonging.berkeley.edu/.

Patriotic Millionaires. https://patrioticmillionaires.org/.

PolicyLink. https://www.policylink.org/.

Poor People's Campaign. https://www.poorpeoplescampaign.org/.

Project Truth, Reconciliation, and Reparations. https://www.projecttruthandrec.org/.

Prosperity Now. https://prosperitynow.org/.

Racial Equity Institute. https://racialequityinstitute.org/.

Relational Uprising. https://relationaluprising.org/.

Reparations 4 Slavery. https://reparations4slavery.com/.

Reparation Education Project. https://www.reparationeducationproject.org/.

Reparations Summer. https://reparationssummer.com/.

RESIST. https://resist.org/.

Resource Generation. https://resourcegeneration.org/.

Roosevelt Institute. https://rooseveltinstitute.org/.

Seed Commons. https://seedcommons.org/.

Showing Up for Racial Justice. https://surj.org/.

Solidaire Network. https://solidairenetwork.org/.

Stanford Center on Poverty and Inequality. https://inequality.stanford.edu/.

Support Genius. https://supportgenius.org/.

Third Wave Fund. https://thirdwavefund.org/index.html/.

United for a Fair Economy. https://www.faireconomy.org/.

United States Solidarity Economy Network. https://ussen.org/.

Way to Win. https:///www.waytowin.us/.

White Men for Racial Justice. https://wmrj.us.hivebrite.com/.

Working Families Party. https://workingfamilies.org/.

ZEAL. https://zeal.coop/.

ENDNOTES

Preface

1. Jake Intrator, Jonathan Tannen, and Douglas S. Massey, "Segregation by Race and Income in the United States 1970–2010," *Social Science Research* 60 (November 2016): 45–60, https://doi.org/10.1016/j.ssresearch.2016.08.003.
2. Chase Peterson-Withorn, "How Much Money America's Billionaires Have Made during the Covid-19 Pandemic," *Forbes*, April 30, 2021, https://www.forbes.com/sites/chasewithorn/2021/04/30/american-billionaires-have-gotten-12-trillion-richer-during-the-pandemic/.
3. "Economic Inequality Basics," Cabon Tax Center, April 2021, https://www.carbontax.org/economic-inequality-basics/.
4. Ben Steverman, "Baby Boomers Are Thriving on an 'Unprecedented' $9-Trillion Inheritance," *Financial Post*, November 19, 2019, https://financialpost.com/personal-finance/baby-boomers-are-thriving-on-an-unprecedented-9-trillion-inheritance.
5. Nick Fortuna, "'Stark Inequality' Points to Retirement Struggles for Many Americans," *Barron's*, September 21, 2021, https://www.barrons.com/articles/generational-racial-wealth-gap-retirement-struggles-51632154247; Pooneh Baghai, Olivia Howard, Lakshmi Prakash, and Jill Zucker, "Women as the Next Wave of Growth in US Wealth Management," McKinsey & Company, July 29, 2020, https://www.mckinsey.com/industries/financial-services/our-insights/women-as-the-next-wave-of-growth-in-us-wealth-management.

Chapter 1: Compounding Unearned Advantage

1. "Power and Privilege," *SAFS Diversity, Equity, and Inclusion Blog*, University of Washington, July 16, 2021, https://sites.uw.edu/safs-dei/2021/07/16/power-and-privilege/.
2. "Basic Statistics," Talk Poverty, Center for American Progress, accessed September 5, 2022, https://talkpoverty.org/basics/.
3. Scott H. Decker, Cassia Spohn, Natalie R. Ortiz, and Eric Hedberg, *Criminal Stigma, Race, Gender, and Employment: An Expanded Assessment of the Consequences of Imprisonment for Employment*, National Institute of Justice, 2010-MU-MU-004, accessed September 5, 2022, https://thecrimereport.s3.amazonaws.com/2/fb/e/2362/criminal_stigma_race_crime_and_unemployment.pdf; Matthew Biddle, "Men Are Still More Likely than Women to Be Perceived as Leaders, Study Finds," press release, University at Buffalo School of Management, August 6, 2018,

https://www.buffalo.edu/news/news-releases.host.html/content/shared/mgt/news/men-still-more-likely-than-women-perceived-leaders-study-finds.detail.html; Lauren Rivera and András Tilcsik, "Research: How Subtle Class Cues Can Backfire on Your Resume," *Harvard Business Review*, December 21, 2016, https://hbr.org/2016/12/research-how-subtle-class-cues-can-backfire-on-your-resume.

4. Bryan Hancock, Monne Williams, James Manyika, Lareina Lee, and Jackie Wong, *Race in the Workplace: Black Workers in the US Private Sector*, McKinsey & Company, February 21, 2021, https://www.mckinsey.com/featured-insights/diversity-and-inclusion/race-in-the-workplace-the-black-experience-in-the-us-private-sector.

5. "Fortune 500," *Fortune*, accessed September 5, 2022, https://fortune.com/fortune500/2022/.

6. Jill Rosen, "Teacher Expectations Reflect Racial Biases, Johns Hopkins Study Suggests," press release, Johns Hopkins University, March 30, 2016, https://hub.jhu.edu/2016/03/30/racial-bias-teacher-expectations-black-white/.

7. Seth Stephens-Davidowitz, "Google, Tell Me. Is My Son a Genius?," *New York Times*, January 18, 2014, https://www.nytimes.com/2014/01/19/opinion/sunday/google-tell-me-is-my-son-a-genius.html.

8. Alana Semuels, "White Flight Never Ended," *The Atlantic*, July 30, 2015, https://www.theatlantic.com/business/archive/2015/07/white-flight-alive-and-well/399980/.

9. C. E. Clark, "Poverty Kills More People Every Year in the U.S. Than Heart Disease or Cancer," Soapboxie, April 15, 2021, https://soapboxie.com/social-issues/Poverty-Kills-More-People-than-either-cancer-or-heart-disease.

10. Jan Ransom, "Amy Cooper Faces Charges after Calling Police on Black Bird-Watcher," *New York Times*, July 6, 2020, https://www.nytimes.com/2020/07/06/nyregion/amy-cooper-false-report-charge.html.

Chapter 2: Wealth and Opportunity

1. Matt Turner, "JAMIE DIMON: There Is a 'National Catastrophe' and 'We Should Be Ringing the Alarm Bells,'" *Business Insider*, May 8, 2017, https://www.businessinsider.com/jamie-dimon-interview-2017-5.

2. George B. Kaiser, pledge letter, Giving Pledge, July 26, 2010, https://givingpledge.org/pledger?pledgerId=220.

3. "Income Inequality in the United States," Inequality.org, accessed September 6, 2022, https://inequality.org/facts/income-inequality/.

4. Chad Stone, Danilo Trisi, Arloc Sherman, and Jennifer Beltrán, "A Guide to Statistics on Historical Trends in Income Inequality," Center on Budget and Policy Priorities, January 13, 2020, https://www.cbpp.org/research/poverty-and-inequality/a-guide-to-statistics-on-historical-trends-in-income-inequality.

5. Jeff Cox, "CEOs See Pay Grow 1,000% in the Last 40 Years, Now Make 278 Times the Average Worker," CNBC, August 16, 2019, https://www.cnbc.com/2019/08/16

/ceos-see-pay-grow-1000percent-and-now-make-278-times-the-average-worker
.html.

6. Juliana Menasce Horowitz, Ruth Igielnik, and Rakesh Kochhar, "1. Trends in Income and Wealth Inequality," in *Most Americans Say There Is Too Much Economic Inequality in the U.S., but Fewer Than Half Call It a Top Priority*, Pew Research Center, January 9, 2020, https://www.pewresearch.org/social-trends /2020/01/09/trends-in-income-and-wealth-inequality/.

7. Josh Bivens, William J. Barber II, Liz Theoharis, and Shailly Gupta Barnes, "Moral Policy = Good Economics: What's Needed to Lift Up 140 Million Poor and Low-Income People Further Devastated by the Pandemic," *Working Economics Blog*, Economic Policy Institute, October 30, 2020, https://www.epi.org/blog /moral-policy-good-economics-whats-needed-to-lift-up-140-million-poor-and -low-income-people-further-devastated-by-the-pandemic/.

8. "Real and Nominal Value of the Federal Minimum Wage in the United States from 1938 to 2022," Statista, accessed September 6, 2022, https://www.statista.com /statistics/1065466/real-nominal-value-minimum-wage-us/.

9. Kevin Stankiewicz, "If You Want the American Dream, 'You Ought to Move to Canada,' Says Ford Foundation President," CNBC, October 18, 2019, https:// www.cnbc.com/2019/10/18/ford-foundations-darren-walker-the-american -dream-is-found-in-canada.html.

10. Masoud Movahed, "Why Is the U.S. Economy Not Growing Fast Enough?," World Economic Forum, November 11, 2015, https://www.weforum.org/agenda/2015/11 /why-is-the-u-s-economy-not-growing-fast-enough/.

11. Pew Research Center, *The Lost Decade of the Middle Class*, August 22, 2012, https:// www.pewresearch.org/social-trends/2012/08/22/the-lost-decade-of-the-middle-class/.

12. Michael Hout, "Social Mobility," *Pathways*, Special Issue 2019, Stanford Center on Poverty and Inequality, https://inequality.stanford.edu/sites/default/files/Path ways_SOTU_2019_SocialMobility.pdf.

13. Alex Davenport, Peter Levell, and David Sturrock, *Why Do Wealthy Parents Have Wealthy Children?*, Institute for Fiscal Studies, September 8, 2021, https://doi .org/10.1920/re.ifs.2021.0196.

14. "Distribution of Household Wealth in the U.S. Since 1989," Board of Governors of the Federal Reserve System, June 21, 2022, https://www.federalreserve .gov/releases/z1/dataviz/dfa/distribute/table/#quarter:129;series:Net%20worth; demographic:networth;population:all;units:shares; Robert Frank, "Soaring Markets Helped the Richest 1% Gain $6.5 Trillion in Wealth Last Year, According to the Fed," CNBC, April 1, 2022, https://www.cnbc.com/2022/04/01/richest-one -percent-gained-trillions-in-wealth-2021.html.

15. Credit Suisse Research Institute, *Global Wealth Report 2019*, October 2019, https:// www.credit-suisse.com/about-us/en/reports-research/global-wealth-report.html.

16. "Report: America's Income Inequality Is on Par with Russia's," CBS News, December 15, 2017, https://www.cbsnews.com/news/report-americas-income-inequality

-is-on-par-with-russias/; Enuga S. Reddy, "The Struggle against Apartheid: Lessons for Today's World," *UN Chronicle*, September 2007, https://www.un.org/en/chronicle/article/struggle-against-apartheid-lessons-todays-world.

17. Alexandre Tanzi and Mike Dorning, "Top 1% of U.S. Earners Now Hold More Wealth Than All of the Middle Class," *Bloomberg*, October 8, 2021, https://www.bloomberg.com/news/articles/2021-10-08/top-1-earners-hold-more-wealth-than-the-u-s-middle-class.

18. Paul Buchheit, "The Inequality to Be Suffered by Our Children," United Steelworkers blog, December 18, 2018, https://usw.org/blog/2018/the-inequality-to-be-suffered-by-our-children.

19. Nathaniel Lewis and Matt Bruenig, "The Wealthiest 1% Inherited an Average of $4.8 Million," People's Policy Project, October 10, 2017, https://www.peoplespolicyproject.org/2017/10/10/the-wealthiest-1-inherited-an-average-of-4-8-million/.

20. Shannon Moriarty, Mazher Ali, Brian Miller, Jessica Morneault, Tim Sullivan, and Michael Young, *Born on Third Base: What the Forbes 400 Really Says about Economic Equality and Opportunity in America*, United for a Fair Economy, September 17, 2012, https://www.faireconomy.org/born_on_third_base.

21. Richard Edwin Marriott and Nancy Marriott, pledge letter, Giving Pledge, November 25, 2013, https://givingpledge.org/pledger?pledgerId=237.

22. Jonathan Ping, "Charlie Munger: The First $100,000 Is the Most Difficult," *My Money Blog*, November 12, 2015, https://www.mymoneyblog.com/charlie-munger-the-first-100000-is-the-most-difficult.html.

23. Thomas J. Stanley and William D. Danko, *The Millionaire Next Door: The Surprising Secrets of America's Wealthy* (Lanham, Md: Taylor Trade Publishing, 2010).

24. Daphne A. Kenyon, Adam H. Langley, and Bethany P. Paquin, *Rethinking Property Tax Incentives for Business* (Cambridge, MA: Lincoln Institute of Land Policy, 2012).

25. "Foundation," Woodside School District, accessed September 6, 2022, https://www.woodsideschool.us/Foundation/.

26. "How Much It Really Costs to Send Your Kid to an Elite College," *Town & Country*, June 28, 2017, https://www.townandcountrymag.com/society/money-and-power/a10207129/cost-of-college/.

27. Gregor Aisch, Larry Buchanan, Amanda Cox, and Kevin Quealy, "Some Colleges Have More Students from the Top 1 Percent Than the Bottom 60. Find Yours," *New York Times*, January 18, 2017, https://www.nytimes.com/interactive/2017/01/18/upshot/some-colleges-have-more-students-from-the-top-1-percent-than-the-bottom-60.html.

28. "How Place Matters for Chicagoans' Economic Mobility," Chicago Community Trust, August 9, 2016, https://www.cct.org/stories/how-place-matters-for-chicagoans-economic-mobility/.

29. "DuPage County Named Most Expensive Housing Market in Illinois," NBC Chicago, April 9, 2018, https://www.nbcchicago.com/news/local/most-expensive-housing-market-illinois-dupage-county/43488/.

30. "Housing Near High-Performing Public Schools Costs 2.4 Times More than Housing near Low-Performing Public Schools," National Low Income Housing Coalition, November 12, 2018, https://nlihc.org/resource/housing-near-high-performing-public-schools-costs-24-times-more-housing-near-low.

31. "Ending Separation through Zoning, Housing, Transportation, and School Integration," *National Civic Review* 110, no. 3 (2021), https://www.national civicleague.org/ncr-article/ending-separation-through-zoning-housing-transpor tation-and-school-integration/.

32. "Fast Facts: Educational Institutions," National Center for Education Statistics, accessed September 6, 2022, https://nces.ed.gov/fastfacts/display.asp?id=84; Veda Burman, "Stanford University Acceptance Rate," Collegedunia, February 17, 2020, https://collegedunia.com/usa/article/c-2074-stanford-university-acceptance -rate.

33. Emmie Martin, "Here's How Many Millennials Got Money from Their Parents to Buy Their Homes," CNBC, March 12, 2019, https://www.cnbc.com/2019/03/11 /how-many-millennials-got-money-to-buy-homes-from-their-parents.html.

34. Anya Martin, "How Parents Can Help with Jumbo Mortgages," *Wall Street Journal*, November 12, 2015, https://www.wsj.com/articles/how-parents-can-help-with -a-home-loan-1447342246.

35. "Mortgage Interest Deduction Is Ripe for Reform," Center on Budget and Policy Priorities, June 25, 2013, https://www.cbpp.org/research/mortgage-interest -deduction-is-ripe-for-reform.

36. Ezra Levin, Jeremie Greer, and Ida Rademacher, *From Upside Down to Right-Side Up: Redeploying $540 Billion in Federal Spending to Help All Families Save, Invest, and Build Wealth*, Corporation for Enterprise Development, 2014, 26, https:// prosperitynow.org/files/resources/Upside_Down_to_Right-Side_Up_2014.pdf.

37. "Policy Basics: Federal Tax Expenditures," Center on Budget and Policy Priorities, December 8, 2020, https://www.cbpp.org/research/federal-tax/federal-tax -expenditures.

38. Thomas M. Shapiro, *Toxic Inequality: How America's Wealth Gap Destroys Mobility, Deepens the Racial Divide, and Threatens Our Future* (New York: Basic, 2017).

39. Grace Enda and William G. Gale, "How Could Changing Capital Gains Taxes Raise More Revenue?," *Up Front* (blog), Brookings Institution, January 14, 2020, https://www.brookings.edu/blog/up-front/2020/01/14/how-could-changing -capital-gains-taxes-raise-more-revenue/.

40. Ashlea Ebeling, "IRS Announces 2016 Estate and Gift Tax Limits: The $10.9 Million Tax Break," *Forbes*, October 22, 2015, https://www.forbes.com/sites /ashleaebeling/2015/10/22/irs-announces-2016-estate-and-gift-tax-limits-the -10-9-million-tax-break/.

41. Taylor Nicole Rogers, "Meet Bill Ackman, the Controversial Hedge-Fund Manager Who Made $2.6 Billion off the Coronavirus Market Crash in March," *Business Insider*, April 9, 2020, https://www.businessinsider.com/bill-ackman -billionaire-hedgefund-manager-made-billions-off-coronavirus-crash-2020-4.

42. Benjamin I. Page, Larry M. Bartels, and Jason Seawright, "Democracy and the Policy Preferences of Wealthy Americans," *Perspectives on Politics* 11, no. 1 (March 2013): 51–73, https://doi.org/10.1017/S153759271200360X.

43. Lee Rainie, Scott Keeter, and Andrew Perrin, *Trust and Distrust in America*, Pew Research Center, July 22, 2019, https://www.pewresearch.org/politics/2019/07/22/trust-and-distrust-in-america/.

44. Andrew Withers, "Compound Interest: 'The Eighth Wonder of the World,'" *Madison Business Review*, James Madison University, April 16, 2021, https://www.breezejmu.org/business/compound-interest-the-eighth-wonder-of-the-world/article_11a24ebe-9e77-11eb-ba00-33aaec328747.html.

45. Nigel Chiwaya and Janell Ross, "The American Dream While Black: Locked in a Vicious Cycle," NBC News, August 3, 2020, https://www.nbcnews.com/specials/american-dream-while-black-homeownership/.

46. "Who We Are," Patriotic Millionaires, accessed September 7, 2022, https://patrioticmillionaires.org/who-we-are/.

47. "Who We Are," One for Democracy, accessed September 7, 2022, https://onefordemocracy.org/about.

48. Home page, In Tax We Trust, https://www.intaxwetrust.org.

49. "We Organize 18–35 Year Olds with Access to Wealth Who Are among the Richest Top 10% of Individuals or Families in the U.S.," Resource Generation, accessed September 7, 2022, https://resourcegeneration.org/whos-in-the-richest-top-10/.

50. Abigail Druhot, "Oscar Mayer Heir Explains Why He Gave Away All His Money at Age 26," *The Heights*, March 1, 2017, https://www.bcheights.com/2017/03/01/collins-talks-giving-away-wealth-working-societal-inequality/.

Chapter 3: White Advantage

1. Garrett Neiman, "It Is Time for White Americans to Take Responsibility—to Dismantle the Return on White Privilege," *Boston Globe*, April 3, 2019.

2. Emmie Martin, "Here's How Many Millennials Got Money from Their Parents to Buy Their Homes," CNBC, March 12, 2019, https://www.cnbc.com/2019/03/11/how-many-millennials-got-money-to-buy-homes-from-their-parents.html.

3. Elizabeth Hinton, LeShae Henderson, and Cindy Reed, *An Unjust Burden: The Disparate Treatment of Black Americans in the Criminal Justice System*, Vera Institute of Justice, May 2018, 20, https://www.vera.org/downloads/publications/for-the-record-unjust-burden-racial-disparities.pdf.

4. Office of Cory Booker, "Growing Momentum for 'Baby Bonds' as Booker, Pressley Reintroduce Landmark Legislation to Combat the Growing Racial Wealth Gap," press release, February 4, 2021, https://www.booker.senate.gov/news/press/growing-momentum-for-baby-bonds-as-booker-pressley-re-introduce-landmark-legislation-to-combat-the-growing-racial-wealth-gap.

5. Jared Abbott et al., *Commonsense Solidarity: How a Working-Class Coalition Can Be Built, and Maintained, Jacobin*, YouGov, and Center for Working-Class Politics,

November 2021, https://images.jacobinmag.com/wp-content/uploads/2021/11/08095656/CWCPReport_CommonsenseSolidarity.pdf.

6. Zaid Jilani, "Telling Liberals about 'White Privilege' Doesn't Make Them More Empathetic," *National Review*, May 29, 2019, https://www.nationalreview.com/2019/05/study-telling-liberals-about-white-privilege-reduces-empathy-poor-whites/.

7. Robert P. Baird, "The Invention of Whiteness: The Long History of a Dangerous Idea," *The Guardian*, April 20, 2021, https://www.theguardian.com/news/2021/apr/20/the-invention-of-whiteness-long-history-dangerous-idea.

8. Cynthia Peters, "The Construction of Race in the U.S.," *Change Agent*, March 2016, 22–23, https://changeagent.nelrc.org/wp-content/uploads/2016/03/The-Construction-of-Race-in-the-US.pdf.

9. Tom Costa, "Runaway Slaves and Servants in Colonial Virginia," Encyclopedia Virginia, January 21, 2021, https://encyclopediavirginia.org/entries/runaway-slaves-and-servants-in-colonial-virginia/.

10. Angela Hanks, Danyelle Solomon, and Christian Weller, *Systematic Inequality*, Center for American Progress, February 21, 2018, https://www.americanprogress.org/article/systematic-inequality/.

11. Kriston McIntosh, Emily Moss, Ryan Nunn, and Jay Shambaugh, "Examining the Black-White Wealth Gap," Brookings Institution, February 27, 2020, https://www.brookings.edu/blog/up-front/2020/02/27/examining-the-black-white-wealth-gap/.

12. Claudio Saunt, "The Invasion of America," Aeon, January 7, 2015, https://aeon.co/essays/how-were-1-5-billion-acres-of-land-so-rapidly-stolen.

13. Zillow, "U.S. Housing Market Has Doubled in Value since the Great Recession after Gaining $6.9 Trillion in 2021," press release, PR Newswire, January 27, 2022, https://www.prnewswire.com/news-releases/us-housing-market-has-doubled-in-value-since-the-great-recession-after-gaining-6-9-trillion-in-2021—301469460.html; "Estimating the Size of the Commercial Real Estate Market in the U.S.," Nareit, accessed September 7, 2022, https://www.reit.com/data-research/research/nareit-research/estimating-size-commercial-real-estate-market-us-2021.

14. J. David Hacker, "From '20. and Odd' to 10 Million: The Growth of the Slave Population in the United States," *Slavery and Abolition* 41, no. 4 (2020): 840–55, https://doi.org/10.1080/0144039x.2020.1755502.

15. Josephine Bolling McCall, *The Penalty for Success: My Father Was Lynched in Lowndes County, Alabama* (Montgomery, AL: McQuick Printing Company, 2015).

16. Equal Justice Initiative, *Lynching in America: Confronting the Legacy of Racial Terror*," 3rd ed., 2017, https://lynchinginamerica.eji.org/report/.

17. Encyclopedia Britannica, s.v. "War on Drugs," July 23, 2020, https://www.britannica.com/topic/war-on-drugs.

18. Kerry A. Dolan and Chase Peterson-Withorn, eds., "Forbes World's Billionaires List: The Richest in 2022," *Forbes*, accessed September 7, 2022, https://www.forbes.com/billionaires/.

19. Michael Fletcher, "White High School Dropouts Are Wealthier than Black and Hispanic College Graduates. Can a New Policy Tool Fix That?," *Washington Post*, March 10, 2015, https://www.washingtonpost.com/news/wonk/wp/2015/03/10/white -high-school-dropouts-are-wealthier-than-black-and-hispanic-college-graduates-can -a-new-policy-tool-fix-that/.

20. Marta Schoch, Christoph Lackner, and Samuel Frieje-Rodriguez, "Monitoring Poverty at the US$3.20 and US$5.50 Lines: Differences and Similarities with Extreme Poverty Trends," World Bank Blogs, November 19, 2020, https://blogs .worldbank.org/opendata/monitoring-poverty-us320-and-us550-lines-differences -and-similarities-extreme-poverty.

21. "Race and Ethnicity in South Africa," South African History Online, updated August 27, 2019, https://www.sahistory.org.za/article/race-and-ethnicity-south-africa.

22. Trevor Noah, *Born a Crime: Stories from a South African Childhood* (New York: One World, 2016).

23. Credit Suisse Research Institute, *Global Wealth Report 2019*, October 2019, https://www.credit-suisse.com/about-us/en/reports-research/global-wealth -report.html.

24. "All the World's Wealth in One Visual," How Much.net, accessed September 11, 2022, https://howmuch.net/articles/distribution-worlds-wealth-2019.

Chapter 4: Male Advantage

1. Alliance for Board Diversity and Deloitte, "Missing Pieces Report: The Board Diversity Study," Deloitte, accessed September 11, 2022, https://www2.deloitte .com/us/en/pages/center-for-board-effectiveness/articles/missing-pieces-report -board-diversity.html.

2. https://hbr.org/2017/04/female-supreme-court-justices-are-interrupted-more-by -male-justices-and-advocates.

3. Linda Babcock, Maria P. Recalde, and Lise Vesterlund, "Why Women Volunteer for Tasks That Don't Lead to Promotions," *Harvard Business Review*, July 16, 2018, https://hbr.org/2018/07/why-women-volunteer-for-tasks-that-dont-lead -to-promotions.

4. Babcock, Recalde, and Vesterlund, "Why Women Volunteer."

5. Amanda Barroso and Anna Brown, "Gender Pay Gap in U.S. Held Steady in 2020," Pew Research Center, May 25, 2021, https://www.pewresearch.org/fact-tank/2021 /05/25/gender-pay-gap-facts/.

6. Stephen Dubner, host, "Is Venture Capital the Secret Sauce of the American Economy?," *Freakonomics Radio* (podcast), episode 482, November 10, 2021, https://freakonomics.com/podcast/is-venture-capital-the-secret-sauce-of-the -american-economy/.

7. Lizette Chapman, "Female Founders Raised Just 2% of Venture Capital Money in 2021," *Bloomberg*, January 11, 2022, https://www.bloomberg.com /news/articles/2022-01-11/women-founders-raised-just-2-of-venture-capital -money-last-year.

8. Julia Boorstin, "VC Funding to Women-Led Companies Falls during the Pandemic," CNBC, March 17, 2021, https://www.cnbc.com/2021/03/17/vc-funding-to-women-led-companies-falls-during-the-pandemic.html.

9. "Physician Salaries Declined over Last Decade," *Oncology Times* 28, no. 15 (August 10, 2006): 30, https://doi.org/10.1097/01.COT.0000293390.79865.16.

10. Claire Cain Miller, "The Gender Pay Gap Is Largely Because of Motherhood," *New York Times*, May 13, 2017, https://www.nytimes.com/2017/05/13/upshot/the-gender-pay-gap-is-largely-because-of-motherhood.html.

11. Cyndy Baskin, "Contemporary Indigenous Women's Roles: Traditional Teachings or Internalized Colonialism?," *Violence against Women* 26, no. 15–16 (2020): 2083–2101, https://doi.org/10.1177/1077801219888024.

12. Maggie, "Iroquois Women," *History of American Women* (blog), May 8, 2008, https://www.womenhistoryblog.com/2008/05/iroquois-women.html.

13. Arizona State University, "What Are the Roots of Gender Inequality? Women's Rights, Race and Reproduction," Newswise, June 1, 2012, https://www.newswise.com/articles/what-are-the-roots-of-gender-inequality-women-s-rights-race-and-reproduction.

14. "Toxic Masculinity vs. Healthy Masculinity," Green Hill Recovery, accessed September 11, 2022, https://greenhillrecovery.com/toxic-masculinity-vs-healthy-masculinity/.

15. Petula Dvorak, "What's One of America's Most Dangerous Jobs? It's Not What You Think," *Washington Post*, September 11, 2017.

16. Claire Cain Miller, "Women Did Everything Right. Then Work Got 'Greedy,'" *New York Times*, April 26, 2019, https://www.nytimes.com/2019/04/26/upshot/women-long-hours-greedy-professions.html.

17. Camila Domonoske, "CDC: Half of All Female Homicide Victims Are Killed by Intimate Partners," *The Two-Way* (blog), NPR, July 21, 2017, https://www.npr.org/sections/thetwo-way/2017/07/21/538518569/cdc-half-of-all-female-murder-victims-are-killed-by-intimate-partners.

18. Soraya Chemaly, "There's No Comparing Male and Female Harassment Online," *Time*, September 9, 2014, https://time.com/3305466/male-female-harassment-online/.

19. Jen Chung, "Subway Harassment Largely Unreported, According to Manhattan Beep's Survey," Gothamist, July 29, 2007, https://gothamist.com/news/subway-harassment-largely-unreported-braccording-to-manhattan-beeps-survey.

20. "About Sexual Violence," It's On Us, accessed September 11, 2022, https://www.itsonus.org/about-sexual-violence/; "How to Report Suspected Abuse," Center for Hope, accessed September 11, 2022, https://www.lifebridgehealth.org/Centerfor Hope/HowtoReportSuspectedAbuse.aspx.

21. Barbara Bradley Hagerty, "An Epidemic of Disbelief," *The Atlantic*, August 2019, https://www.theatlantic.com/magazine/archive/2019/08/an-epidemic-of-disbelief/592807/.

22. "The Criminal Justice System: Statistics," RAINN, accessed September 11, 2022, https://www.rainn.org/statistics/criminal-justice-system.

23. Melissa S. Morabito, Linda M. Williams, and April Pattavina, *Decision Making in Sexual Assault Cases: Replication Research on Sexual Violence Case Attrition in the U.S.*, National Institute of Justice, February 2019, NCJ 252689, 237, https://nij.ojp.gov/library/publications/decision-making-sexual-assault-cases-replication-research-sexual-violence-case.

24. Sara Bastomski and Philip Smith, "Gender, Fear, and Public Places: How Negative Encounters with Strangers Harm Women," Urban Institute, January 1, 2017, https://www.urban.org/research/publication/gender-fear-and-public-places-how-negative-encounters-strangers-harm-women.

25. "Intimate Partner Violence, Sexual Violence, and Stalking among Men," Centers for Disease Control and Prevention, June 1, 2020, https://www.cdc.gov/violence prevention/intimatepartnerviolence/men-ipvsvandstalking.html.

26. Pew Research Center, *Raising Kids and Running a Household: How Working Parents Share the Load*, November 4, 2015, https://www.pewresearch.org/social-trends/2015/11/04/raising-kids-and-running-a-household-how-working-parents-share-the-load/.

27. Sirin Kale, "Surprise! On Average, Women Work Four Years Longer Than Men," Vice, September 22, 2016, https://www.vice.com/en/article/9k9yj5/surprise-on-average-women-work-four-years-longer-than-men.

28. Caroline Criado-Perez, *Invisible Women: Data Bias in a World Designed for Men* (New York: Abrams, 2019).

29. Lauren Caruso, "Women Who Wear Makeup to Work Get Paid More, Study Confirms," *Allure*, May 25, 2016, https://www.allure.com/story/women-wear-makeup-paid-more.

30. Soraya Chemaly, "I'm Tired of Waiting for 'Potty Parity,'" *Time*, January 5, 2015, https://time.com/3653871/womens-bathroom-lines-sexist-potty-parity/.

31. Alisha Haridasani Gupta, "Crash Test Dummies Made Cars Safer (for Average-Size Men)," *New York Times*, December 27, 2021, sec. Business, https://www.nytimes.com/2021/12/27/business/car-safety-women.html.

32. Plataforma SINC, "Medical Textbooks Use White, Heterosexual Men as a 'Universal Model,'" ScienceDaily, October 17, 2008, www.sciencedaily.com/releases/2008/10/081015132108.htm.

33. Kelsey Ogletree, "Women Were Left out of Clinical Trials until the '90s," *Well+Good* (blog), July 6, 2020, https://www.wellandgood.com/women-clinical-trials/. ; Annaliese K. Beery and Irving Zucker, "Sex Bias in Neuroscience and Biomedical Research," *Neuroscience and Biobehavioral Reviews* 35, no. 3 (January 2011): 565–72, https://doi.org/10.1016/j.neubiorev.2010.07.002; Elizabeth Cooney, "Females Are Still Routinely Left out of Biomedical Research—and Ignored in Analyses of Data," *STAT* (blog), June 9, 2020, https://www.statnews.com/2020/06/09/females-are-still-routinely-left-out-of-biomedical-research-and-ignored-in-analyses-of-data/.

34. Caroline Criado Perez, "The Deadly Truth about a World Built for Men—from Stab Vests to Car Crashes," *The Guardian*, February 23, 2019, https://www.theguardian.com/lifeandstyle/2019/feb/23/truth-world-built-for-men-car-crashes.

35. Deyen Georgiev, "How Much Time Does the Average American Spend on Their Phone in 2022?," Techjury, accessed June 3, 2022, https://techjury.net/blog/how-much-time-does-the-average-american-spend-on-their-phone/.

36. Rae Ellen Bichell, "Women, There's a Reason Why You're Shivering in the Office," *Shots*, NPR, August 4, 2015, https://www.npr.org/sections/health-shots/2015/08/04/429005094/women-theres-a-reason-why-youre-shivering-in-the-office.

37. Robert Preidt, "How Does Room Temperature Affect Test Scores?," WebMD, May 22, 2019, https://www.webmd.com/a-to-z-guides/news/20190522/how-does-room-temperature-affect-test-scores.

38. Melinda Gates, *The Moment of Lift: How Empowering Women Changes the World* (New York: Flatiron, 2019).

39. "Gender Parity Accelerators," World Economic Forum, accessed September 11, 2022, https://www.weforum.org/projects/gender-parity-accelerators/.

40. Abigail Adams to John Adams, March 31, 1776, Massachusetts Historical Society, https://www.masshist.org/digitaladams/archive/doc?id=L17760331aa.

41. Shannon Selin, "What Did Napoleon Think of Women?," *Shannon Selin* (blog), March 8, 2019, https://shannonselin.com/2019/03/napoleon-view-women/.

Chapter 5: Intersectional Advantage

1. Office of Faculty Development and Diversity, Harvard University, 2020 *Annual Report*, accessed September 12, 2022, https://faculty.harvard.edu/files/faculty-diversity/files/2019-20_full_annual_report.pdf.

2. Luna Malbroux, "Celebrating Kimberlé Crenshaw and Intersectionality," Ellequate, accessed October 5, 2022, https://www.ellequate.com/blog/celebrating-kimberle-crenshaw-and-intersectionality.

3. Kimberlé Crenshaw, "Demarginalizing the Intersection of Race and Sex: A Black Feminist Critique of Antidiscrimination Doctrine, Feminist Theory and Antiracist Politics," *University of Chicago Legal Forum* 140 (1989): 149.

4. Katherine L. Milkman, Modupe Akinola, and Dolly Chugh, "What Happens Before? A Field Experiment Exploring How Pay and Representation Differentially Shape Bias on the Pathway into Organizations," *Journal of Applied Psychology* 100, no. 6 (2015): 1678–1712, https://doi.org/10.1037/apl0000022.

5. Sinku Ren, "How to Do Intersectionality," *Narrative Initiative* blog, March 8, 2021, https://narrativeinitiative.org/blog/how-to-do-intersectionality/.

6. http://www.timothy-judge.com/Height%20paper—JAP%20published.pdf.

7. https://www.researchgate.net/publication/223613650_Height_in_Women_Predicts_Maternal_Tendencies_and_Career_Orientation.

8. Ashley Mardell and August Osterloh, *The ABC's of LGBT+* (Coral Gables, FL: Mango Media, 2016).

9. Robert W. Livingston and Nicholas A. Pearce, "The Teddy-Bear Effect: Does Having a Baby Face Benefit Black Chief Executive Officers?," *Psychological Science* 20, no. 10 (October 2009): 1229–1236, https://doi.org/10.1111/j.1467-9280.2009.02431.x.

10. Rachel A. Feinstein, *When Rape Was Legal: The Untold History of Sexual Violence during Slavery* (New York: Routledge, 2019).

11. Kate Geiselman, "In Brock Turner's Home Town, We're Raising Kids Who Are Never Told 'No,'" Washington Post, June 8, 2016, https://www.washingtonpost.com /posteverything/wp/2016/06/08/in-brock-turners-hometown-were-raising-kids -who-are-never-told-no/; "U.S. Census Bureau QuickFacts: Oakwood City, Ohio," accessed October 5, 2022, https://www.census.gov/quickfacts/oakwoodcityohio.

12. Victor Xu, "The Full Letter Read by Brock Turner's Father at His Sentencing Hearing," The Stanford Daily, June 8, 2016, https://stanforddaily.com/2016/06/08 /the-full-letter-read-by-brock-turners-father-at-his-sentencing-hearing/.

13. Dan Mangan Macias Amanda, "Jury Finds Jeffrey Epstein Friend Ghislaine Maxwell Guilty in Sex Crimes Trial," CNBC, December 29, 2021, https://www.cnbc .com/2021/12/29/ghislaine-maxwell-trial-ends-jeffrey-epstein-sex-crime-case.html.

14. Emma Ockerman, "The Program That Let Jeffrey Epstein Leave Jail Almost Daily Just Got Scrapped by the Sheriff," Vice, December 18, 2019, https://www.vice.com /en/article/3a8zvb/the-program-that-let-jeffrey-epstein-leave-jail-almost-daily -just-got-scrapped-by-the-sheriff.

Chapter 6: The Exception Factory

1. Norma M. Riccucci, "Tokenism," Encyclopedia.com, accessed September 13, 2022, https://www.encyclopedia.com/social-sciences/encyclopedias-almanacs-transcripts -and-maps/tokenism.

2. Martin Luther King Jr., *Why We Can't Wait* (New York: Signet Classics, 2000).

3. Moira Alexander, "5 Ways Diversity and Inclusion Help Teams Perform Better," *CIO*, September 3, 2021, https://www.cio.com/article/189194/5-ways-diversity-and -inclusion-help-teams-perform-better.html.

4. Rosabeth Moss Kanter, *Men and Women of the Corporation* (New York, NY: Basic Books, 2010).

5. "Black Dude Dies First," TV Tropes, accessed September 13, 2022, https://tvtropes .org/pmwiki/pmwiki.php/Main/BlackDudeDiesFirst.

6. Jeremy Nesoff, "The Myth of a Post-Racial Society after the Obama Presidency," *Facing Today* (blog), Facing History & Ourselves, February 8, 2017, https://facingtoday .facinghistory.org/the-myth-of-a-post-racial-society-after-the-obama-presidency.

7. Mary Daly, *Beyond God the Father: Toward a Philosophy of Women's Liberation* (Boston: Beacon, 1973), 14.

8. Ted Thornhill, "We Want Black Students, Just Not You: How White Admissions Counselors Screen Black Prospective Students," Sociology of Race and Ethnicity 5, no. 4 (October 1, 2019): 456–70, https://doi.org/10.1177/2332649218792579.

9. Deena Prichep, "A Campus More Colorful Than Reality: Beware That College Brochure," *Weekend Edition Sunday*, NPR, December 29, 2013, https://www.npr .org/2013/12/29/257765543/a-campus-more-colorful-than-reality-beware-that -college-brochure.

10. Sam Ruland, "York College Faces Scrutiny for Photoshopped Billboard; College Responds," *York Daily Record*, February 4, 2019, https://www.ydr.com /story/news/2019/02/04/york-college-pennsylvania-faces-scrutiny-photoshopped -billboard-diversity-ycp/2769092002/.

11. Timothy D. Pippert, Laura J. Essenburg, and Edward J. Matchett, "We've Got Minorities, Yes We Do: Visual Representations of Racial and Ethnic Diversity in College Recruitment Materials," *Journal of Marketing for Higher Education* 23, no. 2 (2013): 258–282, https://doi.org/10.1080/08841241.2013.867920.

12. The Education Trust, *"Segregation Forever"? The Continued Underrepresentation of Black and Latino Undergraduates at the Nation's 101 Most Selective Public Colleges and Universities*, July 21, 2020, 26-32, https://edtrust.org /wp-content/uploads/2014/09/Segregation-Forever-The-Continued-Under representation-of-Black-and-Latino-Undergraduates-at-the-Nations-101-Most -Selective-Public-Colleges-and-Universities-July-21-2020.pdf.

13. Christine Tamir, "Key Findings about Black Immigrants in the U.S.," Pew Research Center, January 27, 2022, https://www.pewresearch.org/fact-tank/2022/01/27 /key-findings-about-black-immigrants-in-the-u-s/.

14. Emily Chen and Jenny Dorsey, *Understanding...Respectability Politics*, Studio ATAO, July 1, 2021, https://www.studioatao.org/respectability-politics.

15. Xuan Thai and Ted Barrett, "Biden's Description of Obama Draws Scrutiny," CNN, February 9, 2007, https://www.cnn.com/2007/POLITICS/01/31 /biden.obama/.

16. Ta-Nehisi Coates, "Fear of a Black President," *The Atlantic*, August 23, 2012, https://www.theatlantic.com/magazine/archive/2012/09/fear-of-a-black -president/309064/.

17. Shankar Vedantum, "In Jill Abramson's Firing, Was the 'Glass Cliff' to Blame?," interview with Audie Cornish, *All Things Considered*, NPR, May 19, 2014; Annie Lowrey, "Yahoo's Marissa Mayer and the Glass Cliff," Intelligencer, *New York*, December 18, 2014, https://nymag.com/intelligencer/2014/12/marissa-mayer-and -the-glass-cliff.html.

18. "Discovering the Glass Cliff: Insights into Addressing Subtle Gender Discrimination in the Workplace," Context, Identity and Choice: Understanding the Constraints on Women's Career Decisions, University of Exeter, accessed September 13, 2022, https://psychology.exeter.ac.uk/cic/about/theglasscliff/.

19. Emily Stewart, "Why Struggling Companies Promote Women: The Glass Cliff, Explained," Vox, October 31, 2018, https://www.vox.com/2018/10/31/17960156 /what-is-the-glass-cliff-women-ceos.

20. Larry Kim, "After Shattering Glass Ceiling, Women CEOs Fall Off the Glass Cliff," *Inc.*, October 28, 2014, https://www.inc.com/larry-kim/after-shattering -glass-ceiling-female-ceos-fall-off-the-glass-cliff.html.

21. Ada Stewart, "Women Close Med School Enrollment Gap; Others Remain," *Leader Voices Blog*, AAFP, accessed September 13, 2022, https://www.aafp.org /news/blogs/leadervoices/entry/20200228lv-diversity.html.

22. Seger S. Morris and Heather Lusby, "The Physician Compensation Bubble Is Looming," American Associate for Physician Leadership, January 16, 2019, https://www.physicianleaders.org/news/physician-compensation-bubble-looming.

23. Association of American Medical Colleges, "The Majority of U.S. Medical Students Are Women, New Data Show," press release, December 9, 2019, https://www.aamc.org/news-insights/press-releases/majority-us-medical-students-are-women-new-data-show.

24. Janice Hopkins Tanne, "Neurosurgery Is Highest Paid Specialty in the US, Survey Shows," *BMJ* 367 (December 16, 2019), https://doi.org/10.1136/bmj.l6988.

25. "Information on Women in Neurosurgery," Northwest Neurosurgery Institute, accessed September 13, 2022, https://www.northwestneurosurgery.com/resources/information-on-women-in-neurosurgery/.

26. "Karin Marie Muraszko MD," Michigan Medicine, University of Michigan Health, accessed September 13, 2022, https://www.uofmhealth.org/profile/267/karin-marie-muraszko-md.

27. Edwin Nieblas-Bedolla et al., "Racial, Ethnic, and Gender Diversity of Applicants and Matriculants to Neurological Surgery Residency Programs," *Journal of Neurosurgery* 137, no. 1 (2021): 266–272, https://doi.org/10.3171/2021.7.JNS21906.

Chapter 7: The Minority-Ranking System

1. Amy Chua and Jed Rubenfeld, *The Triple Package: How Three Unlikely Traits Explain the Rise and Fall of Cultural Groups in America* (New York: Penguin, 2015).

2. National Association of Realtors Research Group, *2021 Snapshot of Race and Home Buying in America*, February 2021, https://www.nar.realtor/sites/default/files/documents/2021-snapshot-of-race-and-home-buyers-in-america-02-18-2021.pdf.

3. Christian E. Weller and Jeffrey Thompson, *Wealth Inequality among Asian Americans Greater Than among Whites*, Center for American Progress, December 20, 2016, https://www.americanprogress.org/article/wealth-inequality-among-asian-americans-greater-than-among-whites/.

4. Abby Budiman, "Indians in the U.S. Fact Sheet," Pew Research Center, April 29, 2021, https://www.pewresearch.org/social-trends/fact-sheet/asian-americans-indians-in-the-u-s/.

5. "14 Important Statistics about Asian Americans," Asian Nation, accessed September 13, 2022, https://www.asian-nation.org/14-statistics.shtml.

6. Abby Budiman, "Burmese in the U.S. Fact Sheet," Pew Research Center, April 29, 2021, https://www.pewresearch.org/social-trends/fact-sheet/asian-americans-burmese-in-the-u-s/.

7. Patrick Winn, "The Biggest Group of Current Refugees in the US? Christians from Myanmar," *The World*, PRX/WGBH, May 4, 2017, https://theworld.org/stories/2017-05-04/biggest-group-refugees-us-christians-myanmar.

8. Sarah Pierce and Julia Gelatt, "Evolution of the H-1B: Latest Trends in a Program on the Brink of Reform," Migration Policy Institute, March 2018; "H-1B Petitions by Gender and Country of Birth Fiscal Year 2019," US Citizenship and

Immigration Services, January 21, 2020, https://www.uscis.gov/sites/default/files/document/data/h-1b-petitions-by-gender-country-of-birth-fy2019.pdf.

9. Noah Smith, "It Isn't Just Asian Immigrants Who Excel in the U.S.," *Bloomberg*, October 13, 2015, https://www.bloomberg.com/opinion/articles/2015-10-13/it-isn-t-just-asian-immigrants-who-excel-in-the-u-s-.

10. Buck Gee and Denise Peck, "Asian Americans Are the Least Likely Group in the U.S. to Be Promoted to Management," *Harvard Business Review*, May 31, 2018, https://hbr.org/2018/05/asian-americans-are-the-least-likely-group-in-the-u-s-to-be-promoted-to-management; "The Leadership Representation Ceiling for Asian Americans," Bloomberg, May 27, 2020, https://www.bloomberg.com/company/stories/the-leadership-representation-ceiling-for-asian-americans/; Sarah Mucha, "The Number of Asian Americans Elected to Congress Is at a Record High," Axios, March 18, 2021, https://www.axios.com/2021/03/18/asian-american-congress-representation.

11. Eric Chung et al., "A Portrait of Asian Americans in the Law," *The Practice*, Harvard Law School Center on the Legal Profession, November/December 2018, https://thepractice.law.harvard.edu/article/a-portrait-of-asian-americans-in-the-law/.

12. Jeffrey Mervis, "A Glass Ceiling for Asian Scientists?" *Science*, October 28, 2005, https://www.science.org/content/article/glass-ceiling-asian-scientists.

13. Melinda Shepherd, "Sundar Pichai," Britannica.com, June 6, 2022, https://www.britannica.com/biography/Sundar-Pichai.

14. Grace Dean, "Google Founders Larry Page and Sergey Brin Are Now Worth More Than $100 Billion, Making Them 2 of Only 8 Centibillionaires in the World," *Business Insider*, April 12, 2021, https://www.businessinsider.com/google-larry-page-sergey-brin-net-worth-billionaire-wealth-bloomberg-2021-4.

15. NPR, Robert Wood Johnson Foundation, and Harvard T. H. Chan School of Public Health, *Discrimination in America: Experiences and Views of Asian Americans*, November 2017, https://legacy.npr.org/assets/news/2017/12/discriminationpoll-asian-americans.pdf.

16. Sakshi Venkatraman, "Anti-Asian Hate Crimes Rose 73% Last Year, Updated FBI Data Says," NBC News, October 25, 2021, https://www.nbcnews.com/news/asian-america/anti-asian-hate-crimes-rose-73-last-year-updated-fbi-data-says-rcna3741.

17. Jennifer Lee and Min Zhou, "From Unassimilable to Exceptional: The Rise of Asian Americans and 'Stereotype Promise,'" *New Diversities* 16, no. 1 (2014), https://newdiversities.mmg.mpg.de/wp-content/uploads/2014/11/2014_16-01_02_Lee.pdf.

18. Kelly Wallace, "Forgotten Los Angeles History: The Chinese Massacre of 1871," Los Angeles Public Library, May 19, 2017, https://www.lapl.org/collections-resources/blogs/lapl/chinese-massacre-1871.

19. Muzaffar Chishti, Faye Hipsman, and Isabel Ball, "Fifty Years On, the 1965 Immigration and Nationality Act Continues to Reshape the United States," *Migration Information Source*, Migration Policy Institute, October 15, 2015, https://www.migrationpolicy.org/article/fifty-years-1965-immigration-and-nationality-act-continues-reshape-united-states.

20. Pew Research Center, *The Rise of Asian Americans*, June 19, 2012, https://www.pewresearch.org/social-trends/2012/06/19/the-rise-of-asian-americans/.

21. William Petersen, "Success Story, Japanese-American Style," *New York Times Magazine*, January 9, 1966.

22. Barbara Frankel, "Asian Divide in the C-Suite," DiversityInc Best Practices, September 17, 2015, https://www.diversityincbestpractices.com/the-asian-divide-in-the-c-suite/.

23. Ann Lyon Ritchie, "Historian Examines Japan's Unexpected Alliance with Nazi Germany," News, Department of History, Carnegie Mellon University, November 1, 2019, https://www.cmu.edu/dietrich/history/news/2019/law-book.html.

24. Jennifer Lee, "Honorary Whiteness: The Making of a Model Minority—The Socio-Legal Construction of Race and East Asians as Global Outsiders in the Landscape of a Post-Apartheid South Africa," honors thesis, Johns Hopkins University, May 2016, https://kipdf.com/jennifer-lee-supervisor-beverly-j-silver_5b2f8b15097c478f398b4630.html.

25. Amy Chua and Jed Rubenfeld, "What Drives Success?" *New York Times*, January 25, 2014, https://www.nytimes.com/2014/01/26/opinion/sunday/what-drives-success.html.

26. Rockefeller Foundation-Aspen Institute Diaspora Program, "The Nigerian Diaspora in the United States," *Migration Policy Institute*, June 2015, 1.

27. Monica Anderson, "Chapter 1: Statistical Portrait of the U.S. Black Immigrant Population," in *A Rising Share of the U.S. Black Population Is Foreign Born*, Pew Research Center, April 9, 2015, https://www.pewresearch.org/social-trends/2015/04/09/chapter-1-statistical-portrait-of-the-u-s-black-immigrant-population/.

28. Jeremy Raff, "The 'Double Punishment' for Black Undocumented Immigrants," *The Atlantic*, December 30, 2017, https://www.theatlantic.com/politics/archive/2017/12/the-double-punishment-for-black-immigrants/549425/.

29. Konrad Franco, Caitlin Patler, and Keramet Reiter, "Punishing Status and the Punishment Status Quo: Solitary Confinement in U.S. Immigration Prisons, 2013–2017" *Punishment and Society* 24, no. 2 (2020): 170–195, https://doi.org/10.1177/1462474520967804.

30. Pew Research Center, "11. Economics and Well-Being among U.S. Jews," in *Jewish Americans in 2020*, May 11, 2021, https://www.pewresearch.org/religion/2021/05/11/economics-and-well-being-among-u-s-jews/.

31. "Jewish Members of the 116th Congress (2019–2021)," Jewish Virtual Library, accessed September 13, 2022, https://www.jewishvirtuallibrary.org/jewish-members-of-the-116th-congress; Jacob Berkman, "At Least 139 of the Forbes 400 Are Jewish," Jewish Telegraphic Agency, October 6, 2009, https://www.jta.org/2009/10/05/united-states/at-least-139-of-the-forbes-400-are-jewish.

32. "5 Jews Make Forbes' List of Top 10 Wealthiest Americans," *Times of Israel*, October 6, 2018, https://www.timesofisrael.com/5-jews-make-forbes-list-of-top-10-wealthiest-americans/.

33. Pew Research Center, "9. Race, Ethnicity, Heritage and Immigration among U.S. Jews," in *Jewish Americans in 2020*, May 11, 2021, https://www.pewresearch.org/religion/2021/05/11/race-ethnicity-heritage-and-immigration-among-u-s-jews/.

34. "2017 Audit of Anti-Semitic Incidents," Anti-Defamation League, February 25, 2018, https://www.adl.org/resources/report/2017-audit-anti-semitic-incidents.

35. American Jewish Committee, *The State of Antisemitism in America 2021*, October 25, 2021, https://www.ajc.org/AntisemitismReport2021.

36. Jeffrey M. Jones, "Some Americans Reluctant to Vote for Mormon, 72-Year-Old Presidential Candidates," Gallup News Service, February 20, 2007, https://news.gallup.com/poll/26611/Some-Americans-Reluctant-Vote-Mormon-72YearOld-Presidential-Candidates.aspx.

37. David Plotz, "The Protestant Presidency," Slate, February 12, 2000, https://slate.com/news-and-politics/2000/02/the-protestant-presidency.html.

38. Luis Noe-Bustamante et al., *Majority of Latinos Say Skin Color Impacts Opportunity in America and Shapes Daily Life*, Pew Research Center, November 4, 2021, https://www.pewresearch.org/hispanic/2021/11/04/majority-of-latinos-say-skin-color-impacts-opportunity-in-america-and-shapes-daily-life/.

39. Ekeoma E. Uzogara, Hedwig Lee, Cleopatra M. Abdou, and James S. Jackson, "A Comparison of Skin Tone Discrimination among African American Men: 1995 and 2003," *Psychology of Men and Masculinity* 15, no. 2 (2014): 201–212, https://doi.org/10.1037/a0033479.

40. Lisa Trei, " 'Black' Features Can Sway in Favor of Death Penalty, According to Study," Stanford Report, May 3, 2006, http://news.stanford.edu/news/2006/may3/deathworthy-050306.html.

41. "Cubans in the United States," Pew Research Center, August 25, 2006, https://www.pewresearch.org/hispanic/2006/08/25/cubans-in-the-united-states/.

42. Luis Noe-Bustamante, Antonio Flores, and Sono Shah, "Facts on Hispanics of Cuban Origin in the United States, 2017," Pew Research Center, accessed June 22, 2022, https://www.pewresearch.org/hispanic/fact-sheet/u-s-hispanics-facts-on-cuban-origin-latinos/; "Cuban Americans in Congress," Cuban Research Institute, accessed September 13, 2022, https://cri.fiu.edu/us-cuba/cuban-americans-in-congress/.

43. Patricia Mazzei, "Frank Artiles Apologizes after Getting Reported for Using N-Word, Other Profanities," *Tampa Bay Times*, April 19, 2017, https://web.archive.org/web/20170419044801/http:/www.tampabay.com/blogs/the-buzz-florida-politics/frank-artiles-apologizes-after-getting-reported-for-using-n-word-other/2320782.

44. Nadege Green, "A Miami Theater Group Has a Change of Heart over Blackface," *The World*, PRX/WGBH, June 25, 2018, https://theworld.org/stories/2018-06-25/miami-theater-group-has-change-heart-over-blackface.

45. "Afro-Latinos Are Part of the American Story," *UnidosUS Blog*, February 26, 2019, https://www.unidosus.org/blog/2019/02/26/afro-latinos/.

46. "Poverty," *The State of Working America*, Economic Policy Institute, accessed September 13, 2022, http://www.stateofworkingamerica.org/index.html%3Fp=4193.html.

47. Jamiles Lartey, "Median Wealth of Black Americans 'Will Fall to Zero by 2053,' Warns New Report," *The Guardian*, September 13, 2017, https://www

.theguardian.com/inequality/2017/sep/13/median-wealth-of-black-americans-will
-fall-to-zero-by-2053-warns-new-report.

Chapter 8: Blaming the Victim

1. Emily Badger, Claire Cain Miller, Adam Pearce, and Kevin Quealy, "Extensive Data Shows Punishing Reach of Racism for Black Boys," *New York Times*, March 19, 2018, https://www.nytimes.com/interactive/2018/03/19/upshot/race-class-white-and -black-men.html.

2. Ralph Richard Banks, "An End to the Class vs. Race Debate," *New York Times*, March 21, 2018, https://www.nytimes.com/2018/03/21/opinion/class-race-social -mobility.html.

3. Alexandria Eisenbarth and Rick McGahey, "Why Is Economics Still Largely a White Male Preserve?," Institute for New Economic Thinking, November 17, 2016, https://www.ineteconomics.org/perspectives/blog/why-is-economics-still-largely -a-white-male-preserve.

4. Alvin Powell, "A New Dean Debuts," Harvard Gazette, June 11, 2015, https:// news.harvard.edu/gazette/story/2015/06/a-new-dean-debuts/.

5. Christine Marin, "Mexican Americans on the Home Front: Community Organizations in Arizona during World War II," *Eric Institute of Education Sciences*, April 1987, https://eric.ed.gov/?id=ED315252.

6. Anne Gearan and Abby Phillip, "Clinton Regrets 1996 Remark on 'Super-Predators' after Encounter with Activist," *Washington Post*, February 25, 2016, https://www.washingtonpost.com/news/post-politics/wp/2016/02/25/clinton -heckled-by-black-lives-matter-activist/.

7. David A. Graham, Adrienne Green, Cullen Murphy, and Parker Richards, "An Oral History of Trump's Bigotry," The Atlantic, May 13, 2019, https://www.theatlantic .com/magazine/archive/2019/06/trump-racism-comments/588067/.

8. Lisa Wade, "When Jews Dominated Professional Basketball," *Sociological Images* (blog), The Society Pages, November 25, 2013, https://thesocietypages.org/socimages /2013/11/25/when-jews-dominated-professional-basketball/.

9. Quoted in Jeffrey Goldberg, "Scheming Oriental Hebrew Basketball Players," *The Atlantic*, January 22, 2010, https://www.theatlantic.com/international/archive /2010/01/scheming-oriental-hebrew-basketball-players/34002/.

10. Johnny Roy, "Social Darwinism for APUSH," Apprend, September 29, 2017, https://apprend.io/apush/period-6/social-darwinism/.

11. F. James Davis, "Who Is Black? One Nation's Definition," Frontline, PBS, excerpt from *Who Is Black? One Nation's Definition* (University Park: Pennsylvania State University Press, 1991)., https://www.pbs.org/wgbh/pages/frontline/shows /jefferson/mixed/onedrop.html.

12. James Q. Whitman, *Hitler's American Model: The United States and the Making of Nazi Race Law* (Princeton, NJ: Princeton University Press, 2017).

13. Lycoming College, "Examining the Impact of the Holocaust on the American Civil Rights Movement," Lycoming College, accessed October 6, 2022, https://www.lycoming.edu/news/stories/2017/10/clive-webb.aspx.

14. The Canadian Resource Centre and for Victims of Crime, *Victim Blaming*, August 2009, https://crcvc.ca/docs/victim_blaming.pdf.

15. William Ryan, *Blaming the Victim*, rev. ed. (New York: Vintage, 1976).

16. U.S. Department of Labor, "The Negro Family: The Case for National Action," U.S. Department of Labor, March 1965, https://www.dol.gov/general/aboutdol/history/webid-moynihan.

17. Howard Zinn, *You Can't Be Neutral on a Moving Train: A Personal History of Our Times* (Boston: Beacon, 2002).

18. Jackson Katz, "Violence against Women: It's a Men's Issue," TEDx Talk, TEDx-FiDiWomen, November 2012, San Francisco, CA, video posted on TED.com, https://www.ted.com/talks/jackson_katz_violence_against_women_it_s_a_men_s_issue.

19. Kali Holloway, "Candace Owens Is a Willing Tool of Republican Racists," *The Daily Beast*, October 11, 2020, sec. politics, https://www.thedailybeast.com/candace-owens-is-a-willing-tool-of-republican-racists.

20. Rilyn Eischens, "Right-Wing Celeb Charlie Kirk Thinks George Floyd Is a 'Scumbag,'" Minnesota Reformer, October 6, 2021, https://minnesotareformer.com/briefs/hagedorn-munson-attend-charlie-kirk-speech-in-mankato/.

21. Stephen Moore, "Private Enterprise," WSJ, May 6, 2006, https://www.wsj.com/articles/SB114687252956545543.

22. Jonathan Martin and Sheryl Gay Stolberg, "Roy Moore Is Accused of Sexual Misconduct by a Fifth Woman," *New York Times*, November 13, 2017, https://www.nytimes.com/2017/11/13/us/politics/roy-moore-alabama-senate.html.

23. Becki Gray, "Giving to Charities Should Not Put You at Risk of Harm," *Carolina Journal*, May 10, 2021, https://www.carolinajournal.com/opinion/giving-to-charities-should-not-put-you-at-risk-of-harm/.

24. Michael T. Nietzel, "Philanthropy for U.S. Colleges Up 6.9% in 2021; Tops $52 Billion," *Forbes*, February 17, 2022, https://www.forbes.com/sites/michaeltnietzel/2022/02/17/philanthropy-for-us-colleges-up-69-in-2021-tops-52-billion/; Dalia Faheid, "Fewer Students in Class of 2020 Went Straight to College," *Education Week*, April 6, 2021, https://www.edweek.org/teaching-learning/fewer-students-in-class-of-2020-went-straight-to-college/2021/04.

25. "Pell Grant Recipients as a Peer Metric," University of California, Berkeley, November 2017, https://opa.berkeley.edu/sites/default/files/2015-16_pell_grant_ivy_compared.pdf; Janet Lorin, "Stanford's $1.39 Billion Haul Makes It Biggest Fundraiser," *Bloomberg*, February 16, 2022, https://www.bloomberg.com/news/articles/2022-02-16/stanford-tops-harvard-as-biggest-fundraiser-with-1-39-billion; "Financial Facts," Finance and Treasury, Princeton University, December 17, 2021, https://finance.princeton.edu/financial-facts; Brown University, *Financial Report*, 2021, https://fy21financialreport.brown.edu/financial-report;

John Lippman, "Dartmouth Employees to Get Bonuses as Endowment Returns 46.5%," *Valley News*, October 11, 2021, https://www.vnews.com/Dartmouth -endowment-grows-by-$2-5-billion-42948060.

26. Caroline Suozzi, "Education and Philanthropy: A Topic Brief for Donors," Rockefeller Philanthropy Advisors, December 2, 2021, https://www.rockpa.org/education -and-philanthropy-a-topic-brief-for-donors/.

27. Andrea Suozzo, Ken Schwencke, Mike Tigas, Sisi Wei, Alec Glassford, and Brandon Roberts, "Kipp Foundation—Nonprofit Explorer," ProPublica, May 9, 2013, https://projects.propublica.org/nonprofits/organizations/943362724; Charity Navigator, "Rating for Teach For America," Charity Navigator, accessed October 6, 2022, https://www.charitynavigator.org/ein/133541913.

28. Tara Bahrampour, "At Regis, Academic Rigor and Service, All Free," *New York Times*, March 13, 2002, sec. New York, https://www.nytimes.com/2002/03/13 /nyregion/at-regis-academic-rigor-and-service-all-free.html.

29. Regis High School, "College Profile," Regis High School, accessed October 6, 2022, https://www.regis.org/section/?ID=121.

30. Jennifer Gillespie, ed., "'We Were Just Doing What Needed to Be Done,'" Alumni Stories, Harvard Business School, March 1, 2018, https://www.alumni.hbs.edu /stories/Pages/story-bulletin.aspx?num=6567.

31. "Data," Advancing Racial Equity, Harvard Business School, accessed September 15, 2022, https://www.hbs.edu/racialequity/data/Pages/default.aspx.

32. Bayard Love and Deena Hayes-Greene, *The Groundwater Approach*, Racial Equity Institute, 2018, pp. 3–4, https://racialequityinstitute.org/groundwater/.

33. Gia Nardini et al., "Together We Rise: How Social Movements Succeed," *Journal of Consumer Psychology* 31, no. 1 (2021): 112–145, https://doi.org/10.1002/jcpy .1201.

34. Jason Wingard, "Reverse Mentoring: 3 Proven Outcomes Driving Change," *Forbes*, August 8, 2018, https://www.forbes.com/sites/jasonwingard/2018/08/08/reverse-men toring-3-proven-outcomes-driving-change/.

35. Jennifer Jordan and Michael Sorell, "Why Reverse Mentoring Works and How to Do It Right," *Harvard Business Review*, October 3, 2019, https://hbr.org/2019/10 /why-reverse-mentoring-works-and-how-to-do-it-right.

Chapter 9: The Luck Defense

1. Hilary Burns, "Wealthy University Endowments Report Billions in 2021 Growth," The Business Journals, October 4, 2021, https://www.bizjournals.com/bizjournals /news/2021/10/04/college-endowments-growth-2021.html.

2. Megan Sauer, "Billionaire Ray Dalio: Going Broke 'Was One of the Best Things That Ever Happened to Me,'" CNBC, June 2, 2022, https://www.cnbc .com/2022/06/02/ray-dalio-going-broke-was-one-of-the-best-things-to-ever -happen-to-me.html.

3. "Interview with Steve Forbes," Business Today Online Journal, January 28, 2019, https://journal.businesstoday.org/bt-online/2019/mag-interview-forbes.

4. "French and Raven's Forms of Power: A Simple Summary," World of Work Project, August 3, 2019, https://worldofwork.io/2019/08/french-and-ravens-forms-of-power/.

5. Martin Luther King Jr., "Where Do We Go from Here?," speech, Southern Christian Leadership Conference, Atlanta, GA, August 16, 1967, https://kinginstitute.stanford.edu/where-do-we-go-here.

6. Jeffrey Pfeffer, *Power: Why Some People Have It—and Others Don't* (New York: HarperBusiness, 2010).

7. Julie Battilana and Tiziana Casciaro, *Power, for All: How It Really Works and Why It's Everyone's Business* (New York: Simon & Schuster, 2021).

8. Shoa L. Clarke, "How Hospitals Coddle the Rich," *New York Times*, October 26, 2015, https://www.nytimes.com/2015/10/26/opinion/hospitals-red-blanket-problem.html.

9. Rob Picheta, "Black Newborns 3 Times More Likely to Die When Looked After by White Doctors," CNN, August 20, 2020, https://www.cnn.com/2020/08/18/health/black-babies-mortality-rate-doctors-study-wellness-scli-intl/index.html.

10. Samantha Artiga, Olivia Pham, Kendal Orgera, and Usha Ranji, "Racial Disparities in Maternal and Infant Health: An Overview," Kaiser Family Foundation, November 10, 2020, https://www.kff.org/report-section/racial-disparities-in-maternal-and-infant-health-an-overview-issue-brief/.

11. Colleen Murphy, "What Is White Savior Complex—and Why Is It Harmful?," *Health*, September 20, 2021, https://www.health.com/mind-body/health-diversity-inclusion/white-savior-complex.

12. Elon Musk (@elonmusk), "Working 16 hours a day, 7 days a week, 52 weeks in a year and people still calling me lucky," Twitter, June 11, 2020.

13. Warren Buffett, pledge letter, Giving Pledge, accessed September 15, 2022, https://givingpledge.org/pledger?pledgerId=177.

14. Jon and Karen Huntsman, pledge letter, Giving Pledge, June 18, 2010, https://givingpledge.org/pledger?pledgerId=215.

15. George Kaiser, pledge letter, Giving Pledge, July 26, 2010, https://givingpledge.org/pledger?pledgerId=220.

16. Jonathan M. Nelson, pledge letter, Giving Pledge, n.d., https://givingpledge.org/pledger?pledgerId=256.

17. John A. and Susan Sobrato, pledge letter, Giving Pledge, July 14, 2018, https://givingpledge.org/pledger?pledgerId=292.

18. Melinda French Gates and Bill Gates, pledge letter, Giving Pledge, accessed September 15, 2022, https://givingpledge.org/foundingletter.

19. Eli Broad and Edythe Broad, pledge letter, Giving Pledge, July 1, 2010, https://givingpledge.org/pledger?pledgerId=174.

Chapter 10: Intersectional Equity

1. Troy Segal, "Enron Scandal: The Fall of a Wall Street Darling," Investopedia, November 26, 2021, https://www.investopedia.com/updates/enron-scandal-summary/.

2. Alex Pentland, *Social Physics: How Social Networks Can Make Us Smarter* (New York: Penguin Press, 2015).

3. Deirdre Fernandes, "At Harvard Business School, Diversity Remains Elusive," *Boston Globe*, June 1, 2019, https://www.bostonglobe.com/metro/2019/06/01/harvard -business-school-diversity-remains-elusive/bpyxP4cE1iCQJdLbHQEaQI/story.html.

4. Naz Beheshti, "10 Timely Statistics about the Connection between Employee Engagement and Wellness," *Forbes*, January 16, 2019, https://www.forbes.com /sites/nazbeheshti/2019/01/16/10-timely-statistics-about-the-connection-between -employee-engagement-and-wellness/.

5. Juliana Menasce Horowitz, Anna Brown, and Kiana Cox, "Race in America 2019," Pew Research Center, April 9, 2019, https://www.pewresearch.org/social-trends /2019/04/09/race-in-america-2019/.

6. Kyle "Guante" Tran Myhre, "'White Supremacy Is Not a Shark; It Is the Water,'" *Not a Lot of Reasons to Sing, but Enough* (blog), November 22, 2020, https:// guante.info/2020/11/22/nottheshark/.

7. Ibram X. Kendi, *How to Be an Antiracist* (New York: One World, 2019).

8. Emily Badger et al., "Extensive Data Shows Punishing Reach of Racism for Black Boys," *New York Times*, March 19, 2018, sec. The Upshot, https://www.nytimes .com/interactive/2018/03/19/upshot/race-class-white-and-black-men.html.

9. Reese Rathjen, "New Analysis Shows Startling Levels of Discrimination against Black Transgender People," National LGBTQ Task Force (blog), September 16, 2011, https:// www.thetaskforce.org/new-analysis-shows-startling-levels-of-discrimination-against -black-transgender-people/.

10. Nanette Goodman, Michael Morris, and Kelvin Boston, "Financial Inequality: Disability, Race and Poverty in America," National Disability Institute, accessed October 6, 2022, 26.

11. André B. Rosay, "Violence Against American Indian and Alaska Native Women and Men," National Institute of Justice, May 2016, https://www.ojp.gov/pdffiles1 /nij/249736.pdf.

12. Center for Disease Control and Prevention, "CDC Works To Address Violence Against American Indian and Alaska Native People," Center for Disease Control and Prevention, accessed October 6, 2022, https://www.cdc.gov/injury/pdfs/tribal /Violence-Against-Native-Peoples-Fact-Sheet.pdf.

13. Ruth Igielnik, Scott Keeter, and Hannah Hartig, *Behind Biden's 2020 Victory*, Pew Research Center, June 30, 2021, https://www.pewresearch.org/politics/2021/06/30 /behind-bidens-2020-victory/.

Chapter 11: Antimonopoly

1. Alec MacGillis, "The Tax Break for Patriotic Billionaires," *New Yorker*, March 6, 2016, https://www.newyorker.com/magazine/2016/03/14/david-rubenstein-and -the-carried-interest-dilemma.

2. "Money-Manager Transition," Harvard Magazine, March 1, 2005, https://www .harvardmagazine.com/2005/03/money-manager-transition.html.

3. Tamar Lewin, "John Paulson Gives $400 Million to Harvard for Engineering School," *New York Times*, June 3, 2015, sec. Education, https://www.nytimes .com/2015/06/04/education/john-paulson-gives-400-million-to-harvard-for -engineering-school.html; Will Daniel, "Falling Home Prices Shouldn't Collapse the Financial System, Says Hedge Funder Who Made $4 Billion Betting on the 2008 Housing Crash," Fortune, September 26, 2022, https://fortune.com/2022/09/26 /falling-home-prices-shouldnt-collapse-financial-system-hedge-funder-john -paulson-made-billions-2008-housing-crash/.

4. James Fallows, "When the Top U.S. Tax Rate Was 70 Percent—or Higher," *The Atlantic*, January 25, 2019, https://www.theatlantic.com/ideas/archive/2019/01 /tax-rates-davos/622220/.

5. Sabrina Parys and Tina Orem, "2021–2022 Tax Brackets and Federal Income Tax Rates," NerdWallet, April 12, 2022, https://www.nerdwallet.com/article/taxes /federal-income-tax-brackets.

6. Jake Johnson, " 'Eye-Popping': Analysis Shows Top 1% Gained $21 Trillion in Wealth since 1989 while Bottom Half Lost $900 Billion," United Steelworkers blog, June 22, 2019, https://usw.org/blog/2019/eye-popping-analysis-shows-top-1 -gained-21-trillion-in-wealth-since-1989-while-bottom-half-lost-900-billion.

7. Dominic Rushe, "The Richest Americans Became 40% Richer during the Pandemic," *The Guardian*, October 5, 2021, https://www.theguardian.com/media/2021/oct/05 /richest-americans-became-richer-during-pandemic.

8. Joseph E. Stiglitz, *People, Power, and Profits: Progressive Capitalism for an Age of Discontent* (New York: W. W. Norton, 2019).

9. Dan Mangan, "Bezos, Buffett, Bloomberg, Musk, Icahn and Soros Pay Tiny Fraction of Wealth in Income Taxes, Report Reveals," CNBC, June 8, 2021, https:// www.cnbc.com/2021/06/08/bezos-musk-buffett-bloomberg-icahn-and-soros-pay -little-in-taxes.html.

10. Peter A. Thiel with Blake Masters, *Zero to One: Notes on Startups, or How to Build the Future* (New York: Crown Business, 2014).

11. Warren E. Buffett to the shareholders of Berkshire Hathaway, March 1, 1996, https://www.berkshirehathaway.com/letters/1995.html.

12. Emmanuel Saez and Gabriel Zucman, *The Triumph of Injustice: How the Rich Dodge Taxes and How to Make Them Pay* (New York: W. W. Norton, 2019).

13. "Google Shifted $23 Billion to Tax Haven Bermuda in 2017: Filing," Reuters, January 3, 2019, https://www.reuters.com/article/us-google-taxes-netherlands -idUSKCN1OX1G9.

14. Renu Zaretsky, "Corporate Taxes: Are They Fair? Who Really Pays Them, and When?," Tax Policy Center, March 4, 2020, https://www.taxpolicycenter.org /taxvox/corporate-taxes-are-they-fair-who-really-pays-them-and-when.

15. Galen Hendricks and Seth Hanlon, "The TCJA 2 Years Later: Corporations, Not Workers, Are the Big Winners," Center for American Progress, December 19, 2019, https://www.americanprogress.org/article/tcja-2-years-later-corporations-not -workers-big-winners/.

16. Jason Del Rey, "Leaked: Confidential Amazon Memo Reveals New Software to Track Unions," Vox, October 6, 2020, https://www.vox.com/recode/2020/10/6/21502639/amazon-union-busting-tracking-memo-spoc.

17. Nir Kaissar and Timothy L. O'Brien, "Who Helps Pay Amazon's Low-Wage Workers? You Do," Bloomberg, March 18, 2021, https://www.bloomberg.com/opinion/articles/2021-03-18/who-helps-pay-amazon-walmart-and-mcdonald-s-workers-you-do.

18. Associated Press, "Judge Approves Settlement in Apple, Google Wage Case," Los Angeles Times, September 3, 2015, https://www.latimes.com/business/technology/la-fi-tn-tech-jobs-settlement-20150903-story.html.

19. Daria Roithmayr, "Racial Cartels," Michigan Journal of Race and Law 16, no. 1 (2010): 45–79.

20. Existential Comics (@existentialcoms), "News That Will Cause Stocks to Go up:—A Minimum Wage Increase Is Struck down—Employees Are Prevented from Unionizing—Corporate Taxes Are Reduced..." Twitter, January 12, 2020, 7:52 p.m., https://twitter.com/existentialcoms/status/1216160983875375104.

21. Adedayo Akala, "Cost of Racism: U.S. Economy Lost $16 Trillion Because of Discrimination, Bank Says," Updates: The Fight against Racial Discrimination, NPR, September 23, 2020, https://www.npr.org/sections/live-updates-protests-for-racial-justice/2020/09/23/916022472/cost-of-racism-u-s-economy-lost-16-trillion-because-of-discrimination-bank-says.

22. Jonathan Woetzel et al., How Advancing Women's Equality Can Add $12 Trillion to Global Growth, McKinsey Global Institute, September 1, 2015, https://www.mckinsey.com/featured-insights/employment-and-growth/how-advancing-womens-equality-can-add-12-trillion-to-global-growth.

23. E. Wesley F. Peterson, "The Role of Population in Economic Growth," SAGE Open 7, no. 4 (2017), https://doi.org/10.1177/2158244017736094.

24. Ollie A. Williams, "World's Wealth Hits Half a Quadrillion Dollars," Forbes, June 10, 2021, https://www.forbes.com/sites/oliverwilliams1/2021/06/10/worlds-wealth-hits-half-a-quadrillion-dollars/.

25. "The Richest Get Richer," Reuters, March 15, 2012, https://www.reuters.com/article/idUS425139732120120315.

26. Robert Frank, "Here's Why This Economist Says the 'Perfect' Tax Rate for the Rich Is 75%," CNBC, October 15, 2019, https://www.cnbc.com/2019/10/15/this-economist-says-the-perfect-tax-rate-for-the-rich-is-75percent.html.

27. Saez and Zucman, Triumph of Injustice.

28. "When Income Was Taxed at 94%: How FDR Tackled Debt and Reckless Republicans," FlaglerLive.com, August 14, 2011, https://flaglerlive.com/26685/gc-fdr-and-taxes/.

29. Michael J. Sandel, The Tyranny of Merit: What's Become of the Common Good? (New York: Farrar, Straus and Giroux, 2020).

30. Martin Luther King Jr., speech to striking sanitation workers, Memphis, TN, March 18, 1968, in "All Labor Has Dignity," ed. Michael K. Honey (Boston: Beacon, 2011), 172.

31. Leo P. Brophy, "Horace Greeley, 'Socialist,'" *New York History* 29, no. 3 (1948): 309–317.

32. Michael Hiltzik, "They Tried to Call FDR and the New Deal 'Socialist' Too. Here's How He Responded," *Los Angeles Times*, February 13, 2019, https://www.latimes.com/business/hiltzik/la-fi-hiltzik-socialism-20190213-story.html; Tom van der Voort, "In the Beginning: Medicare and Medicaid," Miller Center, July 24, 2017, https://millercenter.org/issues-policy/us-domestic-policy/beginning-medicare-and-medicaid; "Why Calling Obamacare 'Socialism' Makes No Sense," ABC News, October 1, 2013, https://abcnews.go.com/ABC_Univision/Politics/calling-obamacare-socialism-makes-sense-analysis/story?id=20435162; Fred Sievert, "'Build Back Better'? Beware of the 'Free' Gifts of Socialism, America," Fox Business, November 5, 2021, https://www.foxbusiness.com/politics/build-back-better-free-gifts-socialism-fred-sievert.

33. "McCain, Palin Hint That Obama's Policies Are 'Socialist,'" CNN, 2008, https://www.cnn.com/2008/POLITICS/10/18/campaign.wrap/.

34. Marco Ranaldi and Branko Milanovic, "Capitalist Systems and Income Inequality," VoxEU, December 3, 2020, https://voxeu.org/article/capitalist-systems-and-income-inequality.

35. Robert Faturechi, "The Billionaire Playbook: How Sports Owners Use Their Teams to Avoid Millions in Taxes," Minnesota Reformer, July 15, 2021, https://minnesotareformer.com/2021/07/15/the-billionaire-playbook-how-sports-owners-use-their-teams-to-avoid-millions-in-taxes/.

36. Ken Belson and Kevin Draper, "N.F.L. Signs Media Deals Worth Over $100 Billion," *New York Times*, March 18, 2021, sec. Sports, https://www.nytimes.com/2021/03/18/sports/football/nfl-tv-contracts.html.

Chapter 12: Abolishing Poverty

1. Nick Hanauer, "Better Schools Won't Fix America," *The Atlantic*, June 10, 2019, https://www.theatlantic.com/magazine/archive/2019/07/education-isnt-enough/590611/.

2. Abigail Johnson Hess, "Bill and Melinda Gates Have Spent Billions Trying to Fix U.S. Public Education but Say It's Not Having the Impact They Want," CNBC, February 12, 2020, https://www.cnbc.com/2020/02/12/bill-and-melinda-gates-say-education-philanthropy-is-not-having-impact.html.

3. Teresa Iacobelli and Barbara Shubinski, "'Without Distinction of Race, Sex, or Creed': The General Education Board, 1903–1964," RE:source, Rockefeller Archive Center, January 5, 2022, https://resource.rockarch.org/story/the-general-education-board-1903-1964/.

4. Jeremy Norman, "Andrew Carnegie Donates the First Carnegie Library to His Hometown, Dunfermine, Scotland," HistoryofInformation.com, July 6, 2022, https://www.historyofinformation.com/detail.php?id=3000.

5. Rutger Bregman, "Rutger Bregman Tells Davos to Talk about Tax: 'This Is Not Rocket Science,'" YouTube video, 1:45, posted by Guardian News on January 29, 2019, https://www.youtube.com/watch?v=P8ijiLqfXP0.

6. Nick Hanauer, "Better Schools Won't Fix America," *The Atlantic*, June 10, 2019, https://www.theatlantic.com/magazine/archive/2019/07/education-isnt-enough /590611/.

7. Hanauer, "Better Schools."

8. Megan Ming Francis and John Fabian Witt, "Movement Capture or Movement Strategy? A Critical Race History Exchange on the Beginnings of *Brown v. Board*," *Yale Journal of the Law and Humanities* 31, no. 2 (2021): 520–546, http://hdl .handle.net/20.500.13051/7572.

9. Kelsey Piper, "How 'Movement Capture' Shaped the Fight for Civil Rights," Vox, February 28, 2019, https://www.vox.com/future-perfect/2019/2/28/18241490/movement -capture-civil-rights-philanthropy-funding.

10. Jessica Semega, Melissa Kollar, John Creamer, and Abinash Mohanty, *Income and Poverty in the United States: 2018*, US Census Bureau, report no. P60-266, September 10, 2019, https://www.census.gov/library/publications/2019/demo/p60 -266.html.

11. "Women and Poverty in America," Legal Momentum, accessed September 18, 2022, https://www.legalmomentum.org/women-and-poverty-america.

12. "Poverty Rate by Race/Ethnicity," State Health Facts, Kaiser Family Foundation, October 23, 2020, https://www.kff.org/other/state-indicator/poverty-rate-by -raceethnicity/.

13. University of Wisconsin, Madison, "How Is Poverty Measured?," Institute for Research on Poverty, accessed October 7, 2022, https://www.irp.wisc.edu /resources/how-is-poverty-measured/.

14. Eugene Smolensky and Robert Plotnick, "Inequality and Poverty in the United States: 1900 to 1990," Institute for Research on Poverty, Discussion Paper no. 998-93, University of Wisconsin–Madison, March 1993, https://www.irp.wisc.edu /publications/dps/pdfs/dp99893.pdf.

15. Andre M. Perry and Tawanna Black, "George Floyd's Death Demonstrates the Policy Violence That Devalues Black Lives," *The Avenue* (blog), Brookings Institution, May 28, 2020, https://www.brookings.edu/blog/the-avenue/2020/05 /28/george-floyds-death-demonstrates-the-policy-violence-that-devalues-black -lives/.

16. Angela Davis, "The Meaning of Freedom," speech, Metropolitan State College, Denver, CO, February 15, 2008, Alternative Radio https://www.alternativeradio .org/products/dava013/.

17. Quoted in Jenny Farrell, "Gandhi: The Worst Form of Violence Is Poverty," Culture Matters, October 7, 2019, http://www.culturematters.org.uk/index.php/culture /theory/item/3154-gandhi-the-worst-form-of-violence-is-poverty.

18. Martin Luther King Jr., *Where Do We Go from Here: Chaos or Community?* (Boston: Beacon, 2010).

19. Robert J. Lampman, "Nixon's Family Assistance Plan," Institute for Research on Poverty, Discussion Paper no. 57-69, University of Wisconsin–Madison, November 1969, https://www.irp.wisc.edu/publications/dps/pdfs/dp5769.pdf.

20. Mitchell T. Maki, "How Japanese Americans Fought for—and Won—Redress for WWII Incarceration," History Stories, History.com, April 29, 2022, https://www.history.com/news/japanese-american-wwii-incarceration-camps-redress.

21. Vikram Dodd, "Tackle Poverty and Inequality to Reduce Crime, Says Police Chief," *The Guardian*, April 18, 2021, https://www.theguardian.com/uk-news/2021/apr/18/tackle-poverty-and-inequality-to-reduce-says-police-chief.

22. Muhammad Khalid Anser et al., "Dynamic Linkages between Poverty, Inequality, Crime, and Social Expenditures in a Panel of 16 Countries: Two-Step GMM Estimates," *Journal of Economic Structures* 9, no. 1 (2020), https://doi.org/10.1186/s40008-020-00220-6.

23. " 'It Has Been Proven, Less Inequality Means Less Crime,' " World Bank, September 5, 2014, https://www.worldbank.org/en/news/feature/2014/09/03/latinoamerica-menos-desigualdad-se-reduce-el-crimen.

24. Robert Muggah and Sameh Wahba, "How Reducing Inequality Will Make Our Cities Safer," *Sustainable Cities* (blog), World Bank, March 2, 2022, https://blogs.worldbank.org/sustainablecities/how-reducing-inequality-will-make-our-cities-safer.

25. "Marcus Aurelius Quotes," BrainyQuote, accessed September 18, 2022, https://www.brainyquote.com/quotes/marcus_aurelius_106264.

26. Thomas Paine, *Agrarian Justice*, in *The Essential Thomas Paine*, ed. John Dos Passos (Mineola, NY: Dover, 2008), 167.

27. William MacAskill, "Effective Altruism: Introduction," *Essays in Philosophy* 18, no. 1 (2017): 1–5, https://doi.org/10.7710/1526-0569.1580.

28. "About GiveDirectly," GiveDirectly, accessed September 18, 2022, https://www.givedirectly.org/about/.

29. "GiveDirectly," GiveWell, accessed September 18, 2022, https://www.givewell.org/charities/give-directly.

30. "Research on Cash Transfers," GiveDirectly, December 22, 2020, https://www.givedirectly.org/research-on-cash-transfers/.

31. "Cash Transfers," GiveWell, December 2012, https://www.givewell.org/international/technical/programs/cash-transfers.

32. Rachel Treisman, "California Program Giving $500 No-Strings-Attached Stipends Pays Off, Study Finds," NPR, March 4, 2021, https://www.npr.org/2021/03/04/973653719/california-program-giving-500-no-strings-attached-stipends-pays-off-study-finds.

33. "Participant Story: Laura," SEED, accessed October 8, 2022, https://www.stocktondemonstration.org/participant-stories/laura.

34. "A City Made the Case for Universal Basic Income. Dozens Are Following Suit," *PBS News Hour*, December 27, 2020, https://www.pbs.org/newshour/show/a-city-made-the-case-for-universal-basic-income-dozens-are-following-suit.

35. Emily A. Shrider, Melissa Kollar, Frances Chen, and Jessica Semega, *Income and Poverty in the United States: 2020*, US Census Bureau, report no. P60-273, September 14, 2021, https://www.census.gov/library/publications/2021/demo/p60-273.html.

36. "Poverty in San Francisco," City Performance Scorecards, City and County of San Francisco, accessed September 18, 2022, https://sfgov.org/scorecards/safety-net/poverty-san-francisco.

37. Johannes Haushofer and Jeremy Shapiro, "The Short-Term Impact of Unconditional Cash Transfers to the Poor: Experimental Evidence from Kenya," The Quarterly Journal of Economics 131, no. 4 (November 2016): 1973–2042, https://doi.org/10.1093/qje/qjw025.

38. Joseph Stiglitz, "Share the Wealth as We Recover Health," Noēma, June 9, 2020, https://www.noemamag.com/joe-stiglitz-ray-dalio-share-the-wealth-as-we-recover-health.

39. Kilolo Kijakazi and Alexander Carther, "How Baby Bonds Could Help Americans Start Adulthood Strong and Narrow the Racial Wealth Gap," Urban Institute, January 23, 2020, https://www.urban.org/urban-wire/how-baby-bonds-could-help-americans-start-adulthood-strong-and-narrow-racial-wealth-gap.

40. Aaryn Urell, "Covid-19's Impact on People in Prison," Equal Justice Initiative, April 16, 2021, https://eji.org/news/covid-19s-impact-on-people-in-prison/.

41. Tara O'Neill Hayes, "The Economic Costs of the U.S. Criminal Justice System," American Action Forum, July 16, 2020, https://www.americanactionforum.org/research/the-economic-costs-of-the-u-s-criminal-justice-system/.

42. "NHE Fact Sheet," Centers for Medicare and Medicaid Services, December 15, 2021, https://www.cms.gov/Research-Statistics-Data-and-Systems/Statistics-Trends-and-Reports/NationalHealthExpendData/NHE-Fact-Sheet; Emily Badger and Quoctrung Bui, "Cities Grew Safer. Police Budgets Kept Growing," New York Times, June 12, 2020, https://www.nytimes.com/interactive/2020/06/12/upshot/cities-grew-safer-police-budgets-kept-growing.html.

43. Nelson Mandela, speech for the Make Poverty History campaign, London, UK, February 3, 2005, transcript available at http://db.nelsonmandela.org/speeches/pub_view.asp?pg=item&ItemID=NMS760&txtstr=SLAVERY.

Chapter 13: A Culture of Repair

1. J. Scott Trubey and Bill Torpy, "At Reynolds Plantation, a Vision Comes Together, Then Falls Apart," May 25, 2011, Atlanta Journal-Constitution, https://www.ajc.com/lifestyles/home—garden/reynolds-plantation-vision-comes-together-then-falls-apart/LAJCmOBbXXJVov893furWP/.

2. "Charles Murray," Southern Poverty Law Center, accessed July 22, 2022, https://www.splcenter.org/fighting-hate/extremist-files/individual/charles-murray.

3. Ian Wilhelm, "Ripples from a Protest Past," Chronicle of Higher Education, April 17, 2016, https://www.chronicle.com/article/ripples-from-a-protest-past/.

4. "Ed Whitfield," Community-Wealth.org, January 14, 2015, https://community-wealth.org/content/ed-whitfield.

5. "Black Land and Power," National Black Food & Justice Alliance, accessed September 18, 2022, https://www.blackfoodjustice.org/blacklandfund.

6. Home page, Reparations Summer, accessed September 18, 2022, https://reparations summer.com/.

7. Ed Whitfield, "Nevermind Guaranteed Income, We Want the Cow," Fund for Democratic Communities, January 2, 2017, https://f4dc.org/nevermind-guaranteed -income-we-want-the-cow/.

8. Vanessa Williamson, *Closing the Racial Wealth Gap Requires Heavy, Progressive Taxation of Wealth*, Brookings Institution, December 9, 2020, https://www .brookings.edu/research/closing-the-racial-wealth-gap-requires-heavy-progressive -taxation-of-wealth/.

9. William A. Darity, *From Here to Equality: Reparations for Black Americans in the Twenty-First Century* (Chapel Hill: University of North Carolina Press, 2022).

10. Bryce Covert, "The Typical Member of the 1 Percent Is an Old White Man," Think Progress, May 2, 2014, https://archive.thinkprogress.org/the-typical-member-of -the-1-percent-is-an-old-white-man-afcae20cdafb/; Isabel V. Sawhill and Christopher Pulliam, "Six Facts about Wealth in the United States," *Up Front* (blog), Brookings Institution, June 25, 2019, https://www.brookings.edu/blog/up-front /2019/06/25/six-facts-about-wealth-in-the-united-states/.

11. Chuck Collins, "U.S. Billionaires Got 62 Percent Richer During Pandemic. They're Now Up $1.8 Trillion," Institute for Policy Studies, August 24, 2021, https://ips-dc .org/u-s-billionaires-62-percent-richer-during-pandemic/.

12. "Facts and Figures: Women's Leadership and Political Participation," UN Women, January 15, 2021, https://www.unwomen.org/en/what-we-do/leadership-and-poli tical-participation/facts-and-figures.

13. Home page, Liberation Ventures, accessed September 18, 2022, https://www.liber ationventures.org.

14. Peter C. Baker, "In Chicago, Reparations Aren't Just an Idea. They're the Law," *The Guardian*, March 8, 2019, https://www.theguardian.com/news/2019/mar/08 /chicago-reparations-won-police-torture-school-curriculum.

15. Logan Jaffe, "The Nation's First Reparations Package to Survivors of Police Torture Included a Public Memorial. Survivors Are Still Waiting," ProPublica, July 3, 2020, https://www.propublica.org/article/the-nations-first-reparations-pack age-to-survivors-of-police-torture-included-a-public-memorial-survivors-are -still-waiting.

16. Louisa Schaefer, "'68 Movement Brought Lasting Changes to German Society," DW.com, November 4, 2008, https://www.dw.com/en/68-movement-brought-lasting -changes-to-german-society/a-3257581.

17. "Canada Agrees to Reparations for All Residential School Students," Cultural Survival, accessed September 18, 2022, https://www.culturalsurvival.org/news /canada-agrees-reparations-all-residential-school-students.

18. Jen Kirby, "The Impossible Task of Truth and Reconciliation," Vox, March 24, 2022, https://www.vox.com/22979953/forgiveness-reconciliation-truth.

19. "Basic Principles and Guidelines on the Right to a Remedy and Reparation for Victims of Gross Violations of International Human Rights Law and Serious Violations

of International Humanitarian Law," United Nations Human Rights Office of the High Commissioner, adopted December 16, 2005, General Assembly resolution 60/147, https://www.ohchr.org/en/instruments-mechanisms/instruments/basic-prin ciples-and-guidelines-right-remedy-and-reparation.

20. David A. Graham, "Why Are There Still So Many Confederate Monuments?" *The Atlantic*, April 26, 2016, https://www.theatlantic.com/politics/archive/2016/04 /the-stubborn-persistence-of-confederate-monuments/479751/.

21. Sarah Lynch, "Fact Check: Father of Modern Gynecology Performed Experiments on Enslaved Black Women," *USA Today*, June 19, 2020, https://www .usatoday.com/story/news/factcheck/2020/06/19/fact-check-j-marion-sims-did -medical-experiments-black-female-slaves/3202541001/.

22. Corey Mitchell, "Data: The Schools Named after Confederate Figures," *Education Week*, June 17, 2020, https://www.edweek.org/leadership/data-the-schools -named-after-confederate-figures/2020/06; Kurt Streeter, "It's 2020. Indigenous Team Names in Sports Have to Go," *New York Times*, December 21, 2020, https://www.nytimes.com/2020/12/21/sports/football/chiefs-indians-mascot -names.html; Frank Morris, "The Racial Justice Reckoning over Sports Team Names Is Spreading," NPR, July 11, 2020, https://www.npr.org/2020/07/11/8898 74026/the-racial-justice-reckoning-over-sports-team-names-is-spreading.

23. US Department of Agriculture, *Monthly Reports of the Department of Agriculture* (Washington, DC: Government Printing Office, 1873).

24. DeNeen L. Brown, "40 Acres and a Mule: How the First Reparations for Slavery Ended in Betrayal," *Washington Post*, April 15, 2021, https://www.washingtonpost .com/history/2021/04/15/40-acres-mule-slavery-reparations/.

25. "Truth Commission: South Africa," United States Institute of Peace, December 1, 1995, https://www.usip.org/publications/1995/12/truth-commission-south-africa.

26. "Truth and Reconciliation," Facing History & Ourselves, n.d., https://www.fac inghistory.org/stolen-lives-indigenous-peoples-canada-and-indian-residential -schools/historical-background/truth-and-reconciliation.

27. "South Africa Most Unequal Country in the World: Report," Al Jazeera, March 10, 2022, https://www.aljazeera.com/news/2022/3/10/south-africa-most-unequal -country-in-the-world-report.

28. Honor Keeler, "United Nations Expert Mechanism on the Rights of Indigenous Peoples 8th session," July 24, 2015, https://www.ohchr.org/sites/default/files/Documents /Issues/IPeoples/EMRIP/CulturalHeritage/InternationalRepatriation.pdf.

29. " 'Freedom Is a World in Which We All Have Access to What We Need'—An Interview with Ed Whitfield," Fund for Democratic Communities, May 23, 2017, https:// f4dc.org/freedom-is-a-world-in-which-we-all-have-access-to-what-we-need-an -interview-with-ed-whitfield/.

30. Home page, Fund for Reparations NOW!, accessed September 19, 2022, https:// www.fundforreparationsnow.org.

31. Home page, Reparations Summer, accessed September 19, 2022, https://reparations summer.com/.

32. "About the R4S Portal," Reparations 4 Slavery, accessed September 19, 2022, https://reparations4slavery.com/about-the-r4s-portal/.

33. Rachel L. Swarns, "Is Georgetown's $400,000-a-Year Plan to Aid Slave Descendants Enough?" *New York Times*, October 30, 2019, https://www.nytimes.com/2019/10/30/us/georgetown-slavery-reparations.html.

34. "An Examination of The Times' Failures on Race, Our Apology and a Path Forward" (editorial), *Los Angeles Times*, September 27, 2020, https://www.latimes.com/opinion/story/2020-09-27/los-angeles-times-apology-racism.

35. Cara J. Chang and Isabella B. Cho, "Harvard Pledges $100 Million to Redress Ties to Slavery," *Harvard Crimson*, April 27, 2022, https://www.thecrimson.com/article/2022/4/27/100-million-endowment-for-slavery-redress/.

36. Nigel Roberts, "Illinois City Selects First 16 Black Residents to Receive Reparations," BET, June 23, 2022, https://www.bet.com/article/ovlgoz/evanston-illinois-selects-first-16-black-residents-reparations.

37. Taryn Luna, "California Task Force Suggests Reparations in Report Detailing Lasting Harms of Slavery," *Los Angeles Times*, June 1, 2022, https://www.latimes.com/california/story/2022-06-01/california-to-unveil-groundbreaking-slavery-reparations-report.

38. "Cosponsors: H.R.40—117th Congress (2021–2022)," H.R.40—Commission to Study and Develop Reparation Proposals for African Americans Act, Congress.gov, April 14, 2021, https://www.congress.gov/bill/117th-congress/house-bill/40/cosponsors.

39. "Cosponsors: S.1083—116th Congress (2019–2020)," S.1083—H.R. 40 Commission to Study and Develop Reparation Proposals for African-Americans Act, Congress.gov, https://www.congress.gov/bill/116th-congress/senate-bill/1083/cosponsors.

40. "About NAARC," National African-American Reparations Commission, accessed September 19, 2022, https://reparationscomm.org/about-naarc/; "Our Mission," Project Truth, Reconciliation, and Reparations, accessed September 19, 2022, https://www.projecttruthandrec.org/our-mission; "About," Media 2070, accessed September 19, 2022, https://mediareparations.org/about/.

Chapter 14: A Healing Society

1. "How Common Is PTSD in Adults?," National Center for PTSD, US Department of Veterans Affairs, accessed September 19, 2022, https://www.ptsd.va.gov/understand/common/common_adults.asp.

2. Bessel A. Van der Kolk, *The Body Keeps the Score: Brain, Mind and Body in the Healing of Trauma* (New York: Penguin, 2015).

3. "Fast Facts: Preventing Child Abuse & Neglect," Violence Prevention, Centers for Disease Control and Prevention, May 31, 2022, https://www.cdc.gov/violenceprevention/childabuseandneglect/fastfact.html.

4. "Child Sexual Abuse Statistics," National Center for Victims of Crime, accessed September 19, 2022, https://victimsofcrime.org/child-sexual-abuse-statistics/.

5. "Child Abuse and Neglect: What Parents Should Know," HealthyChildren.org, March 16, 2022, https://www.healthychildren.org/English/safety-prevention/at-home/Pages/What-to-Know-about-Child-Abuse.aspx.

6. Yvonne M. Vissing, Murray A. Straus, Richard J. Gelles, and John W. Harrop, "Verbal Aggression by Parents and Psychosocial Problems of Children," *Child Abuse and Neglect* 15, no. 3 (1991): 223–238, https://doi.org/10.1016/0145-2134(91)90067-n.

7. Matthew J. Breiding et al., Prevalence and Characteristics of Sexual Violence, Stalking, and Intimate Partner Violence Victimization—National Intimate Partner and Sexual Violence Survey, United States, 2011," *Morbidity and Mortality Weekly Report Surveillance Summaries* 63, no. SS8, Centers for Disease Control and Prevention, September 5, 2014, https://www.cdc.gov/mmwr/preview/mmwrhtml/ss6308a1.htm.

8. "Facts about Domestic Violence and Psychological Abuse," National Coalition against Domestic Violence, 2015, https://assets.speakcdn.com/assets/2497/domestic_violence_and_psychological_abuse_ncadv.pdf.

9. Milen L. Radell et al., "The Impact of Different Types of Abuse on Depression," *Depression Research and Treatment* vol. 2021 (April 13, 2021), article no. 6654503, https://doi.org/10.1155/2021/6654503.

10. David W. Brown et al., "Adverse Childhood Experiences and the Risk of Premature Mortality," *American Journal of Preventive Medicine* 37, no. 5 (2009): 389–396, https://doi.org/10.1016/j.amepre.2009.06.021.

11. "Long-Term Consequences of Child Abuse and Neglect," Children's Bureau, April 2019, 9, https://www.childwelfare.gov/pubpdfs/long_term_consequences.pdf.

12. Kimberly Matheson et al., "Traumatic Experiences, Perceived Discrimination, and Psychological Distress among Members of Various Socially Marginalized Groups," *Frontiers in Psychology* 10 (2019), https://www.frontiersin.org/articles/10.3389/fpsyg.2019.00416.

13. Ayman M. A. Omar, Tomasz Piotr Wisniewski, and Liafisu Sina Yekini, "Psychopathic Traits of Corporate Leadership as Predictors of Future Stock Returns," *European Financial Management* 25, no. 5 (2019): 1196–1228, https://doi.org/10.1111/eufm.12244.

14. Aaron Morrison, "50-Year War on Drugs Imprisoned Millions of Black Americans," AP News, July 23, 2021, https://apnews.com/article/war-on-drugs-75e61c224de3a394235df80de7d70b7; Laura A. Pratt, Debra J. Brody, and Qiuping Gu, "Antidepressant Use in Persons Aged 12 and Over: United States, 2005–2008," NCHS Data Brief no. 76, National Center for Health Statistics, Centers for Disease Control and Prevention, October 2011, https://www.cdc.gov/nchs/products/databriefs/db76.htm.

15. Omar A. Almohammed et al., "Antidepressants and Health-Related Quality of Life (HRQoL) for Patients with Depression: Analysis of the Medical Expenditure Panel Survey from the United States," *PLOS ONE* 17, no. 4 (2022), : e0265928, https://doi.org/10.1371/journal.pone.0265928.

16. Sarah Schulman, *Conflict Is Not Abuse: Overstating Harm, Community Responsibility, and the Duty of Repair* (Vancouver: Arsenal Pulp, 2016).

17. Elaine N. Aron, *The Highly Sensitive Person: How to Thrive When the World Overwhelms You*, 25th anniversary ed. (New York: Citadel, 2020).

18. Nedra Glover Tawwab, *Set Boundaries, Find Peace: A Guide to Reclaiming Yourself* (New York: TarcherPerigee, 2021).

19. Ibram X. Kendi, *How to Be an Antiracist* (New York: One World, 2019).

20. Marissa Conrad, "What Is Gaslighting? Meaning, Examples And Support," *Forbes*, March 17, 2022, https://www.forbes.com/health/mind/what-is-gaslighting/.

21. Resmaa Menakem, *My Grandmother's Hands: Racialized Trauma and the Pathway to Mending Our Hearts and Bodies* (Las Vegas, NV: Central Recovery, 2017).

22. John M. Gottman and Nan Silver, *The Seven Principles for Making Marriage Work*, revised and updated ed. (New York: Harmony, 2015).

23. Nirmita Panchal, Rabah Kamal, Cynthia Cox, and Rachel Garfield, "The Implications of COVID-19 for Mental Health and Substance Use," Kaiser Family Foundation, February 10, 2021, https://www.kff.org/report-section/the-implications-of-covid-19-for-mental-health-and-substance-use-issue-brief/.

24. A. Guttmann, "Advertising Spending in North America 2000–2004," Statista, July 1, 2022, https://www.statista.com/statistics/429036/advertising-expenditure-in-north-america/.

25. Anna Cooban, Riley Charles, "Rotterdam May Dismantle Historic Bridge for Superyacht Reportedly Owned by Jeff Bezos," CNN, February 4, 2022, https://www.cnn.com/2022/02/04/business/jeff-bezos-rotterdam-yacht/index.html.

Chapter 15: Embracing Feminine Leadership

1. *Succession*, season 2, episode 10, "This Is Not for Tears," aired October 13, 2019, on HBO.

2. Kimberly Adams, "The Disturbing Parallels between Modern Accounting and the Business of Slavery," *Marketplace*, August 14, 2018, https://www.marketplace.org/2018/08/14/disturbing-parallels-between-modern-accounting-business-slavery/.

3. Scott Christian, "The Epic History of Military Style," *Esquire*, February 2, 2016, https://www.esquire.com/style/a41725/the-epic-history-of-military-style/.

4. Katty Kay and Claire Shipman, "The Confidence Gap," *The Atlantic*, April 15, 2014, https://www.theatlantic.com/magazine/archive/2014/05/the-confidence-gap/359815/.

5. Linda Babcock, Sara Laschever, Michele Gelfand, and Deborah Small, "Nice Girls Don't Ask," *Harvard Business Review*, October 1, 2003, https://hbr.org/2003/10/nice-girls-dont-ask.

6. Tara Sophia Mohr, "Why Women Don't Apply for Jobs Unless They're 100% Qualified," *Harvard Business Review*, August 25, 2014, https://hbr.org/2014/08/why-women-dont-apply-for-jobs-unless-theyre-100-qualified.

7. Hannah Riley Bowles, "Why Women Don't Negotiate Their Job Offers," *Harvard Business Review*, June 19, 2014, https://hbr.org/2014/06/why-women-dont-negotiate-their-job-offers.

8. Lauren Caruso, "Women Who Wear Makeup to Work Get Paid More, Study Confirms," *Allure*, May 25, 2016, https://www.allure.com/story/women-wear-makeup-paid-more.

9. Don Charlton, "This Invisible Problem Is Costing Employers $500 Billion Per Year," *Inc.*, May 20, 2019, https://www.inc.com/don-charlton/this-invisible-problem-is -costing-employers-500-billion-per-year.html.

10. Leslie Picker, "Alpha Males Hurt Alpha: Hedge Fund Managers with High Testosterone Underperform," CNBC, April 19, 2018, https://www.cnbc.com/2018/04/19 /alpha-males-hurt-alpha-hedge-fund-managers-with-high-testosterone-under perform.html.

11. "Unhealthy Testosterone Levels in Men: Causes and Symptoms," Everlywell, accessed September 19, 2022, https://www.everlywell.com/blog/testosterone /unhealthy-testosterone-levels-men/.

12. Gregory Louis Carter, Anne C. Campbell, and Steven Muncer, "The Dark Triad Personality: Attractiveness to Women," *Personality and Individual Differences* 56 (January 2014): 57–61, https://doi.org/10.1016/j.paid.2013.08.021.

13. "The US Gun Homicide Rate Is 26 Times That of Other High-Income Countries," Everytown Research & Policy, Everytown for Gun Safety Support Fund, January 26, 2022, https://everytownresearch.org/graph/the-u-s-gun-homicide-rate-is -25-times-that-of-other-high-income-countries/; "Murder in the U.S.: Number of Offenders by Gender 2020," Statista, October 7, 2021, https://www.statista.com /statistics/251886/murder-offenders-in-the-us-by-gender/.

14. Piero Scaruffi, "The Worst Genocides of the 20th and 21st Centuries," Piero Scaruffi blog, accessed September 19, 2022, https://www.scaruffi.com/politics/dictat.html.

15. Tomas Chamorro-Premuzic, *Why Do So Many Incompetent Men Become Leaders? (And How to Fix It)* (Boston: Harvard Business Review Press, 2019).

16. Jack Zenger and Joseph Folkman, "Research: Women Score Higher Than Men in Most Leadership Skills," *Harvard Business Review*, June 25, 2019, https://hbr .org/2019/06/research-women-score-higher-than-men-in-most-leadership-skills.

17. Zenger and Folkman, "Women Score Higher."

18. Jack Zenger and Joseph Folkman, "Research: Women Are Better Leaders during a Crisis," *Harvard Business Review*, December 30, 2020, https://hbr.org/2020/12 /research-women-are-better-leaders-during-a-crisis.

19. "Why Women Governors May Be Better Crisis Leaders: A Study of States during COVID-19," Wisconsin School of Business, July 14, 2020, https://business.wisc .edu/news/leadership-during-the-pandemic-states-with-women-governors-had -fewer-covid-19-deaths/.

20. Jon Henley, "Female-Led Countries Handled Coronavirus Better, Study Suggests," *The Guardian*, August 18, 2020, https://www.theguardian.com/world/2020/aug /18/female-led-countries-handled-coronavirus-better-study-jacinda-ardern-angela -merkel.

21. Quoted in "Barack Obama: Women Are Better Leaders Than Men," BBC News, December 16, 2019, https://www.bbc.com/news/world-asia-50805822.

22. James C. Collins, *Good to Great: Why Some Companies Make the Leap—and Others Don't* (New York: Harper Business, 2001); Travis Bradberry, Jean Greaves, and Patrick Lencioni, *Emotional Intelligence 2.0* (San Diego, CA: Talent Smart,

2009); Bill George and Warren G. Bennis, *Authentic Leadership: Rediscovering the Secrets to Creating Lasting Value* (San Francisco: Jossey-Bass, 2003).

23. Dale Vernor, "PTSD Is More Likely in Women Than Men," National Alliance on Mental Illness, October 8, 2019, https://www.nami.org/Blogs/NAMI-Blog /October-2019/PTSD-is-More-Likely-in-Women-Than-Men; Benita N. Chatmon, "Males and Mental Health Stigma," *American Journal of Men's Health* 14, no. 4 (2020), https://doi.org/10.1177/1557988320949322; Jarrod B. Call and Kevin Shafer, "Gendered Manifestations of Depression and Help Seeking among Men," *American Journal of Men's Health* 12, no. 1 (2018): 41–51, https://doi.org/10.1177 /1557988315623993.

24. https://bjs.ojp.gov/content/pub/pdf/fvs03.pdf.

25. Lewis Howes, *The Mask of Masculinity: How Men Can Embrace Vulnerability, Create Strong Relationships, and Live Their Fullest Lives* (Emmaus, PA: Rodale, 2017).

26. Leon F. Seltzer, "What Your Anger May Be Hiding," *Psychology Today*, July 11, 2008, https://www.psychologytoday.com/us/blog/evolution-the-self/200807/what -your-anger-may-be-hiding.

27. "Anger—How It Affects People," Better Health Channel, accessed September 19, 2022, https://www.betterhealth.vic.gov.au/health/healthyliving/anger-how-it -affects-people.

28. bell hooks, *The Will to Change: Men, Masculinity, and Love* (New York: Atria, 2004), 11–12.

29. "About Marlo Pedroso," Emergence Project, February 18, 2013, https://emergence projectboston.com/services/bios/.

30. "Get Ready for a 48 Hour Adventure That Can Transform Your World as a Man," ManKind Project, accessed September 19, 2022, https://mankindproject.org/new -warrior-training-adventure/.

Chapter 16: Restoring Connection

1. "Home page, Relational Uprising, accessed September 19, 2022, https://relational uprising.org.

2. Tristan Claridge, "Functions of Social Capital—Bonding, Bridging, Linking," Social Capital Research, 2018, 7, https://www.socialcapitalresearch.com/wp-content/uploads /2018/11/Functions-of-Social-Capital.pdf.

3. Marcela C. Otero et al., "Behavioral Indices of Positivity Resonance Associated with Long-Term Marital Satisfaction," *Emotion* 20, no. 7 (October 2020): 1225–1233, https://doi.org/10.1037/emo0000634.

4. Alan M. Dershowitz, *The Vanishing American Jew: In Search of Jewish Identity for the Next Century* (Boston: Little, Brown, 1997).

5. Dan Rickman, "Does Judaism Discriminate against Women?," *The Guardian*, June 10, 2009, https://www.theguardian.com/commentisfree/belief/2009/jun/10 /judaism-women-feminism-orthodox.

6. Zena Tahhan, "Israel's Settlements: Over 50 Years of Land Theft Explained," Al Jazeera, November 21, 2017, https://interactive.aljazeera.com/aje/2017/50-years -illegal-settlements/index.html.

7. "Israel and Palestine: Whether a Palestinian Who Has Lived..." Immigration and Refugee Board of Canada, Refworld, April 26, 2016, https://www.refworld .org/docid/585a7db14.html; "From the Collection: Jewish Identification Cards" (blog post), Museum of Jewish Heritage—A Living Memorial to the Holocaust, August 17, 2021, https://mjhnyc.org/blog/from-the-collection-jewish-identification -cards/.

8. Ronald A. Heifetz, Alexander Grashow, and Martin Linsky, *The Practice of Adaptive Leadership: Tools and Tactics for Changing Your Organization and the World* (Boston: Harvard Business Press, 2009).

9. Ronald Heifetz, "The Challenge of Adaptive Leadership," *New Zealand Management*, July 24, 2005, https://management.co.nz/article/thought-leadership-ronald -heifetz-challenge-adaptive-leadership.

10. Mark Leary, "Affiliation, Acceptance, and Belonging: The Pursuit of Interpersonal Connection," in Handbook of Social Psychology, vol. 2, 2010, https://doi .org/10.1002/9780470561119.socpsy002024.

11. "Striving toward a World of Belonging without Othering" (blog post), Independent Sector, March 17, 2022, https://independentsector.org/blog/striving-toward-a -world-of-belonging-without-othering/.

12. Brené Brown, *Braving the Wilderness: The Quest for True Belonging and the Courage to Stand Alone* (New York: Random House, 2017), 40.

13. Harvard Diversity Inclusion & Belonging, *Final Report: Pilot Pulse Survey on Inclusion & Belonging*, Harvard University, 2019, https://pulse.harvard.edu/files /pulse/files/pilot_pulse_survey_ib_final_report.pdf.

14. "About Us," Relational Uprising, accessed September 19, 2022, https://relational uprising.org/mission.

15. Julianne Holt-Lunstad, Timothy B. Smith, and J. Bradley Layton, "Social Relationships and Mortality Risk: A Meta-Analytic Review," *PLOS Medicine* 7, no. 7 (2010): e1000316, https://doi.org/10.1371/journal.pmed.1000316.

16. Susan Pinker, "The Secret to Living Longer May Be Your Social Life," TED Talk, TED2017, April 2017, Vancouver, BC, video posted on TED.com, https://www.ted .com/talks/susan_pinker_the_secret_to_living_longer_may_be_your_social_life.

17. Dave Davies, "A Former Neo-Nazi Explains Why Hate Drew Him In—and How He Got Out," *Fresh Air*, NPR, January 18, 2018, https://www.npr.org/2018 /01/18/578745514/a-former-neo-nazi-explains-why-hate-drew-him-in-and -how-he-got-out.

18. Natasha Lipman, "Christian Picciolini: The Neo-Nazi Who Became an Anti-Nazi," BBC News, December 5, 2020, https://www.bbc.com/news/stories-54526345.

19. Thomas J. Saporito, "It's Time to Acknowledge CEO Loneliness," *Harvard Business Review*, February 15, 2012, https://hbr.org/2012/02/its-time-to-acknowledge -ceo-lo.

20. Dan Schawbel, "Why Work Friendships Are Critical for Long-Term Happiness," CNBC, November 13, 2018, https://www.cnbc.com/2018/11/13/why-work-friendships -are-critical-for-long-term-happiness.html.

21. Tomas Chamorro-Premuzic, *Why Do So Many Incompetent Men Become Leaders? (And How to Fix It)* (Boston: Harvard Business Review Press, 2019).

22. Jay Greene, "Bill Gates Acknowledges an Affair with an Employee, Which Microsoft Investigated," *Washington Post*, May 17, 2021, https://www.washingtonpost .com/technology/2021/05/17/bill-gates-affair-investigation/.

23. John Maynard Keynes, "Economic Possibilities for our Grandchildren (1930)," in *Essays in Persuasion* (New York: Harcourt Brace, 1932), 358–373.

24. Willem Roper, "Working More for Less: How Wages in America Have Stagnated," World Economic Forum, November 10, 2020, https://www.weforum. org/agenda/2020/11/productivity-workforce-america-united-states-wages -stagnate/.

25. "Average Annual Hours Worked by Persons Engaged for United States," Federal Reserve Economic Data, Research Department of the Federal Reserve Bank of St. Louis, updated January 21, 2021, https://fred.stlouisfed.org/series /AVHWPEUSA065NRUG.

26. "The Productivity–Pay Gap," Economic Policy Institute, August 2021, https://www .epi.org/productivity-pay-gap/.

27. Michael Moritz, "Silicon Valley Would Be Wise to Follow China's Lead," *Financial Times*, January 17, 2018, https://www.ft.com/content/42daca9e-facc-11e7- 9bfc-052cbba03425.

28. Kabir Sehgal and Deepak Chopra, "Stanford Professor: Working This Many Hours a Week Is Basically Pointless. Here's How to Get More Done—by Doing Less," CNBC, March 20, 2019, https://www.cnbc.com/2019/03/20/stanford-study-longer -hours-doesnt-make-you-more-productive-heres-how-to-get-more-done-by-doing -less.html.

29. Gabriela Miranda, "Employees in Iceland Starting [*sic*] Working 4 Days a Week. It Didn't Hurt Productivity, Researchers Say," *USA Today*, July 6, 2021, https:// www.usatoday.com/story/money/2021/07/06/iceland-worker-study-four-day-work -week-productivity/7871364002/.

30. Michael S. Hyatt and Megan Hyatt Miller, *Win at Work and Succeed at Life: 5 Principles to Free Yourself from the Cult of Overwork* (Grand Rapids, MI: Baker, 2021).

31. Bronnie Ware, "Regrets of the Dying," Bronnie Ware, accessed October 8, 2022, https://bronnieware.com/blog/regrets-of-the-dying/.

Chapter 17: Transforming the Power Structure

1. Parul Sehgal, "Young Jean Lee's Unsafe Spaces," *New York Times Magazine*, July 18, 2018, https://www.nytimes.com/2018/07/18/magazine/young-jean-lees-unsafe -spaces.html.

2. adrienne m. brown, *Emergent Strategy* (Chico, CA: AK Press, 2017).

3. Ben Kamin, *Dangerous Friendship: Stanley Levison, Martin Luther King Jr., and the Kennedy Brothers* (East Lansing: Michigan State University Press, 2014).

4. Martin Luther King Jr. Encyclopedia, s.v. "Levison, Stanley David," Martin Luther King Jr. Research and Education Institute, Stanford University, May 17, 2017, https://kinginstitute.stanford.edu/encyclopedia/levison-stanley-david.

5. Chuck Modiano, "Former NJ Senator and Knick Bill Bradley on Amadou Diallo, 'White Skin Privilege' Relevant as Ever," *New York Daily News*, November 28, 2016, https://www.nydailynews.com/sports/basketball/knicks/knick-bradley-white -skin-privilege-relevant-article-1.2890231; "Ronald Heifetz," Harvard Kennedy School, accessed September 19, 2022, https://www.hks.harvard.edu/faculty/ronald -heifetz; "Jeff Raikes," *Forbes*, accessed September 19, 2022, https://www.forbes .com/sites/jeffraikes/.

6. Kamin, *Dangerous Friendship*.

7. Home page, Community Change Inc., accessed September 19, 2022, https://communitychangeinc.org/; Home page, Organizing White Men for Collective Liberation, accessed September 19, 2022, https://www.owmcl.org/; Home page, Solidaire Network, accessed September 19, 2022, https://solidairenetwork .org/.

8. "Our Stories," Live Share Grow, August 13, 2016, https://www.livesharegrow.org /our-stories/.

9. Home page, Kataly Foundation, accessed September 19, 2022, https://www.kataly foundation.org/.

10. "SEO Career," Sponsors for Educational Opportunity, accessed September 19, 2022, https://www.seo-usa.org/career/team/.

11. Ted Rau, "Sociocracy—Basic Concepts and Principles," Sociocracy for All, August 2, 2020, https://www.sociocracyforall.org/sociocracy/.

12. "Consent Is a Third Option," Circle Forward, accessed September 19, 2022, https://circleforward.us/consent-is-a-third-option/.

13. Ronald J. Gilson and Curtis J. Milhaupt, "Economically Benevolent Dictators: Lessons for Developing Democracies," *American Journal of Comparative Law* 59, no. 1 (2011): 227–288.

14. Mike Isaac, "Uber Founder Travis Kalanick Resigns as C.E.O.," *New York Times*, June 21, 2017, https://www.nytimes.com/2017/06/21/technology/uber-ceo-travis -kalanick.html.

15. Ken Wilber, *A Theory of Everything: An Integral Vision for Business, Politics, Science, and Spirituality* (Boston: Shambhala, 2000).

16. Frederic Laloux, *Reinventing Organizations: A Guide to Creating Organizations Inspired by the Next Stage of Human Consciousness* (Brussels: Nelson Parker, 2014).

17. Bradford Gray, Dana O. Sarnak, and Jako Burgers, "Home Care by Self-Governing Nursing Teams: The Netherlands' Buurtzorg Model," Commonwealth Fund, May 29, 2015, https://doi.org/10.26099/6CES-Q139.

18. Kendra Hicks, "Resist as a Worker Self-Directed Nonprofit: Part One," Medium, January 3, 2019, https://medium.com/@ResistFoundation/resist-as-a-worker-self-directed-nonprofit-part-one-6746a5ce51b7.

19. brown, *Emergent Strategy*.

20. Milena Velis, "LeftRoot's Journal about Liberatory Strategy," LeftRoots, April 2018, https://leftroots.net/introducing-leftroots-journal/.

21. Oguz A. Acar, Murat Tarakci, and Daan van Knippenberg, "Why Constraints Are Good for Innovation," *Harvard Business Review*, November 22, 2019, https://hbr.org/2019/11/why-constraints-are-good-for-innovation.

22. Quoted in Katherine Byrns, "Angela Davis Speaks about Justice and Equality," *Colgate Maroon-News*, February 26, 2009, https://thecolgatemaroonnews.com/10555/news/angela-davis-speaks-about-justice-and-equality/.

23. Quoted in Founderpedia, "Most People Overestimate What They Can Do in a Year and Underestimate What They Can Do in Two or Three Decades," Medium, February 21, 2017, https://medium.com/founderpedia/from-tony-robbins-i-am-not-your-guru-on-netflix-d15a4772ed37.

24. Rob Reich, *Just Giving: Why Philanthropy Is Failing Democracy and How It Can Do Better* (Princeton, NJ: Princeton University Press, 2018).

Conclusion

1. A. J. Christopher, "'Divide and Rule': The Impress of British Separation Policies," *Area* 20, no. 3 (1988): 233–240.

2. Rob Picheta and Mia Alberti, "Prince Harry Says He Left Royal Life Because UK Press Was 'destroying' His Mental Health," CNN, February 26, 2021, https://www.cnn.com/2021/02/26/media/prince-harry-james-corden-interview-scli-intl-gbr/index.html.

3. Home page, Media 2070, accessed September 19, 2022, https://mediareparations.org/; "At the Forefront of Repatriation: New Policy and Impact beyond the United States," School for Advanced Research, April 19, 2017, https://sarweb.org/iarc/iarc-speaker-series/2017-series/at-the-forefront-of-repatriation-new-policy-and-impact-beyond-the-united-states/; "Takeo Rivera," Boston University, accessed September 19, 2022, https://www.bu.edu/english/profile/takeo-rivera/; "Mission and Team," New Media Ventures, accessed September 19, 2022, https://www.newmediaventures.org/mission; Alejandro Lazo, "Former Stockton Mayor Launches Nonprofit to End Poverty in California," CalMatters, February 10, 2022, http://calmatters.org/california-divide/2022/02/former-stockton-mayor-launches-nonprofit-to-end-poverty-in-california/; "Meet Erika," Erika Uyterhoeven for Somerville, accessed September 19, 2022, https://www.electerika.com/meeterika; "Bio," *Jean Theron* (blog), February 12, 2014, https://jeanwilloughby.wordpress.com/about/.

4. Mariame Kaba, *We Do This 'Til We Free Us: Abolitionist Organizing and Transforming Justice* (Chicago: Haymarket, 2021).

5. Ibram X. Kendi, *How to Be an Antiracist* (New York: One World, 2019).

6. Robert Bosman, *4000 Weeks: A Life-Changing Novel* (Canada: 2BeWise, 2011).

7. Rikard A. Hjort, "The Deathbed Fallacy," Medium, February 22, 2018, https://rikardhjort.medium.com/the-deathbed-fallacy-5e54d9639167.

8. Mary Conrow Coelho, *The Depth of Our Belonging: Mysticism, Physics and Healing* (Belize: Produccicones de La Hamaca, 2021).

INDEX

A

accommodations, 212–213
accounting firms, 17
Ackman, Bill, 26
Adams, Abigail, 59
Adams, John, 59
Adobe, 158
Advanced Placement (AP) track, 12
advantage, 7
Advantaged 1 Percent, 146, 148
Africans, 42
Alemu, Asrat, 192
Alphabet, 87
Amazon, 156, 158, 218
American Action Forum, 181
American culture, 239, 244–245
American dream, 17, 20–21, 87, 100,
    171, 180
American economy, 155, 160, 166, 274
American education system, 169–170
  high school graduation rates, 172
American Investment Council, 153
American success story, 5
American tax system, 25, 161–162, 165
America's collective mental health, 217
America's criminal justice system, 69
America's demographic makeup and
    poverty trends, 8, 20
  Black and Latinx representation in elite
    universities, 78–79
  middle class, 5, 21
  working class, 20
Amson-Bradshaw, Georgia, 112
anger, 233
anti-Black racism, 100
Anti-Defamation League, 92
antimonopoly policies, 161

antisemitism, 146
anxiety, 218–219
anxiety disorder and/or depressive
    disorder, 217
apartheid, 21, 40, 42, 90, 102, 182, 193,
    195, 215
Apple, 158–159
Aron, Dr. Elaine, 212
Arrow, Jamie Lee Wounded, 147
Asian Americans, 17, 90
  chance of rising to management or
    political office, 87
  debt rate, 86
  discrimination of, 88
  lawyers, 87
  scientists, 87
Atlanta Braves, 194
audit studies, 8–9
Aurelius, Marcus, 176
Ayan, 112, 285

B
Babcock, Linda, 226
Baby bonds, 179
Baldwin, James, 14
bamboo ceiling, 88
Banks, Ralph Richard, 99
Barber, Rev. William, 27
Barth, Richard, 105
Battilana, Julia, 124
become equitable, 135, 141
  equitable distribution of resources, 164
becoming equitable, 149
Bell, Alicia, 283
belonging, 244–247, 254, 265, 287
benevolence, 125, 267
Berger, Alex, 176

Bezos, Jeff, 67, 156, 218
biases, 66, 78, 130, 144, 234
    institutional, 48, 65
    victim-blaming, 103
Biden, Joe, 34, 80
    Build Back Better, 164
Bill & Melinda Gates Foundation, 59
Black Americans, 42, 79, 86, 88–90,
        94, 101
    discrimination against, 88, 94, 216
    economic disparities between white
        and, 86
    median household income, 90
    poverty rate, 35, 147, 173
Black CEOs, 69–70
Black Land and Power Coalition, 187
Black-led reparations movement, 129
Black Lives Matter, 60, 104, 110, 149,
        192, 277
Black South Africans, 41–42
Blindspot (Banaji and Greenwald), 8
Bloomberg, Michael, 67, 91
BNY Mellon, 111
Bonaparte, Napoleon, 59
Booker, Cory, 33
Born a Crime (Noah), 42
Bosman, Robert, 284
Boston Globe, 31
boundaries, 213–214
Bowles, Hannah Riley, 226
Bowman, Jamaal, 110
Brin, Sergey, 67, 87, 91
British monarchy, 281–283
Brown, Shona, 158
Buffet, Warren, 22, 157, 178
Buffett, Warren, 127
Building Belonging initiative,
        264–265
Burge, Jon, 192–193
Burmese Americans, 86
Bush, Cori, 110
Bush, George H. W., 194
Bush, George W., 138
Business Today, 119–120
Buurtzorg Nederland, 269–270

C
Cable, Daniel, 66
capital gains, 25
capitalism, 27, 165, 268, 270–274
Carlyle Group, 153
Carnegie, Andrew, 39, 102, 169–170
Carnegie, Dale, 118
Carrey, Jim, 284
Casciaro, Tiziana, 124
Chamorro-Premuzic, Tomas, 226–227
charity, 129
Chavez, Luis, 170–171
Chetty, Raj, 99
Cheviot Hills, 37
Chicago Blackhawks, 194
child abuse or neglect
    lifetime economic burden associated
        with, 207
    physical and emotional abuse, 207
    reporting of, 208
child labor law, 164
Children's Health Insurance Program, 181
China Care Foundation, 118
Chinese Americans, 87–89
Chinese Massacre of 1871, 88
Chua, Amy, 85
Civil Liberties Act, 194
Civil Rights Act of 1964, 43
civil rights movement, 102
Clark, Dale, 232
Clarke, Dr. Shoa, 124
class vs race, 43, 99
Clinton, Bill, 41, 101
Clinton, Hillary, 34, 101, 153
Coates, Ta-Nehisi, 80
coercive power, 123
CollegeSpring, 120, 122–123, 125–126,
        129, 143, 169, 205, 209, 231
Collins, Chuck, 28, 110
Collins, Jim, 231
colonialism, 101, 128
colorism, 93
The Commission to Study and Develop
        Reparation Proposals for African
        Americans Act, 199

community investment, 129
community values, 136
compounding unearned advantages, 9–10,
   13–14, 56
   height, 66–67
compound interest, 27
consent-based decision-making,
   265–267
contributive justice, 164
Cooke, Andy, 175
Corden, James, 281
corporate diversity and inclusion
   initiatives, 106
corporate income tax, 157
COVID-19 pandemic, 155, 180–181, 190,
   205, 217, 237, 268
Crenshaw, Kimberlé, 64
Croom, Simon, 208
Crow, Jim, 42
Cuban Americans, 93–94
cultural shift, 196
culture of repair, 191
   benefits, 192
   as a cycle, 192
   federal repair programs, 193
   grassroot institutions in, 199
   by pledging reparations, 193
   in postapartheid South Africa, 195

D
Dalio, Matt, 118
Dalio, Ray, 118
Daly, Mary, 77
Darity Jr., William, 189
"dark triad" personality traits, 228
David, Larry, 216
Davis, Angela, 275
deep conviction, 112–113
DeGraffenreid, Emma, 64
Dell, Michael, 67
Demaris, Lucien, 247
Democratic Party, 34
Difficult Conversations (Stone, Patton,
   and Heen), 34
Dimon, Jamie, 19

discrimination, 64–66, 101, 174, 216
   Anti– Asian American discrimination, 88
   against Black and Latinx populations,
     88, 94
District of Columbia Emancipation Act,
   1862, 195
diversity, 264
dominating voices/conversations, 138–140
DuPage County, 24

E
economic and racial justice, 35
economic inequality, 162, 164–165, 172, 186
economic moat, 157
Economic Opportunity Act, 124
economics, 99
Edison, 37
efficiency-equity trade-off, 154
Einstein, Albert, 27
Elizabeth II, Queen, 282
Ellison, Larry, 91
Emancipation Proclamation, 36
Emanuel, Rahm, 193
Emergence Project, 234
Emergent Fund, 111
Enron scandal, 135
Epstein, Jeffrey, 70
equal opportunity, 19–20
equitable policies, 145–146
Estee Lauder, 111
exceptionalism, 79–81
exclusionary zoning, 24
Executive Order 9066, 88
expert power, 123

F
Facebook, 67
familial relationships, 282
Family Assistance Plan, 175
family values, 37
Farbman, Leo, 283
fatherhood bonus, 51
feminine leadership, 226, 228–230
Ferrazzi, Keith, 118
Finca, Reverend Bugani, 187

firearm homicide rate, 228
Florant, Aria, 190–191
Floyd, George, 104, 107
Folkman, Joseph, 229
Forbes, Steve, 119
Ford Foundation, 20
Fortune 500 companies, 67, 81
Francis, Megan Ming, 172
Franklin, Jason, 283
French, John R. P., 123
frimpong, allen kwabena, 190–191, 275
Fung, Coleman, 120–121

G
Galbraith, John, 174
Gallegos, Ashley, 246
Gandhi, Mahatma, 174, 260
Garner, Dariel, 263
Gates, Bill, 59, 128, 169, 250
Gates, Melinda, 59, 128, 250
GDP growth rates, 21
GE, 37
Gelfand, Michele, 226
gender inequality, 47–50, 60, 65, 176
    car safety, 56
    decision rights, 59
    health care, 56
    parenting, 58–59
    pay gap, 51
    performance ratings, 50
    product designs, 56–57
    risks of sexual assault, 53–54
    venture capital allocation, 51
    victim blaming, 102–103
    violence against women, 53–55
gender norms, 211, 228, 230, 233–234
General Education Board, 170
General Electric, 111
General Motors, 64
genocide, 101
Gen Z, 95, 110, 283
George, Bill, 231
Geshuri, Arnnon, 158
Gifted and Talented Education (GATE)
    track, 11–12

Gilded Age, 155
GiveDirectly, 176–177
Giving Pledge, 127
Gladwell, Malcolm, 66
glass cliff phenomenon, 81
Goldman Sachs, 23, 161
Google, 156, 158
Gottman, John, 216
Graham, Benjamin, 22
Grantmakers for Girls of Color, 111
Great Depression, 1930s, 155
Green Hill Recovery, 53
Green New Deal, 110
Groundswell Fund, 111
Grusky, David, 21

H
Haas, Justin, 283
Hagerty, Barbara Bradley, 54
Hanauer, Nick, 172
Harry, Prince, 281–283
Harvard Business School, 40, 77, 79, 93–95,
    106–107, 135–139, 261, 277, 284
    access opportunities, 138
    access to class airtime, 136–137
    alumni, 138
    business case study, 135
    cash awards, 136
    contributions to reparations, 198–199
    endowments, 153
    screening process, 136
Harvard Kennedy School, 242–243
Harvard Negotiation Project, 34
Haudenosaunee Confederacy, 52
Haudenosaunee women, 52
Haushofer, Johannes, 179
Hawk, Crystal Echo, 194
healing society, 199, 216–217, 219
healthy entitlement, 211
Heifetz, Dr. Ron, 243
height advantage, 66–67
Hennessy, John, 123
Hewlett Packard, 67
Higher Education Act, 124
Hitler, Adolf, 102, 242

Honor Rolls, 117, 120
Howes, Lewis, 232
humility, 149
Huntsman Sr., Jon, 127
Hyatt, Michael, 252
Hyatt, Miller, 252
hypocrisy, 148
Hyun, Jane, 88

I
identity-based abuse, 214
identity-based advantages, 124, 210, 214
identity-based cartels, 159, 161
identity markers, 68–69
Ignatiev, Noel, 92
immigrant groups
    Black immigrants, 91
    Chinese, 87–89
    discrimination against, 87–88,
        91–92, 94
    economic disparities, 86
    immigration policies and, 88, 104
    Indian immigrant population, 86–87
    Irish immigrants, 92
    Jewish immigrants, 91–93, 101
    Nigerian immigrants, 91
    successes of, 85
Immigration Act of 1924, 88
income inequality, 20–21
Indian Americans, 86
individual freedom, 268
inequality, 41–43
informational power, 123
inherited wealth, 21–22
    disparities in, 40
Intel, 158
intergenerational wealth and power, 22,
    39–40
intergenerational wealth transfers, 25
International Repatriation Project, 196
interpersonal and institutional
    relationships, 259–260, 277
intersectionality, 63–64, 208, 210
    impact of, 64–65
    intersectional identity, 66, 68–69, 71

as a legal concept, 64
sanctioned sexual violence, 70–71
Intuit, 158
iPhones, 56, 75
Irish Americans, 101
Iroquois, 52

J
Japanese Americans, 88–89
Jewish Americans, 91–93, 101,
    216, 240
Jewish genocide, 102
Jewish values, 242
Jews or Mormons, 92–93
Jim Crow segregation, 32
Jim Crow segregation laws, 102
Jobs, Steve, 158
Johnson's Medicare, 164
Jordan, Jennifer, 111
Judaism, 239–242
Judge, Timothy, 66
Justice Funders, 111, 199

K
Kaba, Mariame, 284
Kaiser, George, 19, 127
Kalanick, Travis, 267
Kansas City Chiefs, 194
Kanter, Rosabeth Moss, 77
Kataly Foundation, 199
Katz, Jackson, 103
Keeler, Honor, 283
Kendi, Ibram X., 145–146, 214, 284
Kennedy School, 99–100
Keynes, John Maynard, 251
King Jr., Dr. Martin Luther, 76,
    107, 123, 164, 174, 189, 260,
    271–272
KIPP schools, 105–106
Kirk, Charlie, 104
Koch, Charles, 67
Koch Network, 104
Kolk, Dr. Bessel van der, 207
Kopp, Wendy, 105, 119–120
Kushner, Jared, 138

L
Laloux, Frederic, 269
Laschever, Sara, 226
Lateiner, Abraham, 259, 262
Latin Americans, 42, 125
Latinx Americans, 93–94
Layton, J. Bradley, 247
leadership, 225–227, 243
    feminine, 226, 228–230, 234
    qualities and traits, 230–231, 234
    self-centered leaders, 228
    testosterone levels and, 227–228
Lee, Young Jean, 257
LeftRoots, 271
Levison, Stanley, 260–261
Liberated Capital, 111, 199
Liberation Ventures, 111, 190–192, 199, 216
Lincoln, Abraham, 195
Linklaters, 111
Little Fires Everywhere, 129–130
living standards, 20
Livingston, Robert, 69–70, 122
Los Feliz, 37
luck, role in success, 117, 122–124,
    126–130
Lythcott-Haims, Julie, 11

M
Machiavellianism, 228
MacLean, Nancy, 105
Mailman, Josh, 129
Malawians, 41
Malcolm X, 38
male advantage, 47–48, 50–52, 226. *see
    also* gender inequality
    access to wealth and power, 51
    earnings, 51
    likelihood of securing justice,
        54–55, 103
    performance ratings, 50
    power to make changes for
        convenience, 56
Mandela, Nelson, 40, 182
ManKind Project, 234
marginalization, 65, 76

marginalization/marginalized peoples, 9,
    14, 34, 76, 79–82, 89, 101–103, 106,
    109, 111–112, 126, 130, 135, 137–138,
    140, 144–146, 170, 172, 186–187, 193,
    197, 208, 211–212, 214, 244, 258–260,
    264–265, 276
marginalized people and communities, 130
Marginalized 1 Percent, 148–149
marginal tax rates, 155
Markel, Meghan, 281
Marquis, Marriott, 119
marriages, 216
Marriott, Richard Edwin, 22
Marshall Plan, 178
masculinity, 51–53, 225, 232–233
Mayer, Jane, 105
Mayer, Marissa, 67, 81
Mayors for a Guaranteed Income,
    177–178
McCain, John, 164–165
McCall, Josephine Bolling, 38
McIntosh, Peggy, 6
McKinsey, 48–51, 161
Medicaid, 181
Medicare, 181
Menakem, Resmaa, 215–216
Men For Equity and Reproductive
    Justice, 283
Mental Health Alliance, 219
meritocracy, 19–20
#MeToo movement, 51
Mexican Americans, 41, 94, 171, 197
Mexican immigrants, 75
Microsoft, 161
middle class, 5, 172
Milken, Michael, 170
Millennial, 95
Millennials, 283
millennials, 28
minimum wage law, 164
misogyny, 145
Missing and Murdered Indigenous
    Women, Girls, and Two Spirit
    movement, 147, 149
model minority concept, 89–90

monopolies, 156–157
Moritz, Michael, 252
mortgage tax deduction, 25
Mourner's Kaddish, 239–240
Movement Generation, 272
Movement Voter Project, 110
Moynihan, Daniel Patrick, 103
Muhammad, Dr. Khalil Gibran,
    142, 271
Mukherjee, Basundhara, 192
Mullen, A. Kirsten, 189
Muraszko, Dr. Karin, 82
Murray, Charles, 185–186
Musk, Elon, 127, 156

N
narcissism, 113, 228
Narrative Initiative, 66
National African American Reparations
    Commission, 199
National LGBTQ Task Force, 146–147
N'COBRA, 199
NDN Collective, 111, 199
Nelson, Jonathan, 127
neoliberalism, 251–252
Netanyahu, Benjamin, 242
neurosurgery, 224–225
New Economy Coalition, 272
New Media Ventures, 199
New Profit, 121
Nigerian Americans, 87
noblesse oblige, 128

O
Obama, Barack, 80, 145, 165, 197, 230
    Affordable Care Act, 164
    tax proposals, 165
Obama, Michelle, 67, 135
Ocasio-Cortez, Alexandria, 110
occupational segregation, 51
Olin, Chris, 263
Omar, Ilhan, 110
Omidyar Network, 199
oppressive behaviors, 210–211
oppressive systems, 34–35

Orwell, George, 228
Ossoff, Jon, 147
Owens, Candace, 103

P
Page, Larry, 87, 91, 178
Paine, Thomas, 176
Palestinian land, 242–243
paternalism, 113
Patriotic Millionaires, 27, 111
Paulson, John, 153
Pedroso, Marlo, 234
The Penalty for Success, 38
Pencavel, John, 252
Pentland, Alex, 136
people of color, 8, 14, 40, 43, 63, 89
    depiction of, 77
    discrimination, 65–66, 101
    leadership positions, 81–82
    passing as white, 93
    undervalued, 71
    victim blaming, 102–103
Perez, Caroline Criado, 56
Perez, Jessica, 120, 125
Perry, Steve, 137
Persky, Aaron, 70
Petersen, William, 89
Pfeffer, Jeffrey, 123
Pham, Minh, 17
    analyst position in investing firm, 18–19
    education, 17
    hiring process, 18
    internship, 17–18
philanthropy, 5, 25–26, 104–105, 121, 129,
    169, 276
Philip Morris, 37
Picciolini, Christian, 249
Pichai, Sundar, 87
Piketty, Thomas, 162
Pinker, Susan, 248
Pippert, Tim, 78
Pitney, Otis, 263
Pooja, 57–59, 173, 192, 237, 239, 245, 257
Poor People's Campaign, 27, 110
positional power, 123

poverty, 35, 147, 155, 164, 172–173, 178,
    182, 207
  death due to, 174
  reduction programs, 174–182, 189
  War on Poverty, 173
Powell, John A., 246
power, 5, 9, 19–20, 26, 28, 36, 39–40, 42,
    51–53, 55–56, 59, 65, 71, 76–78,
    81–82, 87, 90–91, 94, 100, 105–107,
    109–110, 112, 122–126, 128–129, 135,
    139–141, 149, 156–158, 161, 165–166,
    172, 177, 182, 186–187, 189–190,
    193–194, 197, 208, 210, 213–214, 217,
    230, 233, 242, 249–250, 258–267,
    269–274, 276, 278, 281–282, 284, 287
power/powerful people, 123–124
Pressley, Ayanna, 110
PricewaterhouseCoopers, 17, 111
privileges/privileged, 6–8
Project Truth, Reconciliation, and
    Reparations, 199
promotion game, 10
property tax revenue, 23
psychological pain, 209
psychopathy, 228
Putnam, Robert, 237

R
Race Forward, 66
racial cartels, 159
Racial Equity Institute (REI), 7–8, 108, 284
racial injustice/racial justice/racial
    inequity/racism, 7–8, 33–35, 40,
    52, 57, 66, 68–69, 77–78, 85, 89–90,
    94–95, 99–100, 103, 108–110, 145,
    185, 187–188, 197, 199
racial integration, 75
racist thinking, 143–144
rate of return, 10
Raven, Bertram, 123
Reagan, Ronald, 155, 194, 250
redistribution of wealth, 28
referent power, 123
Regis High School, 106
Reich, Rob, 276

Relational Uprising, 237–238, 241, 250
reparations, 187–192, 194, 199
  around the world, 193–194
  to Black and Indigenous Peoples,
    194, 196
  institutions contributing to, 198–199
  societal repair, 198
  as a solution to racial wealth gap,
    196–197
Reparations 4 Slavery, 198
Reparations Summer program, 187,
    198, 283
Resist Foundation, 270
Resource Generation, 28, 111, 199, 283
respectability politics, 79–80
restorative justice, 217
reverse mentoring, 111–112
reward power, 123
rigged, 6
Ritz-Carlton Lodge Reynolds
    Plantation, 185
Rivera, Takeo, 283
Robbins, Tony, 275
Roberts, Adam, 283
Robin Hood Foundation, 121
Rockefeller, John D., 102, 135, 169
Roithmayr, Daria, 159
Romney, Mitt, 138
Roosevelt's New Deal, 164, 173
Rubenfeld, Jed, 85
Rubenstein, David, 153
rule of seventy-two, 10
Russo, Jr., John, 103
Rustomjee, Parsee, 260
Ryan, William, 102

S
Saez, Emmanuel, 161–162
Salami, Minna, 112
Salinas, Jessica, 283
Small, Deborah, 226
Sandberg, Sheryl, 67
Sandel, Michael, 164
Sanders, Bernie, 153
Sardinians, 248

SAT exam preparation, 124–127
Saunders, Claire, 112
Scarlet, Mik, 112
Schmidt, Eric, 158
Schulman, Sarah, 210–211
Scott, MacKenzie, 111
self-determination, 218
Sen, Rinku, 66
sense of victimhood, 213
sexual violence/sexual harassment/sexual
    assault, 53–54, 190
  as cultural issue, 190
  against Indigenous women, 147
Shabazz, Diallo, 78
Shapiro, Jeremy, 179
sharing resonance, 238
Silicon Valley's Woodside School
    District, 23
Sims, James Marion, 194
Singapore's Central Provident Fund, 179
Skilling, Jeffrey, 135
slavery, 32, 36, 159–160, 175, 182, 191
Smith, Robert F., 111
Smith, Timothy, 247
Sobrato, John, 127
Sobrato, Susan, 127
social capital, 237–238
social entrepreneurship, 117, 126
socialism, 165, 268, 271, 273–274
socialization of men and women, 230
social justice, 76, 138, 154
social mobility, 20–21, 27–28, 63, 89,
    99, 185
sociocracy, 265, 267
socioeconomic advantages, 36
socioeconomic status, 43
Soldier Field, 56
Solidaire Network, 199, 283
Solidaire Network Third Wave Fund, 111
Songhurst, Hazel, 112
Sorell, Michael, 111
South Africa's racial hierarchy, 41
The Squad, 110
Stanford's Center on Poverty and
    Inequality, 21

Stanford University, 117, 123, 125–126
Stephens-Davidowitz, Seth, 12
stereotypes, 144–145
Stiglitz, Joseph, 155–156, 179
Stockton Economic Empowerment
    Demonstration (SEED), 177
Stout, Brian, 264
subprime mortgage crisis, 2008, 153
Succession, 223–224
Sullivan, Becca, 224–225
Sunrise Movement, 110
systemic racism, 100
systems of oppression, 215

T
Tawwab, Nedra Glover, 213
Teach For America, 105–106
teal organizations, 269–270
terrorism attacks, 39
Tesla, 156
Thatcher, Margaret, 250
Theoharis, Rev. Liz, 27
Thiel, Peter, 156
Thornhill, Ted, 78
Tlaib, Rashida, 110
tokenism, 75–77
  as defense against perceptions of bias, 77
  in Hollywood, 77
  for racial integration, 75–76
  rich white men and, 75–82
  worthy of tokenization, 79–80
toxic masculinity, 52–53
traumas, 208–211, 215
trauma therapy, 204, 206–207, 210
traumatized behaviors, 210–211
Trump, Donald, 153
Truth and Reconciliation Commission,
    195
Tubbs, Michael, 283
Tulsa Race Massacre, 1921, 39
Turner, Brock, 70

U
Uihlein, Richard, 104
ultrawealthy, 25

unconscious bias, 8–9
unearned advantages, 8–11, 13, 18, 25, 27,
    140, 213
    access to exclusive neighborhoods,
        24–25, 37–38
    access to gifted and talented
        programs, 13
    beneficiaries of inherited wealth, 22,
        39–40
    capital benefit from, 26–27
    compounding, 9–10, 13–14
    gifted programs, 12–13
    identity-based, 66–67
    individual indulgence, 13
    investments, 23
    parents' financial support, 22–23
    of patriarchy, 55
    ultrawealthy benefit from, 25–26
    wealth and, 21–22
United States immigration law, 88
Upper East Side Regis, 106
Uyterhoeven, Erika, 284

V
validation, 34
Vasquez, Alfredo, 75
verbal abuse, 207, 214
victim blaming, 102–103, 105, 190
Vietnamese Americans, 17
voting preferences, 148

W
Walker, Darren, 20
Walmart, 158
Walton, Jim, 67
Ware, Bronnie, 254
Warren, Elizabeth, 67
Washington, Kerry, 130
Way to Win, 110
wealth
    equitable distribution of, 28
    inequality, 21, 27–28, 32
    transfers, 22
wealthy communities, 23

wealthy liberals, 28
wealthy-versus-middle-class divide, 185
Welch, Jack, 111
Westcott, Chris, 283
white advantage, 8, 39, 43
    access to affluent neighborhood,
        37–38
    dominating voice, 138–139
    favoritism, 65
    free of poverty, 33
    socioeconomic advantages, 36–37
white Americans, 7–8
    economic disparities between Black
        Americans, 86
    spendings, 86
white male economists, 99–100
white privilege, 31–32
white savior complex, 125
white supremacy, 89, 93, 145, 186,
    243–244
white terrorism, 39
Whitfield, Ed, 186–187, 197–198
Whitman, James, 102
Whitman, Meg, 67
Wilber, Ken, 267–268
Willoughby, Jean, 244, 284
Winfrey, Oprah, 6
Witherspoon, Reese, 130
women of color, 263–264
    marginalization of, 65
women's equality, 160
The Working Families Party, 110
World Economic Forum, 21
    gender equality, 59

Y
Yahoo, 67, 81
Young People For, 119

Z
Zenger, Jack, 229
Zinn, Howard, 103
Zuckerberg, Mark, 67, 91, 169, 259
Zucman, Gabriel, 162